The Timber Press Guide to Succulent Plants of the World

The Timber Press Guide to Succulent Plants of the World

A COMPREHENSIVE REFERENCE
TO MORE THAN 2000 SPECIES

Fred Dortort

Timber Press
Portland ▪ London

PAGE 2: *Adenium socotranum*. Photo by Rob Skillin.

Published in 2011 by Timber Press, Inc.

The Haseltine Building
133 S.W. Second Avenue, Suite 450
Portland, Oregon 97204-3527
www.timberpress.com

2 The Quadrant
135 Salusbury Road
London NW6 6RJ
www.timberpress.co.uk

Printed in China

Library of Congress Cataloging-in-Publication Data

Dortort, Fred.
    The Timber Press guide to succulent plants of the world : a comprehensive reference to more than 2000 species / Fred Dortort. — 1st ed.
        p. cm.
    Includes bibliographical references and index.
    ISBN 978-0-88192-995-9
    1. Succulent plants—Handbooks, manuals, etc. 2. Succulent plants—Identification. I. Timber Press (Portland, Or.) II. Title. III. Title: Guide to succulent plants of the world.
    SB438.D67 2011
    635.9'525—dc22
                                                                    2011007949

A catalog record for this book is also available from the British Library.

For Gael

Table of Contents

Foreword

WHEN I STARTED working at the University of California Botanical Garden (UCBG) in 1998 I had the great pleasure of meeting Fred Dortort. Fred worked with the Arid House collection of succulents and cacti, the largest collection of plants in the institution, with over three thousand accessions consisting of approximately double that number of individual plants. At that point he had already been working for nearly twenty years in this living museum, with its rich representation of dry-growing plants from around the world serving as a repository for some of the planet's most endangered species.

Upon meeting Fred I was amazed at his knowledge of the succulents in this large and diverse assemblage. He not only knew the names and taxonomy of seemingly all three thousand taxa, but also their individual growing habits in the wild and their growth requirements in cultivation. I felt lucky to be able to learn from such an avid and enthusiastic authority.

As I got to know Fred I became deeply impressed by not only his knowledge, but also his eagerness to expand that knowledge. Periodically he would disappear, showing up again after several weeks with stories about plant hunting in far-flung places. Tales of local encounters, including charging elephants, flash floods, and camp-site raids filled out his colorful accounts. These stories were woven into the substance of informative—and often quite exhaustive—lectures for UCBG staff and volunteers. Fred's slides of plants growing in their natural habitats have helped us better understand and appreciate these unique plants.

Fred's enthusiasm for conveying his knowledge about these wonderful plants was apparent from the first time I met him. He took great pleasure in educating people about how succulents survive in the often-extreme habitats in which they are found. He began writing articles for the UCBG Newsletter on particular succulent genera or associated groups of plants. These abbreviated presentations, coupled with his writing for professional journals, became the germ of this book.

Seeing Fred's interest and excitement for succulent plants turn into this significant book is very satisfying. A true teacher, Fred has assembled his information in a format that works for a wide audience, particularly for people who are enthusiastic and interested but not necessarily expert in succulent biology or cultivation. The many rich habitat photographs give the reader insight into how the plants grow in nature. Cultural information provides tips for successfully growing these plants at home. This is a book to be appreciated by both experts and beginners alike.

CHRISTOPHER CARMICHAEL
Associate Director of Collections and Horticulture
University of California Botanical Garden
Berkeley, California

Preface

THE FIRST TIME I visited a succulent plant nursery, I felt as if I'd been handed the key to an odd but very interesting room. I saw plants there that resembled flowers, plants that looked like rocks, and plants that fit no familiar description at all. Far from the typical employees of a nursery, the people I encountered at these places, usually the owners themselves, were both extremely enthusiastic and extraordinarily knowledgeable about their plants. In my case their enthusiasm was catching.

Around the same time, I became aware of the University of California Botanical Garden at Berkeley (UCBG). I was intrigued by its scientifically organized collection of plants arrayed against a backdrop of colorful tales of travels and collecting trips as far back as the 1920s to some of the most remote places in the world. Before long I wanted to see some of these exotic places and plants myself. Armed with a paperback book on cacti and succulents, I went out to the great Southwest to look for what I did not realize were some of the rarest, most localized plants in North America.

Over the years I have managed to visit many fascinating succulent habitats. I also have developed a continuing association with UCBG, at times teaching courses there, heading the cactus and succulent propagation program, and at various intervals taking charge of the large greenhouse collections of cacti and other succulent plants. I also began a long series of articles for the UCBG newsletter as well as more formal contributions to the *Cactus and Succulent Journal* and other horticultural publications. The present book is a sort of culmination of these endeavors, intended for an audience I felt was underserved: interested beyond the scope of a beginner but not yet prepared to plunge into the world of botanical monographs and specialized books devoted to individual plant families and genera.

The high points in my experiences with succulent plants, however, have always taken place in the field. It is easy to recapture the wonder I felt at the first sight of a Namaqualand quartz field, where argyrodermas, looking like Easter eggs carved out of sky blue wax, grew so densely that it was almost impossible not to step on them. Or, a lonely Baja California hillside covered with centuries-old bursera trees, 5 feet (1.5 m) across and 8 inches (20 cm) tall, wafting incense into the air at the slightest touch. Or Chihuahuan Desert landscapes where the ground, composed of plates of limestone, rang like bells under my footsteps. Seeing these things made me want to let people know that, first, these places existed on our Earth, and second, these plants which we usually associate with neat little rows of square plastic pots actually are among the most extraordinarily adapted organisms in existence, perfectly suited to their otherworldly homes. If I can convey some of my wonder at the presence of such things and places to some of my readers, I will consider this book a success.

A NOTE ON THE ILLUSTRATIONS

When I first began planning this book I intended to present a balanced mix in the illustrations between habitat shots and cultivated plants, but as I proceeded, my own preference for habitat shots kept interfering. I hope my readers will approve. In the case of some smaller plants, such as haworthias, which often keep hidden in the wild, whether under bushes or literally almost completely underground, cultivated material, planted for display, is necessary to show them at their best. The same applies to many caudiciforms, which in habitat may look like nondescript vines or shrubs, with their most interesting parts hidden beneath the soil. In contrast, however, with some plants, such as agaves, cultivated specimens, particularly if grown in containers, rarely can reach their full size or best proportions, and in the chapters devoted to such plants, the ratio of plants in nature to cultivated plants is greater.

An unavoidable aspect of habitat shots, moreover, is a recognition that many of these localities are disappearing, through habitat loss caused by human activity, possible climate change, and, in some instances, overcollection. Unfortunately, a number of the plants pictured may very well not exist anymore, and some represent species now possibly extinct in the wild. I hope that including pictures of them in their natural surroundings will serve as a record of less-damaged times, and perhaps may inspire some people to take action to help ensure the survival of these plants and their habitats as well.

A NOTE ON TAXONOMY

Most readers will be familiar with basic taxonomic divisions such as genus and species, but several other terms, perhaps not quite so familiar, frequently occur in this book. A *subspecies* (abbreviated subsp.) is a taxonomic classification of less significance than a species, and so is a *variety* (var. for short), with subspecies generally considered somewhat more inclusive than variety. *Forma* (f. for short) refers to an even lesser designation devised for plants with characteristically distinct appearances but indisputably included in a given species.

Because plants in habitat do not come equipped with labels and may not clearly fit within a definite species, the two terms *aff.* and *cf.* also have come into use. *Cf.* signifies that the plant in question is referable to a given species, and probably, though not indisputably, is that species, while *aff.* suggests an affinity with a given species, but with less certainty.

Finally, a *cultivar* indicates a specific-looking example of a plant that has been selected and bred to stabilize its characteristics. Of little if any taxonomic importance, it nonetheless often is attached to particularly attractive or horticulturally desirable plants. Names of hybrids and cultivars are set off by single quote marks.

Many fundamental taxonomic divisions have been thrown into an uproar as a result of DNA testing and other contemporary investigatory methods. Long-established plant families have disappeared and our understanding of the relationships between major groups of plants has in many cases fundamentally changed, particularly among the monocots, which include a number of major succulent groups. I have addressed these changes in the relevant chapters, following the treatments recommended by the Angiosperm Phylogeny Group, but it should be realized that more revisions are surely on their way. The spelling of certain scientific plant names, particularly in *Adromischus* and *Crassula*, is based on the research of English authors Gordon Rowley and John Pilbeam, who have corrected many familiar spellings after checking the original plant descriptions.

A NOTE ON THE PLANT GROUPINGS

Where botanists divide plants into groups based on taxonomic characters and relationships, these botanical differences are often of little interest to horticulturalists, especially when they are invisible to the naked eye. Gardeners want to know about a plant's ornamental value. Does it have colorful flowers, interesting shape, hairy leaves? These of course are characteristics of little botanical significance, though very important in letting people know what plants they might actually want to grow.

The plants in this book are organized first by family and genus. Within that broad arrangement, the subgroups were designed to aid gardeners in figuring out what plants would look like. Some subgroups are easily identifiable, as is the case with the hairy echeverias or the starburst crassulas. Other groups unite plants with a common basic culture. Still other groupings are more arbitrary and vague, but nonetheless horticulturally significant, to make the genus seem like less of an overwhelming mix of unrelated plants. Perhaps some day there will be an agreed-upon horticultural classification for these plants.

Acknowledgments

A BOOK SUCH AS this one can never be the product of one person on his or her own. I have been lucky enough to benefit from the knowledge, skill, and friendship of many other people and I'm very grateful for their willingness to share their expertise with me.

The first group, sadly, consists of people no longer with us. Lila Lillie first introduced me to the real world of succulent plants and taught me much of what I know about how to grow them. Jay Dodson (International Succulent Institute) and Al Irving (UCBG) both shared their knowledge with me and opened up their collections to my amazed eyes. Charles Glass, along with Bob Foster, furthered my knowledge of some of the real rarities, and Charlie, as editor of the *Cactus and Succulent Journal*, encouraged me in my writing and taught me much about how to say the things I wanted to say.

My traveling companions, over many years, many places, and a few adventures, are identified in this book simply as people whose photographs grace and improve it, but Rob Skillin and Kurt Zadnik really deserve to be listed as collaborators or co-authors rather than just contributors. Without their knowledge, planning, energy, and powers of observation, the book would not exist. Rob also has helped me photograph a number of his exceptional plants. Terry Thompson and Kathleen Malan Thompson have been good companions under sometimes-trying circumstances, and whatever I have managed to learn about photography I have learned from Terry.

Brian Kemble (curator of the Ruth Bancroft Garden), Inge Hoffman, Susan Carter (research associate at the Royal Botanic Gardens, Kew), Julia Etter and Martin Kristen, and John Trager (Huntington Botanical Gardens) have all graciously allowed me to use their photographs and have shared their vast knowledge of succulent plants with me as well. The same can be said of Steven Hammer, who also greatly helped with plant identifications, Naomi and Frank Bloss, Mary Parisi and Ed Dunne, and Jerry Wright, all extremely knowledgeable as well as expert growers, who gave me free entry into their spectacular collections. Paul Leondis clarified some issues concerning succulent bulbs. Ernst van Jaarsveld (Kirstenbosch National Botanical Garden in Cape Town), Derek Tribble, and Robert H. Archer (National Herbarium, Pretoria) have all provided valuable assistance in plant identification. I hope any remaining errors on my part will provide them with a bit of amusement rather than indignation.

Everyone at UCBG that I have interacted with for the last thirty-five years has helped me. I want particularly to thank Paul Licht (director) for his enthusiastic support of this project; Chris Carmichael (collections director) also for his support and for writing the foreword; Holly Forbes (garden curator); Meghan Ray (horticultural staff) for her suggestions regarding some of the text; and Bryan Gim (horticulturalist in charge of the arid-growing plants) for his valuable help and friendship.

Tom Fischer and Eve Goodman of Timber Press have been unfailingly pleasant and patient as this project kept going on and on. Linda Willms has demonstrated great dedication with her meticulous efforts with the text. Working with them has been an unexpected pleasure.

And finally, my wife, Gael Fitzmaurice, has read every word of the text with critical astuteness, acted as photographic assistant, put up with my occasional whining when pitching camp in the dark in the middle of Africa, in the rain in Baja, or in the snow in Utah, and in general has been amazingly supportive, for which I will be eternally grateful.

Chapter 1

Succulents in Nature

Even at a glance, succulents seem different from other plants. Compelled by their need to conserve and store water, they have adapted to arid conditions through dramatic alterations to their shapes and structures. Instead of the leaves, stems, and trunks of typical plants, succulents display forms that can resemble columns covered with spines and hair, or heaped piles of translucent, angular pebbles, or the fanciful globe-shaped inhabitants of some science-fiction coral reef. Their odd, sometimes strikingly bizarre appearance is the direct result of their strategy of colonizing difficult and marginal habitats where few other plants can survive. Of course, to survive and grow, succulent plants need water, soil, and light. In this most fundamental respect, they are like any other plant. Most people, however, are attracted to succulents precisely because they seem so unlike ordinary plants.

The hardiness and ease of cultivation of many succulents have helped them achieve enduring popularity. Nearly everyone has at least a passing acquaintance with easy-growing succulents such as the jade plant (*Crassula ovata*), hens and chickens (various echeverias and sempervivums), or donkey tails (*Sedum morganianum* and *S. burrito*). These plants are so ubiquitous, on windowsills, at garden supply shops and discount hardware centers, that it is sometimes difficult to remember that they are representatives of species that exist in nature. Displayed on a shelf in their brightly colored pots, succulents may look like decorative oddities or even living sculptures, but in reality they are highly specialized masters of survival in some of the world's harshest, most extreme environments. Observing these plants in the wild confirms that the very shapes, forms, and textures that endear them to growers also assist the plants in their efforts to survive in the strange and lonely places where many of them grow.

OPPOSITE:
Aloe dewinteri on a steep Namibian cliff face. Photo by Rob Skillin.

Succulent plants by definition have developed methods of storing water internally in times of drought. In this they differ from other xerophytic (dry-growing) plants that may survive long periods without water by producing long, water-seeking taproots or avoid dealing with droughts entirely by lying dormant in the form of seeds until renewed rains start a new generation. Thousands of species from unrelated families have adopted the succulent survival strategy. Almost all the members of the cactus family (Cactaceae), for example, are succulents, and in popular terminology the term *cactus* can stand for any fleshy or spiny desert plant. This is hardly accurate, of course, and the horticultural adage that "all cacti are succulents but not all succulents are cacti," bears repeating, despite a few exceptions. The variety and diversity of all the kinds of succulent plants make it impractical to cover them in any detail in a single volume, and so this book will restrict itself to the "other succulents," those many thousands of species that are not members of the cactus family.

SUCCULENT FORMS

Depending on which plant parts have undergone modification, succulent plants can be termed *leaf succulents* or *stem succulents*, as well as some additional, less self-explanatory designations. In some leaf succulents, fairly ordinary looking leaves have simply become thicker to enable them to store water. The leaves of more specialized plants, however, may have a thick water-retaining epidermis, a waxy coating, or a covering of dense hairs. These highly succulent leaves often develop into precise geometric shapes and may cover the plant so tightly as to obscure its stem. In the most extreme cases, plants of certain highly dwarfed mesembryanthemums (members of the family Aizoaceae) consist of nothing but a pair of fused leaves known as plant bodies. The leaf-pair con-

The compact leaves of *Crassula deceptor*: water-saving geometry.

A three-headed *Conophytum calculus,* each head made of two fused plant bodies. Photo by Rob Skillin.

A young cactuslike stem succulent, *Euphorbia virosa* in central Namibia.

A relatively small specimen of the caudiciform *Adenia pechuelii.* Photo by Kurt Zadnik.

ceals a completely invisible residual stem, no more evident to the observer than the hidden internal leg bones of a python.

In contrast to leaf succulents, stem succulents have transferred the normal functions of leaves to their expanded, water-storing stems. Stem succulents may bear ephemeral, dwarfed, or unrecognizably modified leaves, or be completely leafless. Though almost any cactus could serve as a model of stem succulence, many unrelated plants from numerous families have chosen this path of development as well.

Many succulent plants have both leaves and stems modified to retain water. More exotic succulents include *caudiciforms*, which develop succulence from their hypocotyl, that part of an embryonic plant above the roots and below the stem. A typical caudiciform succulent has an enlarged, partially aboveground tuberous body called a caudex, with more or less ordinary roots below and relatively slender stems and leaves above. Many caudiciforms lose their leaves and stems annually, while the caudex slowly grows and may develop an outer cover decorated by spines or deep fissures and ridges.

The term *pachycaul* refers to another succulent growth form. It is applied to plants with massively thickened, sometimes tree-sized trunks, stems, and branches, and thin, deciduous leaves.

Finally, there are a number of unusual bulbous plants, mostly from southern Africa and cultivated almost exclusively by succulent growers. The bulbs of these plants may become enormous; some kinds have very fleshy leaves, and still others grow with their bulbs partly above

The giant pachycaul *Adansonia za*, dominating its Madagascan thorn forest.
Photo by Brian Kemble.

Bulbine latifolia, resembling an aloe, but a bulb.

GEOGRAPHY

Understanding where the plants originate can provide a key to success in growing them. Succulents grow in a great array of habitats, covering vast, disparate geographic regions. They range as far north as Canada and as far south as southern Argentina and the southernmost tip of Africa.

The most important center of succulent plants occurs in the extraordinarily variable landscape of South Africa and Namibia. For readers unfamiliar with that part of the world, several areas marked on the map (see page 26) and frequently referred to in the plant descriptions merit a brief explanation here. Namaqualand is an arid region spanning the northwest coast of South Africa. The northernmost part of Namaqualand is called the Richtersveld, a desert mountainous area that receives little rain; in the south the Knersvlakte is a vast region covered with fist-sized or smaller chunks of quartz atop rocky,

ground. Since succulence in plants is a descriptive term rather than one that signifies evolutionary relationship or taxonomic organization, it is not too much of a stretch to consider these odd bulbs, denizens of the same environments as more familiar succulent plants, to be borderline succulents as well.

HABITAT AND SURVIVAL

The same exigencies of environment and habitat that have molded the odd and striking forms that attract people to succulent plants have also radically transformed their cultural requirements. Interestingly enough, these transformations often enhance the suitability of succulent plants for cultivation, particularly indoors. Frugal in their needs for both water and supplemental nutrition, they can thrive in the low humidity found inside houses and can be left without care for considerable amounts of time. Given a few daily hours of direct or slightly filtered sunlight, quick-draining soil, and water about once a week in the warm months, with a distinct dry, cool rest in winter, most succulents will thrive for many years.

While many succulents grow with remarkable ease, a substantial number of them need extremely specialized care, often peculiar and even counterintuitive. With many of these atypical succulent plants, failure to understand and pay strict attention to their requirements leads to their rapid death.

The giant *Aloe pillansii* thrives in the arid hills of the South African Richtersveld. Photo by Kurt Zadnik.

On the edge of two monsoons but never wet, the island of Socotra, south of the Arabian Peninsula, supports the bizarre *Adenium socotranum* along with the taller *Boswellia elongata*. Photo by Rob Skillin.

saline soil and receiving 100–175 mm of rain in winter. Beyond the mountains at the eastern edge of Namaqualand lies Bushmanland, almost completely arid year-round and with extreme temperatures from 20°F (–7°C) in winter to well over 100°F (38°C) in summer. Ecologically both the Richtersveld and Bushmanland extend beyond the Orange River into southern Namibia.

The places referred to as karoos, an indigenous term meaning "wasteland," consist of plateaulike areas wedged between the ranges of hills or mountains that block off most precipitation. Located mainly in southwestern South Africa, the largest is the bleak, climatically harsh Great Karoo. Just south of it lies the somewhat less arid Little Karoo, while to the west the Tanqua, Ceres, and Robertson Karoos range from extraordinarily dry to semidry.

Another large and unique selection of succulents lives on the giant island of Madagascar, off the east coast of Africa. East Africa, Somalia in particular, provides a home for many unusual succulents. This region further extends onto outlying islands and the southwestern corner of the Arabian peninsula. Succulent plants in lesser variety can be found in northwest Africa, the Canary Islands, and actually in almost any semiarid spot on the African continent, though rarely in the Sahara Desert itself.

In the New World, Mexico (see map p. 27) harbors a vast and varied assortment of succulents, perhaps second only to South Africa in variety. The drier parts of Central America and the West Indies, Brazil and western South America also support a smaller but distinctive population of succulent plants.

Although it supports a wide variety of endemic cacti, the United States is not home to too many other succulents. A single echeveria and one hechtia grow in Texas, a few small graptopetalums live in Arizona, and xerophytic yuccas occur throughout much of the southern and middle West. Agaves grow in many desert and semi-arid areas, and sedums colonize rock faces as far north as Washington state. A succulent aster and a pachycaulous bursera live in Southern California, also the home of a wide variety of dudleyas, which further extend to a limited degree into Arizona, Nevada, and Oregon.

Oddly, few succulents grow in the vast dry expanses of Australia, but the arid interior of central Asia is home to a few species, as are dry parts of India and even Thailand. Succulents also grow in the mountains of southern Europe.

A natural garden of succulents in the seasonally dry landscape of Oaxaca, Mexico.

DESERTS, FORESTS, AND ROCKY OUTCROPS

People often associate succulent plants with bone-dry deserts, and some, in fact, do grow there. They occur more frequently, however, in semiarid environments marked by extreme seasonal dry periods. Some of these habitats may look deceptively lush during the rainy season, but all plants living there must be able to withstand drought.

Even habitats that bear a superficial resemblance to normal forests offer room for small succulents in the gaps between the larger ones or on rocky outcrops and cliff edges, while many good-sized shrubs and treelike forms will reveal themselves as succulents, complete with spines and enlarged, water-storing stems, after shedding their covering of leaves. Certain succulents inhabit lofty inter-mountain plateaus, desolate rocky mountain passes, mist-covered crags and ridges, or moist tropical forests where they may live as epiphytes. A few succulent plants live in places where the annual rainfall can reach almost 100 inches (2500 mm), in stark contrast to those that grow where it may not rain at all for many years on end.

Many of those plants that grow in the most stereo-typically arid conditions, however, fully exposed to the sun in a desert landscape, begin their lives in the shelter of nurse plants—bushes, shrubs, even cacti or other succulents that provide shade and extra moisture where a seedling can get its start. Many years later, after the death of the nurse plant, the now-mature succulent will remain in sole possession of its apparently eternally sunny spot.

A surprising number of the most interesting succulents grow under conditions as strange and alien as anything on the earth or beneath the sea. These microhabitats include not only picturesque wild lands, but also places that appear to be vacant, gravel-strewn lots. Close inspection of these, however, reveals a flat surface completely covered with translucent quartz pebbles, taken advantage of by miniature succulent plants that use the pebbles as tiny natural greenhouses.

Permanent and diverse communities of succulent plants may form underneath long-lived desert scrub bushes, some of them extending their blossoms just enough beyond the boundaries of the sheltering plants to expose them fully to searching insect pollinators. Other succulent plants have managed to colonize cliff faces so steep that it seems the plants must have been screwed into the rock walls to keep from dropping off. Succulent

Combining autumn color with columnar cactus, *Bursera* forests support smaller succulents as well.

A closer looks reveals a dense population of miniature succulent plants. Photo by Kurt Zadnik.

A Namaqualand quartz field, looking like a barren patch of gravel. Photo by Rob Skillin.

Conophytum ratum poking out through the pebbles in a Bushmanland quartz field. Photo by Rob Skillin.

Yellow-green *Haworthia mucronata* var. *morrisiae* (center), smooth-leaved *Senecio radicans* (left), and spiny *Quaqua ramosa* (right and far left) growing under a bush in the Little Karoo.

Both red and hairy, this *Crassula* aff. *namaquensis* displays multiple survival strategies.

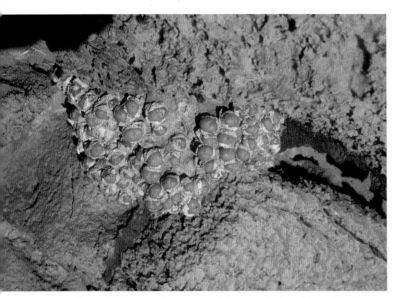

Conophytum saxetanum surviving on dust and fog. Photo by Kurt Zadnik.

plants can survive on apparently bare boulders in full sun, in areas of almost no rain, though closer inspection reveals them to be growing in a tiny bit of wind-deposited grit. These are just a few of the decidedly peculiar habitats where succulents survive and few other plants can.

PHYSICAL TRANSFORMATIONS

Succulents are able to survive in remarkably hostile environments because of the physical transformations they have undergone. Some of these modifications transcend the straightforward development of water-retaining capabilities. For example, crassulaic acid metabolism (CAM), developed independently by almost all succulent plants, enables them to reverse the normal water loss through transpiration that takes place during day time in ordinary plants.

Many succulent plants ensure their survival by controlling the problems of sun, drought, wind, and predation through physical modifications which often enhance their appeal. If the sun is too hot and bright, many succulents shelter their tender green leaves or stems under a cover of protective coloration provided by various compounds that turn them blue, or gray, or red, or brown, even brightly reflective silver or almost any color imaginable.

A number of succulents go beyond this and produce a waxy or powdery, sun-protecting coating, often in delicate shades of pink, blue, or pale lavender, which will rub off at the slightest touch, revealing the green photosynthesizing surface underneath. People generally like fuzzy plants. The fuzz and hairs on the leaves of many succulents often serve as dew traps and provide the plant with just a bit of extra moisture. This adaptation is particularly useful in areas of little actual rain but frequent fog or condensation-inducing extreme day-night temperature differentials.

WINDOWED SUCCULENTS

Probably the most curious stratagem used by succulent plants is the development of windows, portions of succulent leaves which are nearly or completely transparent, letting light deep into the leaf interior. Since one of the major survival strategies in water-conserving succulents is to minimize the ratio of potentially evaporative surface area to volume, the windows manage to expose a much greater number of photosynthesizing cells to light than would be the case with an opaque surface.

Succulents from unrelated families share this trait. Several members of the largely tropical, epiphytic, somewhat drought-resistant genus *Peperomia* in Piperaceae (the pepper family) produce succulent, somewhat scimitar-shaped foliage with a narrow, translucent window that runs lengthwise along the leaf. The windows in other peperomias with even thicker leaves extend over the entire upper leaf surface. Various succulent *Senecio* species in Asteraceae (the aster family) also possess linear windows on their leaves that let filtered sunlight into their interiors.

Many species of *Haworthia*, related to *Aloe* in Asphodelaceae (the asphodel family), and at least one species of the completely unrelated *Crassula* in Crassulaceae (the crassula family) have taken the concept of windows further, combining their almost transparent leaf tips with retractile roots, which pull the plants flush with, or even slightly below, the surface of the surrounding soil. Protected both from burning sunlight and marauding insects or other predators, haworthias with this growth habit obtain a great deal of nurturing sunlight despite almost no visible aboveground presence.

Among the myriad mesembryanthemums in Aizoaceae (the ice-plant family), extremely succulent members of *Lithops*, *Conophytum*, *Fenestraria*, and *Frithia* comprise most of the windowed species, but several other genera, such as *Gibbaeum*, include the occasional window plant. In *Conophytum*, the species formerly placed in the separate genus *Ophthalmophyllum* have plant bodies in which the entire tops are clear as glass. Several other groups within *Conophytum* include plants with largely transparent leaf tips.

Though only a few *Lithops* species have completely clear leaf tips, the remaining species have their own specialized types of windows, forming tessellated or even labyrinthine patterns of translucent tissue interspersed with the highly colored and textured opaque tissue that helps to camouflage the plants in habitat. In the environments where these plants eke out their living, where rain may not fall for several consecutive years, where the sun blazes down, and where hungry insects and rodents patrol the terrain, the combination of near-underground existence, sun filtration, and admission of light to relatively voluminous interior tissue minimizes surface exposure. These factors have undoubtedly ensured the continuing survival of many of these plants.

Domed windows on the leaf tips of *Haworthia springbokvlakensis*.

The glassy windows of *Conophytum praesectum*. Photo by Kurt Zadnik.

ENVIRONMENTAL ESSENTIALS

Knowing where a particular succulent plant originates provides two significant insights into its needs: its growing season and its range of acceptable temperatures. This knowledge makes it possible for a grower to decide, for example, whether there is any point in trying to cultivate it outdoors.

Growing seasons often depend on the time of year that the rains arrive in a given habitat, while the temperature variations that a specific plant can tolerate derive from a combination of geographic location and altitude. For example, most Mexican succulents that grow at altitudes of 4000 feet (1200 m) and higher will survive at least a certain level of subfreezing weather. In contrast, plants from coastal Mexico, can rarely tolerate frost.

TEMPERATURE AND ALTITUDE

Many plants descended from species that once had to survive cold climates often retain their hardiness despite the mild temperatures of their present-day environment. In addition, plants that grow in a rain shadow, the far side of a mountain range where they are cut off from rainfall patterns, often have to put up with particularly cold nights as well as extra-dry conditions.

Nonetheless, it is reasonable to assume that plants native to Somalia, Madagascar, low-altitude regions of Mexico, or northeastern Brazil cannot withstand too much cold, certainly not a hard freeze. In contrast, succulents from the Andes should not have any problems with occasional frosts, and the same can be said for many South African succulents.

With the less frequently encountered species, the more specific the information available about where a plant originates, the better the chances for its successful cultivation. Simply knowing the country of origin is not sufficient. Brazil, for example, covers a great range of climates, and while plants from the northeast tend to be quite sensitive to cold, plants from the south may be quite hardy and resistant.

Habitat elevation often plays a key role as well. Much of the South Africa interior is more than a mile (1600 m) above sea level, but the eastern coast has milder temperatures, and many plants are correspondingly less hardy. With Mexican succulents, altitude generally matters more than latitude, but plants from the far south often cannot withstand as much cold as plants from similar elevations growing nearly 1000 miles (1600 km) farther north.

Moreover, it is not just a matter of altitude and minimum temperatures. Succulents from higher altitudes in the American Southwest, the interior of southern Namibia, and northwestern South Africa—places where winter temperatures routinely drop to far below freezing—obviously will not mind the occasional frost. Yet, some of these plants can be sensitive to excess humidity, presenting challenges even for expert growers.

Many succulent plants from northwestern Africa can take some frost without complaint, and the cacti and succulents of Baja California generally will survive a bit of frost. A number of plants native to tropical and semitropical-appearing localities such as Madagascar, the southwest of the Arabian peninsula, and parts of East African countries such as Sudan and Ethiopia, but which grow at high elevations, may also withstand some frost. To a considerable degree, then, the combination of topography, altitude, and weather equals destiny.

RAINFALL PATTERNS

Rainfall patterns in these environments provides another key to successful growing. Most arid and semiarid regions alternate between distinct rainy and dry seasons; in the majority of cases the rainy season coincides with the warmer months, with winters nearly rainless. Intense summer rains can create near monsoonal conditions on the plains of East Africa, in semiarid Brazil, and even in parts of the Chihuahuan Desert.

In a few cases, however, the reverse is true, where dry summers and winter rain come together to create a Mediterranean climate. California, parts of South Africa, Australia, and South America share this weather pattern with the lands bordering the Mediterranean Sea. The drier areas adjacent to these mild Mediterranean climate zones may seamlessly transition into true deserts.

In eastern South Africa rain generally falls in summer, while in the western part of the country it rains in winter. The succulent plants native to those areas have arranged their growing seasons accordingly. The totality of South African rainfall patterns, however, is more complex.

The winter-rainfall region begins part way up the coast of Namibia and makes a rough curve, extending eastward as it stretches farther south. Furthermore, many areas directly east of its irregular boundary, including places rich in succulent plants, are not really in the summer-rainfall area. For example, the semiarid Little Karoo may receive a bit of rain anytime in the year, though summers there tend toward dryness. Just to the north in the Great Karoo the sparse rains fall in late summer and autumn. Other South African transition zones such as Bushmanland and the Tanqua Karoo rarely receive rain at all, but, once again, occasional storms may arrive at any time of year, most likely winter in the west, summer in the eastern parts.

Northwestern-most South Africa, namely, Namaqualand and the Richtersveld, receive as much moisture from fog as from the winter rains. Across the border in Namibia, the strictly winter-rainfall area narrows and clings closer to the coastal regions as it moves northward; east lies a band where rain may fall any time of the year—or not at all—while farther east the rainy season arrives in summer. Along the Atlantic coast, for a long ways to the north the fog keeps more things alive than the extremely unreliable rain.

On the whole, succulents from summer-rainfall regions behave conventionally, while those from winter-rainfall areas, which include many of the strangest looking, most fascinating succulents, often act very oddly in cultivation.

FOG OR CLOUD DESERTS

Some winter-rainfall dry lands lie near seacoasts situated next to cold ocean currents. This mixture of summer drought and sparse winter rain, hot desert sun and cold ocean water, generates great infusions of fog that blow

Life-giving fog rolling over barren hills in northern Chile. Photo by Inge Hoffman.

onto the land, drawn the farthest during the hottest weather. The resultant environment, known as a fog desert or cloud desert, is ideal for winter-growing succulents. Fog deserts occur in central and northern Chile, western and northwestern South Africa and neighboring Namibia, and the central portion of the Mexican state of Baja California, all places that support an abundance of xerophytes, including extremely strange and interesting succulent plants.

Knowing that a plant comes from a fog desert suggests that it should receive water during the winter months but not necessarily be left completely dry in summer, and that it might benefit from a bit of shade. Plants from nearby regions devoid of fog—often because a range of mountains blocks any sea-borne moisture from reaching them—will probably be able to tolerate more extensive drought in summer along with brighter light. Fog desert plants in general respond well to more water than the regional rainfall statistics of their environment might suggest.

Successful cultivation of cacti and succulents depends upon understanding the habitat in which they grow in the wild. Temperature, sunlight, and climate in general vary tremendously from location to location. Furthermore, the specific area in which a plant is placed, whether a greenhouse, unheated lath-house, or cold frame, an outdoor garden or a windowsill, is absolutely crucial in determining whether a plant will do well, rapidly die, or slowly languish. We will look at some of those factors in the next chapter.

Fouquieria columnaris, one of the larger and stranger denizens of the Baja California fog desert. Photo by Terry Thompson.

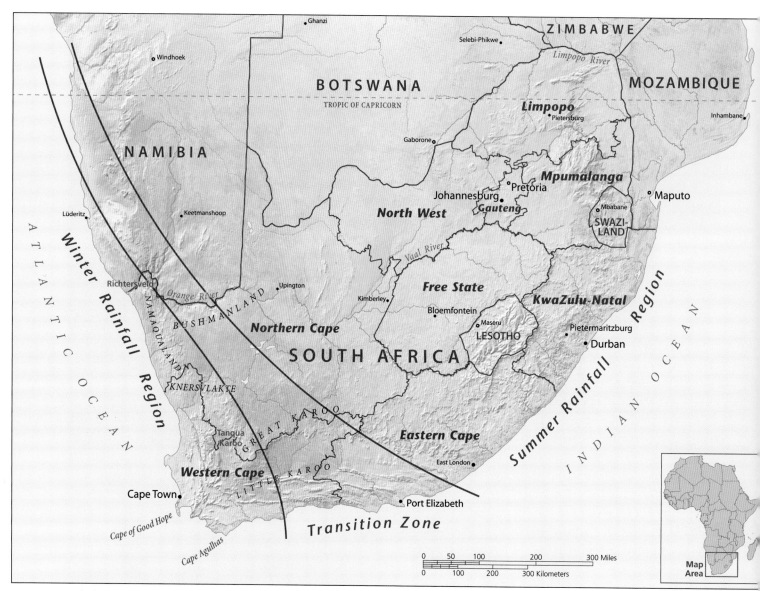

Relief map of South Africa, the primary center of diversity for succulents, showing provinces and rainfall regions. In the east, rainfall generally occurs in summer (November through March), while in the west it comes in winter (June to August). A transition zone separates the two areas. Knowing the region from which a succulent originates is helpful in determining the best watering schedule in cultivation.

Relief map of Mexico, Central America, and the southern
United States. Mexico is home to a vast assortment of succulents, perhaps second only to South Africa in variety, while the
drier parts of Central America support a smaller but distinctive
population of succulents, and a few species are found in the
western and southern United States.

Chapter 2

Succulents in Cultivation

SUCCULENT PLANTS HAVE perhaps gathered more myths about them than any other plant group. Many of these myths center on their cultivation—they should be watered once a month or once a year, or with an eye dropper; they should be planted in pure sand; they must be grown in full sunlight. These bits of succulent plant folklore have arisen in an attempt to make sense of these apparently nonplantlike organisms that still share the vegetative world's fundamental requirements of water, soil, and light. In reality, succulents do differ in how they partake of these essential ingredients, but their habits and requirements are less bizarre than the stories tell and completely make sense when considered in the context of their habitats, whether in nature or as modified by cultivation.

LOCATION

The fundamental combinations of water, soil, and light vary according to the specific locality where the plants are grown. Both overall geographic location and the extremely localized components of the immediate growing

Ideal greenhouse location, light, and water combine to produce a near-perfect cultivated specimen of *Cyphostemma betiforme.*

area influence how succulent plants will grow in cultivation. The basic cultural recommendations given in this book derive from the environment of Berkeley, near the coast of central California, but far away enough from the sea to be out of the zone dominated by coastal fog and overcast. It is an area of moderate temperatures, infrequent winter freezes, and occasional summer days with temperatures in the nineties or slightly higher (above 32°C). During both winter and summer several consecutive days of sunshine may alternate with morning overcast. As is the case with most of California, the rainy season is in winter, and summers typically are completely dry.

Generally speaking, the California climate both to the south and east is hotter and less humid, with more consistent and brighter sunlight. In contrast, farther to the north the intensity of the sunlight slowly lessens; in coastally dominated regions the high temperatures are lower, while inland, though sunnier, hotter, and less humid, the sunlight still is less bright than to the south, and the winters are colder. Along the entire Pacific coast, the light is relatively more subdued, and high and low temperatures are moderated.

To the east of California the rainy seasons generally reverse, with rain in the warmer months, and relatively dry winters, interrupted by occasional winter snowstorms. The humidity tends to be very low. Continuing eastward, humidity increases, particularly in summer, while the light, particularly in winter, steadily diminishes farther to the north. Northern and central Europe have a climate relatively similar to central and eastern North America, but southern Europe, the home of the classic Mediterranean climate of winter rain and summer drought, generally receives more rain and endures considerably colder winters than coastal California.

To summarize, plants grown in areas of brighter and more consistent sunlight, warmer temperatures, and lower humidity generally will tolerate more frequent watering than my basic recommendation, while those grown in areas with less light and heat and higher humidity may do better with somewhat less frequent water. Similarly, plants in sunny, warm climates can tolerate a wider variety of soils, while in less favorable conditions it is important to make sure that soil dries quickly and, especially in winter, thoroughly. This, of course, is a very broad overview, and I will cover the needs of specific plants in the appropriate chapters further into the text.

WATER

The first thing that strikes most people when it comes to growing succulent plants is that their need for water differs from typical plants. Their watering requirements result from a combination of the plants' origins in nature and their specific growing sites in cultivation.

SUCCULENTS FROM SUMMER-RAINFALL REGIONS

The majority of succulent plants come from places with dry winters and summer rainfall. Consequently, most of them benefit from a dry winter dormant period. A simple general rule is to water once a week in the warm months of the year and once a month in winter, though this rule is riddled with almost endless exceptions.

Maintaining a rigid watering schedule can be a road to disaster, and strictly following a calendar has led to the death of innumerable succulent plants. If the surface of the soil remains wet a week after being watered, the plant should be left dry for an extra day, or two, or three, until it actually needs water. During the growing season, when the soil is dry an inch or two (2.5 to 5 cm) below the surface the plant is probably ready for water. Following a very loose watering schedule is particularly important for those succulents that grow in winter; "once a week" may actually turn out to be once every two weeks or even longer during times of low light and low temperatures.

Whenever they are watered it is a good idea to water most succulents deeply, if in a container, with enough water to fill the container to its rim. Deep watering promotes strong root growth.

Among the many exceptions to the once-a-week/once-a-month rule, many common South African succulents, such as crassulas and adromischus, as well as most pachycaul types with thin, deciduous leaves, will do better with more frequent winter water, about every three weeks. In contrast, succulents from arid regions can be watered as infrequently as every eight or ten weeks in winter, while certain species and entire genera do best if left completely dry for their whole dormant period. Leafy succulents, such as echeverias and the Madagascan crown-of-thorn type euphorbias will need more water when resting; about every two weeks usually suffices. A few unusual succulents, such as the succulent dorstenias from East Africa and Arabia, should never completely dry out; providing them with water every week to ten days even in winter works best.

When plants start growing again, as the days brighten and warm up, the pace of their watering should proportionately increase. During the peak growing times the once-a-week rule applies to most succulent plants, but a few types should never thoroughly dry out, and less frequent water every ten days, two weeks, or even less often is best for many particularly dry-growing succulents.

After incorporating all these rules, it is equally important to remember that these directions are approximate, and that some skilled growers water more often, others less. Microhabitats and specific growing situations have a lot to do with that, as well as personal growing habits. In places such as sunny Southern California or the desert states to the east of it, plants can be watered more frequently. A dormant succulent plant that does best here in Berkeley with water every six weeks or so in winter could safely be watered once a month in these areas while a species that when growing should only receive water every ten days or two weeks in Berkeley might be safely watered once a week there. Conversely, in the Pacific Northwest, much of England, and other regions with cold, dark winters, and relatively subdued sunlight even in summer, less frequent watering, sometimes much less, is advisable, whether during the peak of the summer

Echeveria subrigida, a beautiful specimen showing damage on its leaf bases, the effect of residual water eroding its powdery covering.

growing season or the winter rest period. It is remarkable how slowly succulent plants absorb water during dormancy. Though soil in a pot may dry out completely within a week after watering in summer, it may still be thoroughly wet five or six weeks after being watered in winter.

SUCCULENTS FROM WINTER-RAINFALL REGIONS AND FOG DESERTS

Succulent plants that originate in areas of winter rainfall, particularly fog deserts, require quite different treatment. For most of these, the growing period begins typically in early autumn, and during this still-often-warm and bright period many plants will respond to weekly water. Except for regions where sunny winter days predominate, such as much of Southern California, the arrival of winter with its attendant low levels of light mandates a reduction in watering even though plants may be in active growth. As sunlight begins to increase in strength in early spring, the frequency of watering can increase with it until the plants enter into their dormant season, typically from late spring through early summer.

Many dwarf mesembryanthemums come from fog deserts and some of these need absolute summer dryness. Many other fog desert dwellers, however, should receive water every three or four weeks during the summer months. Unfortunately, in northern regions the level of light in winter often is too low to promote healthy growth, and though some winter-growing plants will adapt to a summer watering schedule, a significant number of them will never truly thrive when thrown off their natural growing cycle. As a result, people in much of Europe as well as parts of the United States may encounter difficulties when trying to grow these plants.

The colorful *Lithops optica* 'Rubra', dry for three months and still only halfway through its dormant period, with new growth emerging from the middle of its fading old growth.

SUCCULENTS FROM SPRING- AND AUTUMN-RAINFALL AREAS

A third geographically determined watering regime applies to the many succulent plants that grow somewhat west of the center of South Africa, in the various Karoo deserts (Little, Great, Robertson, Ceres). Many of these plants tend to grow in spring and fall, with relative rest periods in both summer and winter, though most should receive occasional water even then. Since these plants include favorites such as most haworthias and many adromischus, crassulas, and euphorbias, it is worth becoming familiar with the patterns that underlie their cycles of growth.

SUCCULENTS BORDERING WINTER- AND SUMMER-RAINFALL ENVIRONMENTS

A few very interesting succulent plants grow in exotic, remote places such as the islands between the Horn of Africa and Arabia, on the border of winter- and summer-rainfall environments, where they may receive a bit of precipitation at any time of year. Plants native to these areas need some water year-round; nonetheless, winter, with its subdued light and diminished heat, should be a time with less water for them as well.

WATER QUALITY

Finally, a current topic of concern to succulent plant collectors is water quality, particularly the acidity or alkalinity of the water itself. A number of skilled growers assert that water with a pH much higher than 6.0 (significantly lower than tap water) seriously compromises the ability of plants to absorb nutrients (and pesticides as well). There are various methods, more or less elaborate, to acidify water, and it may be helpful to explore these if plants do not seem to be doing as well as they should.

SOIL MIXES

Even though many succulent plants grow only in odd types of soil, it generally is not necessary—and can be counterproductive—to mimic their native ground. Most succulent plants can tolerate a wide range of soils as long as the mix allows for rapid drainage. Every skilled grower will have a favorite soil mix (or mixes), depending on personal preferences arrived at over time in accordance with the specific needs of favored plants and each growing situation.

COMMERCIAL MIXES

Many people have good luck with commercially manufactured succulent soil mixes, although some of these, particularly if based on ground peat moss, should be changed frequently, about every two years, as they may turn toxic over time. Coir, a coconut-based fibrous medium, is often amended with pumice or perlite to increase drainage. Like other soilless mixes it requires regular fertilization, and plants grown in such media will benefit from fairly low nitrogen fertilizers diluted to about one quarter the recommended strength every month or so while actively growing. Some growers provide a weak dose of fertilizer every time they water. Plants cultivated in this manner often grow rapidly; as a result commercial growers frequently favor these types of mixes. Consequently, plants raised this way may suffer after being purchased and treated in a less systematically organized manner.

Planting mixes may also be based on sandy-loamy soil, blended with extra drainage material such as pumice, scoria, perlite, or coarse sand, and the further addition of a little well-rotted leaf mold or other humus product. Avoid water-retaining vermiculite and fine or builder's sand, which turns to something resembling cement in a pot. Plants in such a mix will not be as dependent on applications of fertilizer as plants in artificial mixes, but dilute low-nitrogen or balanced fertilizers a few times a year during the growing season certainly will not hurt. Not as easy to find, but also useful, small amounts of low-nitrogen, timed-release fertilizer may be added to the general mix.

Leaf succulents such as echeverias and their relatives and many haworthias will benefit more from the extra organic matter than will plants from truly arid environments. Some of these very dry-growing plants, particularly some mimicry, stone-imitating mesembs, do best in a soil mix devoid of organic nutrients.

There is no single type of soil mix that will automatically work for everyone, everyplace, but each of the many different standard soil mixes can work well with the majority of succulent plants. Only a relatively few types of plants require anything more specialized than a slight adjustment of the proportions of ingredients in a standard mix, always in combination with excellent drainage.

DRAINAGE

Succulents should never be planted in containers without drainage holes. Traditionally this drainage was supplied by placing pieces of broken crockery over the drain hole,

Duplicating its habitat in the wild, *Graptopetalum paraguayense* flourishes with very little soil in the cracks of a stone wall, along with *Sedum furfuraceum* (above left) and *Pachyphytum hookeri* (partly visible on left).

a technique now largely discredited as leading to rot and providing a comfortable and secure dwelling place in the bottom of the pot for insect pests and slugs. Square plastic containers, with small drain holes on the sides, especially when filled with a fibrous mix, may not need anything extra to promote (or inhibit) drainage. Clay pots, with a larger central opening, drain so well that without something to slow things down most of the soil, or at least the smaller particles, may soon wash right out of the pot. Some fine mesh or screen placed over the hole will solve the problem. Another solution consists of placing a piece of paper towel over the hole or lining the whole bottom of a plastic pot to minimize this erosive effect and give the roots the opportunity to spread throughout the soil and hold it in place themselves.

LIGHT

Soil and water can be controlled anywhere, but adequate light can be a problem. The intensity of light varies greatly from location to location. The farther north, the less intense the sunlight, and therefore the more difficult it becomes to grow, and in particular to flower, the most light-seeking plants. Nonetheless, outstanding conservatory succulent plant collections thrive in relatively northern locations, including several in continental Europe.

Conversely, in the U.S. Southwest and in drier and hotter parts of Southern California, many succulent plants need extra shade to keep them healthy. In the wild, even in true deserts, most plants receive a little beneficial shade at least when young, so direct full sun all day for a potted plant can seriously burn or even kill it. In mild coastal

The brilliantly colored hybrid *Echeveria* 'Mt. Aetna', responding to ideal conditions of light.

California the burning afternoon sun coming through west-facing windows still may severely scorch plants.

PROVIDING ENOUGH LIGHT INDOORS

For purposes of indoor cultivation, gentle eastern sunlight will not burn plants but may not be adequate, bright southern sun will provide the maximum total light but may require additional shade, hot western exposure necessitates extra shade as well, and northern light is insufficient for any but a few plants such as sansevierias. Fortunately, something as simple as a thin curtain placed over a window will generally provide enough shade for even a very exposed situation. In general, the most light a plant can take without burning is best, but exactly what constitutes "the most light" varies greatly. Plants that grow in the open in the Chihuahuan or Namibian desert can withstand blazing sun that would fatally burn a soft green haworthia within a couple of hours.

As a rule gray, brown, blue, and red plants can take more sun than plain green ones. There are exceptions on both sides, so it is important to learn to recognize how sunburn, which manifests itself in irregular, pale, bleached-out patches, differs from good color. For many highly colored or waxy textured leaf succulents the ideal is extremely bright but diffused light, difficult to achieve outside of a greenhouse or cold frame. When grown under inadequate light, many highly colored succulents lose their bright coloration and revert to plain green.

Etiolation is another response to inadequate light. It occurs when the leaves of a succulent become increasingly small and spaced farther apart while the stems grow steadily thinner. With a little experience the damage

caused by either too much or too little light becomes very obvious.

PROVIDING SHADE, VENTILATION, AND HEAT IN A GREENHOUSE OR COLD FRAME

In a greenhouse or a cold frame the situation shifts from determining how to provide enough light to deciding how to keep from providing too much. A greenhouse constructed from glass will require shading, whether from shade-cloth or from the application of shade compound directly to the glass.

If shade-cloth is used it is better to attach it to the outside of the greenhouse instead of the inside, where it will decrease the intensity of the transmitted light but have no effect on heat build up. Depending on greenhouse location, shade-cloth providing shade of thirty, forty, or fifty percent generally works best, with a higher percentage in brighter, hotter areas. In areas of sustained lower levels of sunlight, there may be no need at all for additional shade, but beware the occasional bright, sunny day.

Shade compounds range from simple whitewash to more elaborate mixes, and the use of such products makes it possible to "fine tune" the light transmission within a greenhouse. Adequate light transmission will generate obvious, but blurry shadows. Shadows with sharp, crisp borders indicate too much light. When using a material other than glass, it is best to use translucent rather than clear panels. A number of advanced greenhouse coverings simultaneously transmit and diffuse light as well as repel condensation, and these provide excellent light transmission in combination with relatively low maintenance.

Unheated cold frames essentially act as small greenhouses. Because of their small size and limited internal volume, it is vital to make sure they receive adequate ventilation and shade during warm weather. Temperatures in excess of 100°F (38°C) will not harm most succulent plants, but at 110°F (43°C) or more some plants will suffer. Whether in a cold frame or a greenhouse, vigorous air circulation results in healthier plants, less susceptible both to burning and to fungal or bacterial attack.

Although many succulent plants will tolerate a few degrees of frost, particularly if they are dry, others most definitely will not. A safe general minimum temperature for most succulents is around 50°F (10°C), but some Madagascan and East African plants will do better with a minimum closer to 55°F (13°C). A few succulent plants need much warmer temperatures; for some bottom heat provided with a heating cable or mat is the only way to keep them alive, with a minimum soil temperature of 70 to

75°F (21 to 24°C). The use of bottom heat when rooting cuttings often speeds up root growth as well. These are exceptions, and very warm night and soil temperatures will negatively impact the majority of succulent plants.

GROWING OUTDOORS

Good drainage is vital for all but the hardiest outdoor succulents, and with sufficient drainage many succulents can tolerate annual rainfall of 30 inches (760 mm) or more. Growing on a slope or raised planting area vastly improves drainage. Adding amendments such as pumice, lava rock, or ordinary gravel also helps, particularly in areas with clay soils. The gaps between stones in a rock wall provide a natural-looking, fast-draining setting. There is no limit to how elaborate a succulent garden can be, but relatively simple modifications of the chosen area often will suffice.

Though many succulents come from summer-rainfall areas, they will often adapt to outdoor growing conditions in winter-rainfall regions, particularly when given additional water in the summer months, perhaps every week or two. In such circumstances winter-growing plants will not need to switch growing seasons, but since many of them are specialized for survival under extremely arid conditions it is best to use a bit of caution when placing them in the ground, particularly in summer-rainfall areas. In either case, it is good to give the plants a rest from water for a couple of months.

Many succulents experience freezing temperatures in the wild, but these are rarely combined with rain, and even in winter-rainfall areas the precipitation totals are very small and humidity is low. The worst scenario for an outdoor succulent garden is the combination of rain and freezing temperatures. Under these conditions the cells of the plants can freeze internally, causing them to burst their cell walls and leading to a characteristic "melted" appearance. In such circumstances not much can be done to save the plants.

Consequently, success in growing succulent plants outdoors is very dependent on location and climate. As a point of reference, Berkeley, California, is considered to be in USDA climate zone 10b, with average winter lows from 35 to 40°F (2 to 4°C), but UCBG, with its hillside location, almost always receives a little frost in winter. Broadly speaking, USDA climate zones 10a, 10b, and 11, with average winter lows above 30°F (–1°C), are excellent localities for outdoor succulent gardens. USDA zones 9a and 9b, with average winter lows from 20 to 30°F (–7 to –1°C), are acceptable for at least some plants. Anything much colder, with winter lows below 20°F (–7°C) only support a very reduced variety of succulents. In this book plants described as being slightly frost hardy can safely withstand 28°F (–2°C), moderately frost hardy down to around 24°F (–4°C), and frost hardy, to around 20 (–7°C), with certain rugged exceptions.

Southern California is a paradise for outdoor succulent gardens, central California a bit less so, but in less-hospitable climates the choice of plants to grow outdoors diminishes. The minimal humidity of the desert Southwest enables many succulent plants to survive subfreezing temperatures that might prove fatal to them in moister areas. Growers of outdoor succulent plants in desert regions, however, must protect many of their plants from too much sunlight, rarely an issue in more moderate climates. The Rocky Mountain states will support a small number of hardy succulents (and quite a few cacti) in outdoor situations; again the low humidity helps. Farther east, the combination of fairly high rainfall totals and subfreezing winters limits choices for outdoor succulent growing, although plants such as sempervivums and some sedums will tolerate frigid temperatures and snow as easily there as in their southern European mountain homes.

When planting an outdoor garden it is important to realize how large the plants will ultimately become and to take care not to place large spiny, potentially dangerous plants too close to paths. Succulents outdoors require little fertilizing. Interestingly, more often than not if a plant will survive in the ground it will look better and more natural than a container-grown specimen of the same species. Consequently, it is worth conducting a few experiments to see what will survive outdoors in any given area.

Plants grown outdoors in containers should receive the same general treatment as greenhouse or indoor plants. More sensitive plants will benefit from being sheltered from winter rain, and in the hot months container-grown plants, particularly those in small pots, will dry out rapidly while the soil temperature may rise dangerously. Especially when small, plants in outdoor containers should receive some shade, and newly acquired plants should be exposed somewhat gradually to brighter conditions.

REPOTTING AND PROPAGATION

There are as many ideas about repotting plants as there are about soil mixes, and, once again, there is no single correct method. The types of pots themselves offer some choices. Some people prefer plain terra-cotta pots; others glazed ceramic or plastic containers. Square plastic pots take up much less room than round pots, allowing for more plants in the same amount of space, but cannot compete with ceramic pots in terms of aesthetic appeal. Unglazed terra cotta pots dry out more quickly than the others, which can be either an advantage or a disadvantage depending on circumstances.

Salt and other water-borne minerals build up more quickly in plain terra cotta pots as well, and this can be a serious problem in areas with high mineral content in the water. Mineral buildup can be cleaned easily from plastic pots, but terra cotta pots need to be scrubbed thoroughly to free them from accumulated salts. Soaking previously used pots (both plastic and terra-cotta) in a five- or ten-percent bleach solution for at least half an hour will eliminate any pathogens such as fungi, bacteria, or virus that might be lurking in bits of soil or old roots.

Most growers repot at the beginning of a plant's growing period, though some prefer to repot during dormancy. It is best to pot when the soil is neither too wet nor too dry, often four or five days after watering, as the roots will hold the slightly moist soil in a ball. If too wet, the soil tends to drop off in heavy clumps, destroying roots in the process, and if too dry the small root hairs, through which nutrients are absorbed, will often be damaged as the loose soil crumbles and falls apart. The new container should not be much larger than the previous one as it will take a long time for roots to spread throughout a larger pot, leaving pockets of wet soil that can serve as a breeding ground for fungus and bacteria. In most cases it is a good idea to wait from thirty-six to seventy-two hours after repotting to water the plant, allowing time for any damaged root tips to heal.

LEAF CUTTINGS

Many succulent plants are very easy to propagate. Some grow from leaf cuttings, at times almost too readily. In the case of most *Adromischus* or *Echeveria* species, it is important to detach the whole leaf, particularly the basal portion that attaches to the stem, while other succulents, such as certain *Gasteria*, will root from just a portion of a leaf. After drying off (within a few days in most cases), the leaves can be placed on the surface of a pot filled with medium-coarse sand or perlite, kept semishaded and slightly moist. The leaves often will start sending out roots within several days.

A leaf cutting: *Graptopetalum paraguayense* with new plantlets sprouting from the base of the detached leaf.

A well-rooted stem cutting of *Euphorbia restricta*.

STEM CUTTINGS

Taking a cutting by slicing through or snapping off the stem solves the problem of what to do with an ungainly plant grown too tall for its container. As a bonus, the old stems frequently will produce new growths, which can then be separated after they have reached a reasonable size or started to produce their own roots. Both stem cutting and newly separated plantlets should be allowed to heal over and dry off before placing them in a rooting medium, where they can be treated in the same manner as leaf cuttings. A fully healed over cut should be quite dry, calloused over, or with new semitranslucent skin covering the cut. Generally stem cuttings heal almost as quickly as leaf cuttings, but some, such as thick-stemmed euphorbias, may require several months to heal completely.

DIVISION OF CLUMPS

Clumps may be divided, with any unprotected surfaces allowed to dry and heal over, then replanted and watered after a couple of days. It is important to note that cutting plants potentially exposes them to virus infection, spread through the use of nonsterile tools. Members of the crassula family seem the most susceptible to virus, but plants from other families may be at risk as well. Sterilizing cutting tools by flaming them or dipping them into a five- or ten-percent solution of bleach should become a habit. Alternatively, cutting through stems with a single-edged razor blade and using a new blade for each plant will also prevent infection.

SEED

Growing plants from seed can be more challenging, and with plants that grow easily from cuttings or that clump rapidly it is rarely necessary. With some succulents, however, seed propagation is the only way to produce a mature-looking specimen. Furthermore, in contrast to a batch of genetically identical cuttings, a population of seed-grown plants will exhibit a natural range of variation.

Most seeds will germinate in a mix similar to one used for rooting cuttings. Some germinate quickly and lose their viability rapidly as well. Others such as many mesembryanthemum seeds remain viable for years. Seeds may be quite large or almost as fine as dust, and the smallest ones (typical of the crassula family) often germinate better in a moisture-retaining medium such as damp peat moss. The seeds must be kept moist, but not so wet as to allow the spread of fungal or bacterial rot. Once germinated and past their first precarious months of growth some succulents attain their adult form quite rapidly while others grow and develop extraordinarily slowly.

HORTICULTURAL FORMS AND ODDITIES

Some succulent plants are simply very difficult to keep alive. It is often possible to graft such plants onto the stem of a related but hardier species. Grafting also encourages the production of offsets on slow-growing plants, which then can be detached and rooted on their own.

Grafting is accomplished by cutting through both the plant to be grafted (the scion) and the plant onto which it will be grafted (the stock plant). Their circular cambium layers are placed in contact with each other, and the two are attached, by elastic bands, toothpicks, or any other convenient methods. The two plants effectively merge, with the scion turning into the new growing point of the stock plant, thereby benefiting from its superior vigor. Many rare, slow-growing, and fragile Somali euphorbias are grown this way, often grafted onto the sturdy *Euphorbia fruticosa*.

Variability in seedling group of *Lithops karasmontana* "laterita" red form.

Newly germinated seedlings of *Agave parviflora*, their seed cases still attached. Photo by Terry Thompson.

Grafted *Euphorbia turbiniformis*, rare and almost impossible on its own roots.

Always sought after in cultivation, variegated plants such as this *Agave montana* are almost never seen in habitat. Photo by Brian Kemble.

ties shut off from fresh air, providing ideal environments for fungi and similar pathogens. In such cases, grafting relatively high on a stock will keep the crest safely raised above the soil level. Crests occur in succulents from many genera and may grow successfully for years, but fasciation can also be a symptom of disease or a genetic fault.

Monstruose plants have twisted or otherwise picturesquely deformed growth habits and are sometimes prized as novelties; they usually grow adequately on their own roots. Unusual shapes, colors, or patterning are valued as highly by many succulent growers as by other horticulturalists. Both selective breeding of succulent plants within a species and hybridization between different species have been factors in succulents, with sometimes astonishing results.

At its best, grafting results in plants almost indistinguishable from specimens grown on their own roots, but

Haworthia pumila, variegated and with doughnut shaped tubercles.

Crested *Euphorbia piscidermis,* a grafted specimen. Photo by Terry Thompson.

Variegated plants are rare in the wild and thus highly valued by some collectors. Variegated plants that retain a reasonable amount of chlorophyll will grow adequately on their own, though usually more slowly than nonvariegated ones. Extremely variegated plants, however, are so seriously deficient in chlorophyll that they will do better if grafted, as will some crested plants.

A crested or fasciated plant develops when, for various reasons, growth occurs along a line rather than a single growing point. Crests that develop high on a plant generally have little or no effect on its hardiness, though on the whole crested plants also grow slowly. In some instances, the edges of their irregular growth reach down to the surface of the soil in places, creating hollow cavi-

Crested *Pachypodium lamerei* growing on its own roots. Photo by Terry Thompson.

A highly patterned, select form of *Haworthia truncata* var. *maughanii*.

Echeveria grisea infested with mealy bug.

at times the extra boost the graft receives from its stock plant may produce an unnaturally robust plant that will look swollen and distended in comparison to examples grown on their own roots. Nonetheless, grafting can make it possible to grow delicate plants that otherwise would never survive.

Although tissue culture and other technologically advanced means of growing plants are becoming more common among commercial growers, relatively few collectors and hobbyists need to produce mass quantities of specific plants. Information is readily available for those who wish to try.

DISEASES AND PESTS

Succulent plants, if healthy and given enough water and light, generally resist disease quite well. Excess humidity, however, can be a problem especially when plants are dormant. Some plants from extremely arid areas have very little resistance to bacteria, and humid winters can often prove fatal to them. Moving air aids to prevent fungal and bacterial rot from starting. Appropriate fungicides will alleviate these problems, and garden sulfur or charcoal dust applied to cut surfaces also helps prevent rot.

Insect pests come in all sizes and shapes, with mealy bugs and scale insects being perhaps the most widespread. White fly, the larva of sciarid flies, and aphids will damage plants, and root mealy bugs, hidden beneath the soil, can quickly kill a plant. Various mites can also cause considerable harm and many insecticides have no effect on these small arachnids necessitating the use of miticides. Red spider and related mites thrive in low humidity and infestations can be kept down by the simple

misting of the affected plants. Aloe gall mite causes bizarre and debilitating abnormal growth (sometimes referred to as "aloe cancer"). It is difficult to control and perhaps is best avoided by taking care when acquiring plants. Sow bugs and pill bugs mostly eat decaying material, but they will go after fresh roots as well. Ants place aphids as well as mealy bugs and scale onto plants to obtain the honeydew that these insects secrete. Snails and slugs can quickly wreak havoc on smaller plants, and a panoply of insects awaits those succulents planted outdoors. Nonetheless, it is not hard to keep a small collection clean.

Inspect plants carefully after purchasing them. If possible keep them physically separated from the rest of your plants for a number of days, and treat any infestations quickly. Rubbing alcohol applied with a small brush will kill the insects it comes in contact with, though too much alcohol will damage a plant. A toothpick can help with the physical removal of a few pests, though it will not have any effect on those eggs you do not see, hidden away under spine clusters or by the base of a plant. Insecticidal soaps and other relatively safe, environmentally benign pesticides are increasingly making their way onto the market, but even some of these can damage sensitive plants. Certain groups, such as members of the Crassulaceae, especially those from the New World, along with genera such as *Pachypodium*, *Avonia*, and *Dorstenia* may be particularly sensitive to certain insecticides, or more commonly, the oil-based liquids in which they are suspended.

There are two basic types of insecticides. Contact insecticides kill insects upon touch, while systemic insecticides are absorbed by the plant, turning it toxic to the insects feeding on it. Be extremely cautious when using

Something for horticulturalists to emulate: a natural rock garden of succulent plants in the Richtersveld. Photo by Rob Skillin.

any pesticides in the home or outdoors. There are three levels of safety warnings: "caution" for the least toxic, "warning" for intermediate toxicity, and "danger" for the most toxic. Read the directions, use approved products, and when applying pesticides wear safety equipment such as chemical-resistant gloves, eye protection, approved respirators (not merely dust masks), or even more regardless of whether it seems a little foolish. Being overly cautious has never hurt anyone, while being overly bold can prove quite dangerous, even fatal, when it comes to chemicals.

CONSERVATION AND COLLECTING

In days now long past, collected plants were frequently offered for sale, and trips into habitat typically included collecting interesting specimens. Today such collecting is illegal almost everywhere and a plant collector is committing criminal acts, sometimes with quite severe penalties. It is hard to justify collecting as it was carried out in the past, and the value of conserving plants in the wild is impossible to argue with.

Unfortunately, in many cases the greatest threat to the survival of succulent plants is not collecting but habitat loss and degradation instead, and in most parts of the world relatively little effort is being made to protect the plants in their habitat. Many of the most interesting succulents have extremely restricted habitats, often in underdeveloped and developing countries, and though there are numerous admirable exceptions, in the face of economic opportunity their preservation usually ranks very low on the agenda.

Climate change may also present a serious threat to many succulent plants, which are adapted for survival at the very edge of environmental possibility—one more push may prove too much for them. There have been some minor efforts at habitat restoration and reestablishing species into the wild, but these projects have generally met with only limited success.

On the positive side, a number of growers around the world are propagating many of the rarest and most unusual succulents, which both takes pressure off the wild populations and makes a broad range of species available to the public. The most unusual plants are never going to be commercially common, as even with technologically advanced propagation methods they are still slow and often difficult to grow, and the challenge for the grower always will be to attempt to produce specimens that are as spectacular, and in their own odd way, beautiful, as those that occur in the deserts and the semiarid hills, mountains, steppes, and savannahs of the world.

Chapter 3

Crassula

CRASSULA, THE EPONYMOUS genus of the family Crassulaceae, includes some of the most commonly grown succulent plants as well as some of the most extraordinary. A few species have crossed over into general horticultural popularity, while many have become mainstays of succulent collections. And, still today, from time to time new introductions come along to renew the excitement of enthusiasts, reminding them of the amazing diversity within the genus.

As currently understood *Crassula* comprises about one hundred fifty species—some readily recognizable and others bafflingly variable. Almost any hill within the innumerable natural rock gardens of South Africa's Western Cape and Eastern Cape Provinces will be host to one or more *Crassula* species in the company of various aloes and haworthias, daisies (succulent and otherwise), mesembs, leathery leafed shrubs, and small trees.

In the arid western landscapes of Namaqualand crassulas constitute a significant portion of the largely succulent flora, brightening the rocky ground with a rainbow of leaf color. High on steep granite domes, the smallest cracks are crammed with crassulas, while far below window-leafed and mimicry crassulas share foggy quartz fields with other miniature succulents. In rainier environments low-growing crassulas find shelter amid mossy rocks under a thin canopy of trees, while other moisture-loving species put forth soft-leafed rosettes which flower and die, leaving behind perennial underground rootstocks. Some species even live in seasonal swamps; these, however, tend to be herbaceous annuals rather than succulents. Most crassulas stay put within the boundaries of South Africa or the countries immediately surrounding it, but a few extend far into eastern Africa, even crossing the sea into Yemen and southwestern Arabia.

Crassulas tend to be easy to recognize, but their uniting characteristic is in fact almost imperceptible: their leaves are dotted with hydathodes, a kind of pore that enables wet-growing plants to expel water, but which dry-growing crassulas have reversed, turning them into water-absorbing organs. Crassulas often combine water-conserving frugality with exquisite physical geometry, a geometry founded on their successive pairs of leaves, typically arranged in an opposite fashion on their stems, one pair topped by another rotated 90 degrees. Crassulas have taken this basic form and modified it to a degree rare even among succulent plants. Their five-petaled flowers, typically tiny dull whitish yellow, and often scented in a manner attractive to various small insects but not particularly to people, can in some species form a rounded mass of small white stars. In an exceptional few they are more brightly colored in pinks and reds.

Currently *Crassula* is divided taxonomically into twenty sections, some readily recognizable, others defined by botanically significant but visually obscure details. Some of these sections include species that look nothing alike, while certain species that closely resemble each other are placed in separate sections. For the horticulturalist these fine points of taxonomy do not matter very much, for the lasting fascination of *Crassula* derives from its astonishing variety of shapes, its leaf colors that range from austere blue-white to brilliant red, and—with exceptions—its ease of culture.

TREELIKE AND SHRUBBY CRASSULAS

Some crassulas with short internodes (the spaces between successive leaf-pairs) display a strikingly elegant four-ranked structure, but this opposite arrangement is not as obvious in species with leaves located farther apart on the stem. Among these are the two crassulas with thick succulent stems, rounded or spoon-shaped leaves, and a more-or-less arborescent habit: **Crassula ovata**, the ubiquitous jade plant, from the Eastern Cape and points northeast in South Africa, and its cousin from the West-

Crassula ovata 'Pink Beauty', selected for its flower color.

Crassula streyi, barely recognizable as a succulent plant.

Crassula pubescens growing in a clearing in a moist spot in the Western Cape.

ern Cape, **C. arborescens**. *Crassula arborescens* grows larger than *C. ovata*, to as much as 6 feet (1.8 m) tall, and it has larger leaves as well—silver-gray and heavily overlaid with bluish dots. Both species have a wide distribution in the wild, often growing in large numbers on rocky slopes. The two straddle seasonal rainfall boundaries, and in cultivation they demand little more than bright sunlight, reasonably well-drained soil, and shelter from hard frost.

A few other species take the form of a miniature tree, but with leaves more linear and pointed than round, as well as smaller and less succulent. These include the flat-leafed **Crassula sarcocaulis** and the common **C. tetragona**, with terete (round in cross section) leaves that taper to a point and brittle branches that break off readily and then root from even the smallest piece. In places with a suitably benign climate *C. tetragona* can become a pest.

The less-commonly cultivated **Crassula streyi**, from Natal in eastern South Africa, grows into a treelike small bush, though with decumbent (downward growing, with leaves upturned) rather than erect branches. It is distinguished most obviously from other crassulas by its large spoon-shaped, barely succulent leaves, leathery and with deep maroon undersides. *Crassula streyi* requires a bit more moisture and some protection from the brightest sunlight. Several other species with broad but relatively thin leaves also tolerate more water and less light than the more xerophytically adapted crassulas.

A number of other crassulas share the oval or obovate leaf shape of the jade plant but lack its massive stems and branches. Instead they sprawl over the ground or reach upwards to form small bushes. These include **Crassula cultrata**, an upright grower with a strikingly four-ranked leaf structure, **C. pubescens**, **C. dejecta** (synonym *C. undulata*), and **C. swaziensis** (synonym *C. argyrophylla*). Though their ranges vary, these species do not grow along the fog-bound, northwestern Atlantic coast of South Africa. Instead, they are found in areas that, though often dry, are typically far from true deserts; in some cases the plants grow in rocky outcrops on the edge or even in the midst of forests.

Many forms of **Crassula atropurpurea** and **C. nudicaulis** were once considered distinct species, with varyingly shaped leaves and overall habit. **Crassula atropurpurea** var. **atropurpurea** resembles *C. cultrata*, with multiple erect stems and rather spoon-shaped, sometimes slightly fuzzy leaves. Its foliage turns bright red in good sunlight, unlike that of var. **anomala**, perhaps the most common in cultivation, whose more densely pubescent leaves remain yellow-green. The two varieties come from comparatively well-watered regions of the Western Cape, but varieties from the drier and harsher environments to the northwest have developed a lower, more compact habit less susceptible to desiccation. Among these, **var. *watermeyeri***, with small loose rosettes kept close to the ground, grows in Namaqualand. It resembles **var. *cultriformis***, a plant with a series of very short-stemmed lax rosettes, but with its lowest internodes relatively elongated.

On the seashore not far from the Richtersveld town of Port Nolloth, a plant referable to *Crassula atropurpurea* var. *cultriformis* but with smaller, thickly succulent, and densely arranged leaf clusters forms compact mounds up to almost 12 inches (30 cm) high and wide. These plants manage to maintain a relatively lush appearance despite their bleak environment, an expanse of old beach sand they share with *Fenestraria rhopalophylla* and *Euphorbia ramiglans*, as well as visiting land snails with stark white shells and thick, almost black bodies.

Crassula nudicaulis exceeds even *C. atropurpurea* in its variability and in its number of now-invalid synonyms. It grows over a huge area, from southern Namibia in the northwest, along the southern rim of South Africa, and then northeast into Lesotho and KwaZulu-Natal. Probably the most widely distributed version, **var. *platyphylla*** hugs the ground with flattened, broadly oval leaves, often somewhat blue-gray and crowded together along its stems. **Variety *nudicaulis*** also remains low, with slightly asymmetrical leaves that turn reddish brown in good light. The other varieties have leaves that are more elongated, sometimes pointed or covered with small bristles, and sometimes, as with the Namaqualand-dwelling **var. *herrei***, rather blunt, as thick as broad, and completely smooth. These varieties also usually grow into slightly taller little bushes. It is no wonder that the various types of *C. nudicaulis* were at one time classified into as many as nine separate species. Still retained as valid species because of minute differences in the structure of their inflorescences, both the oblong, round-tip leafed **C. clavata** and the elongate-leafed **C. subacaulis** will turn quite red in good light.

Several other crassulas, a bit less variable and therefore more easily recognized, also grow as small shrubs with elongated leaves. Among these, **Crassula mesembryanthoides** may reach 12 inches (30 cm) or more in height, producing a number of thin branches with long tapering leaves, each cylindrical, green, and clad with small hairs. It is found in drier parts of eastern South Africa.

Farther west, **Crassula macowaniana** grows taller, though in the arid Richtersveld it may hug the ground. It forms a mass of stems densely covered with curved and tapering fingerlike leaves that can be 6 inches (15 cm) long. With a more restricted range within the same region, **C. fusca**, with smaller, often reddish brown leaves,

Crassula cf. *atropurpurea* subsp. *cultriformis*, growing on the dry Richtersveld coast. Photo by Kurt Zadnik.

Crassula macowaniana in the southern Richtersveld. Photo by Kurt Zadnik.

Crassula fusca, colored up nicely under greenhouse conditions.

is another infrequently grown species, as is the oval-leafed **C. cotyledonis**, a low bush with tomentose, blue-white foliage, akin to the leaves of its namesake, *Cotyledon orbiculata*. From wetter, mountainous areas closer to Cape Town, **C. pruinosa** is a small shrub with leaves densely covered with short white hairs.

Also from better-watered, higher elevations and much more widely grown, **Crassula coccinea** has suffered from an overdose of nomenclature, the fate of many pretty plants with a long history of cultivation, and for many years it and a few related species were classified as the genus *Rochea*. It is a small bush composed of usually erect, woody stems cloaked with stiff, barely succulent four-ranked triangular leaves. It belongs to the South African *fynbos* plant community, which consists largely of nonsucculent, drought-resistant plants characterized by long, narrow, leathery foliage. Its terminal heads of tubular scarlet flowers have ensured its popularity even among people otherwise little interested in succulents. Another *fynbos* resident, **C. ericoides**, from coastal districts of the South African south and east, looks like a member of the heath family (Ericaceae), growing into an upright bush with its many densely leafed stems bare at their bases, and with yellow flowers near the tips.

Rather resembling a reduced version of *Crassula ericoides*, **C. muscosa** occurs in almost every region in South Africa where succulent plants grow. A narrow-stemmed,

erect to scrambling plant with branches completely covered with four-ranked, almost scalelike leaves, it resembles a club moss (*Lycopodium*) and was once named *C. lycopodioides*. Very variable, it may have stems leafless at their base or fully clad, freely branching or single-stemmed, larger or smaller. When entirely covered with tiny yellow flowers along their leaf bases, the plants seem like yellow-green fuzzy pipe cleaners.

Typically lush and vigorous, in dry areas occasional plants almost certainly identifiable as *Crassula muscosa*, but considerably thicker and stockier, look almost like **C. pyramidalis**, an arid-growing species that botanically has little in common with *C. muscosa*. The differences between the species become dramatically obvious at flowering, when the monocarpic (taking several years to flower, then dying) *C. pyramidalis* produces a dense head of white to pinkish blossoms directly from the apices of its stems and then expires.

NECKLACE CRASSULAS

Crassula alpestris, another plant that dies after flowering, resembles *C. pyramidalis* in its upright growth habit but has distinct gaps between its paired leaves. It occurs from coastal southern Namaqualand, through the mountains directly to the east, to the semiarid regions farther east still. Its succulent leaves are thin, but spaced out

Crassula coccinea, with the thin, stiff leaves typical of *fynbos* plants.

Crassula muscosa, at home in both arid and better-watered conditions. Photo by Kurt Zadnik.

Crassula alpestris, stretching upward into its terminal inflorescence.

symmetrically along its stem they suggest another group of species known informally as necklace crassulas.

Freely branching, with upright, thin, often brittle stems supporting alternate pairs of flattened, thickly succulent leaves, these crassulas include very widely distributed as well as highly endemic species. With a long history of cultivation, the best known is **Crassula perforata**. It grows from the general vicinity of Cape Town past the curve of southern Africa up into KwaZulu-Natal. Its paired leaves are broadly triangular and yellow-green edged red when provided with good light, and its flowers are pale yellow. Its habitat is overlapped by the generally more western growing *C. rupestris*, an extremely variable species that differs most obviously in its more compact inflorescence and white to pinkish (as opposed to yellow) flowers. Abundant over much of its range, *C. rupestris* forms freely branching clumps a couple of feet (about 60 cm) across and nearly as tall. Some forms of **subsp. rupestris** look almost identical to *C. perforata*, but others may have leaves that are larger, or more pointed, or much thicker, a tendency taken to an extreme by the semiminiature **subsp. marnieriana**, with leaves nearly as thick as broad that completely enclose and surround the stems. Unfortunately, this subspecies, parent and half-sized look-alike of the popular **C. 'Jade Necklace'**, tends to lose its lower leaves, giving older plants a ragged look.

Crassula sladenii, similar to *C. rupestris*, is an untidy looking plant, with several 18-inch (45-cm) tall upright branches and irregularly spaced, almost round, 1- to 1.5-inch (2.5- to 4-cm) long leaves. It has, however, chosen some spectacular locations for its habitat—the rocky midslopes and saddles of apparently desolate Richtersveld and southern Namibian hills and koppies (small hills),

where big clumps of *Euphorbia hamata* and *E. dregeana* live down slope, and surreal-looking trees of *Aloe pillansii* dominate the rounded summits.

Less restricted to true desert lands but still capable of surviving long dry spells, **Crassula brevifolia** typically resembles the necklace crassulas, but its leaves may vary in shape from thick triangles to blunt-tipped ellipses not too different from those of *C. nudicaulis*. It is a species of west South Africa, from southern Namibia down to the southern boundary of Namaqualand, near Van Rhynsdorp and the Giftberg mountain complex. As it grows, it drops its older leaves and develops into an attractive little bush, a bit more than a foot (30 cm) tall and wide.

CRASSULAS WITH SHORT STEMS AND THIN ANGULAR LEAVES

Several *Crassula* species combine the genus's fundamental four-ranked leaf organization with short stems and thin, succulent, sharply angular leaves. A low-growing, spreading plant of this type, *C. socialis*, from the Eastern Cape, produces alternating pairs of broadly triangular leaves that when superimposed on each other look like the four corners of a square. It is a charming little plant, spreading rapidly but never taking up too much space, with each angular, densely leafy rosette rarely as much as an inch (2.5 cm) across and not even that tall except when in flower.

Some forms of **Crassula capitella** resemble the angular versions of *C. socialis*, but the species varies in overall size, leaf shape, and internode length. Some larger forms have leaf-pairs arranged rather laxly on their stems, while others hump up in an impressive display of botanical ge-

A brilliantly colored form of *Crassula brevifolia* from the Richtersveld. Photo by Rob Skillin.

The small-growing form of *Crassula capitella* once called *C. turrita*. Photo by Terry Thompson.

ometry when it comes time to flower, each stem looking something like a four-sided step pyramid surmounted by an elongated inflorescence. Widely distributed over much of South Africa, some smaller forms of *C. capitella* live in exposed, semiarid areas such as the Little Karoo where they attain a brilliant red coloration that will carry over into cultivation with sufficient light. Growing over different rainfall areas, most forms behave well in cultivation; providing sufficient light to keep them from sprawling and elongating is probably the key issue in the cultivation of this species.

STARBURST CRASSULAS

A number of species with alternating pairs of opposite but narrower leaves—some forms of *Crassula capitella* among them—grow into tiny bushes that viewed from above resemble a collection of four-pointed starbursts. Among them, *C. deltoidea*, scattered about from southern South Africa into southwestern Namibia, ordinarily exemplifies the four-pointed star effect. It frequents fairly arid places, facing the sun with sharply angular pairs of almost pure white to blue-white little leaves, though other forms, heavier-leafed and lacking the white overlay, show even more modifications for dry conditions.

Crassula exilis, widely distributed in South Africa and with an outlying variety in Madagascar as well, bears leaves with a ciliate edge and a dotted margin that range from flattened and broadly triangular to narrowly pointed and divided lengthwise into prismatic facets. Its several earlier names, such as *C. picturata* and *C. cooperi*, hint at its long history in cultivation, as these forms, gray-green

leafed, often red underneath and covered with decorative darker spots, are very appealing. Somewhat similar species include the monocarpic *C. congesta*, and high-altitude growers *C. setulosa* and *C. peploides* from the mountainous parts of eastern South Africa.

CRASSULAS WITH ROUNDED LEAVES

A further group of related crassulas includes several species with rounded or broadly pointed leaves. When superimposed, the successive leaf-pairs combine to produce designs of precisely delineated circles, ornate fourfold Gothic quatrefoil windows, and Art Nouveau rosettes.

The most commonly cultivated of these, ***Crassula orbicularis***, seeks somewhat moist, generally shaded places in both the Western and Eastern Cape Provinces, shunning true desert environments. Its rosettes vary from almost circular to rather pointed, with a slightly concave habit that makes them look like shallow, overturned cups composed of overlapping rounded or elliptical green scales. **Var. orbicularis** sends out new orbs on thin runners from one to several inches (about 2.5 to 7.5 cm) long, never forming a solid mass of rosettes. **Var. rosularis**, in contrast, grows in dense clusters, though the differences between the two may be pretty approximate.

Two similar species from farther to the west also seek out shaded places to grow, often on the south side of mountainous slopes where they share their limited space with *Adromischus* and shade-loving *Conophytum* species. The more widely distributed of these, ***Crassula pseudohemisphaerica***, from the west and as far north as Namibia, partly gives way to *C. montana* to the south and east. The two species differ mainly in floral characteris-

Crassula deltoidea, with thicker, more blue-red leaves than normal.

Crassula orbicularis, growing vertically in a shaded, moist spot in the Western Cape.

Crassula pseudohemisphaerica typically forms dense clusters—this one was different. Photo by Rob Skillin.

Crassula barbata, hiding under a bush in harsh country. Photo by Rob Skillin.

tics. Each makes four-ranked, roughly circular rosettes, a bit angular and somewhat rhomboidal. They tend to cluster quite tightly and form masses of slightly cupped rosettes, more typically growing nearly vertically than flat on level ground.

Sharing their territory and extending considerably farther east, **Crassula hemisphaerica** forms small dome-shaped, often solitary rosettes, variously rounded or more ornately four-pointed. In the Little Karoo it grows around the base of bushes, near a possibly hybrid *Euphorbia* allied with *E. anoplia*; close by, large, somewhat sunburned astrolobas sprout in the midst of big clumps of chalk-white *Gibbaeum pubescens*. A very attractive little plant, *C. hemisphaerica* unfortunately often dies after flowering, although it may leave a few surviving offsets behind.

HAIRY CRASSULAS

Always monocarpic, **Crassula barbata** has developed a survival strategy of growing directly underneath small twiggy bushes, which presumably provide it with a degree of protection from both potential predators and the harsh environment in which it generally grows. Its most striking characteristic, leaves thickly fringed with fine, fluffy white hairs that in some cases completely obscure

the plant, makes it look as bearded as its name implies. I have seen it sharing its hidden home beneath a bush with *Haworthia semiviva*, a completely unrelated succulent that also consists of a small rosette densely fringed with white hair. *Crassula barbata* occurs here and there in the Western Cape, including the stony hills and plateaus that border Bushmanland and the Tanqua Karoo, areas of a little winter rain and intense cold and heat.

Two other hairy crassulas also deserve mention. **Crassula ciliata** forms clusters of rosettes fringed at their leaf margins. It is more a coastal and coast mountain species than an inhabitant of the harsh interior deserts and highlands.

Crassula tomentosa, which in some cases is barely tomentose at all, often grows in areas where the combination of winter rain and summer fog results in succulent-rich semiarid, rather than truly desertlike habitats. Its alternating leaf-pairs spiral around each other, resulting in elliptical rather than circular growths. It remains low-growing and over time produces a substantial number of clustered rosettes.

DRY-GROWING CRASSULAS

The fog-bound coastal deserts of South Africa and southern Namibia, along with the even harsher arid lands of the neighboring interior, provide a habitat for a number of truly dry-growing crassulas, strikingly geometric, almost architectural plants designed for survival under difficult circumstances. Looking like little columns or Art Deco styled masonry chimneys, these species hide their stems beneath the thick, densely packed, symmetrical and usually triangular leaves that serve as the "bricks."

Some grow strictly upright, others sprawl; some live in the quartz fields, others in the surrounding hills, and some manage to survive almost entirely on fog within easy sight of the ocean. Striking plants, analogous to some mimicry mesembs, their popularity resulted in a host of species names now reduced to synonymy. Many respond well to cultivation though others often fail to thrive once out of the extreme environmental conditions in which they have developed.

Never far from the Richtersveld and adjacent Namibian seashores, *Crassula plegmatoides* (often incorrectly called *C. arta*) forms upright columns of thick blue-white leaves, slightly fuzzy but otherwise unadorned. It branches quite freely from the base and often grows in sand or gravelly flats where it forms clusters of erect stems up to 6 inches (15 cm) in height and diameter, looking like a complex of faintly segmented, dome-topped little towers. Despite its restricted range and specialized environmental preferences, *C. plegmatoides* is quite easy to grow and propagate, although in cultivation its lower leaves may gradually wither and drop off.

The closely related, also highly endemic *Crassula columella* lives several miles back from the coast in the southern Richtersveld, generally growing on little flat rocky shelves or between small horizontal ridges. Its leaves—basically green rather than blue—redden under the bright sun (see photo on page 163). *Crassula columella* branches freely from the base and though rarely more than 2 inches (5 cm) tall, an exceptionally large plant may cover a 6-inch (15-cm) square of uninviting rock; plants growing on tiny mountain ledges will remain smaller. Its columns of closely arrayed, soft almost velvet-textured leaves taper smoothly and readily branch. Although the plants withstand full sun, in cultivation they also do well with less light than most of their relatives. Perhaps understandably, growers frequently confuse *C. columella* with the similarly named *C. columnaris*.

Crassula barklyi (synonym *C. teres*) also forms round-tipped columns of extremely tightly arrayed leaves. It spreads horizontally and produces many short secondary branches. Its leaves remain smooth, almost leathery, and in good light turn brown or slightly reddish. Unlike the previous two species, its dense, brushlike, fragrant inflorescences emerge directly from the apices of its stems; in this respect it resembles the related *C. columnaris*. *Crassula barklyi* performs well in cultivation if given adequate light and grows fairly rapidly. It is restricted to Namaqualand, typically found between rocks, not far from the sea but not at the seashore itself.

In contrast, *Crassula columnaris* ranges over a very wide area, from the winter-rainfall parts of southern Namibia, through the Richtersveld and Namaqualand, and south and east into the Little Karoo and bits of the Great Karoo as well. It somewhat resembles *C. barklyi*, though less smooth and rounded, but generally remains solitary; even the northern **subsp. *prolifera*** simply puts out a few small secondary stems that surround the central stem. In the extremely bright situations in which it typically grows, *C. columnaris* often remains quite low, more an elongated little dome than a column, and the apical leaves of a single plant can vary from green to yellow-brown to red, resulting in a sort of plaid effect. Some forms of subsp. *prolifera* can be almost black. *Crassula columnaris* puts forth a sessile (stalkless) white to yellow inflorescence similar to *C. barklyi*, but fuller and more symmetrical, and, unusually for a crassula, sweetly scented. The

At the beach, with *Crassula plegmatoides* and snail shells. Photo by Kurt Zadnik.

Crassula columella growing on a stair-step quartzite slope in the Richtersveld.

A dense cluster of *Crassula barklyi,* not far from the sea. Photo by Rob Skillin.

Wedged between rocks in the Ceres Karoo, *Crassula columnaris* prepares to give its all. Photo by Rob Skillin.

flowering stem dies after blooming, and since most forms only have one stem, that pretty much is it for the plant. As a result, despite being common and widespread in habitat, it is not seen too often in collections.

Crassula deceptor, another widespread species, makes short, thick columns, its hard-textured leaves usually heavily marked with raised dark dots that contrast with its overall color of pure, pale blue-white. The closely arrayed leaves may be almost rounded, or broadly pyramidal, or distinctly pointed and upswept, like a collection of little canine teeth—the more upswept versions were once known as *C. cornuta. Crassula deceptor* grows from coastal southern Namibia through the Richtersveld and Namaqualand, and east over the mountains into Bushmanland as well. Often found either in or on the edges of quartz fields, smaller plants of *C. deceptor* blend in with the white quartz pebbles (see photo on page 16). Larger plants, up to about 4 inches (10 cm) tall, are easy to see, as are those growing along the quartzfield margins, which they share with succulents such as *Tylecodon reticulatus* and *Aloe krapohliana.*

Another widespread species confined mostly to arid winter-rainfall regions, the variable **Crassula elegans** perhaps is less smoothly elegant than its name suggests. If most of these densely columnar species have a sort of precisely machined, Art Deco look, *C. elegans* is a little less symmetrical, perhaps more Arts and Crafts in style. It

Crassula deceptor, approaching the upswept form once called *C. cornuta.*

Very variable, *Crassula elegans* can be red or green, tubercled or smooth.

The short-spiraled rosettes of *Crassula alstonii* are unique in the genus. Photo by Kurt Zadnik.

The erect but brittle stems of *Crassula grisea* break all too easily.

Crassula sericea ranges from blue-purple to red-brown to yellow-green.

Variously blue or green and more or less fuzzy, *Crassula namaquensis* thrives in dry surroundings. Photo by Rob Skillin.

is composed of overlapping, thick pairs of alternating, extremely succulent leaves, sometimes decorated with raised white dots, sometimes unadorned, ranging from light lavender to bright red, and more often than not in cultivation, plain green. Its leaves in some cases look almost like green, pink, or red jelly beans stuck closely together, but with their edges distinctly protruding, giving it a somewhat knobby appearance. Though mainly confined to Namaqualand and its fringing mountains, *C. elegans* also extends as far as Bushmanland to the east, pushing beyond the winter-rainfall boundary.

A very different fog-desert species, *Crassula alstonii*, rather than making columns, arranges its elliptically paired leaves into little spheres. It is from the Namaqualand coastal flats where it grows in sandy soil, sometimes as a solitary little ball rarely 2 inches (5 cm) across, occasionally in small groups. *Crassula alstonii*, uncommon in cultivation, looks like nothing else in the genus, although hybrid plants exist that combine its spiraled front with an elongated stem.

Closely related to the columnar species but variously rosette-forming or with elongated internodes, a few additional species with extremely thick succulent leaves have also mastered survival in hard places. *Crassula grisea*, from southwestern Namibia south into Namaqualand, resembles plants such as *C. brevifolia* and some forms of *C. nudicaulis*; that is, it consists of erect stems with opposite pairs of flat-topped, thick, round-tipped leaves which, however, emerge at an angle almost perfectly perpendicular to the stems. Additionally, its leaves are distinctly blue-white in contrast to the greenish foliage of those other species. Finally, rather than forming a bush, *C. grisea* sends up a series of closely packed, completely upright little branches 6 to 8 inches (15 to 20 cm) tall. Though easy to grow, its stems are quite brittle and readily snap off.

Sharing much of the same territory, *Crassula namaquensis* also extends farther south and east as well. Its leaves, typically quite blue and covered with fine hairlike papillae, vary from egg-shaped to noticeably elongated. Particularly in the western part of its territory it is quite abundant, and with its variable foliage it can easily be confused with other species. *Crassula namaquensis* grows in shallow sandy soil on the edges of koppies in the Richtersveld and in rocky depressions in the surrounding hills, usually fully exposed to the blazing sun of these arid parts.

Though some forms of **Crassula sericea**, a third species from the western South African dry lands, resemble *C. namaquensis*, at its most typical *C. sericea* is very distinctive. Its leaves, ranging from near-spherical to hemispherical (the flat side facing upwards) to somewhat elongated, vertically compressed and triangular, are spaced out along its stem. Leaves may be yellow-green or gray or blue, often tipped red or purple, and tinged pink along a lateral keel that divides the upper from the lower surface. The spherical forms look as if a number of small stone-mimicking mesembs had attached themselves at intervals along a succulent stem.

OTHER BLUE-WHITE CRASSULAS

Moving far south and east beyond the fog deserts and quartz fields of the Atlantic coastal regions brings us to the Little Karoo, the home territory of **Crassula tecta** and a host of other succulent plants. With its stem hidden beneath oblong, intricately patterned, rounded leaves of a distinct blue-white hue, at first glance *C. tecta* bears a striking similarity to some forms of *C. namaquensis*. Its tight spherical flower heads rise up 2 to 3 inches (5 to 8 cm) higher than the rest of the plant. *Crassula tecta* gradually clusters but always remains compact. It grows with other crassulas, mesembs (glottiphyllums and gibbaeums), and many other small succulents, on low stony ridges and

Native to Little Karoo quartz fields, *Crassula tecta* resembles more western plants but is easier to grow.

rocky, quartz-strewn flats, where seasonal rains may fall either in spring and autumn or winter and summer.

Still farther to the east, **Crassula perfoliata** grows in a variety of habitats from quite arid to relatively well-watered *fynbos* or semitropical. Befitting a plant with a very wide distribution as well as diverse preferences in growing situations, *C. perfoliata* includes varieties that scarcely resemble each other. **Variety *perfoliata*** and **var. *coccinea*** have erect stems with long, narrow, often channeled leaves (V-shaped in cross section). In contrast, the leaves of **var. *falcata*** and **var. *minor*** grow with their short stem barely visible beneath their overlapping, sickle-shaped or almost rounded leaves. Variety *falcata*, by far the best known and long treated as the separate species *C. falcata*, combines short, almost sideways-growing stems and broad, blue-white foliage with dense heads of bright red flowers. In contrast, var. *perfoliata*, tall, thin, and sparsely branched, with upright, narrow leaves and several loose heads of white blossoms, looks completely unrelated. The other varieties, however, combine elements of each, turning the morphological chaos into a taxonomic continuum. Despite the blue foliage—often a sign of a winter grower—many populations of *C. perfoliata* live in summer-rainfall areas, and the plants cause few problems in cultivation if given adequate light. Even though apparently not closely related to any other sections within the genus, *C. perfoliata* var. *falcata* has been a parent of many popular *Crassula* hybrids, old and new.

UNUSUAL CRASSULAS

Some other choice oddities in the genus demand consideration as well. Restricted to southern Namibia, **Crassula ausensis** includes three varieties of small short-stemmed, tufted plants with longish, bluntly pointed leaves. Discovered in 1998, **var. *titanopsis***, the smallest and most distinctive, occurs in rocky crevices near the south Namibian settlement of Grünau. Its leaves, less than an inch (2.5 cm) long and heavily marked with striking, often contrastingly colored tubercles, conceal its stem, and the plants do indeed resemble tiny clustering mesembs such as *Aloinopsis* and *Titanopsis*, which grow nearby, all of them enduring sun and aridity mitigated by scant, erratic rain.

The aptly named **Crassula mesembryanthemopsis** also resembles *Aloinopsis* and *Titanopsis* but looks entirely different from the bushy *C. mesembryanthoides*. It forms rosettes of soft, somewhat retuse (turned up at the ends) leaves, which grow from a thickened central root. In the wild, as is often the case with succulents with similarly

In the wild, *Crassula mesembryanthemopsis* stays hidden under grit and sand.

The bristly leaves of *Crassula hirtipes* set it apart from other small crassulas. Photo by Kurt Zadnik.

Wild plants of *Crassula susannae* would rarely if ever reach this size. Photo by Terry Thompson.

The tiny rosettes of *Crassula corallina* hide in plain site in its arid surroundings. Photo by Kurt Zadnik.

shaped leaves, it is typically completely buried except for its leaf tips. It grows in dry parts of the western coast of South Africa, in the winter-rainfall regions, and responds well to extremely bright light and sparse winter watering.

Crassula susannae, the only crassula with partially windowed leaves, is a second species with a thickened central root and a way of life centered on remaining nearly invisible. From a very localized area near the north-central Namaqualand coast, it hunkers down with only its frosted, semitranslucent tips exposed. Each truncate leaf-tip terminates in a little *L*, and the pairs of *L*s nest into each other, forming somewhat rectangular rosettes rarely as much as an inch (2.5 cm) in diameter, although large cultivated plants may consist of dozens of tightly compressed individual rosettes. *Crassula susannae* requires very bright light and careful winter water to thrive, but is such a distinctive, pretty plant that it is very popular with growers despite its touchiness.

From the same general region, though more widespread, **Crassula hirtipes** (sometimes still called *C. hystrix*), another of the many outstanding *Crassula* species from the coastal Namaqualand plains, shares its habitat with *C. barklyi* and *C. columnaris* subsp. *prolifera*. The dense coat of long, relatively stiff hairs that covers its leaves distinguishes it from other creeping species. It branches freely and can fill the narrow crevices and cracks among the quartz outcroppings, rocky ridges, and small cliffs where it grows.

A final peculiar little species, much more widely distributed than the previous four, the diminutive **Crassula corallina** forms dense clusters of tiny rosettes, composed of dotted, blue-white, somewhat rounded leaves. The plants grow as little ground-hugging mounds and generally live completely exposed to the sun in arid areas such as the Richtersveld, alongside drought-resistant species such as *Euphorbia friedrichiae* and the giant *Aloe pillansii*. **Subspecies *macrorrhiza***, from Bushmanland and southern Namibia, has tuberous roots and is touchier in cultivation, but bright sun and winter water will generally satisfy both forms of the species.

Many bushy or ground-covering crassulas are not true desert dwellers or specialized inhabitants of extreme environments. Accordingly most of them flourish in cultivation, growing almost as easily as a jade plant. They are ideal for small-scale succulent gardens, mixed plantings in larger containers, or in smaller pots on windowsills. Water once a week in the warmer months, every two or three weeks in winter. They tolerate any kind of succulent soil mix that drains quickly.

Species from southern Namibia and Namaqualand, where the rain falls during the winter, do best when treated as winter growers in locations where the winter light is sufficiently bright. If the weather cooperates, the winter growers should receive water about once a week from early autumn to late spring, but in the depths of winter the length of time between watering can significantly increase; the soil should be reasonably dry before the next watering regardless of how many days have passed. During the summer rest, these crassulas should still receive some water every three weeks or so.

In places with dark winters it is possible to convert many winter-growing crassulas to a summer schedule, though the more sensitive species may not really flourish under a reversed regimen. Most of the columnar, architectural species, along with plants such as *Crassula rupestris* subsp. *marnieriana*, *C. pyramidalis*, and less frequently cultivated species like *C. alpestris*, will further benefit from a particularly quick draining soil mix and extra-bright light. Crassulas as a whole, of course, generally thrive in very bright light, which brings out the color potential of their leaves. Reddish, brown, and blue-white leaves signify a desire for maximum light, while permanently green leaves suggest at least a tolerance for lower light levels.

Among the green-leafed kinds, *Crassula orbicularis* and its close relatives, although not fussy as to water or soil, do best when provided with extra shade. In the wild they often grow in dimly lit spots, but deep shade in habitat translates to moderate light in cultivation, morning or filtered sunlight. Other four-ranked low growers do best with considerably more light, although *C. socialis* tolerates both shade and moderate sun.

In addition to the species, a variety of crassula hybrids have come into the trade over the years. The best of these hybrids, given evocative names such as **'Ivory Pagoda'**, **'Moon Glow'**, and **'Starburst'**, combine the geometric leaf arrangement and intense coloration of the arid-growing species with greater ease of cultivation and sometimes more colorful flowers as well. There are crassulas to fit almost any growing situation, either indoors or outside, justifying their long popularity with growers and enthusiasts.

Chapter 4

Adromischus

WHETHER TUCKED AWAY under brush in the dry hills of the Western Cape, or completely exposed to the burning sun and battering winds of the arid Richtersveld, *Adromischus* species comprise a low-key but significant portion of the South African succulent flora. With an almost unending variety of leaf shapes, colors, textures, and patterns, the genus exemplifies those qualities valued by cactus and succulent enthusiasts. In addition, most adromischus make ideal subjects for a succulent collection: small slow-growing plants tolerant of a certain amount of abuse and able to thrive both in the optimal setting of a greenhouse or the decidedly imperfect conditions of a windowsill.

Consisting of fewer than thirty currently recognized species, *Adromischus* is part of a three-genus subdivision (along with *Cotyledon* and *Tylecodon*) of the crassula family. Although various species range over a good portion of South Africa and southern Namibia, the majority of plants are from central-western and northwestern South Africa, where they share their natural rock gardens with *Crassula* species and various clumping mesembs.

Adromischus includes low, creeping plants that rarely form stems, tufted plants that form loose rosettes, often with somewhat tuberous roots, and plants that slowly produce relatively stocky stems. Although the stem-forming species can develop a certain rugged character, almost without exception people value adromischus because of their strikingly patterned and colored leaves. The scope of leaf shapes found in the genus ranges from almost perfectly round to nearly cylindrical. Often the leaves come decorated with bright spots or black dots, less often with a waxy or powdery coating, a distinct crenulated or horny rim, or a surface roughened with little bumps or distinct, elongated papillae or tubercles.

Determining the species a given plant belongs to can be frustrating. In years past, adromischus were classified largely by their leaf shapes or patterns, features currently thought to have no more taxonomic significance than the absence or presence of freckles on a person's skin. The unending variety of leaf form within the genus led to the description of a large number of species, many now considered invalid.

Furthermore, because of factors such as a preference for spotted leaves instead of plain ones, the representation of a given species in cultivation may not correspond to the natural range of variety as found in nature. As more examples propagated from collected material come into cultivation, this can lead to considerable confusion. An example of this would be seeing a plant with plain, elongated leaves bearing the species name of an adromischus always associated with round, spotted leaves.

The current classification of the plants into five subgroups is based largely on details of their flowering structures, considered a more reliable indicator of relationships. Nonetheless, for horticultural purposes it is entirely appropriate to have informal names indicative of what a plant actually looks like.

The most common adromischus in cultivation include a number of plants with colorfully spotted, flattened, more or less round or oval leaves. In the nursery trade in days past, plants with these patterns and more-or-less circular (orbicular) leaves were generally called *Adromischus maculatus*; plants with longer, more squared off leaves were called *A. cooperi*; and *A. festivus* was used at times for plants with longer leaves, and at other times for plants with rounder leaves. Currently, ***A. cooperi*** is the accepted name for the somewhat rectangular leaved plants, ***A. maculatus*** refers to a larger growing species with generally rounded leaves, rare both in nature and cultivation, and *A. festivus* is an invalid synonym of *A. cooperi*. Most of the plants once called *A. maculatus* are probably more accurately referred either to the extremely variable ***A. trigynus*** or to the equally variable ***A. triflorus***, that is if they are not just random unknown hybrids.

Several other adromischus also come from the Western Cape. These include *Adromischus leucophyllus*, a small species with flattened, unspotted, oval bluish green leaves covered with a white powder, and the somewhat similar but larger *A. liebenbergii*, with flattened, round to spoon-shaped bluish leaves on definite stalks.

Adromischus inamoenus ("not beautiful"), whose name reflects its generally unprepossessing qualities, is another western species. This small plant typically with unmarked blue-green or gray leaves rarely appears in cultivation. *Adromischus caryophyllaceus*, a good-sized species, shares the common aspect of slowly climbing stems and gray-green, sometimes red-margined leaves, but its relatively large flowers, flaring open at their tips, locate it in its own group of distinctive, generally smaller species.

Farther to the east, in the Eastern Cape, *Adromischus sphenophyllus*, a larger species, produces leaves sometimes covered with a grayish wax, sometimes spoon-shaped, and sometimes plain green but wavy edged. Its leaves tend to cluster at the tops of its multiple branches.

Also from the Eastern Cape, with its territory divided into several discrete parts, each with distinct varieties, is

Adromischus liebenbergii, unadorned and not frequently seen. Photo by Kurt Zadnik.

Adromischus maculatus, its name usually applied to other plants.

A very unusual, highly ornamental version of *Adromischus inamoenus,* growing in typical adromischus habitat: a narrow crack in a rock.

Thriving among non-native pine trees, this *Adromischus triflorus* is heavily spotted; other forms have no spots at all. Photo by Rob Skillin.

Adromischus sphenophyllus, spotless but with red-bordered, wavy leaf margins.

Adromischus cristatus f. *poellnitzianus*, with live, white adventitious roots over a coat of dried brown ones. Photo by Terry Thompson.

Adromischus hemisphaericus, rooted firmly into seemingly bare rock. Photo by Kurt Zadnik.

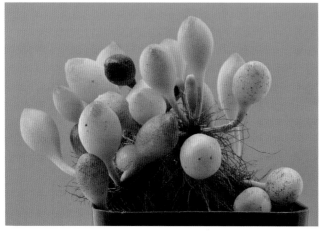

Adromischus cristatus var. *schonlandii*: different varieties of the same species can look very different.

Adromischus alstonii violating the adromischus shade-seeking norm in the Richtersveld.

Adromischus cristatus. This species now includes plants once considered separate species such as **f. *poellnitzianus*** (synonym *A. poellnitzianus*) and **f. *nussbaumerianus*** (synonym *A. nussbaumerianus*). All of its forms typically bear unspotted, flaring green or slightly frosted leaves with a minutely roughened surface and usually a distinct wavy edge. Most varieties of *A. cristatus* slowly produce long stems covered with rapid-growing, mist-absorbing adventitious roots that quickly dry into a shaggy covering of coarse brown hairs. Though **var. *schonlandii*** lacks the wavy leaf tip, and **var. *zeyheri*** lacks the hairs, all the varieties are readily recognizable as part of the *A. cristatus* complex.

The small allies of *Adromischus caryophyllaceus* include species such as *A. humilis* and *A. nanus*, which make little green rosettes, and the similarly rosette forming *A. phillipsiae*. This species has become popular because of its extremely distinctive flowers, proportionately large

red to orange-yellow, downward-hanging elongated bells, displayed along an arching stalk.

Isolated from the other species in its northeast South African habitat, **Adromischus umbraticola** forms dense masses of small slightly elliptical, usually plain (but sometimes "frosted") green leaves that emerge from a mostly underground branching base. Its relatively unadorned leaves, with a propensity to fall off at the slightest touch, may have kept this species from becoming particularly popular in cultivation.

The far west and northwest regions of South Africa are home to a number of species, some very interesting though relatively difficult in cultivation. North of Cape Town and extending into Namaqualand, **Adromischus hemisphaericus** has leaves covered with a distinct waxy glaze, pink or silvery, and often with a crackled surface.

Still farther north, through the Richtersveld and into southern Namibia, **Adromischus alstonii** may have rounded or highly compressed leaves, occasionally spotted, often not. It surprised me to see large numbers of plants growing west of Steinkopf, in stony soil, full sun, and in the company of succulents specialized for survival in harsh environments such as *Cheiridopsis peculiaris* and *Euphorbia filiflora*.

Adromischus montium-klinghardtii grows in the barren, often fog-swept Richtersveld and extends into equally bleak-seeming sections of southern Namibia. It is a low-branching plant with rounded, extremely thick, somewhat flattened leaves that approach the nearly spherical shape of some forms of *A. marianiae*, which live quite nearby. I have seen this species thriving on what seemed like absolutely bare rock along with a few sun-reddened *Crassula* species and tiny equally red and somewhat pathetically shriveled plants of *Conophytum saxetanum*, plants that one typically would assume would both enjoy and need much more light than an adromischus.

Adromischus roanianus and *A. subviridis*, both mak-

Fat-leafed *Adromischus montium-klinghardtii* sharing its inhospitable habitat with *Conophytum saxetanum*.

Adromischus filicaulis, a short, oval-leafed, green form growing in quartzite. Photo by Rob Skillin.

ing their way into collections in recent years, also live in the western reaches of the country, though farther south, where conditions are less harsh.

A wide-ranging species with an array of leaf colors from green to almost silvery-white, sometimes with abundant black spots, and leaf shapes from tear-drops to long, curving cylinders, *Adromischus filicaulis* grows in Namibia, south through the Richtersveld and onto the strange quartzfield habitats of the Knersvlakte in Namaqualand. **Variety *marlothii*** lives farther south and east. The plants known as *A. tricolor*, along with plants frequently mislabeled as *A. mammillaris*, probably fit into this species. The true *A. mammillaris*, a somewhat similar-looking species from farther east, with long, tapering leaves and an elongated erect or creeping stem, is still uncommon in collections.

Probably the best known of the western *Adromischus* species, as well as the most confusing, the most attractive, and the most desirable, is *A. marianiae*. This plant shows up in a bewildering number of forms, many once considered distinct species and now divided into four varieties. All forms grow fairly close to the western seacoast of South Africa and edge into southern Namibia. The leaf forms, shapes, and colors vary so greatly that it makes sense to conserve some old names as horticultural indicators, regardless of botanical significance. **Variety *marianiae*** has long, somewhat spindle-shaped leaves with a definite channeled appearance on one side. It occurs farther south than the others, and the classic type, with very attractive gray leaves mottled with black, lives in semiarid, succulent rich, rather brushy habitat not far from the town of Clanwilliam. Other forms lack the spots or the deeply channeled leaves and grow farther to the north and west. **Variety *hallii*,** a rare, low-growing plant from the South African–Namibian border area, has shorter, more rounded leaves crowded on its stems and of a number of colors, either spotted or plain. **Variety *immaculatus*** includes a number of formerly distinct species and displays a tremendous diversity of leaf shape and color. It includes plants with smooth-textured, elongated, heavily mottled leaves ("*antidorcatum*"), roundish leaves covered with minute bumps ("*alveolatus*"), and a whole panoply of plants ("*herrei*") with leaves that vary from elliptical and teardrop-shaped to wide flaring, compressed, and almost hatchet-blade shaped. Leaf colors in "*herrei*" range from nearly white through orange-brown to purple-black and leaf textures can be smooth, roughened, warty, or covered with papillae resembling little tentacles. The leaves of **var. *kubusensis*** tend to be more-or-less elongated and

Adromischus marianiae var. *marianiae,* from less arid areas than most of the other marianiae varieties. Photo by Kurt Zadnik.

Adromischus marianiae var. *immaculatus* ("*herrei*" form), one of the vast range of shapes taken by this variety.

Adromischus marianiae "Bryan Makin," rare, slow growing and very choice.

smooth or slightly frosted in texture, and sometimes spotted with black dots; one form, found in the coastal Richtersveld growing on bare rock with almost no soil and fully exposed to the sun, has shorter, rather disc-shaped leaves, and once was known as *A. blosianus.*

Other informally named but distinct variations abound, including "Little Spheroid" from coastal Namaqualand; "Bryan Makin," a remarkably pretty form from somewhat to the north of there and named after its discoverer; and a form that grows near Middelpos, by the Tanqua Karoo, far to the southeast of the typical range of the species, on bleak, stony flats dotted with interesting succulents.

Adromischus marianiae and its varieties can be more difficult in cultivation than the other species. Most of its forms grow in areas of summer drought and sparse winter rains, the plants from farther north generally growing under more arid conditions. Consequently, they should have somewhat faster draining soil than most other species and will do best with a fairly strict summer resting period, increased water beginning in fall, extending into winter and spring and then tapering off. If grown in conditions of inadequate winter light, they will respond to summer watering treatment, but must receive very careful and not-too-frequent watering to prevent them from rotting. Their colors and patterns will develop best with quite bright light, more than is typically associated with adromischus cultivation, and they are extremely slow growing, whether as plants or developing from leaf propagations.

Most adromischus will respond well to similar, but less stringent conditions, with a slightly less rigorous dry period in summer, and somewhat reduced water in winter as well. In coastal California that translates to water about once a week in spring and fall, every two weeks in summer, and every two or three weeks in winter depending on the species. If necessity dictates, these plants are less likely to succumb to seasonal water switching than *Adromischus marianiae* varieties.

Plants from summer-rainfall regions, including *Adromischus umbraticola,* forms of *A. cristatus* and *A. trigynus,* and the Namibian *A. schuldtianus,* can take more water in summer, though they will do fine if treated as any of the other typical species. With *A. marianiae* forms the amount of time between watering in rest periods can be increased, to every three or four weeks. Any typical, quick-draining soil mix suitable for succulents will be fine for most adromischus, with additional drainage for the fussier types.

As with most succulents, the maximum light short of burning is best, but many adromischus will put up with less-than-optimum conditions. If the spots on the leaves begin to fade, it is most likely a sign of inadequate light. If kept reasonably dry in winter most species will tolerate considerable cold and several degrees of frost without complaint.

Typically, adromischus are propagated from leaves. In some species, such as *Adromischus leucophyllus*, the leaves detach so readily that it is difficult to maintain a perfect specimen; in other species, the leaves adhere to the stems considerably more securely. Leaves of most kinds root quickly and begin to produce new plants fairly soon, but in taking a leaf cutting, make sure to have the entire leaf including the basal portion.

Some species, such as *Adromischus marianiae*, particularly its more arid-growing forms, are slower and more difficult to root and grow from leaves. *Adromischus phillipsiae* and its allies are extremely difficult, if not impossible, to start from leaves. Stem cuttings work also, and though raising plants from seed takes patience, it is certainly possible.

Some creeping, dwarf-leafed species spread rather quickly, but on the whole adromischus are slow-growing plants that can remain for many years in a 3- or 4-inch (8- to 10-cm) pot. Although not as obviously spectacular as some caudiciforms or fantastically specialized mimicry mesembs, adromischus offers an almost unending variety of pleasing detail for those willing to observe them closely.

Chapter 5

Cotyledon and *Tylecodon*

Now split in two, the formerly united genera *Cotyledon* and *Tylecodon* embody the contrast between summer- and winter-rainfall plants. The pair, along with *Adromischus*, make up a related subgroup of African succulents in the crassula family.

Cotyledon was named in the eighteenth century, a time when succulent plants were being introduced to the emerging world of European natural science. Over the decades, *Cotyledon* became a sort of catch-all designation for a great number of crassulaceous plants, including species from the New World, such as *Dudleya*, as well as the Old. As taxonomic boundaries gradually clarified, one group of plants after another was separated out of the genus. *Adromischus*, for example, was removed in the 1830s. Finally, in 1978, the botanist Helmut R. Toelken combined many species of *Cotyledon* formerly considered distinct. He also devised the genus name *Tylecodon*, an anagram of *Cotyledon*, for the species that did not fit his revised concept of *Cotyledon*.

COTYLEDON

Pruned down to fewer than a dozen species, *Cotyledon* as currently defined consists of small to medium-sized shrubs and bushes with perennial, thickened succulent leaves and upright inflorescences that bear red to yellow, generally pendent, fleshy flowers. The genus ranges across much of southern Africa, in both winter- and summer-rainfall areas and encompasses the much smaller range of *Tylecodon* within its boundaries. Outlying species of *Cotyledon* extend into southern Angola in the west, and in the east grow as far north as Ethiopia and southern Arabia. Regardless of their native habitat, however, cotyledons are universally easy to grow and will respond to the same conditions.

Cotyledon orbiculata, the most commonly cultivated cotyledon, in nature grows over much of southern Africa

and takes on a bewildering number of forms. At various times many of these forms were considered separate species, but the differences, mostly in details of leaf size and flower color, did not justify such a significant designation. *Cotyledon orbiculata*'s plethora of forms include plants with linear, nearly terete leaves arranged in loose rosettes,

Cotyledon orbiculata, a narrow-leafed form from southern Namibia. Photo by Rob Skillin.

Highly glaucous, broad-leafed *Cotyledon orbiculata*.

f. *oophylla* with thick, elongated egg-shaped leaves, and the slow-growing f. *undulata*, which has white, waxy leaves with an undulating edge, almost like graceful, chalk-colored seaweed.

The most frequently grown types of *Cotyledon orbiculata*, however, resemble a slower growing, white- or gray-leafed version of the common jade plant, *Crassula ovata*. Freely branching from a stocky central stem, plants ultimately reach around 2 feet (60 cm) in height and more than that in width. Aside from their pendent, bell-shaped pink flowers, their most striking feature is the white or even silvery waxy coating that covers their thick, spoon-shaped leaves. Other forms of *Cotyledon orbiculata* lack this glaucous coating, among them large all green forms over 4 feet (1.2 m) tall with leaves as much as 4 inches (10 cm) across. In good light the leaves, glaucous or not, develop a red edge.

A second, distinctly different group of species has plants with green, densely hairy leaves and thinner, less succulent stems. The slow-growing, yellow-flowered *Cotyledon campanulata* belongs here as does the more shrubby, but still fairly small *C. tomentosa* with yellow to orange flowers. Its **subsp. *tomentosa*** has wedge-shaped leaves with little notched teeth at the tips and is often confused with **subsp. *ladismithiensis*,** which has longer, toothless leaves.

The remaining cotyledons are small to fairly large shrubs with glabrous (nonfuzzy) leaves. *Cotyledon papillaris*, a low-growing, densely branching plant with wedge- to teardrop-shaped leaves and bright red, recurved flowers comes from western and central South Africa. *Cotyledon cuneata*, also fairly small, with gray-green, red-edged, spoon-shaped leaves and yellow flowers,

atypically inhabits the western winter-rainfall regions of Namaqualand and southern Namibia. *Cotyledon woodii*, a sprawling, good-sized, rather nondescript shrub, produces waxy, oval, almost coin-shaped leaves no more than an inch (2.5 cm) across. *Cotyledon eliseae* is a charming, highly endemic dwarf from 2 to 6 inches (5 to 15 cm) tall with proportionately huge, waxy, bright red pendent flowers on a short stalk. Finally, **C. barbeyi**, a larger plant with loosely arranged, spoon-shaped leaves, grows from eastern South Africa up the east side of the continent as far as Ethiopia, and then across the Gulf of Aden into Arabia.

None of the cotyledons commonly in cultivation presents any problems when it comes to care. Given good drainage the larger forms of *Cotyledon orbiculata* thrive

Left: *Cotyledon tomentosa* subsp. *tomentosa,* with notched teeth and usually misidentified.
Right: *Cotyledon cuneata,* like a small *C. orbiculata,* with sticky, pointed-tipped leaves and yellow flowers. Photo by Brian Kemble.

From the Eastern Cape, *Cotyledon campanulata,* with yellow flowers hanging like bells. Photo by Brian Kemble.

Cotyledon cf. *papillaris,* with pointed leaf tips and reflexed flowers.

Cotyledon eliseae, small, low growing with big flowers.

outdoors in areas of relatively mild climate, such as most of coastal California. They adapt well to winter rain and will tolerate several degrees of frost in a rock garden. The smaller species and forms will do fine in a sunny spot indoors or outdoors if protected from extremes of rain and weather.

Not fussy about soil, cotyledons do well with any standard, well-drained succulent mix. Propagation from stem cuttings (particularly with the thicker-stemmed forms) is easy, from leaf cuttings considerably more difficult. Container-grown cotyledons, regardless of whether they come from summer- or winter-rainfall areas in the wild, do well with regular weekly water in a fairly sunny warm climate in summer, and less water in winter, perhaps every three weeks or so. Though not the most spectacular of succulents, their general hardiness ensures their value in mixed plantings of xerophytic plants, while some of the more attractive forms and unusual species can become small showpieces in their own right.

TYLECODON

Once *Tylecodon* was separated out of *Cotyledon*, it seemed odd that the two ever had been considered members of the same genus. Tylecodons are deciduous; their leaves dry up and fall off at the end of their winter growing season. As a result they must rely on their stems or caudices for water storage. In less obvious but taxonomically significant matters of arrangement of the leaves on the stems, or their usually upright rather than pendent, usually dry rather than fleshy flowers, tylecodons further differentiate themselves from true cotyledons.

When in leaf some tylecodons somewhat resemble cotyledons or even certain types of adromischus. Out of leaf, however, often for half of the year or more, the plants, depending on the species, resemble a lifeless stump, a tangle of dead branches, or a sort of dried up, gray-green onion.

Still somewhat uncommon in cultivation, tylecodons in nature occur only in the winter-rainfall (or more accurately, summer-drought) areas of South Africa and southern Namibia. Tylecodons typically consist of either a thickened trunk or a sometimes completely underground caudex, with a few branches, more-or-less succulent leaves, and generally upright flower stalks that grow from the branch tips. Their stems range from quite large to minute; in those species with a caudex, branches are often tiny and nonsucculent. Leaves run the gamut from flattened spoon-shaped, to linear, to almost completely spherical.

Flowering often starts when the plants are still leafless, with the new leaves following soon afterwards, but blooming also may occur at the end of the growth cycle or during the middle of the dormant period. The flowers vary from small to fairly large, from drably colored to bright yellow, red, or magenta. A number of generally smaller species come with heavily fringed, usually white petals. Although about fifty *Tylecodon* species are currently described, for horticultural purposes it is possible to fit tylecodons into several distinct categories.

A TREELIKE TYLECODON

In a class all its own, ***Tylecodon paniculatus*** is not only the largest species, it also has the widest distribution, from the Cape Peninsula in the south, well into Namibia hundreds of miles to the north. It can reach 6 feet (1.8 m) in height and, with a thick trunk as much as 2 feet (60 cm) in diameter, it somewhat resembles a miniature baobab tree. Its fairly thin, spoon-shaped leaves vary in degree of succulence; in some extremely arid areas the leaves may be smaller and thinner, beaten down by their environment, while in slightly better-watered places the leaves will be considerably fleshier. The plants make a few short, thick branches and send their tall, bright red inflorescences straight up into the air at the height of the summer drought. Though full-sized specimens would be impractical as container plants, even smaller ones have much the same massively imposing look. Wild plants often grow in somewhat shady small canyons, while cultivated plants thrive in the very brightest light; with less light they will become somewhat leggy and unnatural in appearance.

Five feet (1.5 m) tall and a foot (30 cm) thick, *Tylecodon paniculatus* surveys its bleak south Namibian home.

Tylecodon hirtifolius may leaf out later than other species. Photo by Terry Thompson.

Squat-based and long-leafed, *Tylecodon pearsonii* shows its white phyllopodia.

MEDIUM-SIZED TYLECODONS

A second group of tylecodons consists of several medium-sized species that range widely over western South Africa and Namibia, though no single species has a territory as large as that of *Tylecodon paniculatus*. The best known of these grow fully exposed to the sun, whether on rocky hillsides, ledges, or arid flats. **Tylecodon wallichii**, from Namaqualand and points north, and **T. cacalioides**, from farther east in the Little Karoo, both have stems covered in phyllopodia (persistent leaf bases elongated into trun-

Tylecodon wallichii growing in a south Richtersveld succulent paradise.

cated spikes). The two can be hard to tell apart until they flower: *T. wallichii* produces small drab flowers while *T. cacalioides* blooms with much larger, bright yellow flowers. Their dense phyllopodia presumably help to protect the plants from predators, although their toxic sap probably is a more effective deterrent.

Other mid-sized, but much scarcer tylecodons also develop phyllopodia, particularly on their new growths. Among these, the low-growing, Namaqualand mountain endemic **Tylecodon hirtifolius** differentiates itself with its soft, broad foliage and its procumbent growth habit.

Several other tylecodons bear less prominent phyllopodia, rounded or diamond-shaped rather than protruding. **Tylecodon pearsonii**, with almost linear leaves and a few whitish stems, marked with a pattern of phyllopodia resembling pointed fish scales, is a smaller plant, rarely exceeding 6 to 8 inches (15 to 30 cm) in height. It arises from a swollen base and occurs at scattered locations along the west South African arid zones.

With a general resemblance to *Tylecodon wallichii* but smaller, with shorter phyllopodia, and very uncommon in cultivation, *T. rubrovenosus* grows along the hot, dry Orange River watershed. Somewhat atypically for a tylecodon, its pale yellow flowers hang down.

Occupying a small area along the river banks within *Tylecodon rubrovenosus* territory is the rare *T. hallii*. With

In rocks near the Orange River, *Tylecodon* cf. *hallii* endures great heat and little rain.

Tylecodon reticulatus sharing its Richtersveld ridge-top home with *Conophytum gratum* subsp. *marlothii*. Photo by Kurt Zadnik.

a very attractive natural bonsai look, it resembles its more widespread cousins, but lacks phyllopodia, making up for this with its peeling bark and relatively good-sized yellow flowers.

Phyllopodia are usually but not always entirely lacking in the very popular **Tylecodon reticulatus**, but the plant makes up for its relatively unadorned stems by retaining its dried inflorescence for many years, the mass of twiggy dried stems surmounting a main trunk sometimes as wide and thick as it is tall. Out of leaf *T. reticulatus* can appear more like a rounded rock topped by a leafless, angular-branched shrublet than a single plant. It grows from Namibia as far southeast as the Little Karoo.

Tylecodon leucothrix, confined to the Little Karoo, combines a short smooth stem with fuzzy leaves and bright white flowers. The stems of *T. ramosus* are similarly unarmed and peeling, several of them often growing from a tuberous base. It tends to grow in shaded, somewhat sheltered places, often south-facing cliff faces that trap fog and a little extra moisture. *Tylecodon ramosus* has proportionately large leaves and makes dense heads of good-sized pink to green flowers.

With curving red flowers up to 2 inches (5 cm) long, **Tylecodon grandiflorus** grows from the Cape peninsula as far north as Namaqualand, often in places that receive more rain than most tylecodons will tolerate. It is a large but low-growing shrub, often hard to see amid the undergrowth until it sends out its relatively tall inflorescence.

Hairy leaves and stems accompany the swollen, hairy flowers of **Tylecodon ventricosus**, widely distributed and varying from occasional good-sized specimens with phyllopodia-bearing stems to dwarfed plants reduced to a largely subterranean caudex topped by only a few leaves.

Tylecodon ramosus juts out of a sheer quartzite cliff in the Richtersveld.

SMALL TYLECODONS

Many of the more dwarfed species share the Namaqual-and–Richtersveld distribution of most medium-sized species. As well as several fairly widely cultivated (and widely misidentified) plants, a number of these small species are exceedingly scarce both in habit and in cultivation. Many are extreme endemics, native to a few small patches of ground or a few gorges in a single mountain. They often grow in relative shade, and some form surprisingly large masses of small stems in crevices among the boulders. Their combination of localized habitat, diminutive size, and cryptic appearance has created a continuing story of new plant discoveries in *Tylecodon*.

Some small species, such as **Tylecodon schaeferianus**, from the coastal areas, make masses of sparsely branched stems only a few inches (about 8 cm) high, topped by rounded leaves. A particularly small-leafed form was known in cultivation as **T. sinus-alexanderii**. **Tylecodon decipiens**, similar to *T. schaeferianus* but with thicker stems and more oblong leaves, often with a grooved top, also lives near the coast, but has a considerably smaller range. The related Richtersveld endemic **T. longipes**, another small mat-former, also flowers when dormant. Its somewhat spoon-shaped, pale green, occasionally lobed, and slightly tomentose leaves immediately distinguish it from species close to it.

Tylecodon buchholzianus, from farther inland, also makes masses of short, somewhat thicker stems with an oddly grainy surface. Its linear leaves are absent for most of the year, and for some forms in habitat, years can go by with no leaves produced at all other than tiny rudimentary black ridges near the stem tips. The stems of **var. fascicularis** may be pendent.

Tylecodon nolteei, endemic to a few southern Namaqualand hillsides, remains very small, with a few short, very thick branches. Its leaves, often speckled with tiny reddish brown elliptical markings, generally have a covering of fine, faint hairs (called trichomes) as well.

A native of Bushmanland, to the east of the Richtersveld mountains, **Tylecodon sulphureus** has white to pale yellow flowers and generally very short, thick branches covered in rounded phyllopodia that emerge from a tuberous, partially underground base. With only one or two 3- or 4-inch (8- to 10-cm) long stems growing out of a tuberous base, the fringe-petaled **T. bodleyae** grows wedged between rocks in near vertical gorges cut into the single smallish mountain where it is found.

Tylecodon viridiflorus also produces relatively thin, upright stems from a tuberous base, largely underground in the wild. When in bloom its bright yellow-green flowers make it easy to recognize; out of flower, with oblong, slightly spathulate leaves, it resembles many other smaller species.

Tylecodon ellaphieae, with broader leaves, produces a lot of proportionately large, pure white flowers that nod on the ends of their stalks, and its very short stems are equipped with short, stocky phyllopodia. In the case of **T. torulosus**, its brittle stems are unarmed and its short, thick leaves are almost square-shaped.

Even at the height of its growing season *Tylecodon buchholzianus* var. *fascicularis* rarely produces leaves. Photo by Kurt Zadnik.

Good things come in small packages: *Tylecodon* aff. *nolteei*.

Among all these relatively similar tylecodons, the miniature ***Tylecodon singularis*** stands out because of its relatively huge, sometimes solitary leaf, up to 3 inches (8 cm) across, nearly round, green veined white on top and purple below. It benefits from extra fog funneling through its cliff edge habitat in southern Namibia.

MINIATURE TYLECODONS

In contrast to the hill and canyon species, most of the truly miniature tylecodons live on the arid flats of Namaqualand and the Richtersveld, home to so many strange, miniaturized succulents. ***Tylecodon pygmaeus*** lives only in the Knersvlakte, the vast quartz field that covers much of southern Namaqualand. Sparse rains fall there during the few months of winter, accompanied by fogs that deposit as much precipitation, but in summer, despite the persistent fog, the quartz fields are bleak and appear lifeless. To survive there, plants must be small and prepared to go underground during the summer drought. The few tiny zigzagging branches that arise from the small caudex of *T. pygmaeus* bear in turn a few thick, more-or-less heart-shaped little leaves that somewhat resembles conophytums, and which disappear during summer. Its close relatives, which include **T. occultans** and **T. pusillus**, are even smaller, rarely poking their two or three thickened, cordate, rather bristly leaves more than an inch (2.5 cm) into the air.

Discovered by chance by the young daughter of noted South African botanical explorer Ernst van Jaarsveld, ***Tylecodon peculiaris*** takes miniaturization to an extreme, with a 1-inch (2.5-cm) underground caudex surmounted by a single, spherical but deeply cleft leaf no more than a half inch (13 mm) in diameter.

Tylecodon similis, which ranges from small to nearly invisible, creeps into Namibia from South Africa. It has white, fringed flowers and tiny oval leaves, and may sprawl with zigzagged stems or remain compact. Other species extend farther north into southern Namibia, or east into Bushmanland, or even farther southeast into the Little Karoo.

A number of small tylecodons lack the tight growth form of these inhabitants of quartz fields and *kloofs* (gorges). Depending on species, they typically put forth either single or multiple stems that sprawl over the ground or clamber through surrounding vegetation. Less attractive than the more compact dwarfs, these plants, including ***Tylecodon striatus***, ***T. scandens***, and ***T. suffultus***, have not made as much of a splash among growers, although some of them readily thrive in cultivation.

Tylecodon occultans, its heart-shaped leaves its only above-ground parts. Photo by Terry Thompson.

Tylecodon similis, multileafed and barely a quarter inch (6 mm) across. Photo by Rob Skillin.

Tylecodon pygmaeus, its stems kept underground beneath the quartz pebbles. Photo by Rob Skillin.

On the whole tylecodons are not too difficult to grow. As is the case with most deciduous-leafed succulents, the plants signal the end of their growing period—typically in late spring—by dropping their leaves, and start their growing seasons with the appearance of the new leaves, usually in midautumn. Tylecodons with broad geographic ranges tend to be adaptable to a variety of rainfall patterns, while species from small and localized habitats are often quite demanding in their watering needs.

Most of the larger, and in particular, more widely distributed plants should be given occasional water even when they are dormant in summer, perhaps once every three or four weeks. When in growth, if there is good light, water once a week is fine, but the frequency of watering should be adjusted downward in times of low light and overcast skies.

As might be expected the mid-sized tylecodons with strange stems, such as *Tylecodon wallichii*, or other odd features, such as *T. reticulatus*, are very popular with succulent collectors, often being the pride of collections. Without intense light, however, they tend to become leggy, and structures such as phyllopodia diminish in prominence; it is rare to see a cultivated *T. reticulatus* as thick stemmed and nearly hemispherical as they often are in the wild. A number of these species, along with *T. paniculatus*, have earned bad reputations because of their toxic leaves and sap. Sheep and cattle that eat these plants sicken and sometimes die, and although the chance of anything happening to owners of cultivated plants seems slight, a bit of caution when repotting cannot hurt.

Many tylecodons flower before they begin their growth, and a little water as the inflorescences develop will not hurt most of them. Some species, however, in particular those from very restricted habitats in extremely arid places like the Richtersveld, northern Namaqua- land, and southern Namibia should be kept drier when dormant, and in a few cases should not receive any water until growth actually begins. *Tylecodon ventricosus*, for example, can rot quite easily if given water at the wrong time, and similar care should be taken with many of the true miniature species.

In the wild many tylecodons, particularly smaller species, grow in places somewhat sheltered from the sun. In cultivation, however, they all do well with extremely bright light, though once again, some of the miniature species should be given a bit of shade while dormant in imitation of their half-buried existence among the quartzfield pebbles.

They should be grown in soil without too much organic material in it, and above all, they need extremely quick drainage. Surprisingly, a plant probably referable to *Tylecodon torulosus* has survived freezes down into the high teens (around –7°C) at the University of California Botanical Garden in Berkeley. Although a number of tylecodons grow in areas of regular frosts, aside from species such as *T. paniculatus* and *T. grandiflorus*, in cultivation it is probably best to keep them fairly warm; except in the most sheltered, sunny and dry places they will not survive long if planted outdoors.

With their wide range of sizes, their leaves that range from linear to spherical, and their stems often marked either by elongated or geometrically patterned phyllopodia or with attractively peeling bark, tylecodons possess many qualities most sought after by succulent plant enthusiasts. Not surprisingly, they have always been considered extremely desirable plants, and traditionally the hardest thing about growing them simply was finding them. Lately, however, they are becoming a little more common in the trade, although many undoubtedly will always remain rarities.

Chapter 6

Kalanchoe

THOUGH MANY OF its members are popular, almost ubiquitous plants, the genus *Kalanchoe* in the Crassulaceae also includes very interesting, rather rare species as well. Most of the commonly cultivated types originate in Madagascar, and as many other species grow up and down eastern Africa, from South Africa to Somalia, or farther east into Arabia, India, and the frontiers of East Asia.

Befitting its wide distribution in faraway places, its name retains a lingering touch of exoticism. Almost everyone pronounces the genus name "kah-lan-cho" at first, when it actually is properly pronounced as "ka-lan-ko-ee." The origins of the name are murky, possibly coming from a Chinese word, possibly originating in India, and spelled in the typically Greek-derived botanic way in which "ch" is pronounced "k." The close to one hundred fifty species range from tiny leafed, pendent crawlers to small trees, from nearly indestructible to surprisingly difficult in cultivation.

As is the case with many leaf succulents, kalanchoes are not true desert dwellers. They occur mostly in semi-arid habitats, in brush or the sunny edges of woodlands, in places where a decent rainfall is annually interrupted by a much drier—though not bone-dry—season, typically winter. They do not require conditions of intense aridity, and a number are surprisingly tolerant of relatively low temperatures despite their often equatorial homelands. Consequently, kalanchoes tend to do very well in cultivation. A good number of species can be grown outdoors in areas with mild climates, while almost all will thrive given a bit of sun on a windowsill.

The genus is divided into *Kalanchoe* proper and *Bryophyllum*, which often is considered an independent genus. The key distinctions between the two sections relate to flower shape and structure. Though all kalanchoes have four-part flowers, the flowers of bryophyllum types are tubular, sometimes looking like elongated, hanging bells, while the flowers of kalanchoe types typically are up-right, with petals separate or even split in fours down to their bases. For purposes of practical horticulture, however, the several species that produce countless adventitious vegetative buds from a variety of places all are bryophyllums, though not all bryophyllums produce these annoyingly rapid growing incipient plantlets.

KALANCHOES WITH TUBULAR FLOWERS

Bryophyllum types, endemic to Madagascar but naturalized throughout much of the tropical world, come in a fairly wide variety of forms. Some of them are vining, such as ***Kalanchoe beauverdii***, which wends its way among the supporting stems and branches of other plants. If it were better behaved, it would be a nice plant to grow, with stems no thicker than a piece of string and terete to slightly flattened, blackish brown leaves, grooved on top, up to 2 inches (5 cm) long and little more than a quarter inch (6 mm) in diameter. Though its buds develop only at the tips of its leaves, the presence of one plant in a collection inevitably leads to the appearance of many more.

The best known of the adventitious bud producers, however, are a couple of upright growers. ***Kalanchoe daigremontiana*** has fairly good-sized, arrowhead-shaped, flattened leaves. The smaller ***K. delagoensis***, still almost universally known as *K. tubiflora*, has blackish red spotted leaves that curl into a near cylinder. Both species produce enormous numbers of buds, either apically or along the soft teeth on the sides of their leaves, leading to the common name of mother of millions that can be applied to either of them or their hybrids. Children love these plants. Although the plants are a good way to attract people to succulents, they will quickly turn into pests whether in the greenhouse or a rock garden.

The various bryophyllum-type kalanchoes include clambering plants such as ***Kalanchoe campanulata***, which

Kalanchoe delagoensis, attractive but too prolific.

Kalanchoe manginii sometimes grows as an epiphyte and does well in a hanging basket. Photo by John Trager.

The blue leaves of Kalanchoe marnieriana will turn orange in bright sunlight.

produces vast numbers of adventitious buds from its spent inflorescences. The bryophyllum types also include several attractive epiphytic species, such as the small-leafed, better-behaved *K. manginii* and *K. uniflora*. Both have pretty, proportionately large bell-shaped red flowers and often are grown in hanging baskets. They come from moister parts of the Madagascan highlands.

Several bryophyllum types are upright plants with flattened, crenate-margined blue leaves that may turn purple or orange-pink in good light. Among these are the common ***Kalanchoe fedtschenkoi***, and the somewhat similar *K. laxiflora* and *K. marnieriana*. ***Kalanchoe gastonis-bonnieri*** is a striking short-stemmed species with large curving, flattened triangular leaves somewhat resembling a trowel, but up to almost 2 feet (60 cm) long by perhaps 4 inches (10 cm) wide, while *K. suarezensis* grows a bit taller and has similarly shaped but smaller leaves. ***Kalanchoe laetivirens***, which is shorter stemmed than *K. daigremontiana* and smaller than *K. gastonis-bonnieri*, has become popular with growers, perhaps because of its relatively recent discovery.

Other species have serrate-margined leaves marked by small lateral, triangular to arrowhead-shaped lobes, or pinnate leaves in which the lobes are sufficiently separated as to resemble individual leaves. Among these is ***Kalanchoe pinnata***, widespread over warmer parts of the world as a result of its ease of propagation. It has fleshy leaves composed of three to five completely separated lobes, while leaves of *K. prolifera* may have as many as twelve lobes. These plants are used in tropical landscaping, often in modest surroundings as anyone possessing a

Though uncommon in cultivation for the moment, Kalanchoe laetivirens is ready for mass production.

little patch of sandy soil exposed to a bit of sunlight can grow them.

KALANCHOES WITH UPRIGHT FLOWERS

The second large group of kalanchoes, those indisputable members of the genus, includes a wider range of forms, but apart from their flower structure a number of these plants are physically quite indistinguishable from the bryophyllums. ***Kalanchoe rotundifolia***, which grows over much of Africa and has upright stems and bluish leaves that range from round to elongated and are variously smooth or crenate-margined, looks very similar to any number of bryophyllums. It does not produce bulbils, but

Kalanchoe pumila can withstand surprisingly low temperatures outdoors.

Kalanchoe luciae, understandably gaining popularity.

its easily detached leaves rapidly root and start new plants. Some of its forms are quite attractive, and it is somewhat surprising that it has not joined its bryophyllum cousins in attempting to take over the world.

Kalanchoe blossfeldiana, which branches densely and forms clusters of stems with succulent, somewhat spoon-shaped dark green to red leaves, has proven to be a surprisingly hardy garden subject, perhaps unlikely given its Madagascar origins, but it grows at fairly high elevations. Originally with red flowers, it has been hybridized and selected until forms with a rainbow of flower colors can be found at nurseries, where people hardly take notice that it is, in fact, a succulent plant.

The more decorative *Kalanchoe pumila* is not grown quite as often. It also shows up in nurseries and flower shops, however, often in hanging baskets. It is a smaller plant, with pinkish purple flowers and rather wedge-shaped leaves, succulent but brittle rather than fleshy, light purple and glazed over with a thin, translucent white, waxy coating. This succulent grows outdoors as far north as central coastal California, although it requires better drainage and more sunlight than *K. blossfeldiana*.

One of a relatively few South African species occasionally encountered in cultivation, *Kalanchoe thyrsiflora* forms a fairly good-sized, elongated rosette of rounded, somewhat spoon-shaped leaves, with a gray or whitish coating and often red margined. One could be forgiven for thinking it was some kind of *Echeveria*, that is, until it produces its long, tapering, densely flowered inflorescence and subsequently dies.

Differing only in details of its flowering and similarly often monocarpic, *Kalanchoe luciae*, from Zimbabwe, Mozambique, and eastern South Africa, turns glowing red in good light. In the last few years it has become a popular California garden plant, though it is unclear how much frost it can tolerate.

Some forms of the very variable *Kalanchoe lanceolata*, widely distributed throughout East Africa, also die after flowering, while others survive as perennials. From Socotra, an island midway between Somalia and the Arabian peninsula in the Gulf of Aden, *K. farinacea* does not grow as tall and branches more freely, but also has rounded leaves coated with a white bloom.

Coated densely with short, silvery white fuzz, *Kalanchoe citrina* remains compact and attractive when supplied with adequate light. Its pale lemon-yellow flowers gave it its name. The species grows in northeastern Africa and, as is the case with many succulents, crosses over into Yemen, at the southwest tip of Arabia as well.

The more commonly cultivated *Kalanchoe marmorata* is native to Somalia and neighboring regions. Generally low growing, with highly succulent stems, it has leaves that are less rounded at their tips than those of *K. citrina*, and its margins are somewhat crenate. Its main attraction, however, is its leaf markings, as in bright sunlight its bluish leaves become spattered with dark, almost black splashes, leading to its (now archaic sounding) common name of pen-wiper plant. In less light, however, the decorative dark marking may fade into invisibility. As also is the case with several of the Madagascan species, though *K. marmorata* comes from lands noted for their hot climates, it grows at considerable altitude and is surprisingly hardy, surviving several degrees of frost without complaint.

Many other less-often seen continental African spe-

Kalanchoe lanceolata, dying as flowering concludes. Photo by Susan Carter.

A low-growing Socotran endemic, Kalanchoe farinacea. Photo by Rob Skillin.

Kalanchoe marmorata, probably the most commonly cultivated African kalanchoe. Photo by Terry Thompson.

The East African Kalanchoe citrina, rarely cultivated. Photo by Susan Carter.

Kalanchoe humilis, a small creeping species from Mozambique.

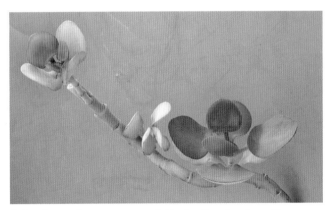

Kalanchoe nyikae, more graceful but rather fragile, with exceptional color. Photo by Terry Thompson.

cies lack *Kalanchoe marmorata*'s cold hardiness. Among them, both *K. nyikae* and *K. humilis* (particularly the Mozambique form also known as *K. figueiredoi*) are worth seeking out. **Kalanchoe humilis**, a medium-sized plant with frequently procumbent stems, has tuberous roots and oval, slightly wedge-shaped leaves about an inch (2.5 cm) wide and twice as long, mottled with a pretty pink-purple color. **Kalanchoe nyikae**, a somewhat more northern species from Kenya and Tanzania, grows taller and more upright, with leaves attached to the stems by a definite stalk (petiole). Its rounded, spoon-shaped leaves have a raised rim that in some Kenyan forms is covered by a pearly deep pink waxy coating that may spread to a lesser degree over the entire leaf, obscuring the underlying, more mundane yellow-purple hue. *Kalanchoe nyikae* is somewhat difficult to propagate from leaf cuttings or even stem cuttings, but it sets seed fairly easily and the tiny seeds will germinate without too much difficulty. The Kenyan **K. fadeniorum** is a bit more commonly grown but not as attractive as *K. humilis* or *K. nyikae*. Although not really difficult to raise, these three species are less indestructible than many common kalanchoes and do not proliferate nearly as rapidly or annoyingly.

Somewhat challenging in cultivation, the distinctive **Kalanchoe bentii** (particularly the form better known as *K. teretifolia*) has clusters of gray-brown leaves shaped like elongated dunce caps, almost circular in cross section and tapering to a point. They grow at the tips of thick, cylindrical, unbranched succulent stems. The species is native to southern Arabia and Somalia, an area of extreme temperatures and varying rainfall, and some forms, at least, can be quite difficult in cultivation, acting more like an erratic winter grower than a typical hard-to-kill kalanchoe. It is best to keep a careful eye on the plant and increase watering as it starts to grow, whatever the season, and decrease it while it is not in active growth.

A number of non-bryophyllum Madagascan kalanchoes also tend to be comparatively shy with offspring. An interesting small species, **Kalanchoe rhombopilosa**, is frequently compared visually to members of the South African *Adromischus*, because of the configuration and coloring of its wedge-shaped leaves. As with many *Adromischus* species, its leaves are speckled and dotted, especially near the tips, with dark spots on top of an overall gray color. *Kalanchoe rhombopilosa* very readily drops its leaves, which sprout and slowly produce new plants. It is another of the Madagascan species that survives coastal California winters outdoors and in the ground, but since it does not exceed 8 inches (20 cm) in height and often is much less, it is generally kept in a small container rather than used in outdoor plantings.

Other Madagascan kalanchoes much better suited for the outdoors in the right climate include several large to tree-sized species. The biggest of these, the appropriately named **Kalanchoe arborescens**, actually becomes a small but indisputable tree, with a single trunk up to about 4 inches (10 cm) in diameter, a swirl of branches, and an ultimate height of close to 20 feet (6 m). Aside from sheer size, however, it is not an interesting plant. The succulent but rather unexceptional stalked leaves are plain green or slightly glaucous, about 2 inches (5 cm) long and half as wide. It is understandably uncommon in cultivation and, as a resident of hot, tropical southeastern Madagascar, it along with almost every other Madagascan endemic is in danger of extinction.

Rather similar and just about as large, **Kalanchoe dinklagei** differs in the form of its immature leaves, which are long, narrow, serrated, and covered with green felt. When mature the leaves lose their serrations; however,

Crowded in its small container, *Kalanchoe rhombopilosa* will lose many leaves during repotting.

plants do not suffer when kept in small containers where they will permanently retain their juvenile leaf form.

These two larger species are uncommon in cultivation, but in contrast a third species, not as large but still capable of reaching 10 feet (3 m) in height, is very well known. **Kalanchoe beharensis**, sometimes called the felt plant, has a stout, slowly branching stem covered with protective sharp-edged, angular leaf scars. Its leaves, up to a foot (30 cm) long, half as wide, and lobed somewhat in the manner of an oak, are covered densely with thin, typically golden-brown, sometimes light green, fuzz. The leaf lobes may turn up enough to make the leaves look entirely crinkled; in other forms this folding is less pronounced.

Forms devoid of fuzz exist alongside selected clones like 'Fang', in which, particularly on their posterior side, the leaves are covered with sharply angular toothlike tubercles. Several other named forms of *Kalanchoe beharensis* have also been selected out. When grown in relatively small containers, the leaves will attain full size but the stems are unable to reach their adult dimensions. Seeing one of the aberrant forms with a 6-inch (15-cm) stem and 10-inch (25-cm) leaves, one might not even recognize it as being in the same species as a normal adult plant.

With proportions that somewhat resemble these potbound forms of *Kalanchoe beharensis*, **K. synsepala** generally remains a short-stemmed plant with disproportionately large leaves. Long and proportionately narrow, the leaves taper to a point and are more-or-less toothed and flattened. They form an approximate rosette at the apex of the stem. Typically, *Kalanchoe* leaves curve up and then arch downward, but *K. synsepala* is unique in the genus because of the stolons that develop from its leaf axils.

Kalanchoe beharensis, the nontomentose green form, over 6 feet (1.8 m) tall. Photo by Brian Kemble.

Kalanchoe orgyalis, a small heavily felted plant. Photo by Brian Kemble.

Kalanchoe synsepala, with a couple of stolons growing out from the central plant. Photo by Brian Kemble.

Kalanchoe tomentosa growing with *Aloe acutissima* in a pocket of sedge. Photo by Inge Hoffman.

These elongate, bend down to the soil, and produce new plantlets which develop roots and become independent as the stolons wither.

A third species, somewhat reminiscent of *Kalanchoe beharensis,* with leaves similarly coated with a bronze felt-like fuzz, **K. orgyalis** also becomes fairly large, close to 6 feet (1.8 m) tall. It branches more freely than *K. beharensis,* its leaves are smoothly elliptical rather than toothed

and gnarled, and its bronze fuzz gradually turns silver as the plants mature. It is another slow grower that will do well in a container for many years.

In botany the term *tomentose* signifies a covering of fuzz, and one of the best-known species is **Kalanchoe tomentosa,** a.k.a. the panda plant. Its leaves and stems are covered with soft, dense, pale blue-gray hair. The slightly concave, elliptical leaves are surrounded by a raised rim

Kalanchoe grandidieri growing near the Madagascan seacoast. Photo by Brian Kemble.

Similar but lower growing and freely branching from its base, ***Kalanchoe eriophylla*** is another highly tomentose species, gray with rusty-red markings on its foliage. It is a charming little plant, easy to grow and very possibly hardy outdoors in mild climates. Though certainly not rare, it deserves to be better known in cultivation.

Finally, there are a number of Madagascan and mainland African species that still are quite uncommon though very worthy of cultivation. Among these, ***Kalanchoe grandidieri***, rare in the wild, is a large stout, knobby stemmed plant with thick, round leaves at its branch tips. It looks something like some forms of *Cotyledon orbicularis*, a miniature thick-trunked and heavy branched tree, and certainly would appeal to collectors of succulent bonsai if it were available. Several other species also share this general form, though with very differently shaped leaves. It is interesting that in a genus so long in cultivation and with so many extremely common species, potential collector's items still remain out there, lurking behind the scenes.

Kalanchoes typically range from almost too easy to pretty easy in cultivation. On the whole they like a soil a bit richer in organic matter than most succulents, very bright light, and a fair amount of water, at least once a week during the warmer months and about every two weeks in winter. Though, as mentioned, there are a few exceptions, even the more delicate kinds provide less of a challenge than many truly difficult succulent plants. Furthermore, as indicated, a surprisingly large number of species will do well outdoors in areas with mild climates given good drainage and a sunny exposure. Many larger species thrive in the ground in Southern California and may be hardier than one might expect. In particular *Kalanchoe beharensis*, whose large branching specimens have the look of a Mid-Century Modern piece of abstract sculpture, capable of providing a form in a landscape unlike anything else, might be worthy of some experimentation.

with a regular pattern of rusty brown stripes and dots, and must once have given someone the impression of a panda's coloration. Easy growing and benefiting from very bright light, *K. tomentosa* has had a long history of popularity. More recently several forms have entered the horticultural trade, selected out of natural variants. One, **'Chocolate Soldier'**, has a basic brown rather than blue-gray coloration. Other forms have much longer hair on the leaves, or more bristly hair, and other variations.

Chapter 7

Sedum, Sempervivum, and Other Old World Crassulaceae

THE GENUS *SEDUM* has given rise to most members of the Crassulaceae other than those largely endemic to South Africa and Madagascar. The Old World components of this sedum-derived aggregation can be roughly divided into two parts. The first part includes *Sedum* itself and genera closely allied with it, largely though not entirely from temperate or even alpine environments. A second distinctive group includes genera native to the Macaronesian floristic region, consisting of the large islands west of the African coast: Cape Verde, the Azores, Madeira, and most importantly, the Canary Islands. A few members of this second group occur in North Africa and southwestern Arabia as well.

SEDUM

More than two hundred Old World species remain within *Sedum* even after the removal of the plants that now make up the primarily Asian *Rhodiola*, *Phedimus* (semisucculent plants, typically used as ground covers), and *Hylotelephium*. Most of the European and Asian sedums consist of small creeping plants, often with imbricate leaves (covering the stem like shingles on a roof or scales on a fish), typically tiny, often from very high altitudes. Many exist as annuals or biennials to cope with their harsh, alpine environments.

Most are not frequently cultivated, and many of the very high altitude species from elevations over 13,000 feet (4000 m) are fairly recently described plants from western China and central Asia. Although these plants could survive in outdoor rock gardens almost anywhere, most of them are so tiny as to have little horticultural potential. Others, slightly larger and less ephemeral, have become common components of succulent dish and rock gardens.

Sedum acre, growing over much of Europe and into central Asia, and **S. dasyphyllum**, with slightly larger leaves, typify many Old World sedums. Their thin stems

are densely clad with tiny succulent leaves, and they root as they creep along the ground. Commonly used in rock gardens throughout the United States, in some areas *S. acre* grows vigorously enough to have turned into an invasive nuisance. *Sedum dasyphyllum*, from countries around the Mediterranean Sea, makes a good candidate for dish gardens, with four-ranked, tiny blue-green leaves that give off a resinous smell if crushed.

Also with partially imbricate foliage but an upright growth habit, **Sedum multiceps**, from the mountains of Algeria, is a small well-behaved plant, suitable for con-

Sedum multiceps grows into a miniature pachycaul. Photo by John Trager.

tainer culture as its mass of densely branched stems rarely exceed 6 inches (15 cm) in height. Its rosettes of small succulent leaves at its branch tips have given it the name miniature Joshua tree, based on a casual resemblance to mature plants of *Yucca brevifolia*. As is the case with many Mediterranean plants, it is a winter grower, dormant in the summer when its leaves tend to shrivel. More sprawling, with procumbent stems and thin, lance-shaped leaves less distinctly crowded toward its branch tips, **S. sediforme** grows on both the north and south shores of the western Mediterranean.

HYLOTELEPHIUM

Probably the most horticulturally popular former sedums are members of the East Asian genus *Hylotelephium*. Among them, **H. sieboldii** (synonym *Sedum sieboldii*) is native to Japan and China. It consists of a number of thin, somewhat pendent, slightly succulent stems, each clothed with almost circular glaucous leaves that emerge from a central rootstock. In fall the plants put forth masses of pink flowers at the tips of their branches. The stems die back to the central rootstock after blooming. **Hylotelephium spectabile**, an erect, branching shrub, also East Asian, has larger spoon-shaped leaves with sprays of similar pink flowers. It is grown widely as a general garden subject.

SINOCRASSULA AND OROSTACHYS

Dry, rocky localities in East Asia from Kazakhstan through Korea and Japan provide habitats for the members of two other genera of small monocarpic succulents, related fairly closely to *Hylotelephium* but quite different in appearance. Instead of creeping or shrublike growth, *Sinocrassula* and *Orostachys* species form small clusters of compact rosettes and do well in rock gardens or in pots, but *Orostachys* in particular prefers places where nights stay cool.

In the case of *Sinocrassula*, the rosettes may be somewhat elongated, the plants resembling some villadias, although with more robust, branching inflorescences. **Sinocrassula indica**, from Himalayan parts of India and surrounding lands, probably is the best known in cultivation.

Several species of *Orostachys* manage to prosper in cold, remote Mongolian and Siberian mountain habitats, while others live in the slightly less forbidding mountain climates of Japan and Korea. **Orostachys spinosa**, in common with some of the other species, produces a ring of larger, sharp-tipped leaves in a kind of fringe around a center composed of much smaller leaves, the whole rosette somewhat resembling a dried sunflower. The tall, densely flowered inflorescence that emerges from the rosette center looks like a miniature *Agave* inflorescence.

The variegated form of *Hylotelephium sieboldii* remains popular with gardeners. Photo by John Trager.

An award-winning *Orostachys spinosa*, looking more like a dried flower than a living plant. Photo by John Trager.

An unidentified *Orostachys* species, showing its inflorescence like an agave or yucca. Photo by John Trager.

Variety *erubescens* produces reddish flowers rather than the typical pale yellow ones. The 2- to 6-inch (5- to 15-cm) rosettes of the Japanese ***O. malacophylla* var. *aggregata*** and **var. *iwarenge*** frequently have a glaucous bloom.

SEMPERVIVUM

Ancient Romans decorated gravesites with sempervivums, believing that the plants' seeming ability to endure any kind of conditions with little need for either soil or water hinted at immortality. This very well known genus includes about forty species that grow over rocky areas in much of central and southern Europe, extending through Turkey as far as the Caucasus Mountains.

Most sempervivums look rather alike. Their larger or smaller artichoke-shaped rosettes are composed of many short, thin, pointed leaves. Some have foliage tipped in black or dark red, and in some clones the entire plant is more-or-less red. Colorful forms have been hybridized from or selected out of widely grown and distributed species such as ***Sempervivum tectorum***, the ubiquitous hen and chickens, and ***S. calcareum***. The most interesting species, however, may be the smaller, hairy kinds such as ***S. ciliosum***, from the Balkans, or the even fuzzier ***S. arachnoideum***, which appears to be covered with spider webs and grows in mountains from Spain and Italy to the Alps.

Sempervivums frequently surprise people with their proportionately large pink or yellow, star-shaped blossoms carried on small stocky flower stalks. After flowering, the individual rosette dies, but sempervivums clump readily and so do attain a sort of immortality after all.

As befits plants that thrive in the detritus found on slate roofs or tucked behind a bas-relief angel wing on an eighteenth-century tombstone, sempervivums prefer thin, rather nonnutritious, fast-draining soil. Most of these typically alpine succulents will do better in a rock garden than in a pot. Although extremely rugged, they are not the best choices for true desert environments, as

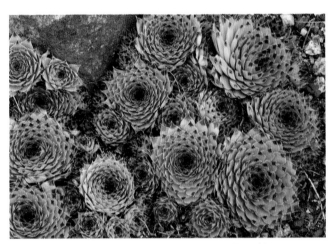

The classic look of a miniature artichoke, displayed by *Sempervivum tectorum* 'Greenii'.

Crowded rosettes of *Sempervivum ciliosum*, from the Balkans and Greece.

The spider web sempervivum, *S. arachnoideum*.

A recent sempervivum hybrid, called "Purdy 90-1."

their succulence has evolved to help them survive frigid, desiccating climates and rocky surroundings rather than to help them endure blazing heat.

ROSULARIA AND PROMETHEUM

Rosularia, with a territory from Eastern Europe through central Asia, produces rosettes quite similar to *Sempervivum*, but the plants often have a caudexlike central stem with a thickened rootstock. They tend to be a little softer looking, and though very hardy, some lack the ability of *Sempervivum* to withstand heavy snows and temperatures below 0°F (–18°C).

Rosularia platyphylla, a central Asian species with a massive taproot, appears in cultivation, as does the species formerly called *R. pallida* but now known as *Prometheum aizoon*. Covered with fine hair, it resembles one of the cobweb sempervivums.

AEONIUM, AICHRYSON, AND MONANTHES

The islands off the northwest coast of Africa, the Canary Islands in particular, are home to a distinctive group of Crassulaceae centered on three genera, *Aeonium*, *Aichryson*, and *Monanthes*.

A few species of *Aeonium* grow in North and even East Africa as well as some other island groups, the rest occur among the canyons, mountains, and seacoasts of the Canary Islands. There, the combination of island isolation and mountainous terrain has led to conditions conducive to speciation, resulting in a species count of around three dozen.

Aeonium arboreum displays the typical aeonium habit of a number of tall, slightly arching branches topped by a dense rosette of green, thin, overlapping leaves, but selected natural and horticultural forms range from brownish red to a purple so dark as to look black. Each rosette sends forth a good-sized inflorescence shaped like an elongated cone and densely covered with bright yellow flowers. After blooming the rosette withers and dies. Since the plants branch freely, however, the death of an individual rosette does not significantly harm the plant as a whole.

Many aeoniums share the general habit of *Aeonium arboreum*, some with rosettes larger or smaller, some more freely branching, some less. Among the more attractive, *A. undulatum* is a good-sized species that sends up a few branches and makes large rosettes of curling, wavy-edged leaves. *Aeonium urbicum* also produces large rosettes, while *A. arboreum* var. **holochrysum**, formerly considered a separate species, is distinguished by its very shiny, bright green leaves.

Aeonium leucoblepharum, from high altitudes in East Africa and Yemen, branches readily and produces heads of smaller yellow-green rosettes. A little less robust, the 4- to 6-inch (10- to 15-cm) rosettes of *A. smithii* are composed of densely hairy, wavy-margined leaves. In *A. balsamiferum* the leaves are even hairier and have a somewhat sticky texture, with thick, fragrant sap.

Lower growing, with thick, ciliate-margined small rosettes, often red-edged and densely branching, *Aeonium haworthii* is one of those succulents that thrives with neglect and often persists in gardens where few succulents would survive. *Aeonium simsii* forms small mats of dense rosettes, composed of red-striped, narrow, thin leaves with white marginal hairs. Even smaller, *A. sedi-*

Aeonium 'Zwartkop', the black-headed aeonium.

The ground-hugging *Aeonium simsii*.

folium forms a short, dense bush rarely more than 6 inches (15 cm) tall, its branches tipped by diminutive, few-leafed rosettes composed of oblong, proportionately thick, small leaves. *Aeonium lindleyi* is similar in size but branches less vigorously. Its leaves, densely fuzzy and sticky to the touch, are filled with sap that has a reputation of being an antidote for the caustic latex of euphorbias—a reputation not entirely justified.

The several aeoniums previously placed in the separate genus *Greenovia* produce small, almost spherical, open-ended rosettes on short stems. When dormant, their rosettes shrink into an open-topped cylinder protected by dried, larger basal leaves. Though most offset sparsely if at all, because of its atypically prolific offsetting habit *Aeonium dodrantale* probably is the best-known species, although the solitary species such as *A. aureum* and *A. diplocyclum* are more interesting.

Two of the most interesting aeoniums usually remain solitary, die after flowering, and generally can only be propagated from seed or leaf cuttings. The unique *Aeonium tabuliforme* grows flat as a dinner plate and about as large, poking out from crevices and cliffs. *Aeonium nobile*, with thick-leafed rosettes up to almost 2 feet (60 cm) in diameter, looks very much like a large *Echeveria* when growing and closes up tightly when dormant. From more arid, interior localities than most aeoniums, its stems remain short and its leaves color up reddish brown, particularly along their margins, in good light.

The species of *Aichryson*, mostly native to the Canary Islands, but with a few from Madeira, resemble small aeoniums, with somewhat less dense, less circular rosettes. The most commonly grown, *A. tortuosum*, a vigorously branching species that rarely exceeds 6 inches (15 cm) in height, also has a popular crested form. Many aichrysons are short lived, flowering after two or three years, then dying, but the branching ones will persist.

Aeonium sedifolium forms a container-sized bush.

Aeonium tabuliforme offsets only very rarely.

Aeonium cf. *diplocyclum,* dormant and shrunken into a cylinder.
Photo by John Trager.

Aeonium nobile, sometimes occurring on barren lava beds, requires more care than most species.

Monanthes polyphylla, with sparkling flowers over tiny rosettes. Photo by John Trager.

Yet another genus almost entirely endemic to the Canary Islands, *Monanthes* consists of fewer than a dozen small to miniature species of monocarpic rosette formers. Their almost hemispherical rosettes, composed of up to one hundred narrow, terete leaves, look like little pompoms. Some, such as the tiny **M. polyphylla**, offset freely and grow as thick mats of 0.5- to 1-inch (13- to 25-mm) wide rosettes, blue in the shade and red in the sun.

In contrast, the slightly larger **Monanthes brachycaulos**, with a thick, almost caudiciform stem, generally remains solitary, although a branching variety exists. Narrow, raylike petals, often with marginal glands covered with droplets of shining nectar, frame their rounded blossoms, which glisten like little star-shaped jewels. These flowers differentiate *Monanthes* from superficially similar *Sedum* species, expanding their horticultural value to more than just that of a small-growing rock garden ground cover.

Aeoniums in particular are very well known in the coastal California landscape, where their growing season coincides with the winter rains. All three genera require no particular soil type other than one that drains reasonably well, and they tolerate a certain amount of frost. They benefit from occasional summer water as well, mimicking the mists and fogs of their island habitats. As island plants, they do not tolerate true desert conditions, though providing additional shade and a bit more humidity, along with cool nights, should enhance the possibilities of their successful culture.

Chapter 8

Echeveria

UNDOUBTEDLY THE BEST known and most widely cultivated of the New World Crassulaceae, the approximately one hundred and fifty species and varieties of the genus *Echeveria* display almost every possible variation on their basic theme of a rosette of succulent leaves. Everyone is familiar with the most common echeverias, whether as components of dish gardens or as the low, mat-forming clusters of blue-green rosettes residing in innumerable garden borders. Along with these everyday plants, however, there are many unusual echeverias with strange shapes, spectacular colors, and odd habits.

Although the largest number of echeverias—well over one hundred species including those most frequently encountered in cultivation—are Mexican in origin, the range of the genus extends south through Central America and along the edges of the Andes to northwestern Argentina and northern Chile. To the north, a lone species, *Echeveria strictiflora*, crosses the Rio Grande and extends a short distance into Texas in the Big Bend region.

All echeverias form a rosette of leaves, whether tight or loosely strung out, which grows out of a longer or shorter succulent stem. Their tubular or bell-shaped, generally yellow, orange, or pink flowers organize themselves in various taxonomically significant arrangements along a stalk that emerges out of the stem at a point below the growing tip of the plant. According to the environments in which they occur, the leaves of echeverias may be rather thin or extremely thick and succulent, equipped for withstanding long periods of drought. Only a few echeverias, however, live in what we would think of as true deserts.

For a sense of a typical echeveria habitat, imagine walking along a Mexican hillside under a light cover of woodland in which short, twisted gnarled oaks are interspersed with taller, long-needled Mexican pines. Occasional outcrops of boulders interrupt the trees. Along their bases, or growing directly out of narrow clefts and

fissures in the rocks themselves, are scattered rosettes of echeverias. Individuals of the same species are variously green or brightly colored depending on how much sunlight falls on any given part of the rock face.

In other likely places, the trees might be denser and taller, or short and scattered, mixed with bushes, grasses, agaves, and cacti. Wherever they grow, echeverias generally seek out steep slopes, some specializing in almost vertical cliff faces. In these settings their rosettes both convey downward-running water to their roots and funnel off any excess.

The Mexican pine-oak forests, at altitudes from 4000 to 7000 feet (1200 to 2100 m), provide a home for many echeverias. Others seek out much greater elevations, sometimes over 2 miles (3 km) high on some of the tallest peaks of Mexico and the outliers of the Andes. A number grow in areas of high rainfall, in high-altitude cloud forests, or lower-lying tropical montane forests where they may live as epiphytes along with orchids and bromeliads. And some do manage to eke out a living in semisheltered places in arid areas. In all these habitats, though, the plants are found in situations of fairly bright light and extremely good drainage.

Plants growing in a forested environment do not grow in the shade of tall trees, but rather in fissures in big boulders or almost perpendicularly on the edges of cliffs, where they receive good light and instant drainage no matter how great the total rainfall. Conversely, those species that typically live in truly arid surroundings usually grow in somewhat shaded spots, again often amid boulders and on cliff faces, where they receive protection from the sun and benefit from runoff patterns when it does rain.

During the dry season, the outer leaves of echeverias wither and form a protective barrier against desiccation, within which the newer growth can survive. As further protection against drying out and too much sunlight, many species have developed a sun-blocking mechanism, either a powdery, often silvery, pink, or blue-white bloom, or leaf colors modified from green to blue, purple, pink, orange, red, or brown. Under conditions of less than ideal light, which often occur in windowsill cultivation, the leaves will revert to their fundamental green and will lose their powdery covering as well.

In the sampling of *Echeveria* species that follows, the plants are divided into subgroups designed to be helpful to prospective growers in figuring out what a particular plant will look like. Some echeverias, such as the hairy-leafed species or the large plants usually somewhat associated with *E. gibbiflora*, form easily identifiable groups that are related to each other, but other groupings are less so. It is hoped that these informal groupings make the genus seem like less of an overwhelming collection of too many kinds of plants.

RAPIDLY OFFSETTING ECHEVERIAS

A number of echeverias form small to medium, fairly rapidly offsetting rosettes with somewhat thickened leaves. Some of these, understandably, are very common in cultivation, others less so. Plants in this category include the extremely common, blue-white ***Echeveria elegans***, with several other former species now included within its taxonomic boundaries, and the smaller ***E. derenbergii***, another rapidly offsetting plant suitable for old-fashioned, mass "carpet-bed" cultivation that may predate the European conquest of Mexico.

Less often grown, the very small ***Echeveria amoena*** has the habit of shedding leaves almost at the drop of a hat. The dropped leaves then form new plants. ***Echeveria diffractens***, relatively recently introduced into cultivation, is a compact, beautiful little species, with a delicate covering of gray powder. It created a stir before people found out how readily its bracts would drop from its flower stalks, and how quickly they would develop into full-sized plants.

COLORFUL MEDIUM-SIZED ECHEVERIAS

Many medium-sized, more slowly clustering echeverias attract attention because of their highly colored or delicately powdered, almost iridescent leaves. Among the most strikingly colored, rosettes of the red-flowered ***Echeveria affinis***, from the mountains of northwest Mexico, turn a dark brown when given sufficient light. Closely related forms become almost black.

From the opposite part of the country, in wet Veracruz lowlands, ***Echeveria racemosa*** forms a broad, thin-leafed rosette to about 6 inches (15 cm) in diameter. Its color can range from yellow-orange to bronzy purple, although the widely grown **var. *citrina*** remains green except for a red rim around its leaf margins, contrasting with its bright yellow flowers.

Also green and with yellow flowers, ***Echeveria pulidonis*** in time forms small clusters of many-leafed rosettes up to 5 or 6 inches (13 to 15 cm) across, its sharply tapered leaves broadly edged in red. It is a central Mexican plant, less fussy than many about water remaining on its leaves, and reasonably outdoor hardy.

A third species with bright yellow blossoms, the very distinctive ***Echeveria lutea*** from San Luis Potosí state, forms somewhat larger rosettes made of many long, nar-

Some forms of *Echeveria affinis* turn almost black, contrasting with their bright red flowers. Photo by Julia Etter and Martin Kristen.

The deeply channeled leaves of *Echeveria lutea* set it apart from other species. Photo by Julia Etter and Martin Kristen.

Echeveria multicaulis may be close to the bottom of the family tree of the genus. Photo by Julia Etter and Martin Kristen.

A thin-leafed form of *Echeveria halbingeri*. Photo by Julia Etter and Martin Kristen.

Echeveria colorata dangling from a rock in company with a selaginella. Photo by Julia Etter and Martin Kristen.

With fewer, thicker leaves and contrasting two-toned flowers *Echeveria halbingeri* var. *sanchez-mejoradae* looks very different from its relative. Photo by Julia Etter and Martin Kristen.

row, deeply channeled leaves. They color up to a grayish brown tone, sometimes tinged with red.

Many other species redden up in bright light, among them **Echeveria multicaulis**, which grows into a small shrub with many rosettes growing on comparatively tall stems. **Echeveria semivestita** also gradually forms a proportionately tall stem, but rarely branches. Its sparse, rather open rosettes are composed of a relatively small number of leaves. The green, long, narrow, and red-rimmed leaves are minutely hairy in **var.** *semivestita* and smooth in **var.** *floresiana*. The flowers stand out, a crowd of pink petals emerging out of distinctly blue sepals.

A second assortment of colorful mid-sized echeverias includes many that appear blue, white, pink, or purple. Some of these attractive plants, such as the 8-inch (20-cm) wide **Echeveria colorata**, or the smaller, cliff-dwelling, freely clumping **E. halbingeri** and its **variety**

sanchez-mejoradae, are coated with a blue-white waxy bloom, which contrasts with their red leaf margins. In two larger growing species, **E. runyonii** and **E. similis**, both from the eastern rim of the Chihuahuan Desert, the coating, thicker and with a slight pearly quality, completely masks the underlying green of their thin leaves.

The more exotic-looking **Echeveria peacockii** remains solitary, and its bright blue-white, pink-edged leaves look almost dusted with powder. A distinct variant, formerly called **E. subsessilis**, has slightly broader leaves, pink

A very pink, very wavy form of the variable *Echeveria shaviana*.

Highly endemic, *Echeveria lilacina* grows near the habitat of some of Mexico's rarest cacti. Photo by Brian Kemble.

Clinging to its sheer cliff face, the miniature *Echeveria cuspidata* var. *zaragozae* is another extreme endemic. Photo by Julia Etter and Martin Kristen.

tinged, and more pearlescent as well. Highly glaucous and colored a distinct purple, *E. prunina*, endemic to a few canyon-edge localities in the southern Mexican state of Chiapas, grows slowly and remains small. It is a beautiful little plant, and as is the case with a number of cliff-dwelling species from areas with high rainfall, does best in cultivation with a logic-defying combination of a rich soil mix and nearly instantaneous drainage.

The 3- to 5-inch (3- to 13-cm) diameter *Echeveria shaviana*, a pine-oak forest species of northeastern Mexican, consists of rosettes of thin, ruffled leaves covered with delicate, almost iridescent pink to blue-purple powder. *Echeveria lilacina*, from lower, drier places, has waxy, thicker leaves coated in glowing white-purple and resembles an object made of porcelain. Still another small echeveria from the Chihuahuan Desert fringe, *E. cuspidata*, is a third attractive, pearly powdered species, with its dwarf **varieties** *gemmula* and *zaragozae* consisting of many narrow, cuspidate (ending in a point) leaves, rounded off at their ends except for their black, sharp but harmless little tips. **Variety** *cuspidata* is slightly larger, growing to about 4 inches (10 cm) across, and has tapering, broader leaves. It also looks like a delicate piece of ceramic sculpture, blue-white with a pink tinge.

SLOWLY CLUMPING OR SOLITARY SMALL ECHEVERIAS

Along with tiny rapidly proliferating species, *Echeveria* also includes a number of equally small species that either offset slowly or remain solitary. Several of these are somewhat difficult in cultivation, while others are seen only rarely.

From Chiapas, **Echeveria bella** does offset fairly freely though never to the extent of making a pest of itself. It forms tight rosettes less than 2 inches (5 cm) in diameter, composed of many long, narrow leaves ranging from bright to yellow-green. At a quick glance it has something of the look of a sempervivum or rosularia, though its yellow flowers shaped like open bells quickly confirm its identity as an echeveria.

Just as small, **Echeveria minima**, from Hidalgo state, forms a glaucous, bluish, dense rosette, with leaves almost truncate at the ends, tipped by a small reddish point. Some forms cluster very slowly, others more rapidly, with more vigorous hybrid plants often masquerading in cultivation as the actual species.

Clumping slowly or remaining solitary, **Echeveria moranii**, from dry, narrow canyon walls in Oaxaca, has very thick, distinctly gray, nonglaucous, almost stonelike leaves edged and tipped with a band of red. Up to 3 inches (8 cm) in diameter, it often fails to thrive in cultivation, generally from a combination of inadequate light and too much water.

Also susceptible to premature death in cultivation, **Echeveria strictiflora** grows at the opposite end of Mexico, the northeast, the territory of the Chihuahuan Desert. The only echeveria to cross over into southwestern Texas, it is a small though not tiny plant, with rosettes up to about 4 inches (10 cm) across, but usually less. With a wide but scattered range, it varies from glaucous gray to brownish or green; some Mexican populations have broader leaves edged in red. As is generally the case with desert-dwelling echeverias, it grows in somewhat sheltered areas, partially shaded by small oaks and similar vegetation, or in shady cracks in rocks. During winter dry periods it may shrink down into near invisibility, but when revived by rains it sends its 8- or 10-inch (20- to 25-cm) tall inflorescence and pink and orange flowers up through sheltering grasses. Plants from farther south, where the summer rains are a bit higher, do better in cultivation but still generally remain solitary. The plants should be watered more sparingly in winter than most other echeverias.

A species from the far Mexican south, in Chiapas, **Echeveria sessiliflora** is about the same size as *E. strictiflora*, with slightly thicker leaves either blue-green or covered with a faintly purple bloom. Easy to grow, it occurs in rocky areas around small oak trees, accompanied by agaves, and epiphytic tillandsias and orchids.

The vast expanse of Mexico lying between *Echeveria strictiflora* and *E. sessiliflora* country includes many rather similar looking small echeverias with gray, brown, or slightly blue-glaucous leaves. Among them, **E. humilis**, from the desert state of Querétaro, may grow among grasses and small columnar cacti. It also sometimes ventures onto the exceedingly dry habitat of the fantastic Mexican cactus, *Strombocactus disciformis*. In these surroundings the echeveria clings to tiny ledges, in contrast to the strombocactus, which grows tightly wedged into solid, vertical rock.

Somewhat similar in general aspect, though less attracted to extreme living situations, **Echeveria bifida** is rarely grown, though fairly widely distributed. Other species, such as **E. xichuensis, E. rodolfii, E. trianthina**, and some not yet firmly identified plants, tend to be much more localized in the wild.

More widely, though not necessarily successfully

Echeveria strictiflora, the only species found in the United States, lives in some of the most arid of echeveria habitats. Photo by Brian Kemble.

Echeveria humilis manages to survive on bare gypsum slopes in arid circumstances. Photo by Julia Etter and Martin Kristen.

grown, *Echeveria longissima* and *E. nodulosa*, from Puebla and Oaxaca states, distinguish themselves from this crowd of species. **Echeveria longissima** forms gray-green rosettes rarely much more than 3 inches (8 cm) across and produces a foot (30 cm) tall inflorescence with long, narrow, deep yellow flowers that flare open at their tips. It rots more readily than most echeverias. A quicker-than-average-draining soil and care with overhead and excessive water will enhance its chances of survival in cultivation.

Echeveria nodulosa, widespread in its southern Mexican habitat, where it often grows as an epiphyte, is immediately recognizable because of the deep purple-red longitudinal line that runs along its midrib, in combination with similar lines on its leaf margins and a deep-maroon tip; plants almost look as if they were painted.

From moist surroundings, this *Echeveria nodulosa* was growing as an epiphyte on an ancient cycad, *Dioon califanoi*.

Echeveria agavoides can reach over a foot (30 cm) in diameter. Photo by Julia Etter and Martin Kristen.

Their rosettes are quite small, but the plants slowly form a stem 6 to 8 inches (15 to 20 cm) tall that in time will freely branch.

THICK-LEAFED ECHEVERIAS

Another batch of species—not particularly closely related—includes echeverias noticeable for their very thick leaves. Thick leaves obviously conserve more water than thin ones, but despite their drought-resistant modifications, their needs in cultivation do not differ from less highly adapted plants.

Very common and with a large number of colorful variants, **Echeveria agavoides** has a tight rosette of angular, point-tipped leaves vaguely reminiscent of an agave and is an easy plant to grow. It does best with more light than most echeverias desire, and in areas that do not experience hard frosts it is an excellent candidate for outdoor growing. Some of its forms multiply rapidly while others offset much more slowly. Generally stemless, its rosettes may approach a foot (30 cm) in diameter. It is widespread in the northern parts of central Mexico, often growing in rocky clearings amid low forests.

Echeveria chihuahuensis can look something like a smaller version of *E. agavoides*, but with rounder, less angular leaf tips. Native to northern Mexico, it may be glaucous blue or plain green, its leaves often tipped with red; though some forms are drab, the most highly colored are very pretty. It offsets slowly, and, at least in dimmer regions of the world, may rot if kept too wet in winter.

Looking a little like a small partly closed up example of *Echeveria agavoides*, **E. purpusorum** rarely exceeds 4

Typically found in dry places, *Echeveria chihuahuensis* manages to find locally moist spots. Photo by Brian Kemble.

inches (10 cm) in diameter. It lacks the marginal coloring of *E. agavoides* but makes up for that by having distinctly speckled leaves, unique in the genus, and keeled leaf bottoms as well. *Echeveria purpusorum* grows slowly, and offsets sparingly and very gradually. It does best with excellent drainage in small pots.

Other highly succulent echeverias produce very different shaped leaves, thick, almost terete, and tapering to a point. **Echeveria craigiana**, from northwestern Mexico, makes a many-leafed rosette. The leaves are sometimes recurving and sharply pointed, sometimes less so, and range from green to brown to glaucous gray. Some forms may intergrade with the neighboring brown to almost black **E. affinis**.

A multiheaded specimen of *Echeveria purpusorum* is a rare find. Photo by Julia Etter and Martin Kristen.

Echeveria unguiculata, a rarity from northeastern Mexico, needs excellent light to keep its vivid patterns. Photo by Julia Etter and Martin Kristen.

Echeveria tolimanensis keeping company with *Mammillaria elongata* in central Mexico. Photo by Julia Etter and Martin Kristen.

Echeveria laui, coated with a thick layer of almost glowing powder.

With more pronounced terete and pointed leaves, the central Mexican **Echeveria tolimanensis** grows into a relatively few-leafed, medium-sized rosette densely covered with thick gray-purple powder. Some forms offset more readily than others, but it never makes a large clump. Given adequate light to maintain its powdery coating, it grows easily enough.

Echeveria unguiculata, a Chihuahuan Desert species, takes the incurved, pointed leaf look to the maximum. Its white-purple powdered leaves are tipped with a sharp, reddish black little spine. It also requires bright light to thrive, and perhaps a little-less-than-average water in winter.

A fourth thick-leafed *Echeveria* worth mentioning, **E. recurvata** is still uncommon in cultivation. Given sufficient light it rather resembles *E. tolimanensis* both in shape and color, but interestingly, it is from Venezuela, where it grows at altitudes of 10,000 feet (3000 m) or more.

Among the prettiest echeverias, the Oaxacan **Echeveria laui**, with thick, rounded, pure-white leaves, grows at lower altitudes than most echeverias and requires some protection from cold. At first glance it looks more like a *Pachyphytum* than an *Echeveria*, though it remains very short-stemmed and in the wild only rarely offsets. It needs very bright light to do well, with the intense yet diffused light provided by some modern greenhouse coverings producing the best results. Definitely less-than-average water in both summer and winter is recommended for growers in less bright locations. In California that does not seem necessary, though it is important to keep water from remaining between its leaves.

SOUTH AND CENTRAL AMERICAN ECHEVERIAS

Though not often encountered in cultivation, a good number of *Echeveria* species come from South America, growing in Venezuela, Colombia, Ecuador, Peru, and even farther south. They cling to the edges of the Andes, often at high altitudes, where their preference for steep slopes and sheer cliffs ensures rapid runoff of excess water in this land of overly abundant precipitation. Their Mexican relatives include species such as **E. penduliflora**.

Perhaps the most commonly cultivated of the South American plants, **Echeveria bicolor** forms smallish, blue-white, red-tipped rosettes, generally at the tops of fairly tall stems, though related forms with thicker leaves remain more-or-less stemless. Several other species develop long stems, branch freely, and turn into rather nondescript small shrubs. As more South American species are

Echeveria aff. *utucambensis,* growing in Peruvian ruins with a succulent *Peperomia.* Photo by Inge Hoffman.

discovered their horticultural availability will undoubtedly increase.

Compact, glaucous species such as **Echeveria andicola**, **E. peruviana** (with a range reaching into Argentina), and **E. eurychlamys**, have obvious appeal, while distinctive species such as **E. utucambensis**, growing occasionally among Peruvian pre-Columbian ruins in the company of shingle-leafed, succulent peperomias, do not really resemble any of the Mexican plants. Many South American species do well in cultivation, but despite their high-altitude origins, are generally not as cold-hardy as most Mexican species.

Echeveria penduliflora, growing pendently in well-watered habitat in Oaxaca state.

HAIRY-LEAFED ECHEVERIAS

One group of echeverias exclusive to central and southern Mexico consists of plants with densely tomentose leaves.

Echeveria cf. *peruviana,* a small species with large flowers. Photo by Inge Hoffman.

Echeveria setosa aff. var. *minor,* with leaves more blue-green than the typical variety.

Echeveria pulvinata, with long stems dangling from the rocks. Photo by Julia Etter and Martin Kristen.

Echeveria gibbiflora, a very purple form growing in an Oaxaca garden.

Echeveria gigantea with Sedum pachyphyllum, Agave salmiana var. ferox, Hechtia sp., and Mammillaria albilanata in Oaxaca state.

Of these, **Echeveria setosa** includes the hairiest plants, 4-inch (10-cm), flat rosettes composed of numerous short green leaves densely covered with fairly long hairs. This is a variable species, incorporating several distinct varieties formerly considered separate species. These include relatively hairless forms, as well as smaller plants with blue-green leaves. Plants remain low and gradually cluster.

Other species, such as **Echeveria pulvinata** and *E. leucotricha*, have developed dense coatings of short silvery-white bristles and appear more fuzzy than hairy. They ultimately become long-stemmed and multi-branched, though *E. pulvinata* branches much more quickly. The two species have dark brown, almost black, marking on their leaf tips, and some forms of *E. pulvinata* turn quite red in bright light. *Echeveria leucotricha* responds well to very bright light as well, its dense fuzz growing increasingly silver-white. *Echeveria pulvinata* has been hybridized extensively over the years, and most of the commonly seen tomentose green echeverias will be one or another of its hybrids. **Echeveria coccinea**, named for its brilliant red flowers, develops a fairly long stem, and has leaves clad in short, silvery hair.

None of these plants is exceptionally difficult, but *Echeveria setosa* can be fussy, with water remaining on its leaves easily leading to trouble.

LARGER ECHEVERIAS

Probably the best known of the larger echeverias, **Echeveria gibbiflora** from central Mexico develops a rosette composed of broad rounded leaves that can reach close to 2 feet (60 cm) in diameter and a 3-foot (90-cm) tall flower stalk. Its green to pale purple to bronzy-red leaves, combined with a habitat that at one time extended right into Mexico City, has led to a long history of cultivation, and the species belongs in the parentage of many echeveria hybrids. A form of the plant produces leaves with upper surfaces covered with blisters, and this oddity, called *E. gibbiflora* 'Carunculata', also has parented many exotic hybrids, attractive or not depending on the eyes of the beholder.

Mostly central Mexican, these large echeverias are certainly not plants of the desert. **Echeveria gigantea**, from southern Puebla and Oaxaca states, even larger than *E. gibbiflora*, and with an inflorescence as much as 6 feet (1.8 m) tall, grows as often in forest clearings as on sunny cliff faces and rocky slopes. Its leaves tend toward an almost metallic-looking blue-green, edged in pink, and it too has been widely used in hybrids.

Looking a bit like a smaller, paler version of *Echeveria gigantea*, **E. pallida** is more easily contained in a medium-sized pot, as it is less likely to topple over under the weight of its own flower stalk. Similar in general configuration but smaller again, with narrower leaves colored bronze-purple rather than blue-green, **E. fulgens**, also has a wide history of hybridization.

Echeveria fimbriata was named because of the minute fringes along the edges of its leaves, an attribute much less distinctive than its brown-orange color, just about that of a pumpkin pie when given proper light. It is more sensitive to cold than many echeverias, but otherwise

does well in cultivation, very gradually branching from its slowly elongating stem.

The northwestern **Echeveria dactylifera**, another large species, remains solitary in nature. Vegetative propagation from cuttings and leaves is fairly difficult. Its rosettes—up to a 1.5 feet (45 cm) across—are made up of very long, proportionately narrow leaves, thick, brilliant red, and occasionally slightly crenulated and wavy.

Probably the most beautiful echeverias are the large slow-growing members of a taxonomically long-confused complex of species consisting of *Echeveria cante* and *E. subrigida*. Both plants were originally considered to be *E. subrigida*, but finally the more northern growing plant (with a quite limited distribution) was determined to be separate and named in honor of a Mexican botanic garden.

Echeveria cante forms a good-sized rosette, always solitary in the wild, with broadly triangular leaves densely covered in silvery-white powder and edged pink. Its leaves are quite brittle and thin, almost papery in texture. Though a well-grown specimen possesses an almost other-worldly beauty, *E. cante* is not that easily cultivated; it is very slow growing, slow to flower, and very difficult to propagate vegetatively, although cultivated specimens sometimes offset.

Echeveria subrigida tends to be more robust. It often grows at fairly high altitudes, on near-vertical rocky cliff faces in regions of substantial rainfall. An inhabitant of the central Mexican plateau, it varies considerably in size and form. The classic type has large triangular, somewhat channeled, sometimes wavy leaves thicker than those of *E. cante*, red-edged and coated with a waxy blue to almost white powder. It is quite variable, however; some forms have smaller rounded or crenate leaves, and

Echeveria dactylifera glows red and rarely if ever offsets.

Echeveria cante, growing near a seep along with xerophytic ferns. Photo by Julia Etter and Martin Kristen.

Echeveria rubromarginata doing well on a crack in essentially bare rock. Photo by Julia Etter and Martin Kristen.

some forms are red-edged plain green, or only slightly glaucous, depending on how much sun they receive. *Echeveria subrigida* remains solitary in the wild (some tissue-cultured forms do offset) and flowers rarely. Though its plainer forms do not compare with *E. cante*, at its best *E. subrigida* is at least as attractive and typically a bit easier to grow as well (see photo on page 29).

Scarce in cultivation and slightly smaller, **Echeveria rubromarginata** shares the extravagant coloration of these two species.

EPIPHYTIC ECHEVERIAS

A final selection of echeverias includes species mainly from the forests of southern Mexico and Central America. Several have adopted an almost exclusively epiphytic way of life, leaving the soil altogether and living in the organic detritus that accumulates on the limbs and trunks of cloud forest trees.

Echeveria australis, along with **E. guatemalensis** and **E. pittieri**, form small, rather loosely organized rosettes on the ends of long, freely branching, straggly stems as does the less exclusively epiphytic Oaxacan **E. macdougallii**. *Echeveria pittieri* produces a distinctive spray of open flowers surrounded by large leafy bracts.

Echeveria rosea, a plant of high-altitude Mexican cloud forests from as far north as Tamaulipas state all the way south to Chiapas, sports an even flashier inflorescence, crowded with yellow blossoms and large red bracts, that manages to compete successfully with the orchids and tillandsias that share its habitat. It is the most frequently cultivated of the epiphytic species, but not the easiest, liking very bright shade, cool night-time temperatures, and a good amount of water.

ECHEVERIA HYBRIDS

The cultivated world of echeverias is filled with hybrids, some rapidly spreading, some quite slow to proliferate and therefore not as commonly grown. The documentation of many *Echeveria* hybrids is quite vague, but most of the large often brilliant red types, such as **E. 'Scarletta'**, have *E. gibbiflora* somewhere in their background.

Echeveria macdougallii growing as a semiepiphyte in a spot with agaves, hechtias, tillandsias, and orchids.

Echeveria 'Scarletta', big and red. Photo by Terry Thompson.

Though sometimes a lithophyte, *Echeveria rosea*, as in this instance, usually grows as a pure epiphyte. Photo by Julia Etter and Martin Kristen.

Echeveria 'Aquarius', highly crisped and pale, glaucous blue.

Echeveria 'Morning Light', with the characteristics of both parents.

Smaller, slower growing, and not common, **Echeveria 'Aquarius'** is an example of one of the nicer, heavily glaucous blue forms. **Echeveria 'Black Prince'**, derived largely from forms of *E. affinis*, both intensifies the characteristics of the species and reproduces and grows more readily.

Echeveria 'Morning Light', a hybrid of *E. shaviana* and what was taken to be *E. subrigida* but was almost certainly *E. cante* instead, combines the form and dense powdery covering of *E. cante* with the pink coloration of its other parent. It is easier to grow than *E. cante*, although just about as reluctant to offset. When *E.* 'Morning Light' was crossed with the true *E. subrigida*, the result was *E.* **'Afterglow'**, a striking plant that has proved hardy in central California gardens, and propagates quite readily as well.

The list and further possibilities of *Echeveria* hybrids goes on and on, ensuring a continuing horticultural tradition. *Echeveria* can also be crossed with related Mexican genera resulting in *Pachyveria*, *Sedeveria*, *Graptoveria*, and so forth.

Species and hybrids alike, echeverias respond to a soil somewhat richer in organic matter than that preferred by most succulents. In general, echeverias should never dry out completely, even in winter when watering them every two weeks or so will keep them healthy, less often in areas of low winter light. When plants are growing actively in the warmer months, weekly watering is best.

Echeverias need bright light, but too much direct sun can burn them; not enough and their distinctive colors mute back into plain green. Ultra-bright indirect light, sometimes difficult to provide, is ideal. In desert climates echeverias definitely will need additional shade to keep

from severe, often fatal scorching. Most of the plants can withstand cold, even a little frost, but some such as *Echeveria fimbriata* or the tropical *E. australis* and other Central American species, along with many South American echeverias, need to be protected from low temperatures.

A few other echeverias can cause problems in cultivation. Some species, such as *Echeveria longissima*, with its small rosettes and proportionately huge flowers, simply rot quite easily, as can *E. prunina* if not carefully watched. A few utterly normal-seeming species, such as *E. craigiana*, grow in crevices completely filled with organic matter and need the difficult-to-supply combination of rich soil and instantaneous drainage; a well-known grower used to mount them on vertical, moss-covered poles. It is important to keep water from standing in the rosettes of almost all echeverias, as this can lead either more or less quickly to rot. *Echeveria strictiflora* and other species from the arid Chihuahuan Desert can benefit from somewhat less-than-average water in winter though they respond well to normal watering during the warmer months.

Propagating most *Echeveria* species is easy, though growing them from their tiny seeds can be more difficult. Since the plants hybridize readily, seed-growing can also be a source of much confusion if not carefully done. Many of the plants will grow from a complete leaf, left to heal for a couple of days and then placed in sand or pumice until it begins to root and produce a small new plant at its base.

As the stems of echeverias elongate over time the rosettes become smaller. Cutting through the stem, letting the cut heal over for several days, and re-rooting the top is a good way to rejuvenate such plants. As a bonus, in most species the old stem will begin to produce offsets, which, when they reach 1.5 to 2 inches (4 to 5 cm) in diameter, can be twisted off, allowed to heal, and planted.

When cutting through a stem, it is very important to use sterile tools, as echeverias are quite susceptible to virus infections, usually spread by contaminated equipment. Use either single-edged razor blades as one-time-only cutting tools, or sterilize other tools by flaming them or dipping them in a 5- or 10-percent bleach solution. Neither sterilizing option, however, is very good for expensive shears.

Mealy bugs are fond of echeverias, and the plants are extremely susceptible to damage from oil-based pesti-cides, so checking them for pests before they can become established is a good idea, particularly around old, dried-up leaf bases.

Echeverias have been popular in cultivation for centuries and probably always will remain so. Some of them are good plants for beginners, while others are difficult to obtain and require skill and luck to grow. Many will do well outdoors in areas with moderate climates. Most can withstand some frost if kept reasonably dry, while the difficult ones can challenge and reward even the most experienced growers.

Chapter 9

Sedum and Other New World Crassulaceae

ALONG WITH *ECHEVERIA*, a number of other New World crassula family members have found their way into cultivation. The best known of these are the couple of dozen species, almost all Mexican, of *Graptopetalum* and *Pachyphytum*. They share their habitat with several other genera of exclusively New World Crassulaceae as well as a large assortment of species of the worldwide genus *Sedum*. Some of these plants have a long history of cultivation. Others, less common, have been valued by generations of growers of succulents, and some still remain quite rare, almost unknown outside their habitat and a few botanic gardens and choice collections.

GRAPTOPETALUM AND PACHYPHYTUM

Typical graptopetalums and pachyphytums have succulent stems ranging from a quarter to a half inch (6 to 13 mm) thick, surmounted by often loosely arranged rosettes of succulent leaves that may be angular or more-or-less elliptical. Many of these plants resemble a long-stemmed echeveria, and some taxonomists have made a case for including *Pachyphytum* within *Echeveria*. Pachyphytums often have leaves rather sparsely distributed along their succulent stems, although many form more obvious rosettes. The stems themselves elongate fairly rapidly in some species; others remain almost stemless for many years.

The best way to tell the two genera apart is by their flowers. *Graptopetalum* flowers look like open, five-pointed stars, usually pale tan or light yellow, with petals sparsely marked with dots. In contrast, *Pachyphytum* flowers are bell- or tube-shaped, generally almost hidden within bracts and thick sepals, and crowded along an arching, scorpioid stalk (like a scorpion's tail). When pachyphytums flower, their pale blue or green outer sepals contrast vividly with their bright orange to red petals.

Pachyphytums and graptopetalums have the same cultural needs as echeverias. They freely interbreed in cultivation and when crossed with echeverias have given rise to the bigeneric *Pachyveria* and *Graptoveria*.

Graptopetalum paraguayense (see photo on page 31), undoubtedly the most commonly cultivated of these plants, is a mainstay of succulent dish gardens the world over. Its stems gradually elongate, curve and droop, with thick, angular-pointed, flattened leaves that form a tight rosette. If given sufficient light, the leaves develop a dense white, waxy coating. Stem cuttings propagate readily and leaf cuttings produce new plants almost as easily though more slowly (see photo on page 34). Curiously, the natural habitat of this extremely common, long-cultivated plant remains unknown. A variant form of the species was discovered fairly recently on a single mountain in northeastern Mexico. Presumably the typical species also arose in some isolated location within the Chihuahuan Desert, perhaps a similar peak rising abruptly from a low plain covered with tick- and snake-infested scrub.

Several other species resemble *Graptopetalum paraguayense*, among them **G. pentandrum**, from western Mexico, and the more southern **G. grande**. Also long-

Graptopetalum amethystinum outdoors at the University of California Botanical Garden at Berkeley.

stemmed, but with thick, elliptical, pale amethyst-colored leaves, the slow-growing **G. amethystinum** has been treasured by generations of growers. **Graptopetalum pachyphyllum** resembles a miniature version of these large branching plants, with 4- to 6-inch (10- to 15-cm) long stems and dense, rounded rosettes 1 or 2 inches (2.5 to 5 cm) across.

Rather than growing on long pendent or decumbent stems, other graptopetalums form short-stalked rosettes that either cluster densely from the base or grow from wiry, 6- or 8-inch (15- to 20-cm) runners. The Oaxacan **Graptopetalum macdougallii**, with long, thin turquoise leaves, will readily start growing in any pot within reach of its runners. Clustering types include **G. rusbyi** and **G. bartramii**, both from southern Arizona.

Many of these short-stemmed graptopetalums are uninteresting but there are exceptions. **Graptopetalum filiferum**, a northern Mexican species that resembles a 2-inch (5-cm) stylized gray sunburst, has been hybridized with echeverias to produce beautiful little plants with evocative names such as **Graptoveria 'Silver Star'**. The somewhat similar **Graptopetalum bellum** (originally called *Tacitus bellus*), discovered not that long ago in the Mexican state of Chihuahua, also makes small clumps of flat, tight little rosettes crowded with grayish silver leaves. In contrast to its drab-flowered, mostly fly-pollinated relatives, its flowers, displayed around the end of the year, look like brilliant red stars.

Except for color and flower form, **Pachyphytum oviferum**, with rounded, egg-shaped, pale blue-white leaves, closely resembles *Graptopetalum amethystinum*, and shares the slow growth of that species as well. Cultivated for decades, it is known from only a single location in the wild.

Many other species also have leaves that range from blue-white to quite intense blue, such as **Pachyphytum coeruleum** and the rarely seen **P. rzedowskii**, while the

Graptopetalum macdougallii on a shady rock face in Oaxaca.

Pachyphytum oviferum, its pale floral bracts surrounding its red flowers. Photo by Julia Etter and Martin Kristen.

Graptopetalum bellum with large red flowers unique in the genus.

Pachyphytum coeruleum has pale yellow bracts and flowers. Photo by Terry Thompson.

Pachyphytum rzedowskii growing with tillandsias and orchids as well as cacti. Photo by Julia Etter and Martin Kristen.

In common with most pachyphytums, *P. saltense* grows pendently. Photo by Julia Etter and Martin Kristen.

The pendent flowers and faceted leaves of *Pachyphytum compactum* distinguish it from other species. Photo by Brian Kemble.

nonglaucous leaves of the uncommon **P. viride** turn red in bright light. From northeastern Mexico, **P. werdermannii** has almost pure white leaves that may flush pink or purple, as do those of **P. saltense**, another rare, recently discovered species. **Pachyphytum glutinicaule** is easily identifiable by its sticky stems, while **P. compactum** has sharply faceted leaves almost like mineral crystals instead of the organic ellipses of the other species. **Pachyphytum hookeri**, another slow-growing species, has small leaves,

blue, or somewhat orange in bright light, green in less (see photo on page 31).

From the central Mexican state of Hidalgo, **Pachyphytum longifolium**, less commonly cultivated, grows to almost 2 feet (60 m) tall, its thick, somewhat spindle-shaped leaves forming a sparse rosette. It grows on crumbling limestone cliffs, sharing a predilection for steep, rocky slopes with most members of its genus.

Sedum morganianum, on a farmhouse porch in rural Mexico.

Sedum dendroideum growing in ground completely covered with other cloud forest denizens. Photo by Brian Kemble.

SEDUM

The genus *Sedum* consists of a great number of plants from all the continents of the Northern Hemisphere, although several Asian species groups have been split off into separate genera. Mexico is home to well over a hundred species.

Among many worth mentioning, the donkey tail, *Sedum morganianum,* has had a long history of cultivation, both in Mexico and abroad. Though known to be native to Veracruz state, its exact habitat remained a mystery until very recently. Its pendent stems, densely cloaked with pale green leaves, drape down as much as 3 feet (90 cm). Unfortunately prone to drop leaves at the slightest touch, if given a fair amount of shade, a soil mix with a good deal of organic manner, and protection from frost, from time to time it will produce velvet-textured crimson-purple flowers.

Sedum burrito, also from Veracruz and comparatively new to cultivation, resembles a less elongated, sturdier version of the donkey tail. It may simply be a variety of it rather than a separate species. Other sedums, such as the small *S. versadense,* also develop stems densely cloaked with pointed leaves, but remain upright.

Many New World sedums hug the ground and spread rapidly. These make good ground covers in generally frost-free climates. The Mexican jelly bean, *Sedum rubrotinctum,* with elliptical succulent leaves that color up bright red in good light, also has been widely grown for many decades. Rather than a true species, it may be a garden hybrid, with the similar but less colorful *S. guatemalense* as a parent. Its other possible parent, *S. stahlii,* has bright red leaves arranged geometrically along its stems.

Sedum lucidum, with shiny, almost semicircular foliage and dense heads of white flowers, and *S. hernandezii* have leaves superficially similar to *S. rubrotinctum* in size,

Sedum versadense var. *villadioides,* may grow epiphytically on trees or lithophytically on rocks.

Sedum stahlii in a California rock garden.

shape, and color. Relatively rare in the wild and in cultivation, they are slow growing, larger, and more upright than *S. rubrotinctum* as well.

Slow and low growing, the dwarf **Sedum furfuraceum** can survive in the ground, but also makes a better behaved container plant than many of its rapidly spreading relatives (see photo on page 31). It has small elliptical leaves covered with rough-textured scurf.

A number of sedums form irregular rosettes of broad, more-or-less spoon-shaped leaves. Among these, **Sedum palmeri**, a good rock garden plant, forms medium-sized rosettes and sends out sprays of yellow flowers. **Sedum dendroideum**, somewhat similar but with less distinct rosettes, grows in the central Mexican highlands. In common with a surprising number of sedums, it is often found in cloud and montane forests, in places where epiphytes cover the trees and the ground itself is a soft mass of variously colored lichens, mosses, and tiny herbaceous plants.

A number of thick-leafed, vigorously branching sedums colonize rocky outcrops, growing variously erect, horizontal, or pendent depending on conditions. **Sedum allantoides** displays blue-white oblong leaves, while the succulent leaves of **S. pachyphyllum** remain yellow-green. **Sedum adolphii** (synonym *S. nussbaumerianum*) has triangular leaves and looks very much like a graptopetalum until it flowers. **Sedum macdougallii** produces small tight *Echeveria*-like rosettes at the ends of thin, succulent stems. Very glaucous, under conditions of intense indirect light it glows with an iridescent, pearly sheen.

Other rosette formers remain low-growing. Somewhat uncommon in cultivation, **Sedum hintonii** (synonym *S. hystrix*), from western Mexico, makes small rosettes of densely hairy, turquoise leaves. It requires more shade than most and fairly careful watering. From northern Mexico, **S. craigii** and **S. suaveolens** also remain short-stemmed and produce *Echeveria*-like rosettes of thick, rounded, highly glaucous leaves. The more southern **S. moranense** develops long stems but remains low to the ground.

Among the many sedums from the United States, a large number are minimally succulent, small creeping ground covers. One of the more succulent species is the western **Sedum spathulifolium**, found in rocky places from California all the way north into British Columbia. Its broad-leafed, whitish rosettes, 1 or 2 inches (2.5 to 5 cm) in diameter, spread by rhizomes and runners.

The most interesting New World sedums, however, are a few Mexican species with a growth form like a little tree, in effect, natural bonsais. Two of these, **Sedum oxy-**

Sedum hintonii, blue and densely haired, with very pale flowers.

Hanging from a rock face, *Sedum allantoides* looks much like a pachyphytum until it flowers.

Sedum moranense, growing on limestone in full sun, where it is brilliant red.

Sedum frutescens, a pachycaulous species, thick stemmed and up to several feet tall.

Thompsonella minutiflora, with a dense, upright inflorescence.

Sedum torulosum, multistemmed and reasonably frost hardy.

Thompsonella cf. minutiflora, with highly crisped leaf margins. Photo by Brian Kemble.

petalum and *S. frutescens*, have smallish, slightly succulent green leaves on fairly thin branches that emerge out of a swollen trunk up to 3 feet (90 cm) tall and covered in peeling bark. *Sedum torulosum* looks quite different, with thick, branching, upright stems that end in dense, glaucous rosettes. Back in the days of freely collected plants, specimens of these species were highly coveted. They are not seen too often now owing to the time it takes to raise them from seed or cuttings to maturity.

THOMPSONELLA

Thompsonella, a genus of infrequently cultivated Mexican plants, deserves to be better known. Most of the half-dozen or so species form compact, stemless rosettes that resemble small delicate echeverias. Their leaves, variously smooth or wavy-margined and sometimes covered with purple to white powder, are perhaps thinner and more brittle than those of echeverias, and their small, open, densely arrayed flowers look more like those of graptopetalums or sedums.

Thompsonellas often occur in quite arid areas, whether slopes or rocky flats where they may share their growing sites with a surprisingly diverse community of plants. As a rule they are less hardy to cold and a little touchier in cultivation than echeverias, and do not grow nearly as readily from leaf or bract cuttings.

Thompsonella minutiflora, with a thickened rootstock and variable leaf shape and colors, probably is most common in cultivation. *Thompsonella platyphylla* forms flattened little rosettes, while the atypical *T. mixtecana* branches from a relatively thick stem up to a foot (30 cm) in height.

Cremnophila nutans with yellow *Sedum*-like flowers.

Villadia aristata, with a white-flowered inflorescence that dwarfs its tiny rosette. Photo by Julia Etter and Martin Kristen.

CREMNOPHILA

The two members of the central and southern Mexican genus *Cremnophila* ("cliff-loving") have been variously placed in *Echeveria* and *Sedum* over the years. They look rather like a pachyphytum with pale yellow flowers. In **C. linguifolia** the flowers resemble an echeveria, and in **C. nutans**, a sedum. Cremnophilas can be slightly touchy in cultivation, needing good drainage. Their best feature is the seasonally deep chocolate brown color of their leaves.

LENOPHYLLUM AND VILLADIA

Lenophyllum and *Villadia* are infrequently cultivated. These primarily Mexican genera resemble sedums but differ in flower structure.

Lenophyllums develop small sparse rosettes and long inflorescences covered with tiny extremely loosely attached leaves that fall at the slightest touch and rapidly produce hordes of new plantlets (see photo on page 198). **Lenophyllum guttatum**, the most commonly grown, has speckled, wedge-shaped to almost terete leaves. Given very bright sunlight and little water, it maintains a tight appearance, but in a collection it generally soon becomes a pest.

Distinctly tubular flowers on tall stalks distinguish the approximately twenty species of *Villadia* from *Sedum*. Plants vary in size and habit from tiny creepers to mid-sized, upright shrublets. **Villadia guatemalensis**, from southern Mexico and northern Guatemala, may grow on steep slopes or as an epiphyte. In bright light it turns completely orange. Other villadias grow among sun-baked rocks, or even in high-altitude peat swamps.

Rosette-forming species, like **V. aristata** from the Sierra Madre Oriental, look like miniature echeverias and contrast with the unkempt-looking, densely leafy upright growers.

As is often the case with succulent plants, the quick-growing kinds of *Graptopetalum*, *Pachyphytum*, and *Sedum* are so widely distributed that people rarely think of these genera as particularly desirable, despite their many uncommon, choice species. Most grow easily, fast or slowly depending on species, and respond to a rapidly draining succulent mix with a decent amount of organic matter, regular (typically weekly) watering in the warm months of the year, and a drier period in winter, with watering reduced to once every two or three weeks. They generally need sun or extremely bright filtered light to maintain good color, and those with white or blue foliage should not be touched or the colorful, waxy protective coating will rub off. A little less water in fall will often promote better color in the plants, many of which can take some frost. The easy one are good subjects for outdoor succulent or rock gardens, while the slower ones do better in containers, either in a sheltered spot outdoors or in a brightly lit indoor growing situation.

DUDLEYA

Not closely related to other New World Crassulaceae, the genus *Dudleya* occupies its own distinctive ecological niche. The three dozen or so members of the genus are almost completely confined to the Pacific coast from southern Oregon through Baja California, their range corresponding in large part to the winter-rainfall region. Most species live near the ocean, many on offshore

Dudleya brittonii, so glaucous it is hard to look at in sunlight. Photo by Inge Hoffman.

Dudleya attenuata, typifying the narrow-leafed species.

islands. Their rosettes range from 1 or 2 inches (2.5 to 5 cm) to almost 2 feet (60 cm) in diameter. Most dudleyas cluster but a few remain solitary.

The most frequently grown species are heavily coated with dense, white powder, but others such as the northern Baja Californian **Dudleya ingens** and **D. cultrata** remain green unless the sun reddens them. Several rarely cultivated dudleyas lose their leaves altogether during their summer dormancy and retreat to their underground tuberous roots.

By far the best-known species, **Dudleya brittonii** forms a large dramatic rosette of many narrow, untapered, pointed leaves, typically but not always pure chalky white. It grows in coastal northwestern Baja California as well as on some adjacent islands. **Dudleya anthonyi**, from farther south on the peninsula, closely resembles the more widely distributed *D. brittonii*, but with smaller, narrower leaves.

Dudleya pulverulenta, with broader, *Echeveria*-like foliage, inhabits the coastal borderlands of Mexico and the United States, but extends much farther east, to the Mojave Desert of California and as far as Arizona. In parts of the Mojave it shares its habitat of rock-strewn, gentle slopes with *Echinocereus engelmannii* and the desert bulb, *Calochortus kennedyi*. When in autumn bloom the combination of brilliant purple cactus flowers, orange-red calochortus blossoms like deeper-colored, larger poppies, and the vivid arching red inflorescences of the dudleya provides one of the prettiest sights of the California desert.

Along with these good-sized plants, several much smaller dudleyas deserve mention. **Dudleya farinosa**, widely distributed along the northern California coast,

The Cedros Island endemic, *Dudleya pachyphytum.*

from the Monterey Bay region as far as southern Oregon, forms clusters of small star-shaped rosettes, generally heavily coated with white powder (farinose).

Other similar species grow south along the coast, among them **Dudleya lanceolata** and the densely clustering **D. caespitosa**. Even smaller, particularly in habitat, **D. gnoma** is one of several species endemic to one or another of the California offshore islands. **Dudleya gnoma 'White Sprite'**, a particularly tiny cultivar, has proven popular both in rock gardens and small containers.

In the driest parts of its central Baja California coastal habitat, another dwarf species, **Dudleya albiflora**, may not exceed an inch (2.5 cm) across, although in less-arid regions it forms good-sized clusters. And, far to the north, **D. cymosa**, which grows both along the central California coast and east to the Sierra Nevada, varies from pure white to either brown- or gray-leafed, but rarely if ever is simply green.

Rather than forming open, flat-leafed rosettes, several other dudleyas grow as tight, closed, though still circular, clusters of terete, finger-shaped leaves. Among them are the prolific Baja species **Dudleya attenuata** as well as the California endemic **D. abramsii**.

Finally, distinct from all the others, **Dudleya pachyphytum**, found in nature only on Cedros Island, west of central Baja California, has extremely thick, stubby leaves, heavily farinose and somewhat faceted at their tips.

Dudleyas start growing when the winter rains fall, so keeping them wet in summer and dry in winter will often have fatal consequences. Coastal plants and those from less-arid areas can withstand summer water better than the inland species. Dudleyas will not thrive in desert climates without additional shade, and warm summer nights disrupt their natural metabolic cycles. Given a bit of protection from the brightest summer sun in moderate, moister climates, such as coastal California, however, they will thrive in gardens or pots, as easily as their Mexican crassulaceous cousins.

Chapter 10

Euphorbia

IN CONTRAST TO THE crassula family, the euphorbia family, Euphorbiaceae, is dominated by a single genus—*Euphorbia*—with at least two thousand species. The majority of these are small to medium-sized, nonsucculent plants, recognizable by their unique floral structure and their white, milky, often irritating sap. Some have entered the horticultural trade as ornamentals while others are familiar garden weeds. As many as five or six hundred species, however, have become adept enough at water storage to be considered succulents.

People unfamiliar with the genus are often amazed by the several *Euphorbia* species that bear a remarkable resemblance to members of the completely unrelated cactus family, but that is just the tip of the iceberg. Within a single genus, euphorbias cover almost the whole range of succulent possibility. Succulent euphorbias also have a huge distribution, both in the New World and the Old, though, in common with so many other succulent plants, they reach their broadest development and widest speciation in South Africa and Namibia.

Although traditional *Euphorbia* taxonomy centered around spination and body shape has undergone numerous revisions, for general horticultural purposes it is still helpful to divide the genus into four groups based on these older criteria. The first group consists of plants from diverse parts of the world with stems thickened for enhanced water storage; though modified, these plants have not undergone drastic structural transformations from their nonsucculent ancestors. A second group, more succulent, more highly modified, and exclusively from southern Africa, includes species with large tuberous roots or greatly thickened stems. Some, but not all, have peduncular spines, derived from sterile flower stalks. They may have persistent leaves, ephemeral leaves, or no leaves at all. The third group, which unlike the first two consists of plants clearly descended from common ances-

tors, is composed of species with stipular spines, often, but not always, in pairs. These plants occur from southern Africa through East Africa, Arabia, and as far east as Thailand, but do not occur naturally in the Western Hemisphere. A last group consists of a large number of strictly Madagascan euphorbias that simply do not fit in with any of the other groups.

EUPHORBIAS WITH THICKENED STEMS AND DIVERSE DISTRIBUTION

The first, less strikingly modified group of species understandably has never attained the popularity of the other groups, though in nature they may dominate their habitat. Included among them are a number of species well worth cultivating by growers who can meet their sometimes specialized needs.

Several semisucculent species originate in North Africa and the islands of Macaronesia. Among these plants, characterized by thin, somewhat succulent branching stems topped by rosettes of nonsucculent, deciduous leaves, **Euphorbia balsamifera** is widely distributed, while *E. obtusifolia* and *E. lambii* are among the Canary Island endemics.

Euphorbia tirucalli, probably the most widespread of any of the succulent euphorbias, was first described from plants cultivated in India. It is widely grown—though rarely cherished—throughout much of Asia and the Americas. Probably native to Africa, it is found in almost the whole southern half of the continent. Under the right circumstances it will reach more than 25 feet (7.6 m) tall and resemble a pine tree. It has roughened, dark brown bark and dense swirls of small branches at the tips of its major limbs that look almost like clusters of pine needles. When kept as a container plant it consists of a mass of slightly jointed pencil-thick green branches with a com-

This *Euphorbia obtusifolia* subsp. *broussonetii* typifies the leafy, marginally succulent species.

Euphorbia leucodendron subsp. *oncoclada*, a tree formed of elliptical segments. Photo by Inge Hoffman.

plement of small short-lived leaves. In suitable climates it is often grown as a hedge, with primary branches thick and stemlike.

Several striking Madagascan tree-sized euphorbias are good candidates for container culture even though they will never reach their mature size when confined to a pot. Among them, *Euphorbia enterophora* has flattened, often brownish branches, while *E. leucodendron* and in particular its **subspecies oncoclada** have round, distinctly jointed branch segments, almost like strings of hot dogs. The intimidating-looking *E. stenoclada* is armed with spikes formed by sharp-tipped, multibarbed, incipient branchlets. *Euphorbia arbuscula*, from the island of Socotra, typifies the look of these arborescent species.

Smaller-growing species of this type have a worldwide distribution. *Euphorbia abdelkuri*, from a small island west of the succulent fantasy island of Socotra (between Yemen and Somalia in the Gulf of Aden), grows into a mid-sized branching shrub with a gray surface that looks like poured cement. Rare and coveted in cultivation, it grows slowly and receives a touch of mist and rain year-round in its isolated home.

New World species include *Euphorbia pteroneura*; *E. phosphorea*, which unfortunately gives no indication of phosphorescence, at least not in cultivation; *E. sipolisii*; and *E. weberbaueri*. They are attractive container plants,

Euphorbia stenoclada, every branchlet ending in a spike. Photo by Inge Hoffman.

with somewhat jointed, upright, sometimes distinctly ribbed succulent stems. From the Chihuahuan Desert, the thin-stemmed, peculiarly named *E. antisyphillitica* forms sprays of gray branches amid the barren rocks.

The shrublike euphorbias really come into their own, however, in the west coastal lands of South Africa and Namibia. Huge colonies of bush-sized euphorbias populate vast areas of the countryside, growing in hemispherical mounds up to 4 or 5 feet (1.2 to 1.5 m) high and across. The most common of these species, *Euphorbia*

The Socotran *Euphorbia arbuscula,* roots exposed because of erosion.
Photo by Rob Skillin.

Euphorbia abdelkuri, endemic to a tiny island and with yellowish white sap.

The Brazilian *Euphorbia phosphorea,* growing with an *Encholirium* species.
Photo by Rob Skillin.

Euphorbia dregeana, looking like a clump of gray reeds.

mauritanica, from nowhere near Mauritania despite its name, brightens up its drab, dry landscape with vivid yellow inflorescences set off by bright green cylindrical branches. Among the numerous other euphorbias that grow beside this species, **E. ephedroides** is wispier and not quite as symmetrical, **E. gummifera** develops bright red seed capsules, and **E. chersina** produces short, blunt-tipped secondary branches. Looking like an oversized clump of thick, gray-green reeds somehow transplanted to a desert, **E. dregeana,** from arid winter-rainfall areas of southern Namibia and northwestern South Africa, branches only from its base.

Euphorbia chersina, picturesquely dwarfed by its habitat. Photo by Kurt Zadnik.

Euphorbia lignosa growing amid rocks over sand in central coastal Namibia.

Euphorbia gariepina in a stony Namibian desert.

In cultivation, it can be difficult to maintain the tight appearance of these species, as they tend to elongate and flop. Nonetheless, several of them have potential as container specimens. When confined to a rocky crevice even obviously old plants of species such as *Euphorbia chersina* may turn into picturesque, dwarfed specimens worthy of show awards. Careful, patient cultivation would give the same results.

Rarely grown but horticulturally worthwhile, several other winter-growing species develop spines from their hardened branch tips. **Euphorbia spinea** resembles the mound-formers, but remains relatively small. Its branches, growing out at right angles from each other, give it a symmetrical, sculptural look. In harsh environments dwarfed forms of *E. brachiata* hug the ground. In common with these two species, the young growth of *E. lignosa* is soft and succulent but matures into hard, woody tissue. It shows up in cultivation from time to time, with straight sharp-tipped branches that grow out from each other at acute angles. *Euphorbia lignosa* matures into a dense, angular, extremely spiky mound, with alternating branches that give it a fiercer look than the more symmetrical *E. spinea*.

Occasionally grown, **Euphorbia gariepina** reaches beyond the Richtersveld and the Orange River (known as Gariep River in the local indigenous language) region as far as northern Namibia. In this species the branches—often distinctly blue-green—curve and taper gracefully, forming a sort of open vase shape. Clumps may be 2 feet (60 cm) across, but environmental factors may dwarf them to half that size.

Resembling a more succulent *Euphorbia gariepina*, *E. hamata* ranges from not far north of Cape Town to southern Namibia, always in the winter-rainfall area. Composed of curved segments that terminate in a hooked twist, the jointed, slightly zigzagged branches that emerge and rebranch from its central stem anticipate the tubercles that mark the stems and branches of many of the more familiar succulent euphorbias. At the relatively well-watered southern part of their range, the plants sprawl laxly but grow more compactly and neatly, with shorter internodes between their joints, as they venture northward into increasingly arid habitat. New branches, along with flowers and ephemeral leaves, start up in autumn from the hooked ends' segmented stems. Plants from the arid north may surround their small flowers with bright red bracts in contrast to the drabber but more typical pale green ones. Uncommon in cultivation, *E. hamata* is nonetheless popular with euphorbia enthusiasts.

A final selection of these euphorbias, adapted to harsh

Euphorbia hamata, the northern, tighter growing form.

From Madagascar, *Euphorbia platyclada* has the smallest flowers of any succulent euphorbia.

Euphorbia aff. *stapelioides*, with features of *E. herrei* as well, poking out of the Richtersveld sand.

conditions through miniaturization, includes the very rare **Euphorbia herrei** and the slightly more common **E. stapelioides**, both from the coastal Richtersveld. Both look like little clumps of sausages, growing prostrate, barely above ground level, with mature plants sized for a 4-inch (10-cm) pot.

Euphorbia juttae, from southern Namibia, forms a tiny densely branched shrub with branches composed of elliptical segments. Its flattened stems grow upward for a couple of inches (about 5 cm), then curve parallel to the ground and bend forward, generally facing northwest.

Euphorbia celata, from the southern Richtersveld, and **E. namuskluftensis**, growing several hundred miles farther north in Namibia, fill longitudinal cracks in rocks with heavily tubercled branches that crawl along or just under the soil, and spring from a central, somewhat tuberous rootstock. The related **E. verruculosa**, distributed approximately midway between the others, with even shorter, densely arrayed branches, looks like a dwarf sprig of broccoli, barely poking above the ground.

Far from the aridity and wind of the South African

Richtersveld, the Madagascan **Euphorbia platyclada** duplicates the low, sprawling growth of these continental African miniatures. Its branches consist of elongated, narrow segments, mottled pink-gray, a quarter inch (6 mm) wide by an inch (2.5 cm) long, that either hug the ground or occasionally climb as much as a foot (30 cm) into the air.

In mild climates, *Euphorbia tirucalli* is hard to kill. It roots from small cuttings and withstands almost anything except regular frost. The Madagascan species, large and small, need protection from frost as well, and a bit more water than most succulents.

Most plants from this first group respond to a soil mix a little richer in organic matter than most succulents need, and *Euphorbia platyclada* benefits from a certain amount of shade as well. Water once a week, or even a bit more in summer, and every two or three weeks in winter works best for them.

The southern African plants are a different story. Both the larger shrubbier species and the smaller ones need almost complete dryness in summer, with water beginning in fall and lasting until late spring. The most dwarfed species are the most sensitive to overwatering, and all of them need a great deal of light and rapidly draining, lean soil.

EUPHORBIAS WITH HIGHLY MODIFIED STEMS FROM SOUTHERN AFRICA

A second euphorbia group consists of species in which the succulent lifestyle has led to more dramatic physical modifications and includes some of the most popular, as well as some of the rarest and most difficult species in cultivation. With only a few exceptions, these euphorbias are confined to South Africa itself or neighboring countries such as Namibia, Angola, Botswana, and Zimbabwe. The only thing these diverse regions have in common is a marked dry season, and even that varies from place to place according to season—winter, summer, or almost any possible combination of months—with annual rainfall from as little as 2 inches (50 mm) a year to as much as 30 inches (760 mm).

Covering this varying expanse of land, habitat, and climate, it is no surprise that the ever-adaptable euphorbias have devised a wide array of succulent responses to environmental vicissitudes. A relatively few species have developed tuberous, water-storing roots and caudices or what essentially are underground succulent stems.

Probably the best-known of the tuberous, caudiciform species is **Euphorbia trichadenia**, from northeastern South Africa and parts of neighboring Zimbabwe. In the wild this plant looks like a small fairly plain shrub, with rambling stems and linear, slightly glaucous green leaves, recognizable as a euphorbia only by its flowers. But hidden underground, the bulk of the plant resides in a greatly enlarged, onion-shaped succulent tuber, which retains more than enough moisture to enable it to survive winter droughts.

The related, smaller **Euphorbia pseudotuberosa** grows farther to the south. At a considerable distance from these two, and not closely related to them, several associated species inhabit a wide expanse of the winter-rainfall area, where they remain leafless and dormant during the summer. With the coming of the winter rains these species present small stemless rosettes of leaves flush with the surface of the soil, giving little indication of the succulent stem or stems below. The best known of these, *E. tuberosa*, has broad, sometimes curly margined leaves; *E. silenifolia* has long narrow, almost linear foliage; and the broad leaves of *E. ecklonii* have an odd quilted texture. In cultivation raising the tubers and underground stems of these geophytes (a collective term for plants with underground storage structures such as tubers, bulbs, corms, and rhizomes) above the soil, displays the entire plant and helps prevent them from rotting. Older, multistemmed specimens of *E. tuberosa* make superb succulent bonsais when grown this way.

This essentially underground mode of life extends beyond South Africa. Perhaps the best known of these geophytes is *Euphorbia primulifolia*, one of a few from Madagascar. Even a cursory look at its flower structures shows that this diminutive plant belongs with the nongeophytic

Beneath the soil, *Euphorbia tuberosa* develops its invisible tuber. Photo by Kurt Zadnik.

Euphorbia trichadenia in cultivation, showing more than the leafy stems which would be all that protrudes above ground in the wild.

Without its characteristic fruit, *Euphorbia ecklonii* might not be recognizable as a euphorbia.

Madagascan species rather than with the South African plants. A small number of other geophytic euphorbias occur in East Africa as far north as Somalia. Combining almost complete invisibility in the field with genuine scarcity, these are practically unknown in cultivation.

Another group of euphorbias, mostly from eastern South Africa, also bear large leaves at the tops of their succulent stems, but unlike the geophytes they grow above ground. *Euphorbia bupleurifolia*, undoubtedly the best known of these, has short, dark brown, woody, sharply tuberculate, rarely branched stems and resembles a highly stylized drawing of a miniature pineapple. As is often the case with euphorbias, it is dioecious, with individual plants either male or female. Its flowers appear at the ends of deciduous peduncles, often before its rosettes of bright green leaves.

Several related species with taller, less distinctly tubercled, plain green and proportionately narrower stems include *Euphorbia clandestina*, with inflorescences hidden close to its stem; *E. pubiglans*, with persistent peduncles and a spray of green, round-bracted flowers; *E. clava* and *E. cylindrica*, with respectively wider and narrower leaves; and the smooth-tubercled, branching *E. bubalina*. The similar but often much larger *E. monteiroi* grows farther north, in a band stretching across southern Angola and northern Namibia through Botswana and Zimbabwe into northeastern South Africa. Most of these plants need some protection from cold, moderately bright light, a reasonably rich though fast-draining soil, and adequate water.

A small group of western South African euphorbias combines prominent leaves with dense, persistent peduncles that harden off into spines after flowering. These

Euphorbia clandestina, half hidden in the Little Karoo.

Euphorbia pubiglans, with its flowers definitely not hidden.
Photo by Terry Thompson.

Euphorbia bupleurifolia, one of the most popular species.

include the tuberous-rooted **Euphorbia oxystegia**; the spiny, densely branched *E. loricata*, up to 3 feet (90 cm) tall and almost as wide; the symmetrically growing dwarf *E. multifolia*; and the somewhat larger, cushion-forming *E. eustacei*. A cultivated, probably hybrid plant sometimes called *E. loricata* neither looks like nor has any particular relation to the actual species. Though they resemble plants such as *E. clandestina*, these euphorbias probably are more closely related to the other peduncular-spined species from farther east, such as *E. horrida*. These rarely encountered plants live in areas of summer drought and should be grown accordingly in cultivation. If kept too wet in summer they have a bad habit of quickly rotting.

In contrast, the spineless leafy euphorbias do well with weekly water in summer, less in winter. *Euphorbia bupleurifolia*, despite enjoying more-than-average water when growing, should be left dry from the time its leaves drop until new growth starts. It also prefers a barely shaded situation.

A few rare species, which certainly look like they belong with this group but probably do not, live many thousand miles away in Somalia and the southwestern corner of the Arabian peninsula. Among these are **Euphorbia hadramautica**, **E. napoides**, and **E. longituberculosa**. All three are small plants that resemble a miniaturized, unbranched *E. bubalina*, but differ from that easily grown species by being extremely sensitive to excess humidity and both over and under watering. Accordingly, the three offer poor prospects for long-term cultivation. Growing them with bottom heat may lead to better results.

Standing out from the succulent scrub of coastal Namaqualand, **Euphorbia schoenlandii**, **E. fasciculata**, and **E. restituta** form a distinct group. Their hard, green, columnar stems are covered with more or less regular patterns of prominent tubercles. *Euphorbia schoenlandii*, up to 4 feet (1.2 m) high, and the slightly shorter *E. fasciculata* remain solitary, while *E. restituta*, extremely localized in the wild, forms small clumps of stems. All have ephemeral leaves and develop sterile peduncles that harden into stout, curving, woody spines. *Euphorbia schoenlandii*, with a more orderly arrangement of tubercles and proportionately smaller, neater-looking spines than the others can survive at least a few degrees of frost outdoors despite its seaside habitat, sheltered from the intense cold of the interior deserts. All three species lean toward the sunny north, and do well in cultivation with extra fast draining soil, less-than-average water in winter, fairly strict summer dryness, and intense sunlight.

These *noordpool* (north pole) plants overlap the range of a larger euphorbia subgroup composed of plants with a single thickened, sometimes underground main stem fringed with a whorl of secondary branches. Reminiscent of a swarm of snakes, the so-called Caput-Medusae Group was named after the mythical serpent-haired Greek demonesses.

Euphorbia multifolia, a rarely seen dwarf species from the Little Karoo. Photo by Terry Thompson.

Euphorbia schoenlandii, growing within sight of the Atlantic Ocean.

A surprisingly large variety of Caput-Medusae euphorbias, called *vingerpols* ("tufts of fingers") in Afrikaans, grow in South Africa or bordering regions of neighboring countries. The best known of these, **Euphorbia caput-medusae**, grows in the hills that run alongside Cape Town. As might be expected in a plant from a well-watered area, it can become quite large, almost 3 feet (90 cm) across. It looks like a great swirl of spiraling and twisting tubercled branches a foot (30 cm) or so in length that emerge out of a central, thickened, cylindrical stem. Unlike most of the other medusoids, however, it lacks a flattened or depressed, branchless area at its apex, the head, as it were, from which the snakelike branches emerge.

The vingerpols once were divided into those with fringed, filamentous flower parts and those without them. Though not presently considered taxonomically significant, the fringed and fringeless medusoid euphorbias form recognizable horticultural associations.

The fringeless-flowered plants, with uniformly green stems and branches, bloom from their distinctly depressed central stem and basal branch areas rather than from their tips. Their range extends eastward from the central southern coastal regions of South Africa. They form a kind of continuum from small to larger depending on the ecological conditions in which they grow. The small end of the continuum includes the generally solitary **Euphorbia gatbergensis** and the slowly clumping **E. ernestii**, both with bright yellow flowers. The brownish-purple-flowered **E. gorgonis** and the green-flowered **E. pugniformis** grow a bit larger. **Euphorbia franksiae** and the commonly cultivated **E. flanaganii**, both with yellow flowers, are larger still. The biggest, **E. woodii**, from warmer, better-watered areas, has a main stem up to 6 inches (15 cm) across, and twenty or more swirling secondary branches that can triple its total diameter.

With similar fringeless, shiny yellow flowers but a very different appearance, **Euphorbia clavarioides**, from high in the mountains of eastern South Africa and neighboring Lesotho, has a main stem that subdivides into many short, somewhat club-shaped secondary stems, eventually forming a large dome-shaped mound up to 3 feet (90 cm) across. In its **variety truncata**, a somewhat smaller disc as flat as a pancake, the myriad secondary branches all reach the same height. At ground level it looks like a sort of knobby green pavement.

Along with a general dwarfism related to more arid conditions, the smaller medusoids tend to have shorter secondary branches, reaching the ultimate with the possibly mythical **Euphorbia brevirama**. Found only once,

Euphorbia gorgonis, from dry areas, remains small. Photo by Brian Kemble.

Euphorbia pugniformis has green flowers, more branches, and grows somewhat larger.

Euphorbia clavarioides, a smaller plant clearly displaying its varying branch lengths. Photo by Brian Kemble.

in 1912, this species forms a tiny flat-topped cylinder with a whorl of secondary branches less than a half inch (13 mm) long. The desire to relocate *E. brevirama*, which may have simply been a stunted or aberrant example of something else, has led to the discovery of a panoply of small medusoids in recent years. Though many of these discoveries undoubtedly will turn out to be just forms of *E. gorgonis* and related species, a few may manage to retain their taxonomic autonomy. Among these, **E. suppressa**, from the Great Karoo, has a relatively large cylindrical body, with many very short, thick secondary branches growing from around its apex, while **E. atroviridis** looks like a smaller version of either *E. clavarioides*, from far to the east, or *E. ramiglans*, from far to the west. Both *E. suppressa* and *E. atroviridis* live in the central South African interior, a harsh region of blazing summer heat, little rain, and bitterly cold winters.

Twin heads of snakes—a paired *Euphorbia esculenta*. Photo by Brian Kemble.

Euphorbia ramiglans, another native of the Richtersveld coast. Photo by Kurt Zadnik.

With flowers looking almost like little daisies because of their fringed processes (appendages of the involucre glands) the other medusoid euphorbias start at the south with *Euphorbia caput-medusae*. An arc of related species stretches both to the northwest and to the northeast. Immediately east grow **E. muirii** and **E. marlothiana**, dwelling in sandy coastal flats and consequently deep-rooted, but also lacking the highly defined central stem that distinguishes most members of this group. Farther up the coast to the east and inland to the north, a number of other medusoid euphorbias come into view, among them **E. fortuita**, **E. esculenta**, **E. colliculina**, and **E. inermis**. All four are medium-sized plants with short, thick, usually light brown or gray-green central stems and concentric circles of secondary snakelike branches. **Euphorbia albipollinifera**, a smaller plant, produces striking little flowers with centers surrounded by feathery white processes, while the fringes of other vingerpol flowers vary from white, to golden yellow, to red. Though individual blooms are small, when they bloom in mass the outer branches of these euphorbias burst with bright color.

North and eastward into Zimbabwe, the few endemic medusoid species grow with larger, more persistent foliage than those from more arid places. **Euphorbia davyi**, up to a foot (30 cm) in diameter, has leaves as much as 1.5 inches (4 cm) long that remain on its secondary stems throughout its summer growing season. It may rot if allowed to get too cold and wet in winter. The related, smaller-leafed **E. maleolens** is one of the easiest of these plants to grow.

Most of the remaining medusoids live along the Atlantic coastal and associated interior deserts. **Euphorbia tuberculata**, which resembles *E. esculenta* and the other eastern plants, first appears not far northwest of *E. caput-medusae*, and follows the winter rain all the way to the Richtersveld.

Restricted to the northern half of this foggy coastal desert, **Euphorbia ramiglans** generally forms a short, stocky main stem with a few branches at the top. In some areas near Port Nolloth ancient plants up to 3 feet (90 cm) across with innumerable branches embed themselves in old sand dunes a quarter mile (400 m) back from the sea. There they flourish in the company of *Crassula plegmatoides*, *Fenestraria rhopalophylla*, and hordes of land snails with pure white shells and fleshy, jet-black bodies.

Euphorbia confluens has greenish flowers, while *E. tuberculata* has whitish ones, and the flowers of *E. ramiglans* have yellow or rust-colored processes. The absolute

Euphorbia namibensis, bent from the wind and growing in pure sand.

This flowering *Euphorbia pentops* was wedged between two rocks, disguising its shape.

Euphorbia friedrichiae, sand blasted but flowering.

Euphorbia braunsii, two plants from farther west than normal benefiting from supplemental water from fog.

differences between the plants are indistinct, and it may be impossible to sustain them as separate species forever.

Back from the beaches, several other rare vingerpols grow in the quartz hills and stony Namaqualand plains or across the border in Namibia. Perhaps the most spectacular of these, **Euphorbia namibensis**, grows in flats composed of nothing but compacted sand, an unpromising habitat that it shares only with a little very sparse grass. Its central stem, displayed well above ground, looks dis-

proportionately massive, as does the whorl of snakelike branches that grows from its top. The plants form scattered colonies bent low against the prevailing western wind.

Wind-blown sand often adheres to the other medusoids from this area on either side of the South Africa–Namibia border as well. These include thick-stemmed plants with very short branches such as **Euphorbia namaquensis**, **E. melanohydrata**, and **E. friedrichiae**. The small **E. pentops**, endemic to a few Richtersveld hills, has distinctive flesh-pink flowers with an emerald-green spot at the base of each glandular process.

A number of western species have main stems subdivided into several upright secondary stems which in turn put out reduced little snakelike branches, so each stem looks like a miniature version of *Euphorbia namaquensis*. These include **E. filiflora** and the green-flowered **E. braunsii**, never common, but found in arid, rocky flats from southern Namibia all the way to the Great Karoo. Closely related to *E. filiflora* but very localized, **E. brakdamensis**, from Namaqualand quartz hills, comes with dark green stems, a dense array of secondary branches,

A multiheaded *Euphorbia multiceps* in Little Karoo scrub.

and green flowers. The extremely scarce Richtersveld-dwelling *E. versicolores* displays its gaudy, multicolored fringed flowers on long stalks.

The bleak, alternately roasting and freezing but always arid Great Karoo provides a home for endemic medusoids as well as some that wander in from the not-quite-so-bleak west. These plants tend to be brown or even purplish, very hard bodied, with short, stiff secondary branches crowned by persistent, hardened peduncles. *Euphorbia arida* has an erect main stem and upright secondary branches that fan out from its apex. *Euphorbia fusca*, with a foot-wide (30 cm) stem, has a distinguishing furrow that runs down its center, missing in the smaller *E. albertensis*. *Euphorbia decepta*, with globular main stem and stiff little branches radiating out in all directions, resembles a World War II maritime mine, as does the smaller *E. hopetownensis*. *Euphorbia astrophora* is small as well, slightly less globular, and has a distinct starburst of dried peduncles at its branch tips unlike the unadorned *E. inornata*. *Euphorbia crassipes* forms its own version of a low dome of hard, brown secondary stems.

As with other assortments of medusoid euphorbias, it seems possible that many of these basically similar species will eventually be swallowed up, in this case into what might seem to be the most distinctive species of all, the widespread *Euphorbia multiceps*. It is found in the Little Karoo, the Ceres Karoo, and far northwest into Namaqualand and the southern Richtersveld. Unlike typical medusoids that look like globes or cylinders topped with snakelike secondary branches, the classic form of *E. multiceps* resembles a miniature succulent Christmas tree. Its central stem is completely obscured by a dense growth of horizontal branches that grow increasingly shorter

from the base of the plant to the top, resulting in an elongated triangle. A colony of these plants looks like a scattering of little green pyramids, growing in the midst of succulent scrub and low brush.

Many of these plants are rare in the wild and uncommon in cultivation. *Euphorbia flanaganii* and its close allies grow easily with standard succulent water and soil, and bright light. The same is true with those plants most closely related to *E. caput-medusae*.

The plants from the west coast of South Africa and Namibia live in a winter-rainfall region, while the plants from the Great Karoo receive most of their rain in late summer and fall, and some of these can prove difficult in cultivation. Summer dryness may be best for the coastal plants, but if the plants decide to grow in summer, we should take advantage of their good nature and water them.

Less-than-average water may be advisable, along with extremely rapidly draining soil, for the most-arid growing species. Even though it is widely distributed, *Euphorbia multiceps* can be a challenge to keep alive. Less water, if any, when dormant, and careful observation during its growing season is the best way to keep this plant alive, and is a good rule for all the arid-growing medusoids.

Many of these plants used to be great rarities in cultivation, but several commercial growers have introduced seed-grown plants in good quantities into the trade. Growing a seedling into a natural-looking mature plant does not come quickly or easily with some of these euphorbias. Others grow well, and a few even tolerate outdoor conditions in the moderate climates where they have become valued favorites with many growers.

Several other species, all related, though lacking the colorful flowers of the medusoids, have blossoms with highly elongated processes, informally called finger flowers and often prominently displayed on long peduncles. Looked at closely the flowers may evoke images of tiny bird heads or ornate coral reef invertebrates. Despite this intriguing quality, the basic appeal of these plants for growers lies in their vegetative habit.

The two most commonly cultivated finger flowers, *Euphorbia globosa* and *E. ornithopus*, often look very similar. Both form a tangle of small somewhat elongated, segmented green stems with a central stem that imperceptibly turns into a thickened root. In the wild, however, or when grown under extremely bright light, the resemblance disappears. *Euphorbia ornithopus* maintains its appearance, but the segmented branches of *E. globosa* turn round as marbles. In nature, as *E. globosa* matures its main stem sinks steadily farther underground, pulling the older branches along with it, while spherical new branches keep developing on top. The result is an extremely low-growing plant that looks like a patch of oversized green peas staking out a turf up to 8 inches (20 cm) wide. In a pot, the main stem and older branches can only descend so far, and the mounds of new branches pile up on top of each other, with more elongated secondary stems that produce the long-peduncled finger flowers uppermost.

Euphorbia ornithopus, **E. tridentata**, and **E. wilmaniae** grow in the same manner, but with tapering, cylindrical, more obviously tuberculate rather than spherical segments. The differences between these three consist mainly of floral details and density of underground stems and tuberous roots.

In contrast, the two remaining members of the group, **Euphorbia planiceps** and *E. polycephala*, have single, large mostly underground stems that branch and rebranch into an almost solid mass of ground-level succulent vegetation. The 0.5- to 1-inch (13- to 25-mm) thick branchlets in *E. polycephala* are more-or-less rounded and solidly packed together, while the branchlets of *E. planiceps*, only half as thick, taper at their tips. Generally flush with the ground, in areas of rocky soil *E. polycephala* may be forced up into a dense mound, to 6 feet (1.8 m) across and 2 feet (60 m) high in exceptional circumstances. When grown in pots it is hard to keep plants compact, and they generally grow into collections of elongated stems similar to *E. ornithopus*.

In coastal central California *Euphorbia globosa* will survive outdoors if given excellent drainage. When grown in the ground in full sun the elongated branches of container-grown plants will gradually be pulled underground, replaced over time by perfect little green spheres. *Euphorbia planiceps* and *E. polycephala* are rare enough that there is little information available about their potential outdoor hardiness.

Another group of euphorbias resembles the finger-flowered species, but with simple, unelaborated flowers. Included here are **Euphorbia pseudoglobosa** and *E. juglans*, with rounded secondary stems, and the cylindrical stemmed **E. tubiglans** and **E. jansenvillensis** (the former with a proportionately huge tuberous root). Sometimes lumped in with these species, though not really resembling them, **E. susannae** has a main stem, ribbed and supplied with dense rows of pointed but harmless little teeth. Very popular with collectors, it branches prolifically with age and each branch can be taken off and

A heap of oblong stems, *Euphorbia pseudoglobosa* would retract underground if not confined to a pot.

Euphorbia jansenvillensis, planted to reveal its underground tuber. Photo by Terry Thompson.

Euphorbia susannae, another Little Karoo plant, nearly hidden in the vegetation.

rooted, maturing into a little hemisphere composed of numerous bright yellow-green or kelly-green stems.

Euphorbia hypogaea, a species traditionally included with the medusoids, may be better situated with this group. It resembles *E. susannae*, with a series of toothy, upright branches emerging in parallel from a large underground main stem. From the very arid Great Karoo, it is considerably more susceptible to rot than *E. susannae*.

Less prone than the finger flowers to distortion and etiolation in cultivation, these euphorbias remain small. A 4- or 5-inch (10- to 13-cm) pot will easily contain a mature specimen of any of them. A note of caution, however: the sap of *Euphorbia tubiglans*, and possibly several of the others, is quite toxic, and I can attest to how painful even a tiny droplet can feel if you manage to get it on your face. Since the plants are completely unarmed, it makes sense that their sap would have good defensive characteristics. Euphorbias, however, seem quite unconcerned with rational consistency, as some of the most poisonous species are heavily armed with sharp spines, and some spineless species have completely nontoxic sap.

Closely related to these dwarf, branching species, *Euphorbia obesa* and *E. meloformis* have been popular in cultivation for the last century. *Euphorbia obesa*, in particular, is a perfect little ball, remaining nearly completely round for years, divided into symmetrical ribs marked by stitching (almost like a baseball), and with its body decorated with arching purple and green bands. Over time these dioecious plants become more cylindrical, the males elongating more than the females. The similarly "obese" *E. meloformis* has distinct ribs. With age it often branches, and its persistent dried peduncles give it a less symmetrical appearance than *E. obesa*.

Euphorbia valida is so similar to *E. meloformis* that, contrary to its name, it may not really be a valid species at all, while *E. symmetrica*, probably just a form of *E. obesa*, is the roundest, its height never exceeding its diameter. Despite looking like specialists in arid land survival, given excellent drainage both *E. meloformis* and *E. obesa* will do surprisingly well in California rock gardens, where their bands of color will intensify in the natural light.

Another large group of euphorbias has clumping cylindrical, ribbed stems, characterized by persistent peduncular spines. These species generally resemble each other, differing mainly in size of stems, specific development of peduncular spines, and minor differences in flowering parts. A few, with stems divided into distinct tubercles, have earned the nickname corncob euphorbias, including *Euphorbia fimbriata*, *E. nesemannii*, and by far the most frequently cultivated, *E. mammillaris*. The latter has a variegated, yellowish white form more common in cultivation than the standard green. Primary stems of the corncob species reach a bit more than a foot (30 cm) in height, and the secondary branches that grow from their base gradually form a loose hemisphere.

Other nontuberculate species such as *Euphorbia enopla*, *E. atrispina*, *E. aggregata*, and in particular, *E. pulvinata*, form masses of hundreds of densely packed branches up to 6 feet (1.8 m) across, like a single huge cushion of stems. *Euphorbia ferox* also grows in dense hemispherical masses, but its particularly stiff, thick, sharp spines set it apart. Though the spines are only modified flower stalks, they will rip your skin off as effectively as a clump of cacti.

Other peduncular-spined species branch less tightly and grow taller. *Euphorbia pentagona* and *E. heptagona*

A young female *Euphorbia obesa*, its flowers turning into three-segmented seed capsules.

Distinctly banded, a small *Euphorbia meloformis* hunkers down in eastern Karoo habitat. Photo by Brian Kemble.

Euphorbia fimbriata, one of the "corncob" species. Photo by Brian Kemble.

Euphorbia heptagona with characteristically orange spines. Photo by Terry Thompson.

Euphorbia pulvinata, mound forming, cold and rain hardy, with larger, longer lived foliage. Photo by Brian Kemble.

Euphorbia ferox, aptly named with stiff, sharp spines. Photo by Terry Thompson.

Yellow blossoms top the thick, gray stems of this *Euphorbia horrida*. Photo by Brian Kemble.

reach as much as 5 or 6 feet (1.5 to 1.8 m) in height. The many forms of **E. horrida** and the closely related **E. polygona** resemble clustering barrel cacti, with thick stems up to 2 feet (60 cm) tall. Finally, the spines of **E. pillansii** have forked tips, while those of large-stemmed **E. stellispina** fork into multiple points, like sharp stars.

Though quite slow growing, *Euphorbia stellispina* is a tough plant that forms spectacular clumps several feet across. In the Western Cape Province I have seen it on stony hillsides with ice still on the ground at high noon. Though not commonly cultivated, if given good drainage it will survive outdoors in central California as well.

Probably the hardiest, *Euphorbia horrida* survives freezes into the teens (about −8°C) without complaint and is a mainstay of outdoor succulent gardens. Generally easy growing, these plants will thrive either in containers or outdoors in suitable climates.

The peduncular-spined euphorbias, along with the finger-flowered species, do best in extremely bright light. *Euphorbia susannae* and its relatives can take less and may need some protection from the brightest sunlight. These euphorbias enjoy a standard succulent soil mix. *Euphorbia obesa* and its relatives require a bit more drainage and should receive somewhat less water, perhaps every ten days or so during the warm months, around every six weeks during their winter rest. The other euphorbias like water once a week in summer, about once a month during winter.

The euphorbias that will survive outdoors adapt well to coastal California rainy winters and dry summers, with occasional extra water in summer. Leaving them dry from midautumn until the rains begin provides them with the rest period that most succulents seem to need. Many of these species are among the best candidates for an outdoor succulent garden, as they really come into their own when given sunlight and space to grow.

EUPHORBIAS WITH STIPULAR SPINES

The third group of succulent euphorbias consists of those commonly called the twin-spined euphorbias. A very distinct subset of these occurs on the island of Madagascar, but hundreds of other, more closely related twin-spined species grow throughout Africa and then to Arabia, India, and as far as Thailand. In these euphorbias sets of paired spines derived from appendages (stipules) found at the base of leaves occur in longitudinal patterns at every node. These twinned stipular spines actually start out as a juvenile pair of double spines, which some species retain, resulting in four spines per node. In other species the spines are fused and seem single, or one pair becomes fused, resulting in three spines. A few species lose their spines with maturity. In all cases the spines are derived from identical structures, evidence of their phylogenic relationship.

It is easy to distinguish these euphorbias from those with peduncular spines discussed previously because of the symmetrical arrangements of the twinned spines, which often emerge from distinctly colored "shields" located along the stems. Aside from the twin spines themselves, however, this large euphorbia group can take on almost any appearance imaginable, from 60-foot (18-m) tall trees to shrunken spheres less than an inch (2.5 cm) across.

Probably of Indian origin but with exact habitat localities lost in antiquity, **Euphorbia trigona**, with long-lasting, blade-shaped leaves distributed along its branches, and **E. lactea**, often seen either as a variegated or crested form, become small trees. Among the most widely cultivated euphorbias, they respond well to container culture.

Other Indian tree or shrublike species include frequently cultivated plants such as **Euphorbia antiquorum** and **E. nivulia** and the less commonly encountered **E. royleana**, from western Himalayan foothills. The latter species produces long-lasting, succulent leaves at the tips of its cylindrical, unsegmented main stem and branches. In habitat it receives regular winter frost, though its ability to endure cool, rainy winters outside is questionable.

The species of tree euphorbia differ from each other both in flower details and in the more obviously varying growth patterns of their branches, dense or sparse as well as vertical or horizontal. Accordingly, even though they share the same general design, tree euphorbias display a significant range of forms. Distributed through Arabia and the Horn of Africa, **Euphorbia ammak**, often mistakenly called *E. candelabrum*, a rarely seen plant from Angola, typifies them. It has a tall main trunk and a burst of erect branches beginning halfway up. Plants with this general shape grow over much of eastern Africa. In the case of the distinctive, wide-ranging **E. ingens**, the horizontal spread of the branches may equal the height of the plant.

Among a large number of strictly South African species, **Euphorbia zoutpansbergensis**, a graceful, slender tree from a very limited area, is diminutive in comparison with the much stouter, taller **E. excelsa** or the lofty **E. grandidens**, with its sparse spray of branches near the very top. Most of these South African tree types live in the frost-free, seasonally dry, somewhat tropical eastern regions. Several species, however, among them *E. triangularis*, flourish at the Kirstenbosch Botanic Garden in Cape Town, which receives winter rains and occasional frosts. A number of the widely distributed tree types have found their way into outdoor gardens in areas with mild climates.

Large specimens of *Euphorbia ingens* dot South Africa's Eastern Cape.
Photo by Inge Hoffman.

Less common, taller, and more slender: *Euphorbia grandidens*.
Photo by Brian Kemble.

Here in full flower, *Euphorbia parciramulosa* has curved, sometimes floppy branches. Photo by Rob Skillin.

Euphorbia cooperi occurs over a large portion of southern Africa and resembles a smaller, laxer version of *E. ingens*, with a shorter trunk. ***Euphorbia parciramulosa***, from the arid mountains of Yemen, is another smaller tree type. ***Euphorbia kibwezensis***, a smallish tree from East Africa, resembles *E. cooperi* and like it makes an imposing specimen, although it is best suited for warm climates. The same applies to ***E. bougheyi***, from Mozambique, with delicate, flattened two-angled stems when young that look like wavy green seaweed, and a thick, three-angled trunk that develops with age.

Several western species from South Africa and Namibia have almost entirely eliminated their trunks and grow in a candelabra shape, with many upright, arching stems. Probably the best known of these is ***Euphorbia virosa***. Up to 8 feet (2.4 cm) tall with a spread twice that

Euphorbia virosa growing just south of the Namibian border. Photo by Rob Skillin.

it has a huge range from just south of the Namibian border all the way north into Angola. Notorious for its highly toxic sap, it must be handled very carefully. It is a beautiful plant, with a short, spiraled primary stem and straighter growing secondary branches bordered with white, horny rims. Its distinctly delineated segments bulge toward the middle and taper symmetrically at their tops and bottoms.

Euphorbia avasmontana, roughly similar in appearance, grows with a short, stocky main stem crowded with upright, less distinctly segmented branches. It shares the hot arid plains of Namibia with ***E. venenata***, distinguished by branch segments that flare out at their bases. Other candelabra species include the rarely seen, aptly named ***E. spiralis***, from Yemen, and the Canary Island endemic ***E. canariensis***, with unsegmented, four-angled stems of an odd olive-green color. Unlike most of the tree euphorbias, candelabra types—*E. avasmontana* in particular—can attain a mature, though miniaturized aspect when grown in a container.

Euphorbia memoralis, from a small zone of chromium-rich soils in Zimbabwe, and ***E. cactus***, from the southwestern part of the Arabian peninsula, form large errati-

Euphorbia spiralis, from Yemen. Photo by Rob Skillin.

cally branched rather than candelabra-shaped shrubs. Despite its name, the latter is no more cactuslike than various other euphorbias.

Euphorbia canariensis presumably evolved from plants native to North Africa, plants similar to **E. echinus** and **E. resinifera**, two Moroccan twin-spined species. *Euphorbia echinus* has cylindrical, branching stems. *Euphorbia resinifera* is shorter growing and forms large mounds of four-angled stems. One of the hardiest succulent euphorbias, it can withstand considerable frost.

An enormous number of small to large shrubby euphorbias inhabit semiarid parts of East Africa, where they grow into spiny bushes of every imaginable variety. The best known of these come from Kenya, Tanzania, and South Africa, areas that are the most thoroughly explored botanically; no doubt other species still await discovery. Many of these plants have largely underground main stems that send out branch-producing rhizomes. Among the larger ones, the widely distributed **Euphorbia grandicornis**, with well-demarcated stem segments and long, very prominent spines, will grow into a thicket-sized shrub if given the chance. **Euphorbia pseudocactus**, shorter spined and less robust, is common in cultivation.

Less dramatically segmented and spined, **Euphorbia coerulescens** once dominated thousands of square miles of the South African interior, though now much of its habitat has been turned into farmland. This very hardy species is excellent for outdoor cultivation. It shares its habitat with other species such as the slimmer growing, slightly less hardy **E. ledienii**.

Concealed amid the rocks or in the grass and brushy veldt, a vast number of thinner-branched twin-spined euphorbias, compact or straggly and often with colorfully contrasting spines and spine shields, cover much of eastern and southern Africa. Perhaps the most strikingly colored, the South African **Euphorbia aeruginosa**, has bright blue-green stems and vivid coppery spines and spine shields. Somewhat similar species include the less distinctively marked **E. cuprispina**, from Kenya; the Tanzanian **E. greenwayi**, with pretty, mottled, blue-green stems; and **E. lydenburgensis**, from northeastern South Africa, with blue stems and bright yellow flowers. Other species may have gray, brown, pinkish, or multicolored stems, and vivid and colorful stripes, particularly when young. Many combinations and colors of spines may actually help camouflage them, as with **E. limpopoana**, which blends in with the reddish soil in which it grows.

While **Euphorbia heterochroma**, a tall-growing, thin-stemmed species, ranges over a good part of East Africa, many others are endemics, restricted to one range of hills or a particular mountain. The abundance of such habitats

Euphorbia aeruginosa, rare in the wild, popular in cultivation.

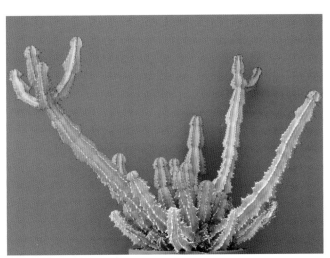

Euphorbia memoralis, imposing, but better suited for a container than the thicket forming species.

Euphorbia greenwayi, representative of its type but prettier than most.

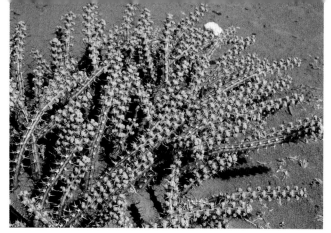

Euphorbia limpopoana, flowering near the northeast border of South Africa. Photo by Brian Kemble.

Euphorbia uhligiana, its tuberous base raised for display.

Euphorbia richardsiae, a heavily branching red-flowered shrub from less arid regions. Photo by Terry Thompson.

has led to a seemingly endless supply of species. ***Euphorbia nigrispina*** is a slender-stemmed plant with black spines. ***Euphorbia cryptospinosa*** and ***E. erlangeri*** are thin stemmed and clambering, with spines reduced almost to nonexistence. ***Euphorbia turkanensis,*** from Kenya, has tall, very thin, spiny stems. ***Euphorbia malevola,*** from Zimbabwe, has distinctly four-angled stems proportionately thicker. A list of these smallish, spiny bushes could go on and on. Well-suited for container culture because of their compact proportions, and often with brightly colored flowers (mostly yellow but sometimes red or other shades) as a bonus, many of these smaller species also do not need quite as much light as their larger relatives.

The Kenyan ***Euphorbia uhligiana,*** a typical-looking thin-stemmed plant, spreads slowly by underground rhizomes but develops surprisingly large tuberous roots. A number of thicker-stemmed euphorbias, also with big tuberous roots, produce fewer rhizomes. Mostly from eastern South Africa, these plants, with thick, segmented stems reminiscent of *E. grandicornis, E. pseudocactus,* or *E. cooperi,* remain restrained in size and spread. Among these, ***E. barnardii*** and ***E. perangusta*** grow with distinctly segmented branches and form mid-sized spiny clusters. ***Euphorbia knobelii,*** brightly striped yellow-green and dark green, is another spiny plant with a limited distribution, smaller than the previous two, with less obviously segmented branches. ***Euphorbia restricta,*** with a very limited distribution and smaller growing still, produces a tuft of rather randomly segmented branches from a short main stem as does *E. richardsiae* (from Malawi), somewhat bigger and pale green.

Almost as large as the thicket-makers but with a limited natural range, ***Euphorbia grandialata*** has distinctly winged segments, colorfully striped light and dark green, and spines about half as long as *E. grandicornis.* The Angolan *E. opuntioides* spreads outward and remains low, with jointlike segments vaguely resembling a prickly pear cactus (*Opuntia*).

Smaller and very variable, the Arabian ***Euphorbia fruticosa*** grows into a rough cushion of spiny stems. The South African *E. vandermerwei* produces a spray of spiny branches that grow from a largely underground stem, which merges imperceptibly into a thickened main root, approaching a true caudiciform habit.

Two groups of related southern African euphorbias have genuinely crossed the divide into caudiciform territory. The first includes ***Euphorbia stellata,*** usually with two-angled, flattened stems held very low to the ground; *E. squarrosa,* larger and generally with three-angled

Euphorbia opuntioides produces segmented, procumbent stems.

Euphorbia brevitorta, with its caudex invisible beneath its branches. Photo by Susan Carter.

Euphorbia stellata, its stems dwarfed by its caudex. Photo by Terry Thompson.

Euphorbia tortirama: relatively few, twisting branches surmount a large caudex.

stems; and **E. micracantha**, typically with four-angled stems, rectangular in cross section. Along with the Kenyan **E. brevitorta**, these three species produce numerous slender, elongated branches from the apex of their proportionately enormous, underground (in the wild) caudex.

Euphorbia buruana, from Kenya and Tanzania, has only a few striped, spiny branches growing from its elongated tuberous base. Larger, with fewer, thicker branches, and main stems that blend imperceptibly into huge caudices and taproots, *E. clavigera*, *E. enormis*, *E. brevitorta*, and most particularly *E. tortirama*—with as many as twenty segmented, twisting, foot (30 cm) long branches—and *E. groenewaldii*—with only half a dozen or so shorter, unsegmented branches—form a continuum that ends with an extreme caudiciform growth form in response to increasingly harsh habitats. The caudices of *E. tortirama* and *E. groenewaldii* can extend 2 feet (60

The smallest above ground, *Euphorbia groenewaldii* may have the largest caudex of all. Photo by Brian Kemble.

Despite their substantial appearance, the branches of *Euphorbia decidua* drop off during its rest period. Photo by Terry Thompson.

cm) underground in very rocky soil, and completely dwarf that part of the plant that exists above the surface. In the wild, *E. groenewaldii* may shed branches in the dry season, and the Zimbabwean geophyte *E. decidua* survives annual drought by losing its crown of thin, spiny branches entirely, its dome-shaped caudex hiding completely underground.

Tree euphorbias respond well to bright sun and a reasonable amount of water during their growing seasons, though many of them will be difficult to maintain in a reasonable-sized container after a while. The thicket growers, such as *Euphorbia grandicornis* and *E. pseudocactus*, also will ultimately become difficult to maintain in a pot, as they want to sprawl, but with an adequately sized container they will behave themselves for a number of years before requiring pruning. A degree of extra care with drainage and water is not a bad idea for the Namibian candelabra types, most of which grow in summer-rainfall areas. Generally, thin-stemmed twin-spined plants do well with normal succulent soil, weekly water when in growth, and bright light. In winter many of these do best with slightly more-than-average water, say every three weeks or so, in contrast to once a month for the thick-stemmed ones, as if kept too dry they will begin to shed their branches.

Though not difficult to grow, the southern African caudiciform euphorbias need a bit more attention in cultivation than the noncaudiciform species. Bright light, fast-draining soil, and water once a week in the growing season, about every four weeks when dormant will do the trick. *Euphorbia decidua* can be fussy, and a more rigorous dry dormancy in winter is probably best. The species

with really large caudices, such as *E. groenewaldii*, need to be treated with great care when they are repotted, as even minor injuries to the caudex may prove fatal; the plants should be watched carefully before resuming normal watering. Despite these warnings, with care these plants will grow well and thrive for decades in containers in a sunny, protected spot.

Though it is possible to root individual branches of the caudiciform euphorbias, in most cases they will simply elongate and never form a caudex. If a rooted branch is cut, however, it often will produce small multibranched growths from the truncated tip, and these can be rooted in turn. They usually will form caudices. (The same technique also works for medusoid plants.) An exception to the rule, **Euphorbia knuthii**, a South African species with a smaller caudex and long, narrow branches, readily forms mature plants from rooted cuttings without further intervention

A small number of memorable twin-spined euphorbias live far from the southern tip of Africa. The tropical-forested landscapes of Nigeria and Cameroon, for example, seem unlikely *Euphorbia* habitats, but a few grow there, in scattered regions of semiarid mountains and plateaus. Among the shrubby, thicket-forming, or small arborescent euphorbias from these seasonally dry, tropical areas, **E. teke** and **E. sudanica** resemble species from southern Africa, but with larger, more persistent leaves.

Farther west, several other closely related but more exotic looking species live in more localized and isolated semiarid pockets. Like the others, **Euphorbia poissonii**, perhaps the best known, ultimately becomes a fairly large shrub, freely branching from a central trunk. Its thick, pale gray stems are covered with upside-down teardrop-shaped tubercles, tipped at the bottom with a solitary spine, and accompanied at its branch tips by a few fleshy, somewhat wedge-shaped, bright green, and sometimes slightly bilobed leaves.

Euphorbia unispina, found sparingly from Ghana east to Togo, differs in its greenish (rather than reddish) flowers and the presence of a few small teeth at its leaf tips. In addition, although *E. unispina*'s tubercles resemble those of *E. poissonii*, they degrade quickly, leaving its pale gray cylindrical stems very smooth. With only these minor differences the two species ultimately may be merged with the generally similar, more eastern **E. venenifica**, from southern Sudan, Uganda, and southern Ethiopia. Another related species, **E. sapinii**, rarely seen in cultivation, is more delicate and smaller growing, with thinner stems and lanceolate leaves. It grows farther

The Nigerian *Euphorbia unispina* grows in semiarid, stony plateaus. Photo by Terry Thompson.

Euphorbia xylacantha produces spiny branches from a short central stem. Photo by Susan Carter.

Well protected, *Euphorbia inaequispina* crawls along the inhospitable ground. Photo by Susan Carter.

Euphorbia ponderosa, one of the larger, and rarer, clustering Somali species. Photo by Susan Carter.

south, ranging from Cameroon through Congo all the way to northern Angola. These species grow slowly and cannot withstand much cold. They need a fairly strict rest period after their leaves drop—which may take place at various times of the year, sometimes more than once a year—until new growth begins. With their unique appearance, these striking, tropical African species will draw enthusiasts like a magnet.

On the opposite side of Africa, the perennially war-torn, desolate-seeming Somali deserts shelter an extraordinary variety of succulent euphorbias, including typical twin-spined trees; thin-stemmed bushes; prostrate types, among them **Euphorbia inaequispina** and the taller *E. longispina*; and a few rare, odd, difficult-to-grow dwarfs resembling *E. bupleurifolia*, such as *E. longituberculosa*. Somalia and adjacent parts of Ethiopia also support a large number of wildly modified twin-spined species that have appropriated the forms of euphorbias from every section of the genus. Three examples of plants that almost

mimic the South African medusoids are the Ethiopian *E. monacantha*, with thin, though spiny, branches radiating out from short, thick central stems, and two more exotic species from Somalia: *E. xylacantha*, yellow with gray spine shields, and *E. schizacantha*, pink-red and yellow-green stemmed with forking spines.

Other, more robust growing Somali species approximate the habit of mounding cushion formers such as *Euphorbia pulvinata*. **Euphorbia mosaica** forms almost solid low mounds of sparely spined stems. **Euphorbia mitriformis**, though less dense, grows taller, with more dome-shaped mounds. **Euphorbia sepulta** forms a low, irregular mound, and the spine shields on its branches more or less merge into longitudinal ridges. Other Somali mound-formers include rarities such as *E. leontopelma*, which looks somewhat like a miniature *E. groenewaldii*; the spiny, densely branching *E. atrox*; and the somewhat larger, gray-stemmed *E. peramata* and *E. ponderosa*. Many Somali species have strangely colored stems—

Not formally described, this new *Euphorbia* species from Cape Guardafui typifies the odd colors and growth habits of Somali euphorbias.

Euphorbia phillipsioides grows more easily than most of its relatives. Photo by Terry Thompson.

Euphorbia columnaris may reach several feet in height, or may loop pendently. Photo by Susan Carter.

yellow, mottled gray, pinkish—no doubt enhancing their survival prospects in the oddly colored, bleached, often gypsiferous soils where many of them grow; in less than ideal light the stems fade to various shades of pale green.

More in the normal fashion of twin-spined euphorbias, *Euphorbia dasycantha* forms a small yellowish gray-stemmed spiny shrub, while the short stems of *E. phillipsiae* and the taller ones of *E. phillipsioides* produce spines of distinctly different lengths, arranged almost randomly.

Like a miniature medusoid, *Euphorbia immersa* displays a radiating spray of short square-sided branches, its aboveground parts dwarfed by its swollen underground caudex. *Euphorbia columnaris*, possibly extinct in the wild because of habitat degradation, has spines shaped like tiny cow horns and stems that are elongated. It may take refuge on the very edge of crumbly cliffs, where it grows into a narrow upright column several feet tall, eventually bending and arching into space.

Euphorbia horwoodii passes through several distinct phases of growth. It ultimately forms a small mound similar to *E. peramata* and *E. atrox*, but it begins life as a nearly spineless, beige to orange, almost perfect sphere. It then starts to develop short, prostrate branches and looks like a miniature starfish or Christmas ornament, an intermediate phase so surrealistically weird that it is a pity it does not last.

The tiny *Euphorbia turbiniformis*, in contrast, never grows beyond the spineless, spherical stage (see photo on page 35). It resembles a 1.5-inch (4-cm) wide, pale brown *E. obesa*. *Euphorbia gymnocalycioides* comes from a relatively well-watered habitat in Ethiopia where it receives as much as 12 inches (30 cm) of annual rain. It also forms a solitary sphere with longitudinal rows of little protruding "chins," reminiscent of the cactus genus *Gymnocalycium*. Each chin is equipped with a barely visible pair of residual spines.

Euphorbia multiclava forms a small cluster of thick, erect, club-shaped stems, oddly ridged and slowly branching dichotomously. Finally, *E. piscidermis* ("fish-skin") has tubercles and spines modified into what looks like a pattern of tiny bright white, diamond-shaped scales (see photo on page 36).

The bizarre *Euphorbia horwoodii*, at an intermediate stage in its life. Photo by Susan Carter.

Euphorbia gymnocalycioides grows slowly though without complaint.

Euphorbia multiclava, fierce looking but impossibly delicate in cultivation. Photo by Susan Carter.

Derived from the ubiquitous, often nondescript twin-spined plants that occur all over countries such as Kenya and Tanzania, as a group—and there are numerous additional species—the Somali euphorbias are true oddities of nature. A few of them, such as *Euphorbia phillipsiae* and *E. phillipsioides*, grow about as easily as typical small twin-spined plants: in a rapid-draining succulent mix, with bright light, protection from temperatures much below 50°F (10°C), and water once a week during the warm months, every three or four weeks in winter.

Euphorbia gymnocalycioides, though much rarer, grows relatively easily with the same treatment but perhaps slightly less light. *Euphorbia leontopelma* responds to a somewhat leaner mix and more dryness in winter, but grows well enough, as do *E. sepulta*, *E. mitriformis*, and rather surprisingly, the always-coveted *E. columnaris*. *Euphorbia immersa*, *E. peramata*, *E. atrox*, *E. multiclava*, *E. schizacantha*, and many other species mentioned here have the distressing habit of rotting if given any water in winter. Fortunately, even small plants can withstand several months of complete drought.

Euphorbia piscidermis is generally grafted onto a hardy species such as *E. fruticosa*, and as a graft does well. On its own roots it is another story, though no doubt someone, somewhere, has managed to accomplish this feat. *Euphorbia turbiniformis* was introduced into cultivation in the 1970s with tremendous fanfare as about the strangest thing anyone had ever seen, but few if any plants from this first distribution survived for long. Grafted specimens are still being produced, and even they can be difficult to keep alive.

Neither the tropical African species nor the Somali plants are really suitable for novice growers. Just finding them can be quite a challenge, and they can be very expensive. They are some of the most remarkable members of a remarkable genus, however, and anyone interested in euphorbias should become acquainted with some of these very rare plants.

MADAGASCAN EUPHORBIAS

Madagascar, famous for its population of endemic mammals, possesses a flora as unique as its fauna, including a large population of succulents. Tree-sized, relatively unmodified euphorbias mingle with other large xerophytic plants in the island's arid southwest, while numerous stipular-spined euphorbias grow in drier spots across the entire island. The spiny euphorbias of Madagascar form a very distinct, readily recognizable group granted status as a subgenus.

Euphorbia milii var. imperatae, flowering in a 4-inch (10-cm) pot. Photo by Kurt Zadnik.

Euphorbia gottlebei, with tufted leaves.

Seed grown, Euphorbia guillauminiana develops slowly but becomes multibranched over time.

Euphorbia rossii grows slowly and needs careful watering.

Euphorbia gottlebei, very bright inflorescences.

Often called the crown of thorns, **Euphorbia milii** is by far the best-known Madagascan euphorbia and is grown throughout the world. It forms a densely branched bush, with paired spines, not particularly succulent woody stems covered with thin green leaves, and typical, nondistinctive euphorbia blossoms distributed near its branch tips. Each flower is surrounded by a pair of bright red bracts known as cyathophylls. **Variety breonii** has much thicker woody stems and larger, showier inflorescences, while **var. imperatae** is a miniature that will flower contentedly in a 3-inch (8-cm) pot. Other *E. milii* varieties, less frequently encountered in cultivation, may bear yellow or even white cyathophylls. As a popular horticultural subject, the crown of thorns has probably been overdescribed, with many minor variations granted unwarranted taxonomic recognition. Additionally, over the last several years many *E. milii* hybrids have entered the market, with much larger cyathophylls in various shades of pink, orange, and yellow.

Other similar species differing from *Euphorbia milii* primarily in bract color, arrangement, and number include **E. duranii** and the slow-growing **E. horombense**. When mature, many of these species form roughly hemispherical mounds up to 3 feet (90 cm) across. Slightly farther afield from the *E. milii* model, **E. croizatii** and **E. delphinensis** have rounder leaves and less gaudy bracts.

As more of Madagascar comes under botanical scrutiny, small localized species keep turning up. These include rarities such as **Euphorbia guillemetii**, with small pinkish bracts, and **E. hoffstatteri**, with variably colored bracts, a tuberous root, thick, spiny stems, and, in some forms, hairy leaves. **Euphorbia rossii**, with beige cyathophylls, and **E. genoudiana**, with pale green blooms, bear narrowly linear leaves. The large bright red bracts of the uncommon **E. gottlebei** set it apart from the other linear-leafed species.

Growing fully exposed to the sun, **Euphorbia didiereoides** puts forth a spray of ascending, arching branches up to 7 or 8 feet (2.1 to 2.4 m) tall, each equipped with distinctive short secondary branches, and tubular cyathophylls that enclose its flowers. Also with enclosed flowers, borne on long, sometimes pendent inflorescences, both *E. perrieri* and *E. paulianii* appreciate more water and a little less light than most of the others in this group.

Euphorbia pedilanthoides, with flowers almost totally enclosed by vase-shaped, tightly tubular scarlet bracts, forms a compact plant with a distinctly thickened base, like a miniature pachycaul, as does *E. kondoi*, its tuberous root contrasting with its slender stems and linear foliage.

Another distinctive rarity, *Euphorbia guillauminiana*, is endemic to a few arid lava beds, where it regularly rebranches, with the new branches all of equal length. The plant ultimately achieves a perfectly hemispherical form up to 2 feet (60 cm) in diameter. Cultivated plants attain such a shape very slowly, but collected plants already have it and command high prices. One wonders about the viability of the species's survival in the wild, although conditions in Madagascar are so precarious that leaving the plants alone might not offer much protection either.

Euphorbia milii and its closely associated species grow easily in cultivation. With a few exceptions, they like very bright light, and most do best with a somewhat richer soil than most succulents and water once a week (or even more frequently) in warm weather, about every two weeks in winter. *Euphorbia milii* itself is marginally outdoor hardy in coastal California; most of the others are both slow growing and somewhat rare, not the best subjects for experiments in frost-hardiness. A few of these species require more care. *Euphorbia didiereoides* should be kept somewhat drier during the winter, as should *E. pedilanthoides* and other tuberous-rooted species. *Euphorbia rossii* will suffer and eventually rot if watered too frequently in winter, and *E. guillauminiana* in particular requires very dry treatment after it drops its leaves; leaving it completely dry for a few months until it makes its new growth will not hurt it, although water every six weeks will do no harm in bright situations. These water-sensitive species also benefit from a leaner, quicker draining soil mix.

Another group of related Madagascan euphorbias has solved the problem of survival in areas of relatively high rainfall by colonizing localized habitats such as bare rock domes that rise above well-watered plains or wildly eroded limestone karst formations known locally as *tsingy*. These plants may slowly branch or remain solitary, and mature into small often spiraling columns. They produce large almost tropical-looking, deciduous foliage and small flowers, surrounded or tightly enclosed by often vividly colored bracts. Some, such as the various

varieties of *Euphorbia viguieri*, are fiercely armed with thick, jagged, often strikingly white spines that contrast with their bright green stems.

Densely covered with smaller spines, *Euphorbia pachypodioides* is purple-green tinged and topped with a rosette of bright green leaves that are purple-red underneath. It puts out an erect inflorescence of a few dozen geometrically arrayed little flowers with purple-red cyathophylls. Others in the group have spines reduced to fringes running down their stems. One of these, *E. leuconeura*, both self-fertile and extremely prolific, grows in areas of high rainfall in eastern Madagascar, where it may live as an epiphyte in tropical forests. Its flowers lack attractive bracts, but when young its leaves are marked with bright white veins. It is sometimes sold as *E. lophogona*, a less common, although certainly not rare plant with fringe "spines" that are more fibrous than in *E. leuconeura*, brown woody stems, dark green leathery leaves, and flowers surrounded by pink or white bracts.

Euphorbia neohumbertii has a stocky green trunk

Euphorbia lophogona, tropical looking, from areas of relatively abundant rainfall.

Euphorbia neohumbertii, thicker bodied and slower growing.

marked with spiraling white leaf scars and bristly spines much like *E. lophogona*. Its enclosing floral bracts are bright red. In the almost identical but more freely branching *E. aureoviridiflora*, the bracts are yellow-green.

Most cultivated plants of this group are small, but with time and root-room they may reach 3 feet (90 cm) or more in height. Though when leafless and dormant they seem very cactuslike, they take much the same care as the *E. milii* group: a fairly rich soil, bright light, and water once a week while in leaf, every two weeks or so after the leaves drop in late fall or winter.

A few Madagascan euphorbias remain mostly underground and produce annual rosettes of leaves. They reveal their relationship with the other Madagascan euphorbias through their blossoms, surrounded with decorative cyathophylls. The best-known of these geophytic species is **Euphorbia primulifolia**, with bright white bracts. It begins to bloom shortly before its new leaves appear. In the wild this and related species, such as *E. quartziticola* and *E. subapoda*, display unremarkable leafy rosettes accompanied by small flowers. In cultivation, however, with their tuberous bodies raised above soil level both for display and to prevent rot, the little rosette-formers suddenly are transformed into fascinating caudiciforms. As with most geophytic succulents, fast-draining soil and some caution when watering is best, but the plants are far from impossible to grow.

Yet another set of Madagascan euphorbias consists of spineless plants that when dormant look like smooth-stemmed columns. Many of these flower before they leaf out, with inflorescences that cover the top of the stem like a decorative hat. The best known of these may be **Euphorbia ankarensis**. Others include *E. millotii*, with thinner, more branching stems and veined leaves, *E. moratii*, and *E. albertii*. Still uncommon in cultivation, they do not need as much light as most of the species mentioned so far. They prefer a good deal of water when growing, but should be kept fairly dry after their leaves fall.

A final Madagascan group consists of dwarf, low-growing species with succulent leaves and stipular spines reduced to small hairs. These plants may spread by underground shoots and rhizomes or crawl along the surface of the soft sandy soil where they grow. **Euphorbia cylindrifolia** forms mats of round branches tipped with small terete, almost black leaves; apricot-colored bracts surround its flowers. It grows vigorously below the surface as well, pushing branches through the drain holes of a pot if given the chance. Rather than producing rhizomes, the much slower growing **subsp. *tuberifera*** forms a caudex.

Euphorbia ankarensis, flowering early in its growing season.

Euphorbia millotii with leaves starting to turn for autumn. Photo by Terry Thompson.

Several species in this group have very decorative leaves with wavy edges and intricately curling margins. Among them are the low-growing, freely branching **Euphorbia decaryi**; the slightly more erect *E. capsaintemariensis*; the tiny extremely slow-growing *E. tulearensis*; and two rare caudex formers, *E. ambovombensis* and *E. suzannae-marnierianae*. The leaves of *E. francoisii* range from rhomboidal to nearly linear and from plain green, to green with pink, to pink and silver, to almost pure silver. These species combine extreme

Euphorbia decaryi var. spirosticha, a form with spiraling stems.

An old plant of Euphorbia ambovombensis with a well-developed caudex.

Euphorbia tulearensis in its southeast Madagascan home. Photo by Brian Kemble.

endemism with near invisibility, resulting in recent years in an explosion of new horticultural introductions from the huge island.

Most of these succulent-leafed species do best with good light, water once a week in the growing season and every three weeks or so in winter. They like a quick-draining soil with some organic matter in it. On the whole, these miniature euphorbias grow easily though very slowly in some cases, and many will never outgrow a 3-inch (8-cm) pot.

In fact, most Madagascan euphorbias are reasonably easy to grow—I have noted some of the exceptions. Most will root from stem cuttings, although obviously this will not work with the geophytes. The succulent-leafed species with tuberous bases will root from cuttings but the resultant plants will form tubers very slowly if at all. Since they do not need too much light and enjoy warmth, some of these dwarf plants make ideal windowsill growers. Given more space, or outdoors in very mild climates, the larger-growing Madagascan species also will flourish, and many will remain content in a container for years.

As a final note of warning, when potting, dividing, or taking cuttings from euphorbias, be careful about the sap. Wash your hands religiously after working with them, and avoid contact with your eyes, nose, or mouth. The sap varies greatly in toxicity, and people differ in their sensitivities as well, but caution never hurts while carelessness can.

Chapter 11

Euphorbia Relatives

THE FEW OTHER genera of succulent plants in the euphorbia family include geophytes, stem succulents, caudiciforms, and small semisucculent trees.

MONADENIUM, SYNADENIUM, AND ENADENIUM

The several dozen exclusively African species of *Monadenium*, the best-known *Euphorbia* relative, grow in an approximately J-shaped arc that starts in Somalia and Ethiopia, sweeps through Kenya and Tanzania, and reaches as far south as northern South Africa before turning west through Botswana and Angola. On the whole, monadeniums come from tropical dry habitats and have not had to adapt to the extremes of cold and utter aridity that many specialized succulents have to endure.

The key difference between the very closely related *Euphorbia* and *Monadenium* lies in their respective inflorescences, with the cuplike fused bracts—called an involucre—that enclose euphorbia blossoms expanded into a sort of hood. Monadeniums often have multiple involucres and in some the hoods flare out dramatically or display brilliant colors, bright red or pink. Also unlike most succulent euphorbias, monadeniums generally retain their lance- or spoon-shaped, sometimes toothy-margined, moderately succulent leaves throughout their growing seasons.

Monadeniums duplicate many growth habits of succulent euphorbias and exhibit a few specifically of their own as well. The less modified forms, such as *Monadenium echinulatum*, the red-flowered *M. coccineum*, the small *M. invenustum*, or the tall *M. arborescens*, consist of relatively thin, somewhat succulent stems with slightly succulent leaves that arise from the tops of poorly defined, sometimes spiraling segments. These deciduous-leafed stems often grow from an enlarged, tuberous root. Quite different, the odd Somali species *M. lindenii* re-

sembles euphorbias such as *Euphorbia lignosa*, forming an irregular mass of thin, woody, sharp-pointed branches.

Each of the various groups of more specialized monadeniums has elaborated one or another of the basic elements found in the less modified species. The most commonly seen plants form a series in which the stems, bearing increasingly defined patterns of prominent tubercles, grow steadily thicker and more succulent. In habitat, as they elongate, the branches hoist themselves up into the air amid the grasses and shrubs of the veldt, or hang pendently from rock faces, to rise up again at their tips like a swarm of snakes. Unlike the more symmetrically arranged medusoid euphorbias, though, they lack a thickened central stem.

The thin, succulent stems of **Monadenium rhizophorum** are divided into overlapping, elliptical, spineless tubercles. In **M. yattanum** the stems are thicker, the tubercles better defined, and the branches more upright. The stems of **M. stapelioides** remain low, crawling along

Left: *Monadenium echinulatum,* relatively unmodified stems with a classic *Monadenium* inflorescence. Photo by John Trager. Right: *Monadenium ritchei* var. *nyambense,* the upright growing variety more common in cultivation. Photo by John Trager.

Above: *Monadenium schubei*, a large multistemmed plant in the Tanzanian bush. Photo by Susan Carter.
Right: *Monadenium* aff. *schubei*, with distinct purple-red stems, has become popular in cultivation.

The Ethiopian *Monadenium reflexum*, with long, downward-pointing tubercles. Photo by John Trager.

Spineless and bright green, *Monadenium ellenbeckii* f. *caulopodium* seems ill equipped for its arid environment. Photo by Terry Thompson.

Monadenium spectabile, red inflorescence bright against the undergrowth in Tanzania. Photo by Susan Carter.

the ground. All three species originate in Kenya and Tanzania, the center of diversity for the genus.

Monadenium lugardae, with inch (2.5 cm) thick stems, upright and covered with flat, diamond-shaped tubercles, crosses over from Zimbabwe and Botswana into northeastern South Africa. In **M. heteropodum** and **M. guentheri** the prominently pointed tubercles come armed with small pricklelike spines at their apices. The tubercles of **M. ritchei** are somewhat dome-shaped rather than pointed; plants may form dense clusters of short, compact stems or grow upright depending on variety.

Monadenium schubei has tubercles so angularly pointed that plants appear to bristle with spines, even though the actual spines at its tubercle tips are quite small and harmless. The rare, thick-stemmed, sparsely branched **M. reflexum**, from Ethiopia, discards its leaves quickly. Slow growing and less resistant to rot than most of the species, when young its proportions evoke the image of a shaggy little cartoon human. Another variation on this

theme, **M. ellenbeckii**, from Ethiopia and Somalia, consists of a cluster of small succulent branches emerging from a central base, but instead of spines or tubercles, its branches are covered with a velvety, kelly green epidermis that looks like corduroy. It generally grows with upright stems although its more frequently cultivated form, **f. caulopodium**, sprawls horizontally.

Instead of precisely patterned tubercles that cover the stems, a second group of tall-growing monadeniums has stems scattered with prominent leaf bases that end in a cluster of small spines shaped like a star or sunburst. *Monadenium stellatum*, a rare species from Somalia with a grooved woody stem, has spiked leaf bases four or five times longer than thick. In **M. magnificum** and its stockier relative **M. spectabile**, the leaf bases are shorter, the

Monadenium spinescens becomes large in time.

Monadenium torreyi, another large-leafed species from less arid surroundings. Photo by John Trager.

Monadenium majus, an underground caudex former with some of the best flowers in the genus. Photo by John Trager.

Monadenium montanum, its caudex raised for display and to prevent rot.

starburst spines not as obvious, but the succulent, long-lasting, terminal leaves themselves come armed with decorative spines along their keeled midrib. The slow-growing Tanzanian *M. spinescens*, as much as 20 feet (6 m) tall in the wild, branches sparsely, with brown, irregularly tubercled spiny stems topped by fresh green, saw-edged, bright green leaves. With flattened, even larger leaves clustered at its stem-tips, *M. torreyi* grows in Mozambique.

In other monadeniums the stems have become reduced, even deciduous, with the tuberous base retaining more of the plant's substance. These geophytic plants, invisible and underground much of the year, include *Monadenium simplex* and several species from seasonally dry parts of Angola and Zambia, which produce stemless rosettes of small leaves after flowering. The Kenyan *M. montanum*, with yellow inflorescences, and the closely related *M. rubellum*, with pink to red involucre hoods, develop annual long thin stems with narrow leaves which may become permanent under the benign conditions of cultivation. With much shorter stems, green and red-striped foliage, and dramatically flaring involucres, *M. erubescens*, from Somalia, matches the exotic appearance of its Kenyan cousin *M. majus* despite the latter's larger, sometimes pubescent gray-green leaves and bright salmon-colored blooms.

DNA testing suggests that the few members of **Synadenium** and **Enadenium** belong in *Monadenium*. Large moderately succulent bushes or small trees, they grow in warmer parts of southern tropical Africa with higher rainfall than most succulent habitats. They resemble some of the relatively unmodified tree euphorbias, although synadeniums retain their large somewhat leathery leaves year-round. The most common in cultivation, **S. cupulare var. rubra** (commonly called *S. grantii*), is markedly reddish purple in its stem and foliage. Easy to grow, with watering needs similar to *Euphorbia milii*, it needs warmth and reasonably bright light. As with many Euphorbiaceae, its sap is reputed to be quite toxic.

On the whole, monadeniums grow without difficulty given bright light and a standard succulent soil mix. Most of the snake-branched or star-spined ones do well with water about once a week in the warmer months, and every three weeks or so in winter. They also need protection from cold in winter. Raising the tuberous bases of the geophytic species above the soil line reduces the risk of their rotting; slightly less frequent water in winter also will not hurt. The less specialized species grow easily, in spite of their tuberous roots. They will tolerate a little less light than the other species as well as more frequent winter water. Along with the spiny, tuberculate species they come readily from cuttings and are frequently cultivated. The caudiciform types, requiring propagation by seed, remain scarce in cultivation despite their popularity with collectors.

JATROPHA AND *CNIDOSCULUS*

Jatropha, another large genus in the Euphorbiaceae, has close to two hundred species, including a number of succulents and a few geophytes. These occur in Mexico, Central America, the West Indies, and parts of South America, Africa, and southwestern Arabia as well.

The most widely grown, **Jatropha podagrica**, from Central America, develops a short, dichotomously branched, somewhat spiny stem with a swollen base. With lobed, peltate (attached at their center) leaves and bright red inflorescences, it is a popular horticultural subject. Although it needs a dry rest after its leaves fall, when growing it enjoys more water than most succulents. Not surprisingly, it cannot withstand much cold.

Another species popular among succulent growers is the geophytic **Jatropha cathartica** (synonym *J. berlandieri*). It has a round underground caudex and a few short stalks surrounded with palmate, fringe-margined, distinctly blue leaves and red-orange flowers. It lives in Texas as well as northeastern Mexico.

Rarely seen, a third caudiciform, **Jatropha lagarinthoides**, grows in warmer parts of eastern South Africa. It produces a short vine from an underground caudex. Widely distributed in Texas and northern Mexico, *J. dioica* (synonym *J. spathulata*) displays a very different growth habit. Its erect, leathery, brownish stems emerge either close together or at some distance from underground rhizomes, and bear spoon-shaped, blunt-tipped leaves. Anyone who travels to the northern Chihuahuan Desert is likely to encounter it, though it is not that frequently cultivated.

Most jatrophas grow into medium-sized, somewhat succulent bushes, often with lobed or palmate leaves and five-petaled flowers, often in shades of red, orange and purple. None of these are grown that frequently, but a

Jatropha podagrica grows in tropical climates but still requires good drainage.

Jatropha multifida grows into a semisucculent bush, prized for its deeply dissected foliage.

number of them lend themselves to succulent bonsai treatment, and a few attain that form naturally under suitable conditions. Representative bush-type species include **Jatropha cuneata** and *J. cinerea*, from Baja California, with spathulate and cordate (heart-shaped) foliage, respectively; *J. capensis*, from South Africa, with wedge-shaped leaves; *J. malacophylla* from western Mexico; the pretty Central and South American **J. multifida**, with leaves as delicately dissected as a Japanese maple; the deeply lobed *J. hyssopifolia*; as well as rarely encountered, dry-growing East African and Yemeni species such as **J. pelargonifolia**, *J. aceroides*, and *J. ferox*. A few of these Old World dry growers live a specialized existence as

Fiercely spined, *Jatropha fissispina* holds its own in the harsh Somali desert. Photo by Susan Carter.

An unidentified *Jatropha* from Argentina, almost certainly not in cultivation. Photo by Inge Hoffman.

From Oaxaca state in Mexico, *Jatropha* aff. *conzattii* and related species make outstanding succulent bonsais.

Cnidosculus basiacanthus, from Peru. The spines on the leaves signal "beware!" Photo by Inge Hoffman.

sand dune dwellers, with very long roots and stems to secure them in their shifting habitats. Consequently they require extremely deep pots when cultivated.

Among the more interesting of these East African types are the rarely cultivated Somali species ***Jatropha marginata***, with long, curling stipular hairs, and *J. fissi-spina*, with pairs of forking spines. Both species develop swollen, caudiciform bases. Under suitable circumstances several of other species may also develop a ground-hugging, contorted appearance: *J. conzattii*, from mainland Mexico; *J. giffordiana* and *J. moranii*, from Baja California; and *J. macrocarpa* from South America.

Cnidosculus, a genus separated out of *Jatropha*, consists of New World shrubs, bushes, and small trees locally known as *mala mujer* (bad woman). These have bright green, sometimes white-veined leaves that stand out in the driest deserts, and which are covered with sharp, ex-

tremely irritating, spiny hairs. Touching the plants will lead to immediate excruciating pain. Understandably, they are rarely grown except in occasional botanical garden collections, where they are kept, one hopes, away from the public. People traveling in arid and semiarid places in the Americas should be aware of these plants and assiduously avoid them.

Most jatrophas grow easily. Raising the caudices of the geophytic species above the soil line will prevent them from rotting. These plants should be kept drier than average in winter. The shrubby plants will remain better behaved if kept in proportionately small pots, where their stems will thicken more readily. For the caudiciform types, standard treatment should work: bright light, good drainage, and water every week or so when in growth, every three weeks or so when dormant. The Baja California plants seem to respond to year-round water despite growing in winter-rainfall areas. Many of the less succulent, tropical growing kinds are better suited for tropical gardens and general greenhouse conditions than situations designed for xerophytic plants. Without a doubt, *Jatropha* species yet ungrown await recognition of their potential for fans of succulent plants.

PEDILANTHUS

A final genus worth mentioning is *Pedilanthus*, with a number of generally similar species distinguished by their odd, almost bird-shaped, typically bright red flowers. Stems of the tropical American **P. tithymaloides** may zigzag, but most species resemble the reedlike gray-skinned euphorbias. The commonly seen **P. macrocarpus** grows in Baja California and Sonora. The similar but slightly smaller **P. cymbiferus** lives much farther south in mainland Mexico along with a few other species, some almost tree-sized. The vivid inflorescences, with flowers hanging down like a beak from the enclosing bracts stand out in the variously brushy or arid areas where the

Pedilanthus species from Oaxaca, like a gray reed with an inflorescence typical of the genus.

plants live, and are the main reasons people grow them. Easily cultivated, pedilanthus responds to normal succulent treatment, with extra warmth and water in the case of *P. tithymaloides*.

Chapter 12

Lithops and Other Living Stones

THE SEVERAL THOUSAND species and more than one hundred twenty genera of succulents known as mesembryanthemums include some of the most extraordinary examples of plant adaptation on Earth. Almost exclusively native to southern Africa, mesembs, as they are informally called, display an astonishing talent for camouflage and an uncanny ability to survive on next to nothing. The group itself is variously considered a distinct family, Mesembryanthemaceae, or, as Mesembryanthema, a subfamily of the family Aizoaceae. Mostly mid-sized to dwarf plants with only a few larger types, the best known are the miniaturized species collectively called "living stones." Of these, the most popular are the members of the genus *Lithops*.

Less well-known to the general public than *Lithops* but possibly the most interesting genus in the family is *Conophytum*. Four more genera of geologically camouflaged mesemb genera particularly deserve discussion, as much for their ability to survive in extremely hostile environments as for their peculiar evolution into something that looks more mineral than vegetable: *Argyroderma*, *Dinteranthus*, *Lapidaria*, and *Pleiospilos*.

LITHOPS

Something about lithops manages to catch the eyes even of people with little interest in plants, evoking associations not normally engendered by small succulents. Their very specific, even counterintuitive growth requirements further complement their other-worldly appearance. Native to a sizable part of South Africa and Namibia, though concentrated in the western regions, lithops manage to thrive in what seem to be desolate wastelands, hot, sometimes very cold in winter, sun-blasted, and subject to droughts that may last for several years. In their forbidding homelands they survive by living mostly under-

ground, with just the flattened tops of their conjoined leaves exposed to the elements.

Each lithops consists of nothing more than a pair of fused leaves known as plant bodies, surrounding a reduced, completely hidden stem. Translucent areas at the tops of the plant bodies act as windows that let light filter deep into the interior of the plants. Consequently, lithops photosynthesize from the inside, protecting themselves from desiccating heat and light. Though a number of succulent plants have independently evolved light-transmitting windows, generally these are simply areas of transparent green or gray. Lithops have taken their windows and made them into unique devices for camouflage.

The windows in the various *Lithops* species may cover the entire exposed tops of the plant bodies, but more often they assume intricate shapes, a maze of lines that hardly seem like translucent windows at all, while the tops of the plant bodies can be marked with opaque lines and colored dots as well. These colorful patterns often duplicate the plants' immediate surrounding. Lithops growing on a hill covered with orange-brown pebbles will be orange-brown; if the next hill has gray pebbles, the lithops there will be gray also. As a result, small lithops plants can be almost completely invisible except at flowering time. Multiheaded clusters and larger rain-swollen individual lithops are easier to see. When shrunken in dormancy, though, even multiheaded lithops hunker down at or below soil level, and, especially if covered up by blowing sand and dirt, seem to disappear.

The combination of just two basic colors of flowers, yellow or white, and an almost unending display of plant patterns and colors has led in the past to wildly divergent ideas about what constitutes a species within the genus. The count of *Lithops* species by different botanists has ranged from as many as three hundred to as few as two. Currently, however, most authorities agree on a total of a

A colony of *Lithops terricolor*, shrunken down and splitting during the Great Karoo dry season. Photo by Rob Skillin.

A cluster of *Lithops olivacea* in full yellow flower. Photo by Terry Thompson.

Lithops divergens var. *divergens* in full growth, gapping wide and less than a quarter inch (6 mm) tall.

few dozen valid species, along with at least that many distinct varieties and forms that show almost every color and pattern imaginable.

Lithops also differ in basic shape. Most have plant bodies essentially fused together, separated at the top by only a narrow furrow, while in a relatively few species the gap between the plant bodies opens wide. Consequently, the plants look two-lobed. The gap-furrowed species include **Lithops divergens**, **L. helmutii**, **L. comptonii**, and the rare **L. viridis**. In cultivation the various gapped species have little in common. *Lithops helmutii*, for example,

multiplies quickly and grows relatively easily, while *L. viridis* and both varieties of *L. divergens* clump slowly if at all and tend to be difficult to cultivate. Even after heavy rains **L. divergens var. divergens**, a tiny greenish plant from Namaqualand, protrudes little more than an eighth inch (3 mm) above soil level.

Lithops flower near the end of their growing season, typically in midautumn. After flowering, the furrow between the plant bodies splits open, revealing a new set arranged at right angles to the old ones. This is when trouble usually begins for people trying to grow lithops.

From this moment, and for the next several months, the plants must be kept bone dry until the old plant bodies shrivel and become literally as thin as a sheet of paper. Watering lithops before the old leaves have completely dried up results in the old plant bodies swelling and choking off the new ones, usually leading quickly to the death of the plant. Holding back water until the time is right will result in the new, brilliantly marked plant bodies bursting through the remains of last year's growth and starting a new yearly cycle. With multiheaded plants the old plant bodies may not all be absorbed at the same rate. It usually will not hurt to wait until they all have shriveled, but lightly watering or spraying just one side of the plant may resolve the situation.

Other than sudden death, the most dramatic way that the yearly transition can go wrong is by what is called "stacking." In this the new growth pokes out long before the old plant bodies have shriveled, giving the appearance of one lithops sitting directly on top of another one. This situation can call for drastic measures. With luck, a little surgery, cutting away the old but still turgid leaves and leaving their cut ends to dry harmlessly, will do the trick.

In the wild lithops may live in winter- or summer-rainfall regions, but for the most part the same culture works for lithops regardless of their origins. Only a few, such as the beautiful pink-purple **Lithops optica** 'Rubra' (see photo on page 30), absolutely refuse to diverge from their built-in calendars and insist on growing in late summer right through winter. Typically, though, in the Northern Hemisphere a lithops will be ready for watering around late April or May and will conclude its growing cycle in late October or November, when the plants begin to split. Even when growing, lithops do not need to be watered too often; every two weeks is generally plenty. Some growers give them water less frequently than that, particularly in midsummer. Though it will not hurt them to go without water for longer than usual, it is a good idea to water them thoroughly when water is given to create good root growth.

In most areas lithops should receive as much light as possible, though in true desert climates a little shade might not be a bad idea. A soil that is low in organic matter is best, but the plants are not terribly fussy about what they are growing in as long as it drains very rapidly. With heavy fertilizing it is possible to grow relatively enormous plants, but these have a tendency to rot during winter.

A few lithops will remain permanently solitary but most gradually cluster and form small clumps over time.

The prettiest clump I have seen was a single plant of **Lithops meyeri** consisting of more than a dozen heads growing in quartz chips on a low saddle in the Richtersveld in far northwestern South Africa. Its almost pearly blue-white coloration closely matched the surrounding pebbles. The plant itself was raised well above the ground and thus readily visible, that is, until you turned your head away and then had to find it all over again.

Lithops grow fairly easily from seed and hybridize freely. True species and varieties usually have better color and markings than random hybrids, but carefully selected clones and hybrids can outshine their unmodified ancestors. Though the basic rules of lithops culture apply to almost all of them, species vary widely in ease of cultivation. The Namibian **Lithops schwantesii** and **L. dinteri**, L. divergens subsp. divergens and the much larger purple **subsp. amethystinum**, and **L. ruschiorum** can all be difficult, as can **L. optica** with its rigid internal calen-

The exceptional color of this *Lithops meyeri* probably results more from environmental than genetic factors. Photo by Rob Skillin.

Besides tan markings, *Lithops otzeniana* also comes in orange and green.

The green color of *Lithops aucampiae* 'Bellaketty' contrasts with the typical red or orange of the species.

Lithops herrei near the Richtersveld coast. Photo by Kurt Zadnik.

Lithops julii subsp. *fulleri,* fully turgid in a desolate part of Bushmanland. Photo by Rob Skillin.

Lithops gesinae: other forms range from brown to red.

Lithops dorotheae, one of the prettiest species and easy to grow.

Lithops karasmontana var. *bella,* growing in lithops-colored grit in southern Namibia. Photo by Rob Skillin.

dar, and **L. otzeniana**, patterned in contrasting colors, as well. Using a slightly different watering schedule with some of these species might help, but many of them simply are fussy and will not tolerate humid climates and long, cloudy winters.

In contrast, the widespread, variable **Lithops lesliei, L. aucampiae, L. bromfieldii, L. hookeri, L. julii, L. olivacea, L. salicola, L. pseudotruncatella, L. verruculosa,** and

L. dorotheae, perhaps the prettiest of them all, grow quite easily. Along with their numerous varieties, these species can provide a novice grower with all the lithops he or she may need.

Other species such as **Lithops herrei, L. gesinae,** and the many forms of **L. karasmontana** fall somewhere in between these two extremes. With correct care, however, lithops can survive for decades in cultivation.

CONOPHYTUM

The range of *Conophytum* is smaller than that of *Lithops*, but in both number of species and variety of form *Conophytum* outdoes its stone-mimicking cousins. As many as three hundred species have been described; around a hundred are currently recognized. Although conophytums share the basic lithops format of individual heads formed from pairs of conjoined leaves, they range from relatively large plants with plant bodies close to 2 inches (5 cm) tall and wide, to vigorous clumpers that produce foot-wide (30 cm) clusters composed of a hundred heads or more, to miniature single-bodied species barely a quarter inch (6 mm) tall or wide.

Unlike lithops, which flower at the end of their growth cycle, conophytums flower as they start to grow. The sudden appearance of flowers is often the best indication that the time to begin watering has arrived. The bursting out of flowers from barely visible fissures in what may seem like small shapeless heaps of dried paper never fails to evoke a kind of wonder to those familiar with the plants.

The classic conophytum shape is that of a cluster of tiny speckled grapes, but others look like flattened, fuzzy buttons or miniature high-peaked saddles, semispherical little blobs, or purple cocktail onions. Almost entirely native to those parts of South Africa and Namibia where the little rain that falls falls in winter, conophytums flourish in a wide variety of microhabitats, from tiny mossy crevices high in the mountains to bone-dry desert flats where they are fully exposed to the most blazing sun and intense aridity imaginable.

Individual conophytums consist of a pair of tightly fused plant bodies with a small slit in the center marking the spot where the leaves will split and the flowers emerge. The edge where the two leaves meet is nearly seamless, and unlike lithops the joined plant bodies look like a single entity. Often conophytums are highly decorated, patterned with red or purple dots and lines. They may have transparent windows on top or be entirely red, purple, or bronze.

Many conophytums do not need quite as much light as lithops, although for indoor gardeners the difference is moot. In typical home-growing situations the plants will benefit from as much light as possible, with very light shade recommended during their dormant periods. A few of the species, the bilobed ones in particular, will even survive outdoors in extremely well drained soil in areas with winter rain and dry summers, providing the plants with a good simulation of their natural conditions.

A little frost will not hurt them, although extensive periods of subfreezing, wet days will certainly prove fatal.

The bilobed species include many of the easiest candidates for cultivation. Though confined to the arid northwestern regions of South Africa, Namaqualand, and the Richtersveld, the bilobes nonetheless can withstand substantial amounts of water and generally resist rot. The variant forms of **Conophytum bilobum**, scattered over its wide range, gave rise to many now-discarded species names, a few of which nonetheless deserve recognition because of their horticultural qualities. The form once known as **C. nelianum** may be the hardiest of these, clumping quite readily and well adapted both to a windowsill or a sunny rock garden. **Conophytum elishae**, with less prominent lobes, also grows easily and multiplies fairly rapidly. Some forms have their edges outlined in red; others are white-skinned, as if glazed. **Conophytum**

Conophytum bilobum in the Richtersveld, home to a huge number of mesembs. Photo by Kurt Zadnik.

Conophytum meyeri, nestled in a Richtersveld *kloof* (canyon wall) and barely bilobed. Photo by Rob Skillin.

bilobum subsp. *altum* gradually forms clusters of proportionately long stems, each surprisingly surmounted by a bilobed conophytum. The other bilobes are much less widespread and mostly less common in cultivation.

Related species include the easily grown ***Conophytum meyeri***, lobed less deeply and sometimes not at all. It quickly forms good-sized clumps of rounded plant bodies, each considerably smaller than *C. bilobum*. ***Conophytum frutescens*** grows even taller than *C. bilobum* subsp. *altum*, ending up as a mass of bilobed plant bodies atop foot (30 cm) tall stems. Native to the east edge of the Richtersveld into Bushmanland, and less easy to cultivate, ***C. regale*** has a bubblelike swelling surrounding its central fissure. From the same general location, ***C. herreanthus*** (synonym *Herreanthus meyeri*) gradually forms tight, low-growing clusters of striking blue-white heads. Species more gap-jawed than bilobed include ***C. hians*** and ***C. roodiae***, the latter with a preference for tiny cracks and potholes high on dome-shaped monoliths of decaying granite.

More numerous than the bilobes, round conophytums also vary tremendously and range from almost perfect spheres, to slightly pointed, to definitely concave, to quite squat. The plants may be plain green, or have bright red markings around their margins or central fissures, slight speckles, or definite patterns of dots and stripes that range from faint to vividly bright. Dozens of conophytums have these characteristics, but I will describe just a few of the most distinct, as well as some of the more commonly encountered ones.

Among the many clustering, small bodied, more-or-less spherical species, in habitat ***Conophytum uviforme*** ("grape-shaped") looks like dense clusters of grapes somehow mysteriously transported to narrow crevices among boulders in the middle of the desert. Its clustering little spheres may be plain green, or grayish, or tinged with purple, their surfaces often but not always marked with a light patterning of dots.

Other species with a generally similar appearance include the very widespread ***Conophytum truncatum***, the easternmost species; ***C. bolusiae***, in nature a rare south Richtersveld endemic, but fast-clumping and easy to grow; and the pale-skinned, usually lightly speckled ***C. flavum***. The Richtersveld-dwelling ***C. saxetanum***, one of the smallest bodied and most rapidly multiplying species, prefers boulders, growing in an eighth inch (3 mm) or so of dusty grit over solid rock—this in an area of blazing sunlight and intense aridity, with perhaps 2 to 4 inches (5

to 10 cm) of rain a year softened only by occasional penetrating sea fogs (see photos on pages 22 and 55).

Similar in general shape and form but more strikingly decorated with marking of dark red, purple, or brown lines and geometrically arranged dots are ***Conophytum obcordellum***, with spidery, night-fragrant flowers; ***C. minusculum***, appropriately tiny-bodied, variously brilliant purple, or marked with mosaiclike designs of curving dark green over a white-green body; ***C. swanepoelianum***, similar though smaller and rarer; and the descriptively named ***C. rubrolineatum***. *Conophytum obcordellum* occurs northwest of Cape Town, along the coast, but does not reach the harsh lands of Namaqualand and the Richtersveld. It shares its somewhat better-watered habitat with many other succulents: crassulas, adromischus, pelargoniums, euphorbias, and many bulbs. This more benign environment explains its relative ease of cultivation.

Conophytum meyeri in Namaqualand, with "lipstick" markings around its fissure. Photo by Kurt Zadnik.

Conophytum roodiae posed for a picture. Photo by Rob Skillin.

Conophytum obcordellum, its spidery, sweet-scented flowers open at night.

Conophytum wettsteinii, piled up like a heap of flat disks on almost bare rock in full sun.

Conophytum minusculum, shrinking down into the soil. Photo by Kurt Zadnik.

Conophytum gratum subsp. marlothii, an old plant of blue-green to purple spheres on long stalks. Photo by Rob Skillin.

Among the larger and squatter species, **Conophytum wettsteinii**, disc-shaped and flattened with plant bodies over an inch (2.5 cm) across, forms odd, almost artificial-looking clumps on bare rock in full sun. It is another of the easier, more reliable species in cultivation. **Conophytum minutum**, in particular its **variety pearsonii**, is also a not-so-minute conophytum that makes tightly packed, geometrical clusters of plant bodies, a sphere formed of spheres. Its **variety minutum** generally is much smaller, with plant bodies averaging little more than half the size of its cousin.

Conophytum gratum, a fairly large-bodied conophytum that eventually becomes quite leggy, is another easy-growing species with potential as an outdoor subject. The very round-bodied **C. calculus** (see photo on page 16), immediately recognizable by its tough, thick, whitish skin, also forms dense, spherelike clusters, composed of fewer plant bodies than those made by C. minutum var. pearsonii. The two species thrive together in full sun in northern Namaqualand quartz fields.

Several of these spherical plants, **Conophytum pageae** among them, may have central fissures surrounded by bright red markings. Such plants are known as lipstick conophytums (see photo of C. meyeri on page 141). Other red-edged species have a somewhat bilobed shape, such as **C. tantillum** or forms of **C. quaesitum**, a species that may seek out crevices where it grows in partial to quite deep shade. Of course, shade in a blazing desert is a relative thing!

Conophytum fulleri is a basically green plant, with a body covered with tiny blisterlike depressions. It lives to the east, in Bushmanland, which, theoretically lies in a summer-rainfall region but is almost completely arid regardless of season. The first one I saw, in late winter

Conophytum fulleri, shriveled during the Bushmanland winter. Photo by Rob Skillin.

Its quarter-inch (6-mm) heads covered with fine hair, the endemic *Conophytum stephanii* grows wedged between Richtersveld rocks. Photo by Kurt Zadnik.

At the eastern end of *Conophytum* territory, bright red *C. ficiforme* f. *placitum* covering the rocks.

In a Knersvlakte quartz field, *Conophytum subfenestratum* can be either green or bright purple-red. Photo by Kurt Zadnik.

(August), clinging to the underside of a small quartz boulder, was so shriveled that at first I thought it was an odd lichen, with strangely rounded fruiting bodies.

Also an eastern species, but from more benevolent conditions farther south, ***Conophytum ficiforme*** has small plant bodies covered with branching, forking lines. It can make large many headed colonies on bare rocks, and in such conditions the plants become completely red, looking like bright little berries. The fuzzy-skinned ***C. ernstii***, two almost cubical species, ***C. angelicae* subsp. *tetragonum*** and ***C. cubicum***, and the distinctly hairy ***C. stephanii*** are all extreme endemics, each restricted to a few scattered stair-stepped gorges and quartzite hills in the Richtersveld, Bushmanland, and surrounding localities.

Conophytum maughanii and ***C. subfenestratum*** look like spherically organized blobs of translucent jelly, ranging from green to bright red, the latter, furthermore with a central fissure reduced to nothing more than a smallish dot. These two grow in Namaqualand quartz fields. Several somewhat similar species, including ***C. pellucidum*** and ***C. lithopsoides***, with heavily patterned and brightly colored translucent bodies and more-or-less transparent windows on their flat tops, often live at fairly high altitudes under almost alpine conditions. Here they flourish in winter in little rocky depressions, at times half-submerged from recent rains, and with a coating of ice all around them. Another mountaintop species, ***C. khamiesbergense***, makes small clusters of rough-edged, tubercled, almost toothy, wide-gapped leaves. Touchy in cultivation, it hardly resembles most conophytums, and in the past was given a genus of its own.

Farther east, mostly in Bushmanland, in the rain shadow beyond the coastal mountains, species even more highly windowed and translucent have made a home. For many years considered as the separate genus *Ophthalmophyllum*, these conophytums look like they are formed from glass, ranging from coke-bottle green to brown to reddish. Some of these plants remain solitary, others clump readily; some are touchy in cultivation, some grow easily but as a group they are quite recognizable. They include species such as **Conophytum friedrichiae**, **C. limpidum**, the slightly fuzzy **C. pubescens**, the clump forming **C. praesectum**, and the mottled **C. verrucosum**.

A few recently discovered conophytums call out for attention. Occupying just an acre or two (0.4 to 0.8 ha) each as their total habitat, they may fill their little patches of quartz -pebbled earth so densely as to form a solid carpet of flowers at blooming time. The best known of these, **Conophytum burgeri**, is purple and covered with permanent layers of silver sheathing made up of old, shriveled plant bodies from former years. It looks something like a cocktail onion. Because it is widest at its base and tapers upward, it was compared to Mount Fuji, even named after that mountain until it was recognized as a conophytum. It remains solitary and grows very slowly. In the wild it normally receives rain in late autumn and early winter. When I saw it in habitat in late winter, it had rained 4 inches (10 cm) a couple of weekends earlier. This was twice the normal annual precipitation, but then it had not rained at all for the previous two years. Despite

Conophytum pellucidum, patterned like a lithops, often withstands hard freezes in its mountain habitat. Photo by Kurt Zadnik.

With magenta flowers and orange plant bodies, *Conophytum praesectum* obviously can thrive in cultivation.

In the hills east of the Richtersveld, *Conophytum pubescens* grows flat-topped like a lithops. Note the minute seedling below to the left. Photo by Rob Skillin.

Conophytum burgeri, slow growing and solitary, with silver sheaths over a purple body. Photo by Rob Skillin.

this, the plants had flowered on schedule each year, as if somehow there was no connection between them and their environment.

Conophytum ratum, growing about 20 miles (30 km) away and confined to a flat patch of quartz pebbles an acre or two in size, looks like a blob of green jelly. Flat-topped, rounded, and well over an inch (2.5 cm) in diameter, it is large for a conophytum. Unlike *C. burgeri*, which pokes its conical head above the ground, *C. ratum* grows flush with the ground, or even makes a slight depression of its own (see photo on page 21).

Tiny ***Conophytum achabense*** is solitary, less than a quarter inch (6 mm) across, and tapers to a little narrow cylinder on top. It lives entirely below the pebbled surface of its improbable habitat. Its spindly purple, proportionately large flowers poke above the pebbles, their unex-pected presence making its discovery in the late 1980s possible. Of course, the ground where these three conophytums live is composed of translucent quartz, in effect providing the plants with their own natural greenhouses.

People rarely cultivate succulents for their flowers, but in addition to their profusion of shapes and habits, conophytums also offer surprising variety at bloom time. Many produce proportionately large flowers, some the size of the fused pair of plant bodies from which they emerge, most often bright yellow or purple. Other conophytums with disappointingly small pale flowers turn out to be highly fragrant when night falls, with a wide array of spicy scents depending on species.

Conophytums, although generally considered to be winter growers, actually display quite a bit of diversity in their cultural needs. The beginning of growth ranges from early winter to early summer. After the new growths have presented themselves to the outside world, the plants should receive water about every two weeks. After several months, when new pairs of leaves become visible inside the split at the top of the plant, or the surface of the plant starts looking whitish, wrinkled, or somewhat stretched, watering should cease. The dry resting period for the plants can last as long as six or seven months. Many smaller bodied species shrivel so much during this time that they seem quite dead.

During this resting state occasional light misting does not hurt, but, as with lithops, the goal is to let the old plant bodies dry up so that they will not block the free emergence of the new ones. If the new growth seems ready but hesitant about emerging, more frequent mistings can help, sometimes as often as every day or two if

The new growth of *Conophytum ratum* bursting through last year's dried sheathing plant bodies. Photo by Terry Thompson.

Conophytum schlechteri, with white flowers unusual for the genus.

Conophytum 'Secret of Suzanne', a hybrid combining brilliant flowers and plant color in the right conditions.

the light is strong enough, until regular watering can resume. Touchier species, such as the *Conophytum pellucidum* group and the ex-ophthalmophyllums, for example, should have their watering cut back, though not eliminated, after the first month or two. Too-frequent watering of these groups after this will result in plants splitting and bursting.

As with most arid-growing succulents, above all, their soil should be very quick-draining. A few of the species, such as **Conophytum obcordellum**, will benefit from a little organic substance in the soil mix, but many of the more specialized species do best with a mix very low in organic matter. Alternatively, the entirely organic, but noninteracting material known as coir (derived from coconut palms), has gained quite a following as a medium for conophytums and other mesembs.

Although the specific needs of conophytums might make their cultivation seem daunting, in reality many grow readily and thrive in containers, and with so many to choose from someone with limited space could assemble a varied collection of succulent plants consisting of nothing but members of this one genus.

ARGYRODERMA

Argyroderma ("silver skin") species resemble carvings in blue-green stone. The best way to describe them is to picture a silvery-blue to blue-green Easter egg cut almost in two along its width, with a V-shaped fissure extending across the cut. Each half of the cut-open egg is actually a leaf, and each year a new set of leaves appears in the fissure, arranged perpendicularly to the preceding pair. The width or narrowness of the fissure can be somewhat useful in determining which of the ten or eleven species a given plant belongs to. The shape of the leaves themselves is also helpful, with some species consistently rounder, others more ovoid.

For the most part, however, *Argyroderma* species are notoriously difficult to distinguish from each other. Some such as **A. delaetii** remain solitary, while others such as **A. congregatum** clump and form clusters of little blue eggs at the ends of short, recumbent stems. **Argyroderma crateriforme**, its leaves sometimes the color of the bluest sky imaginable, lives half buried in the soil, while **A. pearsonii** remains above ground. **Argyroderma framesii** clumps readily. Its individual heads, shaped like eggs placed on end, are smaller than most of the others. **Argyroderma fissum**, the most widely distributed species, is unmistakable; its body consists of a pair of tall, somewhat cylindrical leaves joined only at their base.

The proportionately large yellow, purple-red, pink, or rarely white flowers of argyrodermas emerge from the central fissure, alongside, though usually a bit before, the next set of leaves. The habitat in which they are found is entirely contained within the quartz fields of coastal Namaqualand in a sort of fossilized river delta known as

Argyroderma congregatum, small round bodies forming dense colonies in the quartz fields.

Less prolific, this *Argyroderma crateriforme* holds its seed capsule next to its new growths. Photo by Kurt Zadnik.

Argyroderma pearsonii flowering in a Berkeley, California, succulent garden.

Dinteranthus microspermus subsp. *puberulus*, on top of its pile of quartz pebbles in Bushmanland.

the Knersvlakte. This region consists of flat plains or slightly rolling slopes, covered with small inch (2.5 cm) to fist-sized chunks of quartz atop rocky, saline soil. Hidden among these quartz chunks, or clustering on top of them, in the company of other miniaturized, extremely succulent plants from several families, argyrodermas make their yearly set of leaves, flower, and set seed. And their reproductive abilities in the wild are extremely impressive. In a good year with 2 to 4 inches (50 to 100 mm) of winter rain to supplement the frequent fog that keeps the whole ecosystem surviving, some quartz patches are so dense with argyrodermas that the surrounding landscape seems blue rather than white and it is impossible to walk (even on tiptoe) without stepping on them.

DINTERANTHUS

Dinteranthus may be the most surreal of the living stone genera in looks, habitat, and culture. The genus consists of about half a dozen species and subspecies from Bushmanland and parts of Namibia directly across the Orange River. These species also grow in small quartz fields or in little heaps of crystalline, translucent quartz pebbles. One of the distinguishing characteristics of the genus is its very small seed. The seedlings germinate underneath clear quartz rocks, which act like little greenhouses, transmitting light but sheltering the tiny plants from predators and the elements.

    Dinteranthus, as with the other genera mentioned, comprises plants formed of pairs of fantastically swollen leaves, often with the remnants of last year's leaves around their base. **Dinteranthus vanzylii** looks very much like a lithops. The other species form little spheres, basically gray, with textures either like pearl or marble, sometimes

Dinteranthus vanzylii resembles a lithops and is easier to grow than most dinteranthus.

Here surmounting its own little quartz field, *Dinteranthus wilmotianus* comes from eastern Bushmanland. Photo by Rob Skillin.

with a slight velvety touch. **Dinteranthus microspermus** is covered with dots. Some forms of **D. wilmotianus** have faintly glowing orange ridges along the edges of their leaves. **Dinteranthus pole-evansii** looks like it is made of mother-of pearl. Under optimum conditions of light this species almost glows as if lit from within.

LAPIDARIA

Lapidaria margaretae, the only member of its genus, ranges over a fairly broad area of Bushmanland and neighboring Namibia, encompassing the range of some *Dinteranthus* species, but less restricted to specific localities within that range. *Lapidaria margaretae* also lives in quartz, but in sites that actually have a little soil as well. Though it may grow within a couple of feet (about 60

With geometric, angular plant bodies, *Lapidaria margaretae* grows among, not on top of, quartz pebbles. Photo by Rob Skillin.

Pleiospilos nelii, with heads 4 inches (10 cm) across and brilliant flowers, grows on the edges of the Great Karoo. Photo by Rob Skillin.

cm) of *D. microspermus* in some locations, the lapidaria lives on the stony flats while the dinteranthus keeps to its little mounds of pure quartz pebbles. With rose-colored tips on blue-chiseled leaves, *L. margaretae* looks like a collection of prismatic chips of quartz, at least until they send out their yellow flowers.

PLEIOSPILOS

Far from the seacoast, around the edges of the arid intermountain Little and Great Karoos, another genus of stone imitators has staked out its territory. Copying chunks of granite instead of white or bluish quartz, *Pleiospilos* species resist cold, heat, drought, and frost without complaint. Commonly called split rocks, the few species consist of angular pairs of very thick, soft leaves, gray or reddish and covered with dots that mimic the angular chunks of rock in which they grow.

Pleiospilos nelii has thick, half-ovoid leaves, often several pairs at a time, as much as 4 inches (10 cm) tall, wide, and thick. In the field it actually looks less like a rock than it does a pile of something unpleasant deposited by a good-sized quadruped. Other than that, *P. nelii* is an adorable little plant, the entry point of numerous children's fascination with succulents. When it, or any of the more angular-bodied **P. bolusii**, **P. simulans**, or **P. compactus** flower, their shimmering 3- or 4-inch (8- to 10-cm) diameter yellow and orange-red rimmed flowers belie any resemblance to rock. Though some of the most interesting pleiospilos were split off into the genus *Tanquana*, the remaining members of the genus, though

This plant of *Pleiospilos compactus* was growing with ice on the ground at noon.

neither as rare or difficult to grow as the other living stones, still manage to enchant collectors.

Dinteranthus species look impossibly fragile, but winter temperatures in Bushmanland can drop to below 20°F (–7°C) and in summer reach well over 100°F (38°C). *Lapidaria* withstands the same extremes of heat and cold. The rainfall patterns of Bushmanland change from winter rain in the west to summer rain in the east, but the overwhelming fact about the region is its near complete aridity. Namaqualand and the Little Karoo can seem almost lush by contrast. In parts of the region rain may not fall for several consecutive years, and there is no coastal fog to ameliorate the dryness. *Dinteranthus* species span the boundary between areas of winter rainfall and those with summer rainfall, but in cultivation it is best to keep them drier in winter. The plants should receive considerably less water than a lithops, normal watering every two or three weeks and dry in winter, or conversely, a mild misting every several days that moistens the surface of the soil but never soaks it. With this alternative treatment it is unnecessary to wait until the old plant bodies completely shrivel. The same regimen also works for the more recalcitrant conophytums. Humidity is the enemy of *Dinteranthus*, and in humid climates they may suddenly rot for no apparent reason.

Though they are from the same environment, lapidarias are much easier in cultivation. Regardless of the rainfall schedule in their habitat, they will do well with water every ten days to two weeks in the warm months and a dry rest in winter.

Also easy to grow, *Pleiospilos* species like regular water in the warm months every week to ten days and a dry rest in winter. Although they come from a strict winter-rainfall region, *Argyroderma* species are not difficult to grow either, and can be switched to warm season growth, with water about every two weeks in the warmer months, then dry in winter. Treating argyrodermas as winter growers in places with very bright, sunny, usually dry winters and low atmospheric humidity might be worth a try, but it is not necessary. It is also not necessary to let their last year's leaves wither away to nothing before starting to water them again.

All of these plants want a very fast-draining soil mix, low or completely devoid of organic matter. All of them thrive in very bright sun. *Pleiospilos* will grow well on a sunny windowsill. The others, particularly *Dinteranthus*, are more difficult, but all grow well from seed and are readily available from succulent nurseries for those in the mood for a bit of adventure.

Chapter 13

Dwarf Mesembryanthemums

ALONG WITH THE living stones (*Lithops* and related genera), a number of other mesembs have undergone extreme morphological modification as a response to their difficult environments. Some of these have become equally miniaturized and almost as stonelike in appearance. Others, though also dwarfed, consist of more than just a few "plant body" succulent leaves. Some are closely related to the more commonly seen living stones, while others at most are distant cousins, but all of them are less commonly encountered and all require equally stringent growing techniques to survive in cultivation.

TANQUANA AND DIDYMAOTUS

Now separated from *Pleiospilos*, the three species of *Tanquana* live farther to the west, largely in the bleak Tanqua and Ceres Karoos. Extremely localized, **T. archeri** and **T. hilmari** imitate rocks, remain small, and cluster only sparingly. *Tanquana hilmari* resembles a dwarfed *P. nelii* covered with translucent dots. *Tanquana archeri*, less round and slightly larger, has fewer dots. Both individual head and clump size increase in the more widely distributed, often two-toned **T. prismatica**, which manages to survive uncamouflaged. Its emergent leaves, which are rounder in young plants, more prismatic in mature ones, are blue-gray or turquoise, while its persistent older leaves are colored purple and orange by the sun.

Didymaotus is monotypic. Its single species, **D. lapidiformis**, is shaped like an elongated hexagon and grows under harsh circumstances in the Tanqua Karoo. Convincingly disguised as a small gray-brown rock, it rarely clusters. At flowering time it produces two pink-white to purple blossoms from bracts on opposite sides of its central cleft.

Less easy to cultivate than *Pleiospilos*, *Tanquana* and *Didymaotus* prefer dryness in both winter and summer, doing best with water about every two weeks in spring and fall. They need extremely bright light and quick-draining soil with little organic content. When the lateral buds of *Didymaotus* appear, watering should cease while the old leaves wither and the new ones develop.

Tanquana prismatica, here in the Ceres Karoo, can reach a surprising size. Photo by Rob Skillin.

If not in flower, *Didymaotus lapidiformis* would be nearly invisible in its stony home. Photo by Brian Kemble.

The toothless *Schwantesia herrei* f. *major* readily shows its relationship to *Lapidaria*. Photo by Terry Thompson.

Dracophilus proximus, a clump 5 inches (13 cm) across growing on bare carbonate rock in the Richtersveld.

SCHWANTESIA, NELIA, JUTTADINTERIA, AND DRACOPHILUS

Related to *Lapidaria margaretae*, members of the small genera *Schwantesia*, *Nelia*, *Juttadinteria*, and *Dracophilus* form clumps of very thick, glaucous, sometimes waxy, succulent leaves, often with harmless teeth arrayed in ridges toward their leaf tips. Unlike lithops and conophytums, the long-lasting old leaves of these small mesembs do not annually dry into protective sheaths. Their preferred habitats include imperceptible cracks in the side of a boulder, with room for no more soil than you could pinch between your fingers, or high-altitude desert flats, with below-freezing nights and essentially zero humidity.

The most compact growing of these, *Schwantesia* species, follow the general course of the Orange River, from winter-rainfall areas in the west to summer rain in the east, but always in settings of intense aridity. Schwantesias resemble small heaps of geometric blue stones, with leaves variously pebbled-textured, as in **S. borcherdsii**, or smooth. The easternmost, **S. ruedebuschii**, has leaves tipped with small teeth. Other species such as **S. herrei** or **S. pillansii** are toothless.

The faceted leaves of **Nelia schlechteri**, the most widely grown of its genus, seem carved out of blue soap or wax. Unusually for a mesemb, *Nelia* flowers open in the morning and their white blossoms remain open for several days and nights. Their Richtersveld and Namaqualand habitat overlaps the southern boundary of the mostly Namibian *Juttadinteria*, which grows taller and often less compactly. Many of its ten species, such as **J. simpsonii**, **J. elizae**, and **J. ausensis**, have teeth; others, such as **J. suavissima** and **J. albata**, do not.

Closely related to *Juttadinteria*, *Dracophilus* forms thick-leafed, compact, low-growing clusters. Native to arid coastal southern Namibia and the Richtersveld, its four species, along with similar coastal dwelling mesembs, will not tolerate extreme cold during their winter growing season. The leaves, toothed or smooth depending on species, can be pure sky blue, contrasting with the buff, carbonate boulders and surrounding flats where they often grow. Rather than artful camouflage, their best survival tactic may be their choice of habitat. With few insects here other than occasional extremely slow-moving, flightless, amazingly well camouflaged grasshoppers, or bizarre, lumbering, black armored crickets, the scarcity of predators may be a factor in the plants' success.

These plants need maximum sun and a quick-draining soil devoid of organic matter. Ideally, with bright sun during their winter growing season, they can take water about every two weeks. During periods of low light, they should stay dry regardless of what their "schedules" suggest. Schwantesias from summer-rainfall regions could be treated much like summer-growing lithops, with water every two weeks or so from late spring through midautumn. Again, erring on the side of dryness will not hurt.

GIBBAEUM AND MUIRIA

Paralleling *Argyroderma*, several of the twenty or so *Gibbaeum* species also colonize quartz fields, though in the Little Karoo instead of the Knersvlakte. Most readily recognized by their unequally sized plant bodies, these spherical, angular, or elongated species are always somewhat asymmetrical. Some clump rapidly, others quite slowly.

Gibbaeum pubescens—some clusters can reach 2 feet (60 cm) in diameter.

Gibbaeum album most resembles an argyroderma and similarly specializes in quartz fields.

The fused but disparate plant bodies of Gibbaeum shandii show very clearly.

The rocklike Gibbaeum petrense looks like a freely clustering Lapidaria or Schwantesia.

The largest clusters are formed by species such as **Gibbaeum pubescens**, with elongated leaf-pairs covered by dense, short, silver-white hairs; **G. pachypodium**, similar, though green; and **G. heathii**, with clusters of small round, pale green heads up to a foot (30 cm) across. Short hairs also cover the elongated bodies of **G. shandii**, while the fuzzy covering of **G. dispar** gives it a velvety texture. **Gibbaeum album**, which is white and glabrous (without hair), specializes in quartz fields, sometimes accompanied by the angular-leafed, stonelike **G. petrense**. **Gibbaeum nebrownii** and **G. johnstonii**, the latter with a flattened, windowed top, are among the smallest species. They look more like conophytums than gibbaeums, but they retain the unequal leaf-pairs of the genus.

Rainfall patterns vary in *Gibbaeum* habitat, but on the whole the plants do best with very little if any water in both summer and winter, and with water every two weeks in spring and fall. The smaller species are most sensitive to overwatering, and the light misting technique may work best for them. They need lean, rapidly draining soil and very bright sun.

Set down in the middle of *Gibbaeum* habitat, **Muiria hortenseae** looks like a cartoon, a slightly incurved upright gray-green egg, perhaps 2 inches (5 cm) tall, squat at the base, tapered at the top, and covered in fine, short hair. Each muiria is formed from two plant bodies with no indication of a seam except a slight apical indentation. Their white flowers literally burst through the top of the plant bodies. Muirias can form clusters of as many as half a dozen heads, but even a large plant looks like a small crowd of individual cartoon eggs. People instantly adore muirias; perhaps they fulfill some biologically determined concept of what we think of as cute.

Muirias may receive rain both in summer and winter,

An old five-headed *Muiria hortenseae*.

A conclave of cultivated muirias, all bursting into flower.

sometimes contrasting colored basal sheaths composed of the remnants of old growths, range from round to elliptical to quite elongate.

In the round-topped *Cheiridopsis cigarettifera*, the sheaths bear a fancied resemblance to a cigarette holder; similar species include *C. brownii*. With alternating pairs of completely dissimilar leaves, one pair flat on the ground, the other facing upward, *C. peculiaris*, from a patch of stony soil in the southern Richtersveld, remains solitary or occasionally forms small clumps. *Cheiridopsis pillansii*, from a slightly less hostile part of the Richtersveld, forms good-sized clusters of joined, rounded leaf-pairs ranging from purple to pale green. During wet winters individual plants can grow as large as hard-boiled eggs. In the sheathless, widely distributed *C. denticulata*, the narrow, curving, sometimes toothed leaves are largely separate. Several species, such as *C. verrucosa*, are spotted, or very rarely, as in *C. umdausensis*, covered with raised white dots.

Yellow-flowered *Cheiridopsis brownii*—a few other species have red flowers.

but never very much. They flower at the end of their growth cycle, then shrink dramatically, but do not remain dormant as long as similar plants from Namaqualand or the Richtersveld. The soil where they grow is a kind of gray clay sludge, topped by quartz pebbles and variously colored round rocks, each about the size of a muiria. In their very localized habitat muirias grow abundantly, and it is necessary to take care to avoid stepping on them. With a reputation for being difficult to grow, a need for intense light, and a propensity to rot any time of the year, they are not easy to find in cultivation.

CHEIRIDOPSIS

The approximately thirty species of *Cheiridopsis* thrive in a variety of northwest South African habitats: quartz fields, coastal sandveldt, interior hills, and stony flats. Their pairs of variably fused leaves, often protected by

Cheiridopsis peculiaris with its sets of very different leaf pairs.

Cheiridopsis denticulata, a vigorous but not very dentate-margined plant. Photo by Kurt Zadnik.

Unusual because of its tubercles, Cheiridopsis umdausensis is also an extremely rare endemic.

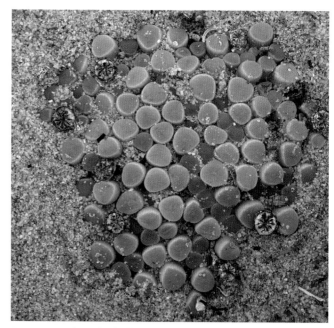

Fenestraria rhopalophylla, buried up to its window tips 300 feet (90 m) back from the ocean. Photo by Kurt Zadnik.

Frithia pulchra, similar to Fenestraria but unrelated.

Cheiridopsis do well with winter water every two weeks and summer dryness. The quicker growing ones will survive outdoors in reasonably frost-free areas, but under these conditions they usually become much larger than normal and often look like a small uninteresting ice plant rather than a specialized Richtersveld dwarf.

FENESTRARIA AND FRITHIA

Though widely separated and not closely related, the plants of these two genera are superficially very similar to each other. Commonly called baby toes, *Fenestraria rhopalophylla* grows near the Atlantic coast, sometimes in old beach sand just yards (meters) from the high tide line. Its cylindrical leaves remain buried in the sand with only their smooth, windowed tops visible, enabling light to pass down into their photosynthesizing interiors. **Sub-**species *aurantiaca* has yellow flowers. Although the winter rainfall in their habitat rarely exceeds 4 inches (100 mm) a year, the almost everyday fog provides them with enough moisture for survival. In cultivation light watering at fairly frequent intervals, every ten days to two weeks, will keep them growing. In the wild they can attain a surprising size, and if given appropriate treatment they will grow fairly rapidly.

Frithia pulchra, from northeast South Africa, can be most easily distinguished from *Fenestraria* because of its textured, almost granular, leaf tips. It remains small, also buried in the ground to its leaf tips, and has purple blooms. *Frithia pulchra* **f.** *minor*, possibly a variety or even a distinct species, has white flowers. In habitat *F.*

pulchra receives surprisingly high rainfall during summer, but it grows in thin, rapidly draining, rocky soil. In winter it should remain dry.

ALOINOPSIS, DEILANTHE, AND TITANOPSIS

The related, relatively few species of *Aloinopsis*, *Deilanthe*, and *Titanopsis* form small rosettes, usually with flattened, spathulate (spoon-shaped), often highly decorated leaves.

Aloinopsis species, essentially succulent rosettes on top of a tuberous root, have adapted to their various habitats by developing leaves that copy the color and texture of the stony soil in which they are found. Species from brown ground have brown leaves, from gray ground, gray, and species endemic to quartz fields or limestone areas come with whitish or blue leaves. Little white protrusions like incipient teeth cover the leaves of *A. lodewykii* and *A. malherbei* as well as the angular rather than flattened leaves of *A. luckhoffii* and *A. setifera*. Other species such as *A. rubrolineata*, *A. spathulata*, and *A. rosulata* have leaves patterned with rounded tubercles. In contrast, the tiny speckled gray leaves of *A. schooneesii*, growing out of a disproportionately large tuberous base, resemble little rounded pieces of granite.

Aloinopsis generally bloom with yellow flowers, silky textured and sometimes red-striped. *Aloinopsis spathulata*, with magenta to pink blossoms, is an exception. Growing near Sutherland, site of the lowest recorded temperature in South Africa, it is also extremely frost hardy, a possible outdoor grower at higher elevations in the U.S. desert southwest. *Aloinopsis* species grow over a broad west-to-east range, including both winter- and summer-rainfall areas, but perhaps are best treated as spring and fall growers, watered very sparingly in summer and with dry winters.

Deilanthe consists of three species closely related to *Aloinopsis*, with spreading, soft, unmarked fleshy leaves distinguished by an almost plush or velvety texture. *Deilanthe peersii*, the best-known species, has attractive blue leaves and a large tuberous root. Not quite as cold hardy as *Aloinopsis*, they do well with the same basic care.

Titanopsis species grow farther north than the others, from southern Namibia in the west, through Bushmanland and east to the Great Karoo. The plants form tight rosettes, their leaves so closely held together that only the tips, completely covered with irregular patterns of warty

Aloinopsis malherbei, growing in stony desert pavement. Photo by Rob Skillin.

Aloinopsis spathulata, flowering in one of the coldest, bleakest parts of South Africa. Photo by Rob Skillin.

Aloinopsis schooneesii, with leaves like granite pebbles.

Titanopsis hugo-schlechteri, orange bodied in orange Bushmanland sand. Photo by Rob Skillin.

Titanopsis schwantesii, from extremely harsh, arid areas. Photo by Kurt Zadnik.

tubercles, show. ***Titanopsis calcarea***, the best-known species, was allegedly discovered by someone walking over limestone rocks who only gradually realized that the stones he stood on actually were plants. The tips of its variously colored leaves have tubercles of varying size that resemble little translucent pearls. ***Titanopsis hugo-schlechteri***, growing in orange-pink sand, is orange-pink, while ***T. schwantesii***, from limestone-colored soil, is bluish white. Along with their warts, the patterns on the leaf surfaces of titanopsis look almost like they are fashioned out of some kind of exotic reptile skin.

Though remarkably hardy to cold, titanopsis also are extremely susceptible to excess humidity and water. Even when growing they should not receive much water, only every two to three weeks. Most titanopsis should be kept dry in winter, and probably in early summer and spring as well. ***Titanopsis fulleri*** grows farther to the east, and can be watered a little earlier in the year. *Titanopsis hugo-schlechteri* flowers contentedly in western Bushmanland, where the winter rains average 2 inches (50 mm) a year and there is absolutely no fog or humidity. Plants prefer an extremely fast draining soil almost devoid of organic matter and as much bright sunlight as possible. Some people grow the plants in a limey soil, but the consensus opinion is that it is unnecessary. When grown under the right conditions, they will show their bright yellow flowers toward the end of their growing season.

Various *Aloinopsis* can make good candidates for outdoor growing. At the Huntington Botanical Garden in Pasadena, Southern California, a clump of *A. schooneesii* has thrived outdoors for years. *Titanopsis* can also survive outdoors in arid places such as Bakersfield, California,

but in wetter climates success with *Titanopsis* in the ground seems improbable.

MONILARIA, MITROPHYLLUM, MEYEROPHYTUM, AND OOPHYTUM

Two pairs of radically dimorphic leaves make up an entire season's growth for these four genera. *Monilaria* and *Oophytum* grow in the surreal quartz fields of the Knersvlakte, while *Mitrophyllum* and *Meyerophytum* live in the coastal regions of the Richtersveld to the north. They survive on the winter rain, supplemented with the fog that frequently creeps in from the cold Atlantic waters.

The six species of *Monilaria* ("string of pearls") consist of upright stalks a few inches high that look like columns of beads, topped during the growing season by two pairs of new leaves. The first set, completely fused, forms a kind of hollow collar. The second pair of leaves, fleshy, elongated, and joined only basally, grows through the center of the collar. At the first touch of sparse winter rain the collar leaves burst through confining sheaths made of dried growths, with the second, elongated pair following almost immediately. In species such as ***M. moniliformis*** and ***M. pisiformis*** the second pair of leaves glistens with shiny papillae, bumps composed of large water storing cells. In ***M. chrysoleuca*** the papillae are so large that the plants have been compared to velvety green pipe cleaners.

Monilarias have a short growing period, only a few months in midwinter. At the approach of spring their second leaf-pair dries up and the year's growth shrivels and turns into a little dry globe, a new bead on top of the column of previous growths. The plants endure the long dry season until, eight or nine months later, the first light rains and heavy fogs wake them up, they send new paired leaves through the top of the string of pearls and begin another cycle. The stalks slowly clump and multiply over the years, occasionally forming 6-inch (15-cm) tall thickets possibly a couple of centuries old.

The half dozen species of *Mitrophyllum*, growing in gorges, quartzite ridges, and sandy basins in the southern Richtersveld, take the theme of foliar dimorphism even farther. A resting mitrophyllum looks as dead as a dormant monilaria, merely a dried up sheath on a shorter or longer stalk, for as much as three-fourths of the year. The plants wake up all at once, as a pair of soft, fat, united leaves bursts through the sheath, elongates, and spreads apart. After a few days more a second leaf-pair emerges, upright and completely conjoined with a little notch on top that resembles the bishop's miter for which the genus is named.

All basically similar, mitrophyllums differ primarily in the size of their leaves and the length of the internodes between them. Old plants of **Mitrophyllum mitratum** and **M. grande**, with very short internodes, consist of a dense thatch of past sheathing leaves with the newest pair on top. In contrast, **M. clivorum**, with long internodes, forms a clump of stalked branches, with only its last season's dried sheaths obvious.

Mitrophyllum grande with both sets of leaves visible. Photo by Kurt Zadnik.

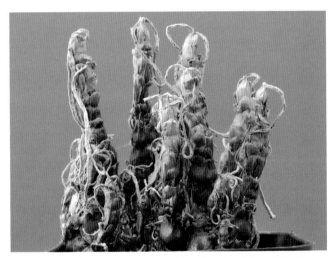

Monilaria pisiformis, dormant and looking dead, in cultivation.

Monilaria chrysoleuca flowering in Namaqualand. Photo by Rob Skillin.

Mitrophyllum grande, dormant but starting to revive.

Meyerophytum meyeri in a quartzite hill in the Richtersveld.

Oophytum nanum, flowers almost open in the Knersvlakte quartz. Photo by Rob Skillin.

Mitrophyllums seek out relatively shaded areas, such as the walls of canyons (called *kloofs*), where they receive protection from the sun and survive largely on consistent fog-borne moisture. Even though the plants themselves can become fairly good sized (*Mitrophyllum grande* can stretch 6 inches (15 cm) from leaf tip to leaf tip when in full growth), typically they grow in cracks in rocks or tiny ledges on cliff faces, in almost no soil at all.

Meyerophytum meyeri, the single species of *Meyerophytum*, enjoys its own version of foliar dimorphism, first producing small round sheathing leaves followed by a second pair, fused for about a third of their length, then forking. Though typically treated as a miniature in cultivation, in the wild plants of *M. meyeri* can reach over a foot (30 cm) across, with dozens of short branches that each terminate in a little Y. They share their kloof and ridge habitat with mitrophyllums and benefit from the same moisture-providing fog. **Meyerophytum meyeri var. holgatense**, with slightly larger leaves and purple flowers with white centers, lives on the arid coast, near the regions where diamonds are mined and trespassers are unwelcome.

Monilaria, *Mitrophyllum*, and *Meyerophytum* species have unusual cultural needs. In late fall or early winter their new leaves swell inside the sheaths of the old growths. At this time watering should begin, but even during their growth period they only need water about every two weeks. After three or four months, in late winter their leaves lose turgidity, signifying the start of dormancy. At this time stop watering and leave them absolutely dry for the next eight or nine months. They may look dead during this time but they are not; watering them during their dormancy will soon prove fatal. A standard mesemb mix will suit them, and they should get maximum available light, although mitrophyllums will also tolerate slightly less light.

Oophytum, with three species from the Namaqualand quartz fields, lacks the extreme dimorphic leaves of its cousins, but shares their need for complete summer dryness. Their flowers range from white to purple, and the plants themselves form columnar clusters of little elliptical bodies. **Oophytum oviforme** is more egg-shaped and larger than the rounder **O. nanum**, but both are dwarf plants. Growing completely exposed amid the white quartz pebbles, plants can turn bright red-brown. Unlike the argyrodermas that often grow next to them, oophytums are difficult to cultivate except in areas of very bright winter light. They should receive either sparse winter water or more frequent, but very light mistings.

Chapter 14

Small, Medium, and Large Mesembryanthemums

ALTHOUGH IT IS obviously impossible to provide complete coverage of the almost innumerable species of mesembryanthemums, in this chapter I will highlight some of the other more popular genera, more unusual forms, and horticulturally significant mesemb groups.

FAUCARIA, STOMATIUM, AND ODONTOPHORUS

Easy to grow, *Faucaria* species have gained the informal name tiger's jaws because of the pointed but harmless teeth lining the sides of their wedge-shaped leaves. Plants consist of alternating pairs of these thick, triangular leaves, and though they cluster freely, they always remain compact. Most faucarias live in the Eastern Cape Province of South Africa, a few edge west into the Little and Great Karoos. They often grow in the thin shade provided by other dry-growing plants but may also live fully exposed to the sun on rocky patches.

By far the most common in cultivation, *Faucaria tigrina* has leaf margins edged in white teeth that attenu-

ate into whiskerlike tendrils. Very similar but more solidly green, the widespread *F. felina* ranges from the borders of the Little Karoo to near the Indian Ocean coast. *Faucaria tuberculosa*, its leaves covered with irregular, usually white tubercles, has fewer but chunkier teeth. Almost toothless, with raised white leaf margins, *F. bosscheana* grows at the eastern end of the Great Karoo. In common with the other faucarias, which have yellow flowers, the atypical white flowers of *F. candida* open in the afternoon.

Faucarias do well with a standard mesemb soil mix and like water once a week during warm weather. In winter they should be kept dry, although water once a month or so will not hurt them. Most are reasonably frost resistant, and in appropriate climates they will thrive in a well-drained outdoor setting.

Stomatiums look a little like faucarias but their toothed leaves, smaller and somewhat oblong rather than wedge-shaped, plus their looser clumps make it easy to differentiate between the two genera. As many as forty *Stomatium* species have a wide, sporadic distribution over

Faucaria tigrina, toothed, tubercled, and red.

Stomatium suaveolens, the only toothless species. Photo by Rob Skillin.

An unidentified but highly toothed *Stomatium* from a high, bleak South African plateau. Photo by Rob Skillin.

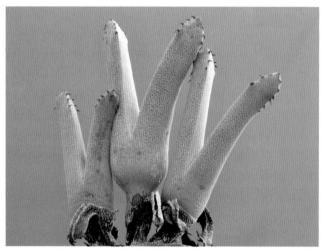

Odontophorus angustifolius var. *protoparcoides,* toothed leaves on a stick. Photo by Terry Thompson.

much of South Africa, some living in western winter-rainfall areas, some in the eastern interior, and some in the central Karoos. Their usually scented flowers open late in the day or in the evening. **Stomatium agninum** has few teeth, the rare **S. geoffreyi** has many. **Stomatium suaveolens**, from western South Africa, is toothless, while **S. alboroseum** has teeth and occasionally bicolored flowers as well; both inhabit high-altitude intermountain plateaus, along with other species difficult to identify.

Stomatiums generally grow easily. Most like weekly summer water and relatively dry winters. Some will adapt to outdoor growing in winter-rainfall areas. They are reasonably frost resistant, particularly if kept dry.

Odontophorus, a third, less frequently cultivated genus of toothed plants, is endemic to the Richtersveld. The more frequently encountered species resemble a stomatium or schwantesia on a stalk. **Odontophorus angusti-**

folius forms dense clumps over a foot (30 cm) across. The occasionally black-toothed **O. angustifolius var. protoparcoides**, from arid, windswept, boulder-pocked Richtersveld mountains, remains more compact. **Odontophorus marlothii** grows upright, with leaf-pairs at long intervals on its branching stems. Eventually it bends down and spreads over the surrounding ground. Generally blue-toned when grown in the lower light of cultivation, in the wild *Odontophorus* species may color up, particularly during their summer dormancy.

GLOTTIPHYLLUM, BIJLIA, AND DIPLOSOMA

Although commonly grown, *Glottiphyllum* ("tongue-leaf") rarely achieves its potential in cultivation. The approximately twenty medium to small species extend in all directions beyond their Little Karoo center of diversity, though they do not venture as far as the western winter-rainfall areas. Their paired, thick, more-or-less elongated leaves, for which they were named, grow distichously in most species, one pair after another on the same plane, like partially expanded fans either laid down flat on the ground, or elevated just slightly above it. A smaller number of species reach upward with growths formed by alternating leaf-pairs. Under ideal conditions the leaves of some smaller species assume a somewhat spherical instead of elongated shape. Glottiphyllum leaves, usually very smooth, with a texture reminiscent of hard wax or plastic, generally are green in cultivation. In habitat, however, particularly in the dry season, they turn brilliant red, purple, blue-white, or bronzy-purple. Glottiphyllums offset but never form massive clumps. Almost without exception they bloom with large silky yellow flowers.

Some species, such as **Glottiphyllum grandiflorum**, from locations with climates moderated by a degree of coastal proximity, remain green in the wild. Species from somewhat harsher conditions, such as the widely distributed **G. longum**, **G. linguiforme** ("tongue-shaped tongue-leaf"), the commonly grown **G. nelii**, or the closely related, even smaller **G. pygmaeum**, stay bright, shiny green when growing but can color up vividly, almost as if painted, during their rest periods. Species from drier areas display the most exotic colors. For example, the leaves of **G. neilii** (not to be confused with the separate species G. nelii) from the Great Karoo, range from blue-green to almost metallic bronze, while the sun-loving **G. oligocarpum** has a thick, waxy, pebble-textured skin that turns blue-white and pearly iridescent.

From relatively well watered regions, *Glottiphyllum grandiflorum* becomes quite lush. Photo by Rob Skillin.

Compact growing, *Glottiphyllum pygmaeum* colors up in bright sunlight.

From the Great Karoo, *Glottiphyllum neilii* has developed protective coloration and a compact habit. Photo by Rob Skillin.

Glottiphyllum cruciatum, a spectacular clone in southern California.

Among the species with alternating leaf-pairs, **Glottiphyllum cruciatum** can turn a glowing orange-red, while the notably asymmetric leaf-pairs of **G. peersii** have bright white lines along their keeled edges. The 6- or 7-inch (15- to 18-cm) long leaves of **G. regium**, the largest species, curve gracefully upward to the sun.

Unlike many mesembs, overwatering will not kill glottiphyllums. Instead it turns their leaves swollen, soft and laxly green, obliterating their individual characteristics. Most kinds will take frost and can survive outdoors in rock gardens, but with more rain than they are designed for they will enlarge and swell unnaturally. Glottiphyllums do best in proportionately small containers with very lean soil, maximum light, and water only about every two weeks in spring and fall, with less in summer, and almost none in winter.

The two species of *Bijlia* live in the southern Great Karoo, a region of blazing summer heat, subfreezing winter nights, and intense aridity. They share their flat, stony habitat with *Glottiphyllum neilii*, in company with particularly dry-growing aloes, euphorbias, tylecodons, monsonias, and lithops. **Bijlia dilatata**, the better-known species, forms three- or four-headed little clusters made of paired, broadly triangular leaves turned upward at their apex, like the prow of a rowboat. Tan-yellow in the wild, in cultivation it is not easy to keep the plants either properly colored or compact enough, although given very bright light, mesemb soil mix, and water about every two weeks in the late summer through autumn they are not difficult to at least keep alive. Although frost does not bother them, rain and high humidity will minimize their survival prospects outdoors in all but the driest climates.

In cultivation it is difficult to keep *Bijlia dilatata* as tight growing as this. Photo by Rob Skillin.

Rhinephyllum pillansii, called the raspberry *vyggie* (a generic term for mesembs) in reference to its dense covering of white tubercles.

Rhombophyllum dolabriforme, baking in the Great Karoo sun.

The second species, **B. tugwelliae**, forms much larger clumps, but it lacks the interesting asymmetrical design of *B. dilatata*.

Rarely seen or cultivated, the two species of *Diplosoma* resemble tiny glottiphyllums with only one pair of leaves per growth. The leaves are oblong, flat on the ground, and forked into a Y in the rare Knersvlakte endemic **D. retroversum**, and semispherical and covered with translucent bumps in the more widespread, more southern **D. luckhoffii**. Both species receive water only in winter. In summer they shrink and almost disappear from sight; in cultivation a complete summer dry period is necessary. Fairly frequent misting after they wake up is probably the best course, but the plants are not easy to keep alive for long.

RHINEPHYLLUM, RHOMBOPHYLLUM, AND PSAMMOPHORA

With pointed or oblong leaves sometimes lightly toothed and often coated with little white dots like a strawberry, *Rhinephyllum* has something of the look of a stomatium or titanopsis, though less extreme. **Rhinephyllum broomii** is probably the best known. **Rhinephyllum pillansii** is more heavily tubercled. Though easy to grow, rhinephyllums are uncommon in cultivation.

Rhombophyllum, with just two species, is distinguished by its odd-shaped leaves, rhomboidal in the appropriately named **R. rhomboideum**, and tubercle-covered, curved, thin, and shaped like a carpenter's hatchet in the more commonly grown **R. dolabriforme**. These plants, from the border area between the Eastern and Western Cape Provinces, generally grow under semi-arid conditions, but *R. dolabriforme* also ventures into truly bleak surroundings. Given standard succulent care, they will do well. They can also survive outdoors in well-drained rock gardens, though in such situations they may grow much larger than in the wild.

Usually smooth-leafed and restricted to the winter-rainfall region from southern coastal Namibia through the Richtersveld, the four species of *Psammophora* are best known for their habit of collecting sand on their leaves, which secrete a slightly sticky substance. **Psammophora longifolia**, with blunt-tipped, oblong, vaguely three-angled leaves, is the most common. It rarely grows more than 4 or 5 inches (10 to 13 cm) tall or wide, though other species can become shrublike. As with most plants from their habitat, psammophoras need dry summer rests and not too much water even during their growing season.

HEREROA, BERGERANTHUS, NANANTHUS, AND RABIEA

Several small clumping mesembryanthemum genera form a visual continuum, with longer, narrower, or broadly wedge-shaped leaves. *Hereroa*, widely distributed in both South Africa and Namibia, and *Bergeranthus*, from southeastern South Africa, often look very much alike, tufted plants with long, upcurved leaves that taper to a soft point. Neither causes particular difficulty in cultivation, requiring bright light, a standard planting mix and, since they do not occur in the driest areas, regular watering, with perhaps reduced frequency in summer and relatively dry winters. **Hereroa calycina** and several other species from more arid regions tend to be smaller, with textured foliage. Members of both genera will adapt to outdoor growing in areas with suitable climates.

Nananthus, with thick, tuberous roots similar to those of the closely related *Aloinopsis*, grow as low clusters of thick, usually broadly triangular, wedge-shaped leaves. Some species have a pebbly texture, others are leathery or smooth surfaced, but in general they tend to look rather alike. Several, such as **N. wilmaniae**, have gray, heavily textured foliage while others are green. Some have longitudinal ridges along their upper surfaces. Their flowers, completely yellow or striped with red, resemble those of *Aloinopsis*. Nananthus live in the central and eastern parts of the South African interior, where extremes of cold and heat are the rule. They need winter dryness. During the rest of the year they need water no more than once a week, though less will not hurt. Rather nutritionally deficient soil and lots of light suit them. They generally remain small.

Resembling a broader-leafed nananthus or a toothless faucaria, the half dozen species of *Rabiea* share the harsh inland habitat of *Nananthus*, and, if anything, are hardier. They do well in the ground even in places where the winter rains arrive during their natural dormant period. If given adequate light they will be covered with white dots, especially **R. albinota**, and can color up nicely. Popular rock garden plants in South Africa, they are not very well known outside of their native land.

ANTIMIMA, ANTEGIBBAEUM, TRICHODIADEMA, AND MESTOKLEMA

Along with the smaller mesembryanthemums, many medium and larger mesembs cover the South African landscape. Considered as individual growths, the approximately one hundred species of *Antimima* would be considered true miniatures, but they develop into many-headed clumps a foot (30 cm) across or more, some with linear, densely packed branches winding around themselves like ribbons as they grow. Most are from extremely arid, summer-drought regions, but they do reasonably well in cultivation. Several, such as the turquoise-bodied **A. dualis** or the pink-tinged *A. pygmaea*, remain compact and are appropriate subjects for small containers. Considered part of the genus *Ruschia* until not long ago, *Antimima* still exists in a state of some taxonomic uncertainty.

In contrast, *Antegibbaeum* consists of a single species, **A. fissoides**, from winter-rainfall parts of the Little Karoo and farther west. It makes little clusters of oblong blue-green leaves and produces exceptionally brilliant, large magenta flowers.

Immediately recognizable because of the starbursts of

Rabiea albinota, widely separated in nature, growing next to *Crassula columella* in a garden setting.

Antimima pygmaea, looking like a coral reef inhabitant transported to a desert. Photo by Rob Skillin.

Antigibbaeum fissoides, in the hills between the Richtersveld and Bushmanland. Photo by Rob Skillin.

Trichodiadema bulbosum planted to show off its tuberous base.

Mestoklema arboriforme, with its varnished-looking rootstock exposed.

tiny bristles at the tips of their small, cylindrical, densely packed leaves, the approximately three dozen species of *Trichodiadema* grow over much of South Africa and into Namibia. The diadem of "stars" is a bonus; trichodiademas are cultivated because of their thick tuberous roots, raised up for display in cultivation as a sort of mesembryanthemum caudiciform. **Trichodiadema bulbosum** and **T. densum** are the best known, but others are grown from time to time. In the wild trichodiademas occur almost everywhere succulents grow, even venturing into some winter-rainfall regions.

Although they lack the crown of bristles, the half dozen species of *Mestoklema* resemble trichodiademas on steroids, as it were. Rather than very small shrubs, they are quite large, up to 3 feet (90 cm) or more in height in some species, with woody branches, persistent, spiky flower stalks, and huge, orange-brown, glossy tubers, underground in nature. The plants grow mostly in cen-

tral South Africa, from coastal regions and far into the interior, in all but the most arid areas. With their tuberous bases and thick stems and branches they hardly look like other mesembs, although their small cylindrical leaves and orange or pink flowers give them away.

The most commonly cultivated, **Mestoklema arboriforme**, and the even larger, though less neat-growing **M. tuberosum**, created something of a sensation among growers when they were introduced into the United States, as their huge tuberous bases seemed indicative of great age, but in reality, particularly when planted in the ground, they develop relatively quickly. In milder climates the plants do very well outdoors, and with their massive, almost artificially polished-looking bases, also lend themselves to container culture. Mestoklemas present no particular problems under cultivation. A standard soil mix and standard water regime will work fine.

Whether called *Dactylopsis digitata* or *Phyllobolus digitata*, this species is one of nature's true curiosities. Photo by Kurt Zadnik.

Brownanthus cf. *pubescens*, jointed like a succulent bamboo.

Like hunched over pilgrims with flowers on their backs, *Phyllobolus digitata* in bloom.

Psilocaulon cf. *dinteri*, stretched out on a Richtersveld beach.

PHYLLOBOLUS AND OTHER SHORE DWELLERS

Only one nonconforming member of *Phyllobolus* out of over thirty species has achieved a certain renown. The typical members of the genus, often found growing by the Atlantic coast, creep along unprepossessingly, dying back almost into nothingness during their summer rest period. They are rarely cultivated, though surprisingly attractive species occasionally show up in specialist collections.

The exception is **Phyllobolus digitata**, long known as *Dactylopsis digitata* ("fingerlike finger"). The plants occur in several places in the Knersvlakte. Each of their growths consists of two closely paired leaves, jointed and growing at an angle like a finger and thumb. When fully turgid, plants resemble pale green rubber gloves sticking out of the ground, the count of fingers depending on the size

of the plant. A particularly large plant may have over a dozen finger and thumb combinations. The "fingers" feel exactly like they look, like a rubber glove blown up with air. **Variety littlewoodii** resembles a miniature version of the typical plant with half-sized "fingers" 3 inches (8 cm) tall, and "thumb" and "finger" set apart at a greater angle.

During less rainy winters the plants are much smaller, and in the dry summers they shrink away into shriveled husks, producing their white flowers at the end of their dormancy. Their growing season lasts three or four months, during which time the scanty rain is supplemented by fog. Still, in a good year dense stands of turgid plants color the quartz fields green. Afterwards the plants endure the next eight or nine months with no water at all. Their extraordinary appearance led to odd theories about their cultivation, but in reality, though not easy to grow, they are far from impossible. They need intense light, extremely fast draining soil devoid of organic matter, and water about every two weeks during the few months of their winter growing season.

Other rarely grown mesembs from the South African seacoasts include **Brownanthus pubescens**, with jointed stems and sometimes looking like a miniature bamboo. Also jointed but prostrate, **Psilocaulon dinteri** lies flat on Richtersveld beaches, looking like a eurypterid, the long-extinct sea scorpions of four hundred million years ago.

DROSANTHEMUM, DELOSPERMA, LAMPRANTHUS, AND ICE PLANT RELATIVES

Many genera and hundreds of species of ground-covering and shrub-forming mesembs go under the very loosely applied rubric of ice plant. The name originated from the shining water-storage cells on the leaf surfaces of many species, glistening like ice crystals, but it has expanded to include many not necessarily closely related plants that spread and clump readily. For example, whether by human agency or not, several **Carpobrotus** species have colonized many coastal areas of the world where they cover untold hundreds of square miles of seashore and highway embankments. A few ice plant types deserve special mention, however. Despite their general rampant growth habit, true miniatures such as **Delosperma sphalmanthoides** are tucked away within almost every genus, awaiting horticultural discovery.

Starting with some of the more compact growers, **Cylindrophyllum**, with cylindrical leaves and pale yellow blossoms, remains medium sized and is occasionally cultivated. **Conicosia**, though often short-lived, has managed to establish itself in both Australia and the Cal-

A large *Ruschia* species coloring up the bleak countryside south of Namibia. Photo by Rob Skillin.

Much smaller, this spiny *Ruschia* aff. *centrocapsula* grows farther south in Namaqualand. Photo by Kurt Zadnik.

ifornia coast. The thirty-plus species of **Cephalophyllum**, winter growers with smaller and larger growing versions, are valuable because of their sometimes bicolored, extremely showy flowers, with a great diversity of colors found among the different species. **Cephalophyllum**

Cephalophyllum compactum, brilliantly yellow flowered.

The brilliant orange flowers of *Lampranthus glaucoides* almost defy photography.

Mesembryanthemum crystallinum established along the Baja California coast. Photo by Terry Thompson.

Mesembryanthemum barklyi, a Namaqualand species with neat, geometrically arranged foliage.

alstonii has bright red flowers, **C. compactum** flowers are shining yellow.

Oscularia deltoides, spreading but relatively restrained, has toothed, blue-white leaves and almond-scented, small pink-lavender flowers. *Ruschia*, still in-

cluding more than two hundred species, ranges from large mounding shrubs to a few smaller plants such as **R. spinosa** and **R. centrocapsula** that, very atypically for the family, have stiff spines.

Drosanthemum, *Delosperma* and *Lampranthus* are the classic ice plant genera, each with well over a hundred species. Of the three, delospermas tend to have small sometimes hairy or glistening leaves and relatively small flowers. They range as far north as Somalia and Yemen, though their center of distribution is in eastern South Africa. With larger leaves, *Drosanthemum*, from much of South Africa and Namibia, spreads vigorously; some species mound up. Its large shining flowers of almost every color have ensured its popularity as an easy, reliable ground cover. **Drosanthemum bicolor** is multicolored.

Smaller growing, shorter, and not quite as hardy, *Lampranthus* species produce solid masses of flowers of extraordinary brilliance. Though less suited for ground covers, they still deserve a spot in any dry-growing garden that can accommodate them. Outstanding species include yellow- to orange- to red-flowered **L. glaucoides**, the red- to pink-, sometimes yellow-flowered **L. roseus**, and the purple-flowered **L. haworthii**.

Lastly, to the genus that gave its name to this entire aggregation of plants, *Mesembryanthemum* itself. Rarely cultivated, often quite unattractive, and generally dying after flowering, the species do not look like any of the other members of this enormous group. Their leaves, typically triangular and flattened, may also be cylindrical or round; larger versions of the triangular ones may have wavy margins and resemble the sinuate foliage of *Kalanchoe beharensis*.

Many species are covered with water storage cells that give them the crystalline look exemplified by **Mesembryanthemum crystallinum**, a small-leafed but widely spreading species that has managed to take hold in warm, dry seashore localities worldwide. Though smaller species typically are annuals, larger species can be long lived. Often mounding, with floppy leaves and capable of covering large areas of arid landscape, stands of some of these larger plants look something like a vegetable trash yard. Other larger species, however, such as **M. barklyi**, with sharply geometric shapes and a more restrained growth habit, could prove rewarding subjects for cultivation, which in a loose, sandy soil should be problem free.

Chapter 15

Anacampseros and Its Relatives

ALTHOUGH BASED ON their vegetative appearance it might seem unlikely, *Anacampseros* and other members of the *Portulaca* complex share a relationship with mesembryanthemums, cacti, and the Madagascan tree-like succulents of the Didiereaceae. Botanists long believed that the unique set of chemicals that give a particularly glowing quality to the flowers of these families implied a relationship between them. DNA analysis has confirmed the connection, although further muddling the situation by suggesting that major divisions within the old Portulacaceae may be as closely related to cacti and the other families as to each other. This finding has led to the division of the group into a greatly reduced Portulacaceae, and several new families. Other major taxonomic changes may well be forthcoming, but for now, at least, it still makes sense to discuss these fairly closely related plants within a single chapter. First we will look at five Old World genera: *Anacampseros* and *Avonia* in Anacampserotaceae, *Talinum* in Talinaceae, and *Portulacaria* and *Ceraria* now ensconced in Didiereaceae. Then we will consider four New World genera: *Cistanthe*, *Lewisia*, and *Phemeranthus* in Montiaceae, and *Portulaca* in Portulacaceae.

ANACAMPSEROS

The best-known succulent genus of the *Portulaca* alliance, *Anacampseros*, ranges over much of South Africa, and enters Namibia and Botswana as well. Several rather uninteresting affiliated species live in South America and Australia. In the wild, anacampseros show up almost anywhere succulents can live, on bare rocks fully exposed to the sun or in the partial shade of the miniature worlds found beneath sparsely branched shrubs. Some seek out the relative shelter and richer soil of eastern South Africa, while others have colonized the inhospitable empty lands of the northwest. Within its less than twenty species

Anacampseros displays a surprising variety, with considerable variation found in individual species as well, making field identification difficult.

No anacampseros become large, but several have a spreading growth habit. Their branches are more-or-less densely clad with loose rosettes of wedge-shaped succulent leaves, which in bright light often turn a distinctive purple-brown. Various species of this type occur over the whole geographic range of the genus, from Free State and KwaZulu-Natal in eastern South Africa to Namaqualand in the far west. Among them are ***Anacampseros rufescens***, ***A. telephiastrum***, ***A. lanceolata***, and ***A. arachnoides***.

As a rule, as the plants move from the relatively lush central and eastern parts of the country to the more arid regions of summer drought in the north and west, their leaves (and often overall size) steadily shrink. Relatively robust plants such as ***Anacampseros lanceolata* subsp. *nebrownii***, from about 100 miles (160 km) northeast of Cape Town, dwarf the very rare *A. pisina*, from drier, climatically more extreme regions to the north and west. The smaller plant retains the proportionately large leaves of this group, but its generally shrunken form demonstrates the effect of environmental stress as does its tuberous root.

In contrast to the nearly hairless (glabrous) leaves of *Anacampseros lanceolata* and *A. rufescens*, *A. arachnoides* has leaves streaked with strands of cottonlike material. Along with differences in seed structure, the distinction between plants with glabrous and tomentose leaves counts a great deal in determining the taxonomic divisions of the genus.

With its broader leaves, *Anacampseros telephiastrum* may resemble *A. rufescens*. Like many anacampseros, it is quite variable. Leaves may be larger or smaller, and plants range from having stems solidly covered with leaves to largely bare stems with a rosette at the apex.

A second group of anacampseros species, especially

difficult to sort out, consists of smaller plants with small densely packed leaves, generally quite tomentose, and with stems that tend to grow into little upright columns. These plants include a number of quite distinct forms previously considered separate species, though currently only three species names retain universal acceptance: *Anacampseros filamentosa*, *A. albidiflora*, and *A. baeseckei*.

Anacampseros filamentosa includes three subspecies: **filamentosa**, **tomentosa**, and **namaquensis**. Often considered a distinct species in its own right, subsp. *namaquensis* is very variable with both tomentose and hairless forms. Examples of subsp. *filamentosa* also exhibit a great deal of variety, with plants more or less densely covered with fuzzy wool. Taxonomically speaking, the significant difference between subsp. *filamentosa* and the white-flowered *A. albidiflora* is primarily a minute difference in seed size. The two species are hardly distinguishable.

Anacampseros baeseckei may be easier to recognize, but it too shows a lot of variation, forming dense masses of highly tomentose, densely leafed little columns, shorter or taller according to both environment and heredity. Farther east, in the heart of Bushmanland, a distinct form of *A. baeseckei*, which may merit taxonomic status of its own, sends up a few leafy columns bristling with long, attractively orange-brown hairs.

A third group of anacampseros consists of several dwarfed species, not necessarily closely related, that form short-stemmed rosettes. These attractive miniatures include **Anacampseros marlothii** and **A. subnuda**. Considered a form of *A. rufescens* by some, *A. marlothii* grows at high altitudes and forms dense clumps of *Sempervivum*-like thin-leafed, green rosettes. The eastern South African *A. subnuda* and its **subspecies lubbersii** have shiny, rounded leaf-tips that turn bright pink in good light.

Anacampseros telephiastrum, very variable, with flowers ready to open later in the day.

Anacampseros aff. *pisina*, from a dry habitat, with reduced leaves and a somewhat enlarged stem.

Anacampseros lanceolata subsp. *nebrownii*, typical of the larger growing species.

Anacampseros baeseckei, with columns of leaves densely clad in feltlike hairs. Photo by Kurt Zadnik.

From the mountains of central South Africa, *Anacampseros marlothii* maintains a low profile suited for dry, semialpine conditions.

Anacampseros cf. *subnuda* subsp. *lubbersii*, short, shiny and with flowers very typical of the entire genus.

Anacampseros subnuda—with denser hair it would look like *A. baeseckei* and its relatives.

Anacampseros retusa, near the Atlantic Ocean not far north of Cape Town. Photo by Rob Skillin.

Widespread in western South Africa, *A. retusa* rarely receives enough light in cultivation to retain its tight rosette. If grown perfectly it can be a beautifully symmetrical little plant, with single heads not more than 1.5 inch (4 cm) across. In time it forms compact little clumps.

Other diminutive rosette formers are smaller still and stranger. One such plant, **Anacampseros wiesei**, sometimes considered a variety of *A. retusa*, comes from a highly localized, quartz field in the Knersvlakte. It forms tiny rosettes, almost invisible under dense cottony fibers.

Other infrequently cultivated miniature anacampseros similarly live hidden away in the harsh hills and stony flats of northwestern South Africa and southern Namibia. The cryptic Richtersveld species **Anacampseros karasmontana**, covered with long strands resembling threads of cotton-wool, usually remains pulled down low amid the sandy soil and quartz pebbles of its sun-blasted

Anacampseros wiesei, a quartz field miniature, leaves almost invisible under dense white wool.

habitat. Also densely tufted with fuzzy wool, extremely tiny, and exceedingly rare, the white-flowered *A. scopata* finds its home in a kloof or two on a single southern Richtersveld hillside. Even a multiheaded specimen, growing out of a miniature caudexlike stem, will never reach an inch (2.5 cm) in diameter.

Anacampseros comptonii, just slightly larger, has chosen a most unlikely habitat. It lives in the mountains at the southeast edge of Namaqualand, where it develops an almost completely buried caudex about a half inch (13 mm) tall and broad. From this a few tiny rounded leaves come forth to produce an approximate rosette. *Anacampseros comptonii* grows in natural pans of shallow, sandy soil that overlie rocky plates. These fill with water in the winter rainy season, resulting in the plants' complete submergence for surprisingly long periods, even though in cultivation they need dry treatment to survive.

The large-leafed anacampseros of the first group thrive in cultivation. Some will tolerate a few degrees of frost and winter rain if planted out in well-drained soil in areas of moderate climate. Most anacampseros are self-fertile, and the tendency to produce numerous seedlings can lead to an overabundance of them in a collection. Furthermore, if kept next to each other, new plants of various kinds will spring up in the same pot, making identification difficult. Other than that, in containers they present few problems, requiring reasonably bright light, a typical fast-draining succulent soil mix and regular watering with a fairly dry rest period in winter. Their usually large, glowing cerise to pink or sometimes white flowers, however, generally do not open until late afternoon, and even then only under conditions of bright sunlight.

The more dwarfed plants benefit from brighter light, the more densely white haired ones liking more light. The smaller plants also prefer somewhat more rigorous drainage and dormancy.

The tuberous-rooted and miniature anacampseros will produce a specimen plant in a 2-inch (5-cm) pot, but they can challenge even an experienced grower. They need extremely good drainage, very bright light, and, in common with some of the second group, are treated best as winter growers, with a dry summer rest period. In places with very bright light in winter it is possible to grow these plants in accordance with their natural cycles. In regions with less reliable winter sun, such as coastal central California, a fairly dry rest in summer, more water in spring and autumn, and occasional winter water when the weather is bright enough to justify it will work. Where the winter sun is even dimmer, switching the plants to a summer watering schedule is an option, but success may be transitory and limited.

Extremely robust examples of the rare, usually cryptic *Anacampseros karasmontana*. Photo by Rob Skillin.

Anacampseros comptonii, emerging from an underground rest. Photo by Kurt Zadnik.

AVONIA

Considered a division within *Anacampseros* until the early 1980s, *Avonia* provided a taxonomic home for about a dozen species of plants that all seemed quite similar to each other and different from everything else. Ranging in size from small to genuinely miniature, individual plants of *Avonia* consist of tufts of elongated branches radiating from either a nearly hidden main stem or a partly underground caudex. Although the stems bear leaves along their entire length, these leaves, reduced to little more than green specks, stay concealed beneath dense sheaths of overlapping white stipules. Consequently, avonias bear more resemblance to clusters of little white worms than they do to a typical member of the vegetable kingdom.

Most avonias inhabit arid regions of northwestern South Africa, often hiding among quartz blocks in the Richtersveld, Bushmanland, and adjacent Namibia. A single species, **Avonia rhodesica**, occurs far to the east and north, in the Transvaal region and Zimbabwe and then, after a several-thousand-mile gap, shows up in Somalia as well.

The white-shingled branches of avonias may remain low to the ground or reach up into the air; some will rise up as they get ready to flower, and they may follow the sun during the course of a bright day. Their extraordinary appearance has given rise to various theories about the plants, for instance that they mimic bird droppings. The extensive avonia colonies that crop up in plain sight and full sun on otherwise barren sandy, gravelly flats certainly are not dependent on these forms of camouflage, however. In fact, they sometimes thrive in areas where grazing goats have chewed almost everything else into nonexistence. Maybe avonias just do not look like food, or, perhaps the plants simply are extremely unpalatable.

Though all avonias, by definition, produce small clusters of branches completely covered by their overlapping silvery white scalelike stipules, there is a considerable range in the appearance of the various species. The broadest branches of the genus belong to **Avonia papyracea**, from the Karoos of western South Africa, and its northwestern **subspecies** *namaensis*. In this species the rounded stipules may give the plants a sort of "puffy" look.

Similar, but with narrower branches and a perhaps sleeker appearance, **Avonia albissima** ("whitest") occupies much of the same territory, but also grows farther to the north in Namibia, and east into Bushmanland. Despite its name, individual plants of *A. albissima* may have scales marked by a dark spot near their tips.

Variations in scale shape and form provide much of the difference in *Avonia* species. In contrast to the smoothly rounded scales of *A. papyracea* and *A. albissima*, **A. ruschii** has scales that flare out at their tips, while the shaggy scales of **A. recurvata** result in a looser coverage that allows a peek at the residual green leaves beneath.

Avonia papyracea, thick stems with rounded scales and always very white, in Bushmanland. Photo by Kurt Zadnik.

Avonia albissima, often with dark spots despite its name. Photo by Rob Skillin.

With one exception the other avonias sort themselves out along a continuum of size and shape. Some, like **Avonia ustulata**, rebranch into little tangles, some are shaggier, some with more pointed stipules, some grayer or darker colored, and so forth. **Avonia quinaria subsp. alstonii** and, to a lesser degree, its smaller, rarely cultivated cousin *A. quinaria* subsp. *quinaria*, however, look entirely different. These are small caudiciforms with a flat-topped, partly underground caudex. Multitudes of short, narrow, but otherwise typical avonia branches grow from the caudex, along with the occasional surprisingly large flower, silvery white or slightly pinkish in subspecies *alstonii*, red-purple in subspecies *quinaria*. Widely distributed over most of *Avonia* territory, they attain surprisingly large dimensions, many having a caudex 4 to 6 inches (10 to 15 cm) or even more in diameter, topped with hundreds of inch-long (2.5-cm) branches. The centers of

Avonia recurvata, one of five *Avonia* species on a single tiny Bushmanland hill. Photo by Kurt Zadnik.

Avonia quinaria subsp. *alstonii*, an old plant, also growing in Bushmanland quartz. Photo by Kurt Zadnik.

old plants may rot out, turning them into semblances of ghostly sea anemones, strangely relocated from the ocean to the white pebbles of a Richtersveld quartz field.

Avonias are not easy in cultivation, although many of them reseed quite readily and produce new plants to continue on in case the older ones perish. They grow in both winter- and summer-rainfall areas, but more importantly they grow in regions of low rainfall and minimal atmospheric humidity. Watering them about every ten days in spring and fall, and occasionally during bright winter days, in combination with summer dryness should keep them relatively happy. In dimmer areas, a regimen of infrequent water beginning in spring and continuing through fall may work. Alternatively, observing the plants closely, watering them when they are actively growing and drying them off when they are not is worth a try. In any case, a particularly rapid draining mix and

extremely bright light are necessary for their survival. In areas of minimal humidity they can withstand a fair amount of frost, but damp air will kill these fantastic-looking plants quicker than cold.

TALINUM

The genus *Talinum* has undergone extensive revision and has lost many of its succulent members. One of the remaining ones, **Talinum caffrum**, ranges from Namibia and South Africa as far north as Kenya. Plants form a fairly good-sized tuberous root and thin branches, vining or sprawling with semisucculent, lanceolate leaves that resemble the foliage of some *Anacampseros* species. Plants should receive a bit of shade and standard succulent soil and water.

PORTULACARIA AND CERARIA

With one intriguing exception, the few species of *Ceraria* and *Portulacaria* consist of small bushes or fairly large shrubs with somewhat succulent stems, branches, and leaves. Distinguishing which of the two genera the plants belong to can be difficult, as the key difference between them consists of the placement of their inflorescence—lateral in *Ceraria* and terminal in *Portulacaria*. For practical purposes, it is easier to tell the plants apart by the relative size of their leaves—smaller in *Ceraria*, larger in *Portulacaria*.

Both genera are found in South Africa and Namibia, often in extremely localized and desolate habitats in the areas near the Atlantic coast. By far the best known of the group, **Portulacaria afra**, ranges far from its relatives over a much wider area, from the Little Karoo east through most of the rest of the country. Known locally as *spekboom*, plants of *P. afra* consist of a spray of erect, somewhat arching branches, fleshy and dark brown or almost purple, covered with secondary branchlets that bear 0.5- to 1-inch (13- to 25-mm) wide, fleshy, medium green leaves. Easy to cultivate, spekbooms have been grown for centuries in Europe as well as in South Africa. In warmer regions of the United States they are used as loose, low, succulent hedges. Though shy blooming in containers, in suitable areas such as Southern California plants allowed to grow to maturity in the ground flower fairly readily.

Confined to the surroundings of the Orange River in southern Namibia and the Richtersveld, **Portulacaria armiana** is a much more interesting plant. Though also a

An old plant of *Portulacaria pygmaea,* with tiny barely visible white flowers.

Ceraria namaquensis—some forms grow or can be groomed into interesting shapes. Photo by Terry Thompson.

changes of its own. Formerly classified in *Ceraria,* it shares the same general habitat as *P. armiana,* but extends into the foggy desert coasts of the Richtersveld as well as the arid interior. Plants consist of a semihemispherical, partially underground caudex that produces a few short, rather woody succulent branches covered with slightly peeling bark. In the wild these branches remain short and plants gradually form a mound up to a foot (30 cm) across and half as tall. Their succulent, bluish green leaves have an odd, spathulate, almost rectangular shape, and they produce tiny pinkish white flowers in small clusters from the tips of their irregularly shaped branchlets. Small but striking caudiciforms, mature plants of *P. pygmaea* remain rare in cultivation. Their branches will root, but it is not clear if the rooted cuttings ever develop a caudex.

The true cerarias grow into good-sized shrubs, with branches covered with rows or minirosettes of tiny elliptical, almost terete succulent leaves resembling miniaturized versions of portulacaria foliage. Though not extreme succulents, the peculiar texture of their whitish gray to pale brownish purple stems, midway between leather and shiny plastic, has a certain intriguing, unworldly quality. Nothing else exactly resembles them, though the organization of their foliage does resemble some of the Madagascan Didiereaceae. Unlike many large-growing succulent shrubs, cerarias produce a reasonable facsimile of their mature form as small plants in a container. In parts of southwestern Namibia characterized by extremes of wind and weather plants grow very low to the ground, taking the form of a natural bonsai, perhaps something to aim for in cultivation. Neither the somewhat smaller **Ceraria fruticulosa** nor the larger *C. namaquensis,* up to 6 feet (1.8 m) tall, are common in cultivation, but they do show up from time to time as interesting oddities.

As indicated earlier, *Portulacaria afra* is easy to grow, and any generalized succulent-growing regimen will work. Because of their restricted, odd habitats, the other species would seem likely to be quite touchy, but that does not seem to be the case. With its variable habitat, *P. pygmaea* may be subjected to frequent fog during the otherwise dry Richtersveld summer, but it grows in fogless regions as well. In cultivation it seems to do best with extremely bright light and not too much water any time of year, with just a moderate drop in the frequency of watering to encourage partial summer dormancy. A similar approach seems appropriate for *P. armiana,* although unlike many summer-dormant plants it does not react badly if watered out of season.

densely branched, bushy shrub, its leaves, of an almost rubbery texture, can reach about 2 or 3 inches (5 to 8 cm) in length and sometimes have a strange, bluish yellow color. The most striking feature of this species is its enormous, perennial flower stalk, emerging unexpectedly from an otherwise modestly proportioned plant and stretching 6 to 9 feet (1.8 to 2.7 m) towards the sun.

Portulacaria pygmaea, the miniature standout among this group of plants, has undergone a few taxonomic

From the arid Chilean coast, this *Cistanthe* species was growing among cacti and terrestrial bromeliads. Photo by Inge Hoffman.

When growing, the summer-dormant *Cistanthe guadalupensis* resembles some succulent composites. Photo by Terry Thompson.

Ceraria namaquensis loses its leaves during the summer drought in the wild, but in cultivation retains its leaves year-round, and it tolerates water whether in winter or summer. In areas of lower light, such as Europe or northeastern North America, more care with water both in summer and winter is probably a good idea. The plants do not seem particularly fussy about soil as long as it drains quickly.

CISTANTHE

Previously classified variously as *Talinum* or *Calandrinia*, *Cistanthe* species grow in dry parts of South America and Mexico. One in particular, **C. guadalupensis**, is prized by collectors. Endemic to Guadalupe Island off the coast of Baja California, it is a summer-deciduous plant with a stocky stem and short, rounded branches. In active growth it makes a rosette of slightly succulent, bluish leaves. Well-grown specimens need extremely bright light to keep from etiolating and make interesting additions to any collection of caudiciforms and pachycauls. Several similar species, longer stemmed and with very succulent leaves, live along the dry coast of Chile. Except for their typical *Portulaca*-type flowers, magenta, wide open, and five-petaled, the plants look almost exactly like Mexican Crassulaceae such as *Pachyphytum*.

LEWISIA AND PHEMERANTHUS

Although most *Lewisia* species are known as Pacific Northwest rock garden plants, **L. rediviva**, the bitterroot, ranges far beyond the coastal mountains into the semiarid landscapes of states such as Idaho and Montana and south into the truly dry Great Basin. In central Utah I have seen it right next to the extremely arid-growing *Sclerocactus spinosior*. Basically, it is a geophyte, with a small rosette of thickly succulent, but fairly ephemeral leaves that grow from a thickened, tuberous root. After its leaves drop, it sends out a flower stalk with very *Anacampseros*-like flowers.

A second species, as narrow in its range as *Lewisia rediviva* is widespread, is the closely related **L. maguirei**

At over 9000 feet (2700 m) elevation, this *Lewisia maguirei* was close to a stand of bristlecone pines.

Phemeranthus brevifolius, found in pockets of sandy soil in Utah's pinyon and juniper country.

A Brazilian example of the South American portulacas, mostly unknown in cultivation. Photo by Rob Skillin.

(synonym *L. rediviva* subsp. *maguirei*), endemic to a few black limestone outcrops high in the mountains of central eastern Nevada. With a slimmer tuber than the bitterroot, *L. maguirei* also retains its terete, lanceolate, succulent leaves a little longer. Undoubtedly difficult to grow and extremely rare, it is just as well that *L. maguirei* remains sequestered in its isolated mountain home.

Essentially under the radar of succulent plant growers, several species of *Phemeranthus*, western mountain and plateau endemics, nonetheless deserve acknowledgment as succulent plants. **Phemeranthus spinescens**, a compact, creeping plant, forms low, many-branched mounds tipped with elliptical succulent leaves in basalt formations east of the Cascades in Washington State. **Phemeranthus brevifolius** is smaller but with large flowers that are generally pink, occasionally white. This species looks almost identical to some higher-altitude *Anacampseros* species. It lives on slick rock slopes and thin, sandy soil in the mountains of Utah, Arizona, and New Mexico, and would make an interesting addition to collections of cold-resistant succulents.

PORTULACA

Portulaca species are native both to South America and Africa. The best-known species of the namesake genus of the family, **Portulaca grandiflora**, is a widely grown annual originally from Brazil. It has many small branches covered with semisucculent, linear leaves and large bright flowers in many colors. Most portulacas, many of them annuals, are fairly weedy and of no real horticultural interest. Some species from dry parts of Argentina and Brazil, however, deserve a closer look. These are less sprawling and have more succulent leaves and proportionately large vividly colored flowers. Many of them die back in late autumn, but their tuberous roots send up new shoots every spring. Although they enjoy more water than most succulents when in growth, they remain content in a 3- or 4-inch (8- to 10-cm) pot. Very rarely grown and difficult to identify, these small South American plants have definite horticultural potential. These portulacas, along with many other relatively unknown succulent members of the alliance, deserve wider recognition among growers, though few can be expected to attain the popularity of either *Avonia* or its *Anacampseros* cousins.

Chapter 16

Pelargonium and *Monsonia*: Succulent Geraniums

Growing up in Southern California I thought pelargoniums, or geraniums as everyone called them, were not much better than weeds, common plants of no real interest. As I became interested in succulents, however, I began to learn about some uncommon members of the Geraniaceae, the xerophytic pelargoniums and their relatives the succulent monsonias. Mostly winter growers and adapted for survival under hostile circumstances, these South African and Namibian plants have little in common with their domesticated cousins.

PELARGONIUM

Deciding which of the numerous species of *Pelargonium* is a succulent and which is not requires us to consider the rather arbitrary nature of the term *succulent plant*: a plant with morphological modifications that enhance the storage of water. To a greater or lesser degree, almost all pelargoniums fit the bill, yet no succulent collector would consider a typical flowering "geranium" to be a succulent. The pelargoniums thought of as rare and desirable suc-

culents are those that are stranger and more difficult to cultivate. In other words, there are no objective criteria, just a general, not always unanimous, agreement by the people concerned.

In any case, a fairly large number of *Pelargonium* species have caught the attention of succulent growers while remaining almost unknown to the rest of the horticultural world. Among these are several with thick, succulent stems and a disproportionately small amount of foliage. Valued primarily for their striking shapes, their flowers are considered a kind of bonus. One of them, ***P. crithmifolium***, a good-sized plant with an extensive range along the Atlantic coast as far north as Namibia, has finely dissected leaves and knobby branches sometimes almost as thick as an arm. These branches reach outward in all directions from a shortened central stem, then curve upward. The zigzagging inflorescences persist and dry into pointed tangles after the white, red-centered flowers drop.

Also with dissected leaves and smaller, mostly white flowers, ***Pelargonium carnosum***, from Namaqualand and

Pelargonium crithmifolium retains its woody inflorescence after flowering. Photo by Rob Skillin.

Pelargonium carnosum, low to the ground in its home on the desolate Richtersveld coast. Photo by Rob Skillin.

Pelargonium crassicaule, a survivor of many hard years, with new growth emerging from the old.

Pelargonium klinghardtense, very slow growing, in almost pure sand. Photo by Kurt Zadnik.

north into the Richtersveld, can occasionally reach 18 inches (45 cm) in height, but usually is considerably smaller. In the harsh conditions of the windy, arid Richtersveld coast, plants composed of a few, thickly succulent branches hug the ground. Sharing this coastal habitat, the dwarf *P. crassicaule* has sparse, crinkled, ovate leaves (sometimes lobed) covered more-or-less densely with soft, silver-blue hairs, and extremely thick, more or less horizontally growing stems, often blasted almost black by the harsh winds. In habitat, old plants of *P. crassicaule* may resemble little weather-beaten boulders, no higher than they are wide, with sprigs of foliage poking out and a few flowers, mostly white marked with purple, on top.

From the Richtersveld and across the Orange River into Namibia, the slow-growing *Pelargonium klinghardtense* has a few upright, smooth, pale, extremely succulent stems and sparsely distributed leaves, themselves marginally succulent and whitish green. Its white flowers complete the picture of a striking but somewhat bleached looking plant up to 2 feet (60 cm) tall growing in sand or in cracks in the sun-bleached rocks. Somewhat similar but smaller, with a waxy coating on its thick, cylindrical stems and hardened, persistent petioles (leaf bases), *P. ceratophyllum* continues farther north into Namibia.

A second succulent pelargonium lifestyle consists of keeping the main stems or tuberous roots underground to survive extensive dry periods. Many of these species form rosettes of leaves so finely dissected that they resemble the fronds of ferns. Others have entire, lobed, or distantly pinnate (featherlike) leaves. In the wild, the plants seem essentially stemless, leafy rosettes flush with the ground or raised up on long petioles. During their dormant period, usually summer, the plants disappear from view.

Several of them, such as *Pelargonium dolomiticum*, an atypical summer grower that ranges from central Namibia east to Gauteng Province in South Africa, and *P. aridum*, develop fairly good-sized, dome-shaped caudices. In cultivation, raising the caudex above the soil level will help prevent the plants from rotting as well as increase their eye-appeal.

Others, such as fern-leafed *Pelargonium rapaceum* and *P. appendiculatum*, with thinner, less dramatic tubers, do better with their leafy rosettes kept at soil level. From the Eastern Cape, another summer grower, *P. bowkeri*, resembles them, but is easier to keep alive than many of this type. The foliage of *P. pinnatum*, though obviously pinnately divided, is not so finely dissected; it grows in dry parts of central-southern South Africa, from Ceres east to the town of Albertinia. Long cultivated, *P. triste*, widespread though restricted to the winter-rainfall area, grows larger and lankier than most of these geophytic species.

Pelargonium hirsutum gradually forms a mound of old leaf bases; it has striking flowers, dark purple and basally white, as well as variably pinnate leaves. Simple-leafed geophytes include *P. barklyi*, whose rounded leaves have a convoluted, blistery surface; the rare *P. ellaphieae*, with elongated, lanceolate leaves; and *P. sibthorpiifolium*, with ovate leaves covered with fine silky hairs and resembling those of *P. crassicaule*, but dark gray-green rather than bluish white. It branches above the soil surface, but the branches remain small and keep very close to the ground.

The fern-leafed *Pelargonium appendiculatum* often produces its narrow yellow flowers before it leafs out.

Pelargonium bowkeri successively puts out a variety of foliage during its summer growing season.

With large red flowers and dense foliage, *Pelargonium fulgidum* seems unsuited for its very arid habitat. Photo by Kurt Zadnik.

A third, varied assortment of succulent pelargoniums does not resemble either the very thick-stemmed species or the geophytes. **Pelargonium crassipes** has fern-leafed foliage but forms an erect, somewhat branching stem. Its petioles persist, become dry and hard, and bend downward, providing the plant with a degree of protection from predators. Several other species have modified stipules, thin and barely bristly in the case of the erect-growing Richtersveld species **P. fulgidum**, noted for its large bright scarlet flowers. In **P. echinatum** the stipules have developed into definite spines, though the plant itself is a fairly normal looking small shrub, with thin branches and white flowers decorated on their upper petals with little red-violet hearts. **Pelargonium hystrix**, from locali-

ties in Bushmanland and the Tanqua and Ceres Karoos marked by extreme temperature swings and intense aridity, has short, thick, mostly horizontal succulent stems covered with stocky, sharp, triangular stipular spines.

The unlikely looking **Pelargonium gibbosum** produces long, thin clambering stems that swell disproportionately at each branching node, ultimately resembling a mass of sausages strung out on long, tangled strings. **Pelargonium cotyledonis**, from isolated St. Helena Island in the middle of the South Atlantic Ocean (where Napoleon was exiled), has crinkled, lush green, sort of bubble-textured leaves, a fairly thick, branching succulent stem, and dense clusters of large white flowers. **Pelargonium xerophyton**, from dry northwestern South Africa, and **P.**

Pelargonium cotyledonis, probably the only cultivated succulent from the island of St. Helena. Photo by Terry Thompson.

Surprisingly rare in cultivation, Pelargonium sericifolium produces its gaudy, two-toned flowers in a few spots in the southern Richtersveld.

Pelargonium xerophyton, a miniature winter-growing succulent bush.

magenteum, which ranges east to the Little Karoo, form dense, intricately branched, ultimately hemispherical little shrubs covered with small crisp-margined leaves.

A Richtersveld resident, **Pelargonium sericifolium** differs from most of the succulent pelargoniums in its production of masses of 2-inch (5-cm), brilliantly colored, cerise and magenta flowers. A spreading plant, it remains low to the ground and seems less succulent than many other species, though it shares its stony habitat with conophytums, arid-growing medusoid euphorbias, and other dry-living specialists. Lastly, with long stems that clamber through and over nearby growth, **P. praemorsum** puts forth large beautifully veined blossoms that look like butterflies (see photo on page 181). Each blossom is up to 4 inches (10 cm) in diameter. The plant sometimes grows at the very tops of granite domes, where extra moisture collects during the winter rainy season, temporarily turning these bleak outcrops into little garden spots.

With relatively few exceptions the more highly modified succulent pelargoniums such as these grow in the winter and should be rested in summer. Rapidly draining soil and water every ten days or two weeks once the new leaves develop is best. It is difficult to keep the proportions of thick-stemmed species such as *Pelargonium crithmifolium* as compact in cultivation as in the wild; they tend to etiolate unless kept in the brightest possible light. Though the larger species are not terribly fussy about receiving occasional water when dormant, many geophytes need complete dryness once their leaves drop and their rest period begins. Finally, even though St. Helena is far from a desert, *P. cotyledonis* should also be watered quite sparingly.

MONSONIA

The members of the second succulent genus of Geraniaceae, for a long time known as *Sarcocaulon*, have now been placed within *Monsonia*, which otherwise consists of small, sometimes annual, herbaceous plants, occasionally with somewhat tuberous roots. The other monsonias are of little if any interest to succulent growers, and the ones under discussion here will be the ex-sarcocaulons.

Inhabitants of some of the most desolate parts of winter-rainfall areas in Namibia and South Africa, these monsonias regularly endure conditions of extreme drought, aided by the waxy composition of their bark, which keeps them from desiccating entirely. In habitat they may remain leafless for several years at a time. Everything about them is bizarre except their pretty flowers, symmetrical, good sized, five-petaled, papery textured, and reminiscent of moisture-loving, horticulturally popular species of *Geranium*.

The succulent monsonias come in two forms. One type has reduced simple ovate leaves and very spiny stems. In habitat several of these species form a stout upright stem that, after reaching about an inch (2.5 cm) in height,

Living on uninviting desert pavement, *Monsonia patersonii* greets the start of a wet winter with a burst of flowers and foliage. Photo by Kurt Zadnik.

Monsonia ciliata makes its home in the slightly more hospitable Namaqualand flats.

This large tall, very spiny bush, *Monsonia spinosa*, lives on top of an eroded granite dome. The large white flowers in the background belong to the clambering *Pelargonium praemorsum*.

produces absolutely horizontal branches up to a foot (30 cm) or more long. The plants look like they are hugging the ground, but actually they are raised just above it. **Monsonia patersonii**, from northern Richtersveld coastal sandy flats, becomes covered with bright pink flowers during a good rainy season, with colonies of the plants lending patches of vivid color to the generally barren landscape. An even spinier variant, sometimes considered the separate species **M. lavranii**, coexists on the red

sandy plains of southwestern Namibia with hoodias, dry-growing bulbs, dwarfed euphorbias, and, rather surprisingly, an occasional wandering chameleon.

The several yellow-flowering species include the low-growing **Monsonia ciliata** and **M. flavescens**, and the brighter yellow-flowered **M. spinosa**. The latter, up to 3 or 4 feet (90 to 120 cm) tall, is often found in somewhat sheltered nooks on tops of weathered granite domes and koppies, where the plants receive a bit more moisture.

This very spiny *Monsonia crassicaule* was growing in the very arid south Namibian winter-rainfall area, though others grow in summer-rainfall parts of South Africa. Photo by Rob Skillin.

Growing in a mix of cracked rock and sand, *Monsonia multifida* flourishes in some of the driest places on the planet. Photo by Rob Skillin.

The northernmost species, ***Monsonia mossamedensis***, ranges from central Namibia into Angola, both in the summer-rainfall interior and the northern Namibian Atlantic coast. Rather than winter rainfall, the Skeleton Coast, as it is called, receives essentially no rain at all, and plants there have to survive on fog alone. In the interior *M. mossamedensis* can become a fairly large bush, with spiny brown branches and bright pink flowers, though in the winter dry period it looks pretty sad, growing near the equally leafless *Cyphostemma bainesii* and withered-looking stapelias.

The widespread, white-flowered ***Monsonia crassicaule*** lives in both winter- and summer-rainfall areas from Namibia to the Great Karoo. I have seen it growing amid rocks with ice still on the ground at high noon. This very tough plant becomes surprisingly large, with stems 2 inches (5 cm) thick radiating out in all directions.

Monsonia vanderietiae, from the Eastern Cape, is a small summer-growing species and probably the easiest in cultivation. It flowers readily as well, with its usually white, occasionally pink, 1-inch (2.5-cm) flowers making it look something like a miniature ground-hugging rose bush.

Monsonia spines develop from the main vein of their leaves; plants often will produce small leaves from the tips of their mature spines. Consequently, one should not brush off old dried leaves, as it will impair spine production.

The species in the second, mostly spineless, group of succulent monsonias do not branch in the normal sense of the word. Rather they have strange, more or less horizontally growing little stems shaped like tiny deep-keeled boats. Even mature plants rarely outgrow a 3-inch (8-cm) pot. Most of the spineless monsonias bear extremely tight, finely dissected, fern-leaf foliage, often covered with fuzz, and frequently with just a few leaves per plant.

There are fewer species of these plants, and all of them grow in the intensely arid regions of the Richtersveld and nearby southern Namibia. They are extremely localized in the wild. ***Monsonia peniculinum*** is restricted to a few absolutely arid spots in southwestern Namibia, and ***M. multifida*** to a few miles along the mouth of the Orange River on both the Namibian and the South African sides. Sometimes the latter grows in pure orange sand at the base of carbonate rock formations accompanied by a few fenestrarias, some quick-growing annuals, and very little else. Its varicolored flowers may be white with a pink center, all pink or completely white.

From the southeastern Richtersveld, ***Monsonia herrei***, another highly endemic species, has foliage that looks like tight little clumps of blue-gray parsley, but also has stems armed with long spines. The ovate leaves of the spineless ***M. inerme***, endemic to southwestern Namibia, resemble those of the larger species.

Somewhat surprisingly considering their natural habitats, these plants, though looking as if they should be nearly impossible to keep alive, are not that hard to grow. A little water during their dormant period will not hurt them, and they may produce foliage at almost any time of year. The best rule is to water them sparingly when they are actively growing and leave them dry when their foliage drops until it starts up again. The wax that impregnates their surfaces burns almost like a candle, and both dead and living plants are sometimes used as kindling by the local people. Fortunately, the small human population in *Monsonia* habitat does not present much of a threat.

Both monsonias and pelargoniums from the western parts of their range have a fairly brief growing season in winter and early spring, and even the ones from farther east should receive less water in summer than in spring or fall. *Monsonia crassicaule* will survive outdoors in suitable settings, as will *Pelargonium crithmifolium*, *P. magenteum*, and *P. crassipes*. The cultural needs of the two genera basically are similar, and for those capable of providing warm, extremely bright winter situations, any of these plants are worth a try.

The thick-stemmed pelargoniums can be propagated successfully by cuttings, and with more limited success, the spiny monsonias also. The tuberous pelargoniums and boat-stemmed sarcocaulons only come from seed. Though these succulent geraniums are not that easy to find in cultivation, specialist growers often raise at least a few varieties of these exotic cousins of some our common garden plants.

Chapter 17

Stapelia and Other Thick-Stemmed Succulent Milkweeds: Stapeliads

ONE OF THE more dramatic casualties of the taxonomic upheaval of the last several years has been the milkweed family, Asclepiadaceae, now officially vanished from existence. Though milkweeds of all sorts, succulent or not, were widely recognized as close relatives of the Apocynaceae, the smaller, less-familiar oleander family, DNA analysis has demonstrated that the asclepiads are genetically nested within the confines of the oleanders and their relatives.

Currently considered a subfamily of the Apocynaceae with the intimidating name Asclepiadoideae, the asclepiads have further undergone taxonomic revision. Many new genera have been created and a few older ones sunk, generating confusion, in no small part because the authorities themselves are not in complete agreement. Fortunately, many individual species names have remained the same, providing at least a modicum of stability when searching through older books or plant labels.

The many members of the milkweed subfamily, regardless of form, habit, or appearance, share the most complex flower structure of all dicotyledons. In common with orchid flowers, the most complex of the monocots, the individual pollen grains in the asclepiads are combined into bodies known as pollinia. Most visibly, however, the five-part flowers have two distinct tiers. The first is a corolla consisting of five outer petals called lobes, usually partially fused and often star (or starfish) shaped. The second is a very complex inner five-lobed structure called a corona, often surrounded by a pentagon-shaped ring known as an annulus.

The most familiar succulent milkweeds consist of small to medium-sized plants that produce sets of thickened stems, variously prostrate, decumbent, or erect, from their bases. Together they form the tribe Stapelieae within the larger subfamily, and as a general term they are called stapeliads. These plants, many of African origin but with additional species from the Mediterranean,

Arabia, and parts east, though organized in a bewildering, still shifting number of genera, actually show less vegetative diversity than most succulent groups. And, uniquely among succulents, they are primarily valued for their endlessly varied flowers.

Not that long ago, someone looking for interesting stapeliads might turn first to *Stapelia*, *Huernia*, and *Caralluma*. After the subsequent taxonomic shakeout and ensuing reconfiguration, however, finding the same plants would now mean wading through *Orbea*, *Orbeopsis*, *Tromotriche*, *Tridentea*, *Quaqua*, *Pachycymbium*, and more. Additional name changes have also taken place in several of the smaller stapeliad genera.

HUERNIA, CARALLUMA, AND *STAPELIA*

Stapelia and *Caralluma* have endured the most nomenclatural fragmentation, but *Huernia* still remains fairly intact. One of the most popular genera, it is also one of the easiest to grow. Its several dozen species extend from South Africa north and east through Kenya and Somalia and into southwestern Arabia.

Plants form branching clusters of succulent stems, usually under an inch (2.5 cm) thick and rarely more than 6 inches (15 cm) long. The stems typically have four or five distinct longitudinal ridges that are often marked with small teeth, and which are the source of the minute, ephemeral leaves. Vegetatively, huernias are quite similar, differing most obviously in the size and arrangement of their teeth.

Their flowers, borne on short pedicels, range from wide open, broad-lobed little stars as in ***Huernia verekeri*** to partially closed, campanulate (bell-shaped) blossoms. They exhibit a wide range of colors, patterns, and textures, most often in shades of buff or pale yellow, but running the gamut from almost white to almost black.

Of ambiguous origins, the plant associated with the

A look into the interior of *Huernia* aff. *caespitosa*.

Huernia loeseneriana, with smaller, though intricate, flowers.

Huernia confusa, annulus shining and presumably attractive to pollinators. Photo by Kurt Zadnik.

Huernia hystrix, one of the larger, more baroque huernia flowers.

Huernia primulina, one of the least elaborate flowers in the genus. Photo by Kurt Zadnik.

uncertain name **Huernia caespitosa** nonetheless illustrates basic huernia flower design: an ornate open bell tapering into a tube and downward to a five-lobed corona deep in its interior. Many huernia flowers are densely spotted and dotted. In others the insides of the flowers are covered with a mass of protuberances and tubercles. **Huernia insigniflora**, *H. zebrina*, *H. confusa*, and several others have flowers with a distinct, contrasting annulus that looks like a bright raised ring set like a doughnut above the sunken corona.

Huernia procumbens combines a thick annulus with a long-lobed, starlike corolla. **Huernia hystrix** has perhaps the most heavily decorated, tubercled flowers of all, and *H. primulina* perhaps the most austere. **Huernia oculata**, from semitropical northern Namibia and southwestern Angola, combines ease of culture with striking flowers, purple-bordered with a round, pure white center, like a little eye.

Among the many species with bell-shaped flowers, **Huernia levyi**, from the more tropical climates of northern Namibia through Zimbabwe, has flowers elongated into expanded tubes; the round-segmented *H. kennedyana* has small flowers with almost tentacle like processes; *H. loeseneriana* has blossoms marked with concentric, raised red lines; and *H. reticulata*, from the west coast of South Africa, combines its upright, sharply tuberculate stems with flowers covered inside by dense, purple, glassy hairs over a broad annulus, the whole yellow splotched with purple in reticulated patterns.

Also with campanulate flowers but very different vegetatively, **Huernia pillansii** has stems totally covered with dense rows of little teeth so elongated as to look almost like hairs. **Huernia pendula** grows pendently, drooping over rock edges with thin stems up to a few feet long and small purple-red flowers.

In habitat huernias usually grow in partial shade,

whether in crevices in rocks, or more commonly, underneath the cover of larger bushes and shrubs. In such places they benefit from a slightly richer soil and protection from the sun.

Caralluma, once one of the largest stapeliad genera, now includes very few South African plants. Its more than fifty remaining species grow through the drier parts of the rest of Africa, and southern and western Arabia. One of them, *C. europaea* (also known as *Apteranthes*), crosses the Straits of Gibraltar into southern Spain. It is fairly easy in cultivation.

Some carallumas resemble larger huernias and are sprawling plants. The spectacular **Caralluma socotrana**, from the supremely exotic island of Socotra, is one ex-

ample. More often, however, carallumas grow as dense clusters of thick, upright, often distinctly four-angled stems. A number of these types, from unpromising habitats in the middle of the Sahara Desert, Somalia, or the Arabian hinterlands, produce tight umbels of flowers looking like 8-inch (20-cm) wide balls perched on the top of a 2-inch (5-cm) thick stem. Among them are the jet black **C. penicillata**, the red-black and vile smelling **C. speciosa**, or the bright yellow and pleasantly apple-scented **C. somalica**. In a number of others such as **C. gracilipes** and **C. priogonium**, the stems elongate as they produce their flowers and the inflorescences die back after blooming, before new stems begin to grow. In India **C. frerei** (synonym *Frerea indica*) can become almost vinelike, and retains its good-sized leaves for much of the year, perhaps hinting at the appearance of the pre-succulent ancestors of the stapeliads.

Carallumas range from fairly easy in cultivation to almost impossible. The larger, upright plants from the North African and Arabian deserts generally will not survive in cultivation for very long, succumbing to a combination of rot and almost unavoidable mealy bugs.

Like *Caralluma*, the genus *Stapelia* has also been pruned down to a fraction of its former size. It currently consists of small to mid-sized, mostly South African plants with spreading but generally upright stems, less distinctly four-angled than the Saharan carallumas, sometimes hairy or fuzzy, or even velvety, with soft, upward-directed, pointed tubercles. As is the case with

Huernia pillansii, with flowers less interesting than its spike-covered stems.

Caralluma socotrana in full flower in the blazing sun of Socotra. Photo by Rob Skillin.

Caralluma socotrana flowers close up. Photo by Rob Skillin.

Caralluma speciosa, from the Horn of Africa. The ball-shaped heads of dark flowers with red interiors are about to open. Photo by Susan Carter.

Caralluma somalica, with flowers like C. speciosa but in yellow. Photo by Susan Carter.

Stapelia gigantea with huge flowers in the Eastern Cape. Photo by Inge Hoffman.

Stapelia grandiflora, out to attract flies.

Corolla lobes reflexed almost backward, Stapelia hirsuta var. comata faces the world.

most stapeliads, their flowers are fly pollinated, and on close inspection sometimes quite vile smelling, covered with hairs and other things that flies find interesting.

Blossoms can be huge, purple-brownish, floppy, and starfish-shaped up to a foot (30 cm) or more across in the case of **Stapelia gigantea**, from eastern South Africa and north to Tanzania. Not quite as large or floppy but even hairier is **S. grandiflora**, native to most of the summer-rainfall parts of South Africa. **Stapelia hirsuta** is more western and has a deeply reflexed corolla and hairy, tufted margins. These larger flowers, usually brownish yellow to brownish pink, often covered with a network of darker lines, are relatively similar to each other.

Other stapelias, however, many with smaller flowers, encompass a whole range of colors. The eastern South African **Stapelia clavicorona** and **S. unicornis** are pale yellow. **Stapelia engleriana**, from the Great and Little Karoos, has dark purple-red flowers marked with concentric white lines and petals so backwards-reflexed that seen face on the flowers look round. In the purple-pink flowers of **S. paniculata var. scitula** the concentric lines have become heavy ridges with an almost leathery look.

A few species have gaudy flowers. **Stapelia glanduliflora** in the southwestern Cape has white flowers covered with thick white hairs hanging down like little walrus tusks. The multicolored flowers of **S. flavopurpurea** from the Western Cape north to Namibia are a vivid mix of yellow, purple, and white.

Though vegetatively most stapelias seem like either bigger or smaller versions of each other, the large-flowered **Stapelia gettliffei** has long, thin, limp stems, while bicolored **S. pearsonii**, growing fully exposed in central Namibia, has longitudinally grooved stems that can turn purple and almost black in bright sunlight. The larger

The smaller, heavily textured flowers of *Stapelia paniculata* var. *scitula* come in bunches. Photo by Terry Thompson.

Orbea namaquensis in flower in the Richtersveld.

Stapelia flavopurpurea, with a very different type of flower.

Orbeanthus hardyi, easy to flower and to root.

stapelias do well in cultivation, but some of the odder plants, particularly from winter-rainfall or fairly tropical regions, can be touchy.

ORBEA, ORBEANTHUS, ORBEOPSIS, AND *PACHYCYMBIUM*

The most common stapelia in people's collections, unfortunately, is now **Orbea variegata**. In fact, plants formerly in *Stapelia* have found their way into sixteen other genera, a few of them now invalidated.

Vegetatively similar to stapelias, orbea flowers feature a distinct, round annulus surrounding their corona. From northwestern South Africa **Orbea namaquensis** resembles a larger *O. variegata*, with striking gold-toned flowers lying flat and extending outward beyond the perimeters of the bushes that shade the plants themselves.

With narrow, toothless, ground-hugging stems, **Or-**

beanthus hardyi (synonym *Stultitia hardyi*), best known of its genus, nonetheless has flowers quite similar to *Orbea*. It is easy in cultivation.

Orbeopsis and **Pachycymbium** species were formerly included in either *Stapelia* or *Caralluma*. They comprise plants with distinctly toothed stems and multiple flowers that bloom in dense fascicles. Widely distributed in northern South Africa and bordering countries and very variable, **Orbeopsis lutea**, an attractive former caralluma with long, narrow-lobed, often very smelly, yellow to dark purple flowers, may be the best known of these in cultivation.

TRIDENTEA AND TROMOTRICHE

Most *Tridentea* and *Tromotriche* species also once were stapelias, though a few were carallumas. Tridenteas resemble an erect-stemmed stapelia with usually dark, flattened flowers lacking hairs. Tromotriches tend to have long, narrow, rhizomatous stems and flowers with marginal hairs.

Tromotriche longipes, relatively easy to grow for a Richtersveld endemic, sets its bizarrely attractive starfish flowers on the ends of long pedicels that protrude beyond the bushes under which the plants take shelter. The flowers are stiff with arms adorned with many lateral ridges. *Tridentea pedunculata*, with similarly almost toothless stems, resembles *Tromotriche longipes* both in plant and flower form, but its light brown to lemon yellow corolla lobes turn pure white toward the center of the flower, where they contrast with the almost black, spiderlike lobes of its corona. *Tromotriche longii*, a cliff-dwelling species from the Eastern Cape, also deserves mention because of the shiny texture and occasionally bright orange color of its shorter, broader corolla lobes.

DUVALIA AND DUVALIANDRA

Most of the dozen and a half species of *Duvalia* come from the summer-rainfall parts of South Africa and adjacent lands. Some grow as far west as the Richtersveld and southern Namibia, and others show up in East Africa as far north as Somalia.

Several, such as the widespread *Duvalia polita*, have dark-toned, but vividly colored, often mottled flowers with a distinct annulus similar to an orbea or huernia. The typical *Duvalia* flower, however, consists of a five-lobed corona set into a circular disk bounded by an annulus, with five narrow, almost linear corolla petals. Examples include *D. modesta*, from the Eastern Cape; *D. pubescens*, the most northwestern species; *D. angustiloba*, from centrally located arid regions such as the Great Karoo; and the closely related *D. gracilis*, from slightly farther

Tromotriche longipes, under a desiccated bush in a Richtersveld quartz field. Photo by Rob Skillin.

Duvalia pubescens, short stemmed and nestled between rocks. Photo by Kurt Zadnik.

Tromotriche longipes blossoms up close. Photo by Rob Skillin.

Duvalia aff. *angustiloba,* with appropriately narrow lobes. Photo by Terry Thompson.

east. With similar, narrow-petaled, rather drab flowers, *D. parviflora*, from the Little Karoo, has nontubercled, elliptical stems that resemble little clustered potatoes.

Most duvalias have a compact growth habit, their more-or-less angular stems so densely arrayed as to create a matlike effect. Duvalias behave better in cultivation than many stapeliads, as they do not require continually larger containers and rarely rot suddenly for no discernable reason.

The anomalous Socotra endemic, **Duvaliandra dioscoridis**, resembles a lumpy-stemmed, rather amorphous duvalia or small caralluma. It has had a checkered taxonomic history since its discovery.

PIARANTHUS

Despite its fairly small flowers, the few-specied genus *Piaranthus* nonetheless is popular among growers because of the compact size of the plants, their relative ease of cultivation, and the bright colors of their star-shaped blossoms. Though most species live in regions of summer drought, they avoid the very driest places.

Piaranthus punctatus produces flowers that resemble little starfish with a bright yellow corona and buff-colored petals heavily marked with striking red lateral stripes. The flowers are more-or-less similar to the flowers of most other species. Despite its Namaqualand–Great Karoo home, this species is easy to cultivate.

Piaranthus geminatus, from the Little Karoo, shows considerable variety in its flowers. **Piaranthus atrosanguineus** (synonym *Huerniopsis atrosanguineus*) has larger flowers, shaggy, velvety red, and odiferous. It and a second ex-*Huerniopsis* live far to the north, in summer-rainfall territory, but still manage to be more difficult to grow successfully than typical *Piaranthus*.

ECHIDNOPSIS AND NOTECHIDNOPSIS

The members of *Echidnopsis* as originally constituted had a strange, disjunct distribution, extending from Namaqualand all the way north and east to Somalia and Arabia, but with almost no representation in the huge middle portion of that range. In the mid-eighties the genus was divided in two, the northern plants left as *Echidnopsis*, the two southern species now called *Notechidnopsis* (*not* in this case meaning "southern"). The two genera resemble each other, with spineless stems patterned in tessellations like a little corncob. The longish, narrow stems can either hug the ground or partly rise up. Their smallish, variably colored flowers remain close to the stem.

Echidnopsis malum has migrated circuitously from *Pectinaria*, finally landing in *Echidnopsis*. It has small ground-level flowers tightly closed up into spheres that look remarkably like little apples. The most widespread species in cultivation, **E. cereiformis**, from the Horn of Africa and Arabia, grows easily. **Notechidnopsis framesii** and other South African species are considerably more difficult to grow and thus uncommon in collections.

PECTINARIA, OPHIONELLA, AND STAPELIOPSIS

Many other former species of *Pectinaria* have ended up either in the new genus *Ophionella*, or in a separate section of the older genus *Stapeliopsis*. In any case, these are small plants, mostly from western South Africa, with prostrate stems that sometimes burrow underground. Their distinctive flowers have petals that close up at their tips, looking like little orbs with slashed sides.

The flowers of **Pectinaria articulata**, one of the few species left in the genus, open at the truncated apex and look like a hollow five-lobed fruit sliced in half. **Stapeliopsis saxatilis** has ovoid, reddish, almost tulip-shaped flowers, while the corolla tips of **Ophionella arcuata** gape open like a nestling bird with a five-lobed beak.

Piaranthus geminatus, with corolla lobes outstretched. Photo by Kurt Zadnik.

None of the plants are particularly common or easy in cultivation. The couple of Namibian species moved into *Stapeliopsis* have flowers like open-ended urns and are quite difficult.

STAPELIANTHUS

Crossing the ocean from Africa to the island of Madagascar brings us the genus *Stapelianthus*, with about half a dozen *Huernia*-like species. *Stapelianthus* flowers resemble those of *Huernia* as well, somewhat campanulate with an open star-shaped apex, often in bright colors and patterns. With stems covered by elongated, almost hairlike tubercles, and hairy flowers as well, **S. pilosus** resembles *Huernia pillansii*. **Stapelianthus madagascariensis** is the most attractive species and the most frequently cultivated. It has pale yellow flowers with bright red dots and stems mottled gray-pink, an unusual color scheme shared by several other unrelated Madagascan plants. Stapelianthus are fairly rare, unable to withstand cold, and susceptible to sudden rot if kept too wet in winter.

Many stapeliads from the eastern half of South Africa or southern East Africa, the region of summer rain and winter droughts, are easy to grow. This includes most huernias, many stapelias, some orbeas and duvalias, and a scattering of others. They enjoy a soil with a fair amount of organic matter, somewhat filtered light, and water throughout the warmer months. In winter they should be kept quite dry. While they actually like decent humidity when growing, they do better with a dry atmosphere when dormant. Because they flower on their new growths, which tend to keep moving outward, they can take up considerable room, and do best in relatively wide, shallow containers.

Touchier stapeliads from farther west in South Africa may respond best to a relatively strict summer rest period. If they continue to grow in winter, they should receive water during sunny weather, though not more often than every ten days or so.

Many winter growers can withstand considerable cold if they are dry and humidity remains low, while plants from East Africa and Madagascar should be protected from cold. Most of the Arabian and Saharan plants are extremely difficult to grow. Growers have had some success by keeping plants in soil heated by cables, and never letting the soil temperature get below 70 to 75°F (21 to 24°C).

All stapeliads can be magnets for mealy bugs, and they should be checked for these pests regularly. Fungus also attacks the plants, but the easier ones tend to be more resistant. They will root from cuttings, but it is best to keep the cut-off part above soil level, and just let them root along the length of their stems.

EDITHCOLEA

Several other genera of stapeliads have developed growth habits quite different from the more typical groups. Most of these are highly specialized, masters of survival in some of the harshest, most arid parts of southern and eastern Africa.

Perhaps the most spectacular stapeliad flowers of all, beautiful in an exotic way rather than just bizarre, belong to the genus *Edithcolea*. Native to Somalia, Kenya, and northern Tanzania, edithcoleas provide a challenge to anyone trying to grow them. The plants differ from the others mentioned so far, with stiff, angular stems and fairly sharp little spikes at the tips of their tubercles.

Edithcoleas can form large clumps in the wild as they grow along the ground in hot, rocky, arid places. Their remarkable Persian rug flowers are the reason for their persistent popularity in cultivation. These can stretch to 6 inches (15 cm) across, open stars with Gothic arch–shaped petals that terminate in graceful, pale yellow, lanceolate points. The rest of the flowers have an intricate network of purple and olive-green lines and are provided with fine hairs that give them an appearance of plush velvet.

Unfortunately, simply keeping edithcoleas alive long enough to flower can be problematic. The best results I have seen were achieved by growing them in a bed of little more than coarse sand with electric heating cables

Edithcolea grandis making a statement when in bloom. Photo by Susan Carter.

On a steep Namibian hillside, this spiny *Quaqua mammillaris* seems well defended.

under the soil. Otherwise, humidity, cold, and excess water can all prove quickly fatal for edithcoleas.

Edithcolea grandis is best known. The smaller, drabber *E. sordida*, generally considered a subspecies of *E. grandis*, comes from Socotra.

QUAQUA

Quaqua consists of about twenty mostly western South African species formerly listed as carallumas. Quaquas typically produce clusters of good-sized upright stems covered with prominent tubercles. In *Q. mammillaris* and *Q. armata* the tubercles terminate in stout-looking spines.

Quaquas bloom from the upper portions of their stems and may bear numerous, oddly colored, not very large flowers. In *Quaqua ramosa*, from parts of the Little and Great Karoos, farther east than the others, the tubercles are less spiky and the flowers so deep purple that they look black (see photo on page 22).

Extremely striking looking, quaquas unfortunately rot quite easily in cultivation. Keeping them dry in summer and in as bright a situation as possible in winter will help, but they are not easy plants to grow and maintain in good condition.

TAVARESIA AND HOODIA

Both species of *Tavaresia*, though from summer-rainfall areas well to the north of *Quaqua* territory, share that genus' propensity for a quick, dramatic demise in cultivation. Tavaresias are compact plants, with short, erect stems arrayed with small tubercles tipped with slender, almost hairlike spines. When grown in good light the stems turn dark brown, almost black, in striking contrast to the white hair-spines.

Tavaresia barklyi, found from southern Angola east across much of northern South Africa as well as parts of Namibia and Zimbabwe, and the very similar *T. angolensis*, produce proportionately enormous flowers shaped like an old Victrola horn, a large tubular funnel that flares open at the end. The plants grow quickly and flower fairly easily, but they are quite delicate. Their flower buds can drop off after the slightest touch, and excess cold, humidity, or water in winter will quickly prove fatal to the plants. Because they do grow well under the right conditions they show up in cultivation from time to time. With their Art Deco colors and huge flowers they make attractive additions to a collection despite often succumbing to adverse conditions after several years.

Even more frustrating to grow are the spectacular, upright, spiky, clustering members of the genus *Hoodia*, now with new fame as the source of a "magical" weight-loss compound. The dozen or so *Hoodia* species can attain considerable size, with stems over 3 feet (90 cm) high in *H. currorii* and even taller in *H. parviflora*, both from northern Namibia and Angola. *Hoodia gordonii*, from central Namibia through northern South Africa, is just slightly smaller.

Typical hoodia flowers resemble inside-out umbrellas, either disc- or pentagon-shaped and usually pink or reddish, sometimes yellow. Those smaller hoodias previously considered trichocaulons have small, more standard star-shaped blossoms. Among them, *Hoodia pedicellata*, a coastal strip dweller from central and northern Namibia, is almost spineless, with a corncob look to its 6- to 10-inch (15- to 25-cm) sprawling stems. In its arid habitat it can rely on little more than fog to survive.

In contrast, the larger hoodias, scattered across a wide swathe of territory from southern Angola to Bushmanland and the Great Karoo, always occur in extremely arid places out of the reach of coastal fog. Mature hoodias may grow in rocky outcrops or completely in the open; they often start life as seedlings sheltered by nurse plants that they outlive.

Many species grow in the winter-rainfall area, and many of these live in places where winter temperatures drop well below freezing. Combine these somewhat contradictory conditions with rainfall totals of 2 to 4 inches (50 to 100 mm) a year and essentially zero humidity and you have the ideal circumstances for raising the plants. Without these conditions, hoodias are notoriously difficult to keep alive, but they are such impressive plants and

Hoodia parviflora, stems 3 feet (90 cm) tall, flowering in northern Namibia. Photo by Brian Kemble.

Hoodia gordonii, a true desert dweller, in southern Namibia.

their flowers are so distinctive that people keep trying, using techniques such as bottom heat, and perhaps, prayer.

LARRYLEACHIA AND LAVRANIA

The next genus, difficult even to assign a name to, exemplifies the stapeliad group's taxonomic ups and downs. The old genus *Trichocaulon* consisted of very arid growing plants with smallish, star-shaped flowers. Some tricho-

caulons had elongated, erect-growing stems with spiny tubercles. Others had stems that grew in shapes that defied easy description—call them blobs. More-or-less cylindrical, but lumpy and covered with rounded tubercles, these blobs look more like sea-squirts than plants.

The decision was made to transfer the spiny species into *Hoodia*. After considerable taxonomic controversy, four remaining species were placed in *Larryleachia*. A fifth species, somewhat different than the rest, was called *Lavrania*. Both new genus names commemorate eminent succulent plant explorers. All species look very much alike, with differences based on details of their flowers.

Possibly because of its name, **Larryleachia cactiformis**, from the Richtersveld and Bushmanland, is probably the best known. Looking more like a tessellated blob than something with the form of a cactus, in good growing conditions it will eventually produce a few branching stems up to 6 inches (15 cm) tall and 2 inches (5 cm) thick. Its flowers, little stars on short peduncles and highly variable in color, emerge from the top of its stems.

Overlapping the range of *Larryleachia cactiformis*, **L. perlata** extends into Namibia as well. It can reach as much as a foot (30 cm) in height, while **L. marlothii**, the most widely distributed, is smaller, about the size of *L. cactiformis*, but more freely branching and with smooth rather than papillose corolla lobes.

Larryleachia aff. *perlata*, a crested plant from southern Namibia's desolate interior. Photo by Kurt Zadnik.

Larryleachia marlothii, flowering while growing on a pile of stones. Photo by Rob Skillin.

Pseudolithos migiurtinus, flowering in Somali badlands. Photo by Susan Carter.

These extraordinary little plants inhabit some of the bleakest patches of earth and rock imaginable, where they survive on almost no rain at all. I have seen them in barren, sandy Namibian soil, completely exposed to sun, great heat, and regular winter frosts, or, closer to the coast, almost defying gravity by growing straight out of soilless cracks in jagged carbonate rocks. Though most grow in winter-rainfall areas, larryleachias absolutely will not tolerate excess humidity, particularly in overcast weather. In areas without extensive winter sunlight the best strategy is to water them cautiously about every two weeks in summer and leave them completely dry for the several cold and wet months of the year.

PSEUDOLITHOS

For champion blob plant of the whole group, however, it is necessary to travel across Africa to Somalia, where *Pseudolithos* ("false stone") was discovered in the late 1950s. Plants share the inflated spongy texture of larryleachias, but have somewhat more protuberant tubercles that vary in size and are arranged in erratic but definite patterns across their bodies. They may grow slowly into small cylinders or remain blob-shaped, and slowly branch by adding smaller, subsidiary blobs. Their small fringe-margined flowers, produced from near the tops of the plants and more open or closed according to species, can be self-fertile, but the seedlings damp off at the drop of a hat. They require good heat, maximum light, water about twice a month when they are growing, and bone-dry conditions during the winter months. When cultivated in conditions of intense heat and aridity they can take considerably more water and very slight shade.

As its matures, *Pseudolithos cubiformis* becomes less cubelike. This plant is about to flower.

Pseudolithos migiurtinus will form small branching columns over time, while the aptly named *P. cubiformis* and the even more bloblike *P. horwoodii* remain low. *Pseudolithos caput-viperae* forms clumps of fat, low stems; with its patterned tubercles mature plants actually do suggest a collection of snake heads. The two remaining species, with more elongated stems, and marginally easier to grow, resemble *Duvaliandra.*

WHITESLOANEA

To complete this discussion, the extraordinary *Whitesloanea crassa,* also from Somalia deserves mention. This stapeliad grows into a fairly large granite gray, almost perfect cube and produces a pale yellow flower spotted with red, superficially looking much like a huernia. When it was rediscovered some years ago, much was made of the grave danger of extinction the plants faced from being eaten by nomadic Somali tribespeople. A number of plants were collected, sold for extravagant prices, and more-or-less vanished from sight shortly afterwards. Since then, however, growers have had some success in raising plants from seed, cultivating them in a manner similar to pseudolithos.

Many of these highly specialized plants enjoy surprising amounts of water when they are actively growing. Larryleachias should always receive less-than-average water, and the others can be unforgiving if watered out of turn. They need a very fast draining soil, and when dormant they all should be left absolutely dry. Many grow readily from seed, and *Tavaresia*, *Larryleachia*, and *Pseudolithos* do reasonably well in cultivation if given the right conditions. Since they are slow-growing, compact plants, they can remain in a small container for many years. Quaquas will grow and spread under ideal growing conditions, and some will take a slightly richer soil than the other genera, that is, until they rot off. Hoodias will look great until they too almost inevitably rot and die.

Chapter 18

Succulent Milkweeds with Vining and Caudiciform Habits

BESIDES STAPELIADS, THE succulent milkweeds also include other genera with a variety of approaches to the succulent lifestyle. In this chapter we will consider two more groups of asclepiads. The first of these includes vining plants in the genera *Hoya*, *Dischidia*, *Ceropegia*, and the so-called dead sticks in the genera *Cynanchum*, *Sarcostemma*, and *Rhytidocaulon*. The second group of asclepiads that have attracted the attention of collectors comprise genera with a caudiciform habit: *Fockea*, *Raphionacme*, *Brachystelma*, and *Matelea*.

HOYA AND DISCHIDIA

Hoya and the closely related *Dischidia* comprise vining plants that barely fit the definition of a succulent. Growers of succulent plants, however, often manage to sneak a few species, out of a couple of hundred, into their collections.

Hoya and *Dischidia* species are native from India through New Guinea, northern Australia, and even southern China. Most hoyas grow more-or-less wholly as epiphytes. As a result, even though they are from tropical regions with heavy rainfall, they have to be able to withstand considerable dryness, and so have evolved relatively thick, succulent leaves. Dischidias tend to be smaller and thinner leafed. Both genera bear umbels of waxy, five-pointed flowers, often small and campanulate in dischidias and frequently larger and star-shaped with a distinctly marked corona in hoyas.

In some hoyas, such as the diminutive *Hoya serpens*, the flowers are covered with papillae and look like little fuzzy stars, while in the very well known *H. carnosa*, the white flowers with dark red coronas are so thick and waxy that they look artificial. *Hoya pubicalyx*, from the Philippines, looks very much like *H. carnosa*, while *H. australis* has similar flowers as well, though its leaves are oval-shaped rather than pointed at their ends. *Hoya shepherdii*

has long, thick, narrow leaves with a channeled upper surface and resembles a collection of string beans. A horticulturally popular plant often called *H. purpureo-fusca* has both outer petals and inner corona colored largely pink and purple. *Hoya macgillivrayi* has large pendent, partially closed, purplish pink flowers that look almost like the blooms of a stapelia. The more succulent *H. kerri*, with flowers with a sharply defined five-lobed, almost purple corona, has extremely thick obovate leaves deeply indented at their tips, making them look like hearts on a stem. Many other species of *Hoya* are cultivated, often more tropical and less resistant to drying out, such as the small neat-growing *H. bella*.

A *Hoya* species, clinging to a tree and ready to flower, in Malaya.

Generally easy to grow, hoyas respond well to a fast-draining soil with some organic matter. They often resent being repotted, and do well in proportionately small pots where they can stay for many years without com-

Collected in the 1950s under the name of *Hoya minima*, this plant is better called *H.* cf. *serpens*.

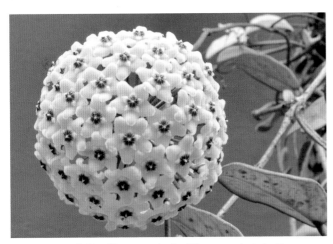

Hoya carnosa's familiar waxy ball of flowers. Photo by Terry Thompson.

Hoya kerri, with heart-shaped leaf in the background, and flowers oozing thick perfumed nectar in the foreground.

plaint. They do best in bright but filtered light, and in summer like water once a week or a little more often, and perhaps every two weeks in winter. The old bloom spikes flower year after year as they elongate. Some hoya flowers have an intense nighttime fragrance of cinnamon or other spices that, although wonderful at first, can become almost overpowering. Hoyas in general, and the more succulent species in particular, can be slow growing, so patience is a virtue when cultivating them.

CEROPEGIA

Many of the approximately two hundred species of *Ceropegia* superficially resemble *Hoya* species. Plants in both genera often are scrambling, thick-stemmed vines, frequently with scattered, fairly succulent leaves. Largely African, ceropegias also extend across most of southern Asia, but unlike hoyas they grow in semiarid habitats.

Ceropegias and hoyas are not closely related, however, and other than the fundamental five-part make-up shared by all members of the family their flowers are dissimilar. Ceropegia flowers have corollas elongated into tubes and sometimes expanded at the base. The corolla lobes may be completely open, united at their tips in a sort of birdcage, or expanded into an umbrella, complete with a handle. Downward-pointing hairs in the tube trap pollinating insects. After pollination the hairs relax and allow the insects to escape.

In some species, such as the very common rosary vine, **Ceropegia woodii**, the drab purple-pink-brownish flowers are small and reveal their strange design only under a degree of scrutiny. Among the many much larger flowered species, **C. ampliata** produces 2.5-inch (6-cm) long

Ceropegia woodii, tubers, leaves, and small flowers.

Ceropegia ampliata, wih birdcage flowers and stems like thick wires. Weedy *Lenophyllum* intrudes in the background.

Ceropegia somaliensis, with thick, bare stems twining around its supporting shrub. Photo by Susan Carter.

Ceropegia lindenii, another Somali rarity, with open-tipped flowers. Photo by Susan Carter.

green and white flowers that somewhat resemble open-ended lanterns.

In other ceropegias the flowers attain a mechanical-looking complexity that almost defies belief, looking like a parachute drop from an old-fashioned county fair, or a robot hybridized with some undersea creature out of a science-fiction movie. In ***Ceropegia sandersonii*** and ***C. elegans***, the 3-inch (8-cm) long flowers begin with fused corolla lobes that form a tube that flares widely two thirds of the way up, then contract into linear posts, then widen again and merge into a parachute or umbrella-like platform.

The rarely grown ***Ceropegia somaliensis*** has long stems, lush leaves, and flowers in which the corolla lobes abruptly join and narrow into a single support, then widen into a sort of fringed globe. The flowers of the somewhat more common *C. haygarthii*, from southeastern South Africa, have much the same look, with an even hairier globe and a tube spotted in patterns of red.

Another rarely seen Somali species, ***Ceropegia lindenii***, has flowers with widely outstretched corolla lobes, while in *C. radicans* the joined lobes flare out midway up and then rejoin into an elongated beak. ***Ceropegia robynsiana***, from tropical Africa, also forms a beak, which veers off at a sharp angle, looking like the head of a heron or a crane.

The round-leafed *Ceropegia woodii* and the closely related but narrow-leafed *C. linearis* have thin stems and persistent, semisucculent foliage. They make small tubers as they root along their stems. Although they are diminutive plants, given time they can spread almost like a ground cover beneath a greenhouse bench.

The very large flowered plants, such as *Ceropegia*

sandersonii, lack the tubers though some species have fleshy roots. Their considerably thicker stems resemble fat, insulated electrical wires, set sporadically with short-lived, succulent leaves. In a few species, such as ***C. cimiciodora*** and ***C. stapeliiformis***, both from eastern South Africa, the mottled, purple-brown stems have become thick and succulent. The plants crawl along the ground, then elongate and twine among surrounding shrubs before producing their wide-open, *Stapelia*-like blossoms.

Ceropegia dimorpha, from Madagascar, has thick, stiff stems heavily armed with sharply pointed modified leaf bases. At flowering time its unarmed branch tips elongate, narrow dramatically, and scramble as much as 10 feet (3 m) through nearby shrubs until they produce apical flowers. Afterwards the entire elongated portion of the stem dries up and drops off, and the plant awaits the next flowering season.

Ceropegia dimorpha, its flowering upper stem not yet present. Photo by Brian Kemble.

Several other Madagascan species, among them ***Ceropegia armandii***, ***C. bosseri***, and especially ***C. adrienneae***, have thickly angular, segmented, sometimes oddly colored stems, pink and gray, which from above look like a chain of little sculpins or other chunky, rock-dwelling fish.

Several species with still another growth habit come from the Canary Islands. Among them are ***Ceropegia dichotoma*** and ***C. fusca***. Their thick, succulent stems grow straight up into the air rather than hug the ground.

The tuber-forming ceropegias are very easy to grow, requiring moderately bright light, any decently draining soil, and enough water to keep them from drying out in summer, a little less in winter. They thrive on neglect and make good house plants. The thicker-stemmed ceropegias require more light but not full sun, faster drainage, and a little more care with water including a distinct winter rest. The thickest-stemmed species should receive water no more than once every four weeks or so. The Canary Island species grow in fall and winter, and should be left relatively dry in summer. They also do well with fairly bright light and any soil mix suitable for succulents.

CYNANCHUM AND SARCOSTEMMA

Other elongated asclepiads include the mostly Madagascan *Cynanchum*, very similar to the thicker-stemmed ceropegias, but with small less ornate flowers. The flowers of ***C. perrieri*** and associated species are star-shaped, while those of ***C. marnieranum*** look like a little birdcage formed out of the narrow corolla lobes, separated then rejoined. Some species can become quite large, clambering for many feet through *Euphorbia* trees and other good-sized plants. A few other very rarely cultivated species have tuberous roots and send out annual vining growths.

Species of *Sarcostemma*, found over much of the drier regions of Africa and into Asia as well, ramble rather than climb, but vegetatively are rather similar. Sarco-

Ceropegia dichotoma, lanternlike flowers on sturdy, upright stems. Photo by Terry Thompson.

Cynanchum aff. *perrieri*, a rather uninteresting plant with interesting little flowers.

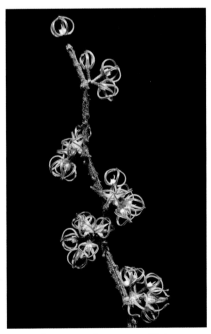

Cynanchum marnieranum, with larger, closed-lobed birdcage flowers. Photo by Kurt Zadnik.

Sarcostemma species, covering a Namaqualand hill like a thicket of dead sticks.

A good-sized *Fockea capensis,* in a 12-inch (30-cm) pot.

stemmas tend to have thicker, mostly leafless, often gray-green stems. Some species can form thickets that cover an entire hilltop. Their flowers are unprepossessing five-pointed stars.

Not surprisingly, neither *Sarcostemma* nor *Cynanchum* is encountered too often in cultivation. Both genera are included among those called dead stick plants, either affectionately by aficionados of such things, or as straightforward descriptions by people with less exotic tastes.

RHYTIDOCAULON

Occasionally found in specialized collections, the largely East African and Arabian *Rhytidocaulon* species may be the most aptly termed members of the dead stick group. They resemble thick-stemmed ceropegias or elongated carallumas vegetatively, unarmed, often unbranched plants typically mottled gray-green, with their flowers held very close to their stems. The flowers themselves may have open corollas and look like small stapeliads, or have united corolla lobes similar to some types of ceropegias. Culturally, they are more like East African caral-lumas, their cousins; in other words, difficult to keep healthy, easy to overwater, and susceptible to rot.

FOCKEA

Probably the earliest of the caudiciform asclepiads to be cultivated and one of the most interesting is *Fockea,* from southern and eastern Africa. Although it is a fairly small genus, its species display considerable diversity. They all produce nonsucculent, usually ovate, often wavy edged leaves, and small flowers with spiraled petals, but

Fockea multiflora, completely different-looking, looping through a supporting tree in northern Namibia. Photo by Rob Skillin.

their stems and tuberous roots assume a number of interesting shapes.

The commonly cultivated species develop large furrowed, hemispherical bases. The most desirable of these, the Great Karoo–inhabiting **Fockea capensis** is usually, though inaccurately, called *F. crispa.* It has highly wrinkled (crisped) leaves and develops a large slightly silvery caudex that twists upward from its thickened roots. Ornamented with odd projections and tubercles, the caudex tends to grow below ground as well as above, so when the plant is repotted it should be raised up. A specimen of this species was long proclaimed the oldest container plant in Europe, having arrived in Vienna in 1796.

Fockea edulis, from coastal South Africa, resembles a plainer, less baroque *F. capensis*. It grows more rapidly, and its species name refers to its occasional use as a food product by some indigenous people in its home territory.

Fockea angustifolia, rarely cultivated but widely distributed from Namaqualand through much of southern Africa, keeps its caudex completely hidden underground. In habitat the only visible evidence of the plant consists of a small tangle of stems with narrow, dark gray-green leaves that emerge from a single spot on the soil surface.

Other fockeas, from more northern semitropical desert regions, look entirely different. Instead of caudiciforms they grow into thick-stemmed shrubs with branches that twist and twine through surrounding growth, almost like short, succulent-stemmed lianas. Some of these plants can become surprisingly large, almost trees themselves. Two examples are *Fockea multiflora* and *F. schinzii*, both from Namibia, southern Angola, east to Zimbabwe and north into Tanzania.

RAPHIONACME AND BRACHYSTELMA

A second variation of caudex-forming milkweeds consists of the genera *Raphionacme* and *Brachystelma*. These species form a large somewhat disc-shaped caudex that annually sends out short leafy branches in the first genus, and low rosettes of tufted, often somewhat fuzzy, non-succulent leaves in the second. In the wild the plants look like small nondescript shrubs, as their caudices remain underground.

The flowers of *Raphionacme* are relatively simple compared to many asclepiads. **Raphionacme hirsuta**, from eastern South Africa, sends out several stems of oval, slightly fuzzy leaves and clusters of smallish greenish purple flowers. Other raphionacme flowers may be somewhat different colored or slightly pendulous. Planted as if in nature, with its caudex underground and invisible, a raphionacme would attract no interest, but for even a chance of survival the tubers of both *Raphionacme* and *Brachystelma* should be kept above soil level.

Brachystelmas are valued in part because of their large, sometimes disgusting smelling, flowers, which occur either singly or in umbels. They come in a wide vari-

A *Raphionacme* species with purple flowers is quite unremarkable in the wild with its caudex underground.

Brachystelma barberae, in deceptively lush leaf.

ety of typical asclepiad colors and shapes, from white to black, often spotted or provided with vibrating hairs, either star-shaped with open corolla lobes or birdcage-like, with joined lobes.

These plants can challenge even expert growers. When they begin to put out their leaves they need a good deal of water. Some brachystelmas grow in misty mountains where the total precipitation can approach 100 inches (2500 mm) a year, though others grow in semiarid grasslands. In any case, and with both genera, as soon as their growing season ends and their leaves begin to fall, they must be kept absolutely dry or else they will quickly succumb to rot and turn to unpleasant mush. The mountain plants are a bit easier to grow, but harder to find, while the grassland species need a leaner soil mix.

Brachystelma barberae, a grassland species and probably the most common brachystelma in cultivation, makes an umbel of thin-petaled, purple and white flowers. **Brachystelma foetidum**, also from grasslands, has more standard *Stapelia*-like star flowers complete with a terrible odor.

Matelea cyclophylla flowers close up.

Matelea cyclophylla, a stapeliad flower on a Mexican caudiciform.

MATELEA

A final caudiciform milkweed brings us to western Mexico. **Matelea cyclophylla**, though still not common in cultivation, is one of the most desirable New World caudiciform succulents. The plant consists of a caudex, at first dome-shaped, but soon turning into a less regular mass of furrows and ridges, topped by a vining stem that bears deciduous, more-or-less heart shaped leaves. At first glance the plant resembles one of the many rather anonymous caudiciform cucurbits, but its dark purple, star-shaped flowers immediately prove it to be a milkweed. The flowers look more appropriate for a huernia or stapelia than for a vining Mexican caudiciform. Mateleas have become popular among collectors, both for novelty value and because of the surprisingly rapidity with which they can achieve a look of great, weathered age.

Matelea and *Fockea* both respond well if given an average, quick-draining succulent soil mix. As plants that grow under other plants, they do not require intense light. During the warmer months they should receive normal water, once a week or so, and while resting they should not dry out completely, with water supplied every three or four weeks.

Cynanchum and related genera require similar care, with water perhaps given slightly more frequently when dormant in winter. As befits most plants from tropical dry lands, they also need protection from temperatures much below 50°F (10°C).

Raphionacme and *Brachystelma* need somewhat brighter light. When growing they should never completely dry out, but any water during their dormant period will probably prove fatal. They are not easy plants to grow.

Chapter 19

Adenium and *Pachypodium*

BEFORE SWALLOWING UP the asclepiads, the Apocynaceae comprised only two genera of indisputably succulent plants, *Adenium* and *Pachypodium*. For many years, however, as far as succulent collectors were concerned these two genera exemplified everything exotic, spectacular, and almost unobtainable. Now that many species of both genera have become readily available in cultivation they still remain high on the list of most-desired plants for many growers.

Straddling the line between caudiciforms and pachycauls, adeniums and pachypodiums range over many arid parts of Africa and have ventured as far as the southwestern tip of Arabia. *Pachypodium*, with a number of species in southern Africa, has additionally diversified into a range of bizarre forms in Madagascar. *Adenium*, in contrast, never reached Madagascar.

ADENIUM

With about ten species, *Adenium* displays less diversity of form than its cousin. Most species live in East Africa, from Somalia to eastern South Africa, a couple have moved farther west, and others can be found in Arabia and Socotra. Plants bear a superficial resemblance to oleanders, nonsucculent members of their family from the Mediterranean shores of North Africa. Envision an oleander with gray-brown, somewhat leathery skin rather than woody bark, with reduced leaves, and with a large caudex or thick, succulent trunk and you will have an idea of how an adenium looks. Though species differ from one another in regard to the size and shape of their base, whether the base is largely under or above ground, and the size and shape of their leaves and flowers, small adeniums, such as those typically found growing in containers, look pretty much alike. Given time and room to grow, however, the differences between species become apparent.

The earliest described and most widely distributed species, *Adenium obesum* grows both in East Africa from Kenya through Mozambique, and across a wide swathe of the semidesert Sahel region just south of the Sahara. Although the species name implies a fat, greatly swollen base, plants of *A. obesum* rarely develop a hugely enlarged caudex. They can, however, become quite large, and all their parts, stems, branches and roots, are thick and succulent. Old specimens sometimes lie almost prostrate in the sandy soil in which they are found, looking something like an outstretched, bleached skeleton topped by bouquets of bright red flowers.

Adenium arabicum, from across the Red Sea in southern Arabia as far as Oman, develops the huge, flattened caudex that suggested the name *obesum*, and the two species are superficially similar. Plants become large, are rapid growers under ideal circumstances, and put out what looks like a miniforest of trunklike stems from their caudex.

From Somalia and neighboring lands, *Adenium somalense* typically forms a thick, branching, single trunk well over 10 feet (3 m) tall. **Variety *crispum***, a much

Adenium obesum, not as obese as some. Photo by Susan Carter.

A mid-sized *Adenium arabicum*, from Yemen, showing its caudiciform base. Photo by Rob Skillin.

smaller form, is a rare endemic from the Somali coast. It also keeps its caudex, which is shaped like a football on end, underground. Unlike all other species, the petals of its flowers curl and fold in on themselves.

Several of the adeniums from much farther south in Africa usually lack massive, aboveground caudices, and rely on the combination of underground storage organs and their overall succulence to get them through dry years. These include *Adenium swazicum*, one of the more cold-hardy species, and *A. multiflorum*, a large freely branching plant, both from eastern South Africa and surrounding countries. *Adenium boehmianum*, from north-central Namibia and southern Angola, can grow twice as tall as a person. From southeastern Namibia, western South Africa, and partway into Botswana, *A. oleifolium* remains low, rarely more than 1 or 2 feet (30 to 60 cm) tall, but branches vigorously and can make a rounded mound of stems, all above a good-sized usually underground caudex that may poke slightly above the soil surface.

Saving the best for last, the island of Socotra provides a home for the truly fantastic *Adenium socotranum* that develops a boulderlike caudex as much as 8 feet (2.4 m) across and at least as tall. Surmounting the caudex are several thick but dwarfed-looking stems that look as if

Adenium multiflorum, growing in the eastern South Africa. Photo by Brian Kemble.

Adenium socotranum—could the island's flora have been designed by Dr. Seuss?
Photo by Rob Skillin.

Flowering at a small size, Adenium 'Crimson Star' is one of an increasing number of hybrids.

they'd been placed there as an afterthought. Still rare and highly coveted in cultivation, it is a much slower grower than the other adeniums, although it develops its swollen base as a very young plant. *Adenium socotranum* leafs out in late summer or fall and, unlike the other species, in areas of suitable light is best treated as a winter grower.

Valued almost as much for their blossoms as their forms, adeniums are sometimes called desert roses because of their beautiful flowers. Most species will, if grown properly, bloom profusely, displaying masses of usually red blossoms, sometimes red-tipped with white interiors. Since 1990 plant propagators have been breeding *Adenium* hybrids for increased frequency and ease of flower production and intensified color. Names such as 'Crimson Star' and 'Volcanic Sunset' give some idea of their results.

Adeniums, though inhabiting arid regions, respond well to water in cultivation and will thrive with frequent watering when they are actively growing, every five days or even more in hot weather. Most species go dormant in late fall and drop their leaves. These must be kept very dry throughout the winter; plants will readily withstand four months with no water at all. *Adenium swazicum* can tolerate more winter water than the others. Some forms of *A. obesum* along with various hybrids that may retain their foliage during winter should receive water then as well, though on a reduced schedule. For most species, however, water given during dormancy may prove fatal. In spring the first new leaves signify that it is time to begin regular watering once more.

Adeniums like heat, and in hotter and drier parts of Arizona they will survive winter outdoors with some slight shelter. Rather surprisingly several species and many hybrids do well in parts of Florida and tropical countries such as Thailand, especially in areas with relatively dry winters. Cloudy, humid winters are another thing entirely, and adeniums cannot be counted on to survive outdoors in places with that kind of climate.

They need lots of light, but are not too fussy about soil as long as it drains quickly. Like oleanders, adeniums have toxic sap, but their epidermis does not puncture that easily and under normal circumstances there is no reason to worry about having them around the house.

PACHYPODIUM

The first pachypodium I saw astonished me because of its bright silver color; not its leaves nor flowers, but its entire spiny stem looked as if it had been sprayed with silver paint. Not all pachypodiums have this silvery, sun-reflecting epidermis, but whether silver-skinned or not, as a group they offer a tremendous amount of variety, from fairly good-sized trees to living canteens to spreading caudiciforms many times wider than tall. The approximately 20 *Pachypodium* ("thick foot") species have a disjunct distribution, with five species scattered across parts of the southern tip of Africa and the rest inhabiting Madagascar, often in extremely localized situations.

The South African species display several distinct forms. The first, shared by ***Pachypodium succulentum*** and ***P. bispinosum***, consists of a number of fairly thin, spiny branches radiating out from a large elongated caudex, typically completely underground. Both of these species have deciduous, narrow, dark green foliage as well and look almost identical except when in flower. *Pachy-*

Similar but different, *Pachypodium bispinosum* has bell-shaped, partly tubular flowers.

Pachypodium succulentum, with open white flowers and an elongated caudex.

The aboveground caudex of *Pachypodium saundersii* may reach 3 feet (90 cm) in diameter.

From northern Namibia, *Pachypodium lealii* var. *lealii* can grow into a 20-foot (6-m) tall tree. Photo by Rob Skillin.

podium succulentum, widely distributed in arid parts of central and eastern South Africa, presents its flowers splayed wide open, its petals slightly spiraled into a star, white to pink with a red midrib. *Pachypodium bispinosum*, with a more restricted range intersecting that of *P. succulentum*, produces smaller campanulate blossoms, pink to red on the outside and white within. It also is often a bit more compact in its growth form, but not reliably so. In cultivation, the caudices are usually raised above the soil line, both for purposes of display and to lessen the possibility of rot.

Pachypodium saundersii (synonym *P. lealii* var. *saundersii*) has a different mode of growth, with a large aboveground caudex and sparse, thickened branches. Unlike *P. succulentum* or *P. bispinosum*, its spiny epidermis is silvery white, and its long-tubed flowers are white as well. Native to the Eastern Cape region of South Africa, *P. saundersii* can reach a couple of feet (60 cm) in diameter at the base, with twisting branches as much as 3 or 4 feet (90 to 120 cm) long. Small plants can flower in a 4- or 5-inch (10- to 13-cm) pot.

In contrast, **Pachypodium lealii var. lealii** may reach as much as 20 feet (6 m) in height. It may have a thick, relatively cylindrical trunk, several trunks that emerge close to the ground, or a broad caudexlike base with a

Pachypodium lealii var. *lealii*, fragrant white flowers. Photo by Kurt Zadnik.

The half man, *Pachypodium namaquanum,* frequently chooses surrealistically bleak spots for a home. Photo by Rob Skillin.

The most treelike of the Madagascan pachypodiums, *Pachypodium rutenbergianum* shuns the driest locations. Photo by Brian Kemble.

much thinner main stem that continues upward. Its fragrant, frilly white flowers resemble those of *P. saundersii,* but the plants are quite different from each other, and its habitat, in arid, semitropical northern Namibia and Angola, is separated from that of the smaller plant by many hundreds of miles.

Though all the mainland African pachypodiums come from dry regions, **Pachypodium namaquanum,** commonly known as the half man, specializes in extremely arid sites on both sides of the Namibian border. Usually single-stemmed, up to 8 feet (2.4 m) tall and about a foot (30 cm) thick, plants very rarely produce a secondary stem growing parallel to the main one. With its trunk covered densely by long spines and topped by tufts of wavy-edged leaves and clusters of tubular, yellow and green, purple-tipped flowers, *P. namaquanum* looks nothing like any other pachypodium. Solitary or in small groups, plants grow on stony ridge tops and lean to the north—the direction of maximum light. From a distance, or silhouetted against the sun, they resemble a line

of partially bent-over people; thus their popular name. *Pachypodium namaquanum* often makes its home on steep slopes or the edges of cliffs, where the plants experience maximum possible drainage, even though they are already growing in areas of near zero humidity, total summer drought, and minimal winter rain.

The pachypodiums of Madagascar range from pachycaulous trees to low-growing forms that almost defy description. The few tree types have long, narrow leaves, fiercely twin-spined stems, and white flowers. Slightly less succulent than the others, **Pachypodium rutenbergianum** branches more freely and actually looks something like a normal tree, albeit a spiny one. **Pachypodium lamerei** and **P. geayi,** notable for their bright silver surfaces, develop more succulent, cylindrical trunks, thickest in the middle. Their apical secondary branches only form after the plants reach flowering size, although **P. lamerei subsp. ramosum** branches while still relatively small. All these have rather broad, elongated leaves except for *P. geayi,* with narrow, almost linear foliage with

A stand of *Pachypodium lamerei* in a seasonally well-watered part of Madagascar. Photo by Brian Kemble.

In the dry season, *Pachypodium geayi* stands leafless with a few dangling seed pods. Photo by Brian Kemble.

a pink midrib on its underside. These more-or-less arborescent pachypodiums can reach well over 20 feet (6 m) in height.

Most of the other Madagascan *Pachypodium* species look like wine flasks or canteens, with an almost spherical caudex that tapers sharply into one or more thick rebranching main stems that grow out of the top as if they were handles for the living "jugs" they surmount. One of these species, **P. decaryi**, is almost spineless and white-flowered, with few secondary branches. In shape it rather resembles an adenium. More heavily spined, **P. ambongense**, with a less sharply differentiated caudex, occupies a place halfway between the arborescent types and the "flasks." Most of the other flask types have yellow flowers, with their paired spines thicker or thinner according to type. Species such as the variable, yellow-flowered **P. rosulatum**, from granite domes in south-central Madagascar, and the rare, red-flowered **P. baronii**, from a few steep-sided limestone karst formations in the island's far north, keep their basic spherical flask form

Pachypodium rosulatum, ensconced in a pocket of thin soil along a granite rock face. Photo by Brian Kemble.

even as they grow to maturity. Others such as **P. densi-florum** and **P. horombense** branch more freely, basally as well as apically, and sprawl into irregular, many stemmed clumps with age.

Pachypodium baronii var. windsorii growing on a karst *tsingy* formation. Photo by Inge Hoffman.

Pachypodium horombense branches rather quickly, though this is an old plant.

Pachypodium baronii var. windsorii, red flowered.

Pachypodium densiflorum, leafless and wedged next to a boulder. Photo by Inge Hoffman.

In recent years as more obscure parts of Madagascar become known botanically, several new flask-bodied pachypodiums have been discovered and subsequently have entered into cultivation. Most of these newer discoveries resemble related plants such as *Pachypodium densiflorum*, but often live in very restricted habitats where isolation has led to their differentiation. These include **P. bicolor**, **P. inopinatum**, and the white-flowered **P. eburneum**, all of which have created a stir among succulent collectors. **Pachypodium makayense**, with large yellow, white-throated flowers and relatively thin spine pairs, though closely related to *P. rosulatum*, has shorter stems and a very chunky caudex up to a foot (30 cm) wide and high. In time many of these relatively newly found plants may be submerged in older existing ones, but they will remain horticulturally desirable regardless of their ultimate taxonomic status.

One final Madagascan pachypodium that does not need a DNA analysis to justify its distinctiveness is the fantastic **Pachypodium brevicaule**, which some enthusiasts consider the most spectacularly odd succulent plant of all. While the other low-growing species have rounded caudices and variously short or long secondary branches, in *P. brevicaule* the extremely reduced branches have shrunk into almost invisible, leaf-bearing nubs fused to the top of a main stem that slowly grows wider but not taller. Hidden among quartz boulders the same color as their white-silver skin, centuries-old plants reach over 3 feet (90 cm) in diameter but no more than 5 or 6 inches (13 to 15 cm) in height. They have been described as looking like a heap of potatoes all fused together. Perhaps

Pachypodium eburneum, a localized variant species with white flowers.

Pachypodium brevicaule, 8 inches (20 cm) wide and 2 inches (5 cm) tall, leafing out.

comparing them to a giant, petrified amoeba is more evocative if not particularly glamorous. Plants live at altitudes up to 6000 feet (1800 m). With their low, irregular caudices obscured by grasses, they escape notice except when their bright yellow flowers open on the ends of their long pedicels. Unfortunately, great numbers of *P. brevicaule* have been collected and sold, and the rare Madagascan pachypodiums in general are caught between overcollection and unremitting habitat destruction.

Perhaps surprisingly, most pachypodiums come well from seed, though *Pachypodium brevicaule* grows quite slowly. The plants are not particularly difficult in cultivation. Since they bear leaves while growing, and drop them when they enter their dormant period, simply observing the plants will provide the most essential information about their needs.

While in leaf pachypodiums like regular weekly watering. Plants often will swell up and become quite turgid within a day or so after a good drink. Generally speaking, a pachypodium with a soft or wrinkled trunk should have some water, although, unfortunately, one that has lost its roots and is in danger of rotting from soaking wet soil will exhibit the same symptoms. When dormant (in winter) pachypodiums should be left fairly dry, watered perhaps every three or four weeks.

Pachypodiums like rapidly draining soil and need very bright light, although Madagascan tree types such as *Pachypodium lamerei* will tolerate somewhat less than the more highly succulent species and as a result do quite well as house plants. These tree types are reasonably hardy outdoors in sheltered parts of Southern California, but will not survive outside in colder and wetter regions. Among the smaller Madagascan species, *P. decaryi* seems extra

sensitive about excess water in winter and *P. eburneum* requires higher minimum temperatures than the others.

Some South African pachypodiums withstand fairly low temperatures and even some frost if dry. *Pachypodium namaquanum* is a winter grower, although in cultivation it may leaf out as early as mid to late summer. Even though some of the places where it grows can be surprisingly cold in winter, they also are regions of essentially zero humidity. Since this species seeks out areas of maximum drainage even in its arid homelands, I'd be astonished if it could survive outdoors in anything but a true desert climate. Even grown in a greenhouse in coastal California, *P. namaquanum* can be a bit touchy, as it needs extremely bright light exactly when skies are at their darkest. Seed-grown plants, however, sometimes will switch to a summer growing season.

Pachypodium brevicaule has a reputation for being difficult as well. Slower growing than the other species, it is not a bad idea to water plants somewhat less frequently, perhaps every ten days when they are growing and dry for up to six or eight weeks at a stretch in winter. More generous treatment will result in more rapid growth, but these relatively lushly grown plants may abruptly turn to mush after several years; with drier treatment they will thrive for decades.

The Madagascan tree species and the South African caudiciforms are probably the easiest to grow, but all of the pachypodiums are worth giving a try. Since growers finally learned how to pollinate their long-tubed, usually dioecious flowers pachypodiums have become much more widely available. Species such as *Pachypodium lamerei* even show up—sometimes under the misleading name of Madagascar palm—in general nurseries from time to time.

Chapter 20

Senecio and *Othonna*: Succulent Asters

THE LARGEST FAMILY of dicotyledonous plants is the Asteraceae, commonly known as the aster, daisy, or sunflower family. For many years the family was named Compositae and its members composites. By whatever name, this family includes surprisingly few succulents. Though vast numbers of Asteraceae, specifically the varied African daisies, cover South Africa, the South African succulent asters are confined to the genera *Senecio* and *Othonna* and have much more limited distributions. In the rest of the world succulent asters are even fewer.

On the Southern California coast and adjacent islands as far south as northern Baja California, two closely related pachycaulous composites, **Coreopsis gigantea** and **C. maritima**, raise their bearded heads as much as 6 to 8 feet (1.8 to 2.1 m) into the seaside air. Their tall, sometimes branching stems and finely dissected foliage, with a brushy layer of old leaves reaching down their trunks,

gives them an exotic look that contrasts with their very sunflower-like yellow blossoms. Not often seen in collections of succulents, they thrive in California native plant gardens, or any well drained spot in areas with moderate temperatures, winter rainfall and summer drought.

A mid-sized Mexican pachycaul plant, often called **Pittocaulon praecox**, but kept in *Senecio* by some, is more truly succulent, with thick, slowly branching stems. Its thin deciduous leaves drop before it sends out its yellow daisy flowers. It is widely distributed in Mexico, growing both on rocky slopes high in moist mountains, or in much drier areas in the company of cacti and agaves.

SENECIO

Though relatively few of the more than one thousand species of *Senecio* have distinctly succulent characteris-

Shaggy-headed *Coreopsis gigantea* grows not far from the beach houses of Malibu, California.

Pittocaulon praecox, more stunted than typical, from a dry Oaxacan slope.

tics, they occur in almost every arid and semiarid corner of continental Africa and adjoining areas. A number of botanists separate many of these plants into the genus *Kleinia*, the chief criteria being small details of their flower parts. Not all botanists accept the split as valid, however, and most horticultural books call them all senecios, a tradition which I will follow. If rayed, the flowers look like daisies; those without rays resemble little brush tips, sometimes drably colored white or pale yellow, but often in bright shades of red, orange, or purple.

Off the northwest African coast, the Canary Islands provide a home for **Senecio kleinia** (synonym *Kleinia neriifolia*), a plant that looks like an enormous green pencil protruding from the ground. The main stem and few branches are marked with faint longitudinal striping and bear small thin, triangular leaves.

Many succulent senecios grow with similar elongated, cylindrical stems. Probably the best known of these is **Senecio articulatus** from western South Africa. It forms small chains of segmented pale blue stems with distinctive curvilinear marking. Its slightly succulent, long-petioled, triangularly pinnate leaves fall from the stems fairly rapidly, and its sausage-shaped segments disjoint readily and root almost as easily. **Senecio kleiniiformis** has never been found in the wild and may actually be a hybrid. It resembles *S. articulatus*, but has thick, succulent leaves.

Other somewhat similar species occur widely in Africa. The thin, segmented stems of **Senecio pendulum**, sometimes called the inchworm plant, crawl along the ground and occasionally hump up, then burrow beneath the soil surface. The species is from Somalia and other countries in the Horn of Africa, and crosses the Red Sea into Yemen as well. One of the more striking senecios of this type, **S. stapeliiformis** (synonym *Kleinia gregorii*), grows in dry underbrush from eastern South Africa as far north as Kenya. Its bright red, nonrayed flower heads grow almost straight up at the end of a tall peduncle. Another senecio with cylindrical, candy-striped stems and red to magenta flowers, **S. picticaulis**, an East African plant, produces terete little apical leaves, and grows from a soft, rather shapeless basal caudex.

Senecio longiflorus, distributed over much of Africa and beyond, forms 3-foot (90-cm) high clusters of narrow stems much like many shrubby euphorbias that accompany it in drier parts of its habitat. **Senecio hebdingii** and **S. descoingsii**, Madagascan members of this complex, have narrower cylindrical, upright, longitudinally striped stems up to a foot (30 cm) or a little taller, and cluster much like a smaller *S. longiflorus*.

Senecio articulatus, leafless but not totally dormant.

Senecio stapeliiformis, a striped dead stick with a bright pompom inflorescence in the Kenyan undergrowth. Photo by Susan Carter.

Candy-striped *Senecio picticaulis*.

Senecio medley-woodii: succulent rosettes topped by yellow daisies.

Senecio longiflorus, accompanied by *Sarcostemma* sp., in Namibia.

Senecio ballyi: slightly succulent leaves rise from hidden water-storing roots.

Senecio mweroensis, and especially its **subspecies saginatus** (synonym *Kleinia saginata*), from East Africa, has shorter, thicker, brightly marked, very succulent, jointed, upright stems. Across the Red Sea in Yemen, **S. deflersii** (synonym *Kleinia obesa*), may be the oddest of this type. It has erect, often solitary green leafless stems up to a foot (30 cm) tall and 3 inches (8 cm) thick, and dense yellow inflorescences that look like encased pom-poms. Younger plants resemble a large cucumber emerging straight up from the ground; mature specimens look like a branching cluster of cucumbers.

A second succulent senecio variation consists of plants with broad succulent leaves, often organized either tightly or loosely in rosettes, and with less highly modified though still succulent stems. As with the previous group, plants that fit this pattern occur in various parts of Africa and surrounding areas. **Senecio medley-woodii**, from eastern South Africa, forms rosettes of broad, wedge-shaped leaves covered—if given sufficient light—with brown-gray scurf. Its yellow, rayed flowers look like daisies. From Kenya, **S. ballyi** has an underground rootstock from which its short stems, white-striped succulent leaves, and bright red inflorescences emerge. Also East African, as far north as Somalia, red-flowered **S. sempervivus** subsp. **grantii** has thick succulent stems

Succulent leaves and stems rising from a tuberous base keep *Senecio sempervivus* alive during Yemeni droughts.

tipped with rosettes of equally succulent leaves. Its **subspecies sempervivus** lives across the sea in Yemen. More compact, its branching stems originate from a swollen base, and its brush-shaped florets are pale purple rather than red.

An uncommonly cultivated but attractive form of *Senecio talinoides* from the Western Cape.

With tomentose leaves white as snow, *Senecio haworthiodes* occasionally produces yellow-orange inflorescences. Photo by Terry Thompson.

Less strongly rosulate (rosette-forming), the East African **Senecio implexus** has sprawling branches turned up at their tips and fuzzy elliptical leaves. Similar in growth habit but with spoon-shaped green leaves that turn purple-red in good sunlight, *S. jacobsenii* (synonym *Kleinia petraea*), also East African, looks like a crassula, but its bristlebrush, unpleasant-smelling, bright orange inflorescences give it away. With thinner leaves, tightly and often vertically arranged, the Madagascan *S. crassissimus* looks very much like one of the many kalanchoes from that island. Several other Madagascan senecios, such as *S. decaryi* resemble it as well.

A few South African species grow with cylindrical stems and blue, terete, often pointed foliage. The best known, **Senecio talinoides** subsp. **mandraliscae**, has suffered from an overabundance of names. It sends out a profusion of procumbent stems. In appropriate climates it can serve as a ground cover. Its leaves smell like licorice if they are cut or broken. Other subspecies of *S. talinoides* are difficult to distinguish: taller or neater growing, or with much longer, narrower leaves. **Senecio ficoides**, more erect growing and less spreading, has somewhat narrower foliage with rudimentary light-admitting window-stripes. With proportionately longer and narrower leaves, *S. acaulis* from the Western Cape remains compact. It has a few short stems, thus contradicting its name, which signifies no stem at all.

Senecio haworthiodes, from Namaqualand, has elongated, tapered leaves covered with dense white pubescence on upright stems up to 18 inches (45 cm) tall. It does well given very bright light. Despite its habitat, it does not need winter-growing treatment. Also coated in white but tightly clustering and almost stemless, *S. scapo-*

Along with its short stem, *Senecio scaposus* var. *caulescens* has distinctly broader foliage than var. *scaposus* itself.

sus has long tapering leaves. In **var. addoensis** the leaves are flattened and slightly lobed, while **var. caulescens** has blunt-tipped foliage and slowly forms a short stem. *Senecio scaposus* comes from dry parts of southern central South Africa.

A number of other senecios have developed a unique leaf structure, striped with transparent windows in the forms of clear lateral lines. These range from species with sausage-shaped leaves to ones with rounder, and finally spherical foliage, variously crowded on short stems or arranged more sparingly on longer ones that creep along the ground. **Senecio hallianus**, from the southern Great Karoo, is a small infrequently seen plant, with leaves crowded in clusters along short stems. The leaves, little more than an inch (2.5 cm) long, are elongated and almost cylindrical. They taper abruptly into a tiny point, and a translucent window strip runs along their upper surface.

Senecio citriformis, with blue leaves shaped like lemons.

A very round-leafed form of Senecio radicans from the Little Karoo.

Taxonomically confused, rarely grown, and hard to keep compact, Senecio sulcicalyx is equipped for survival in dry places.

Senecio citriformis ("lemon shaped") forms a compact bush with thin stems crowded with small bluish, ovoid apiculate (tapering to a point) leaves. It is fairly widespread from the Little Karoo west, but its distribution pales in comparison with the related **S. radicans**. This very variable plant occurs across most of the western half of South Africa and into Namibia. Its leaves share the translucent longitudinal windows of *S. citriformis* and range from quite elongated and elliptical to ovate to nearly hemispherical. They are arranged less densely along the stems, and the plants themselves, though typically germinating in the relative shade found beneath a bush, extend their branches for several feet along the ground in every direction (see photo on page 22).

In contrast to the widespread *Senecio radicans*, the horticulturally popular **Senecio rowleyanus** (the string of beads) is endemic to a small region in Eastern Cape Province. With stems clad thickly with almost perfectly spherical little leaves and cinnamon-scented white brush-tip inflorescences, it has gained popularity as an ideal plant for a hanging basket. Each leaf has a single, wider window-strip.

A much smaller species, **Senecio sulcicalyx**, which includes plants also known as *S. iosensis* (synonym *Kleinia pusilla*), resembles *S. radicans*, but occurs in much drier circumstances. Instead of sending out long creeping branches, it remains tightly clustered. It grows in Namaqualand, often in tiny crevices in otherwise quite solid rocks, in company with mimicry crassulas and mesembs. Its thickened, water-storing roots help it to survive in its bleak habitat.

A final two senecios from the winter-rainfall areas of western South Africa and southern Namibia have adopted a pachycaulous approach to life. **Senecio cephalophorus** and **S. corymbiferus** both form trunks that resemble those of thick-stemmed tylecodons. *Senecio corymbiferus*, more widely distributed, also grows taller, up to 3 feet (90 cm) high. Its leaves, terete and tapering at their apex, drop during the summer dry season, and its flowers lack rays. *Senecio cephalophorus*, smaller and primarily found in the Richtersveld, produces yellow flowers with rays, but it is most easily distinguished from *S. corymbiferus* because of its evergreen, thicker leaves, more flattened and grooved on top, with their edges folding over towards the center.

Most senecios do very well in cultivation with standard succulent soil, light, and water. *Senecio rowleyanus* grows best with slightly less light and a less sharply defined rest period. *Senecio kleinia* along with species from northern Africa are winter growers, though they should

This *Senecio corymbiferus,* growing in Namaqualand, looks very much like a *Tylecodon.* Photo by Rob Skillin.

OTHONNA

Othonna differs most obviously from *Senecio* in usually having rayed flowers, frequently yellow but in a few cases pink to magenta. Its several dozen species range from easily grown succulent ground cover types such as the commonly cultivated **O. capensis** and the smaller, rarely seen **O. sedoides** to strict winter-growing geophytes, caudiciforms, and miniature pachycauls, some of them barely known or coveted collector's items. Most of the winter growers come from the Western Cape, Namaqualand, and the Richtersveld, and extend across the Orange River into southern Namibia.

Not common in cultivation, **Othonna triplinervia** occurs considerably farther east than most of the more succulent othonnas, but it too grows in winter and lies dormant in summer. It may be upright or procumbent, and persistent leaf scars pattern the short trunk. As is the case with many othonnas, its leaves are only slightly succulent, oval, narrower at the base, and distinctly blue-green.

With similar foliage but a totally different way of life, several geophytic species from Namaqualand hide their vital parts underground. Somewhat more common, **Othonna intermedia** grows in quartz fields along with hordes of mesembs and other miniatures. Its fairly fleshy leaves remain close to the soil surface and form a loose rosette, while its flowers, yellow and looking more like a dandelion than a daisy, rise a few inches higher. **Othonna rosea,** from farther north, has a more elongated stem and fewer, less symmetrically arranged, glaucous leaves. Its bright magenta flowers, distinctly rayed, are the only reason it would normally attract attention as its succulent parts keep several inches underground. In a typical Nam-

not be left bone dry during the dormant period. Most of the South African winter-growing species convert readily to a summer growing regimen, although the pachycaulous plants and species such as *S. sulcicalyx* should be treated as winter growers.

Senecio deflersii should receive water somewhat less frequently both when growing and when dormant, and needs very quick drainage. Some East African species, such as *S. picticaulis* and any of the thicker-stemmed species, should be observed carefully and given less water when they are not actively growing whatever the season, although they enjoy water once a week when they are active.

Most senecios will grow readily from cuttings and divisions. *Senecio talinoides* subsp. *mandraliscae* in particular can spread too vigorously under optimum conditions outdoors, though it is easily controlled. Many South African species tolerate at least a few degrees of frost if dry, and *S. kleinia* and the ground covers take light frost and winter rain without complaint.

Othonna intermedia, with *Phyllobolus digitata* in the background, after a Knersvlakte rain. Photo by Kurt Zadnik.

aqualand setting, I found it growing on an outcrop of quartz boulders along with miniature aloes, tylecodons, haworthias, various mimicry crassulas, conophytums, anacampseros, an interesting medusoid euphorbia, and a host of other small succulents. From 50 feet (15 m) away, this great variety of life appeared to be a jumble of bare white rocks.

From farther north in the Richtersveld and across the Orange River, **Othonna cakilifolia** also has pink-purple flowers and a geophytic lifestyle but instead of oval leaves its foliage is deeply pinnate with jagged, narrow lobes. Yet another geophyte, **O. auriculifolia**, with irregularly, less deeply lobed leaves, may send up multiple stems from its woody underground caudex.

Looking like little trees with nonsucculent blue foliage, the pachycaulous othonnas include a number of superficially similar species with thick trunks up to 2 feet (60 cm) tall and as much as 6 inches (15 cm) in diameter at their base. Though uncommon in cultivation, these plants actually grow fairly abundantly in dry, but not totally arid, localities up and down the western coast of South Africa and southern Namibia. The aptly named **Othonna arborescens** from Western Cape, branches freely, grows as much as 2 feet (60 cm) tall, and has peeling bark on a proportionately thick trunk.

Othonna arbuscula is a shorter-growing, less striking Richtersveld species with a trunk not much thicker than its numerous branches. **Othonna pachypoda**, also found

in the Richtersveld, can reach a foot (30 cm) in height, and, as suggested by its name, develops a thick, squat base. It shares part of its territory with the somewhat larger, wider ranging **O. retrofracta**, which extends into Namibia, and is most easily distinguished by its often lobed leaves. Mostly Namibian, **O. furcata** also edges over into the Richtersveld. It is a little taller growing than the other pachycaulous othonnas, and its smooth, gray bark most easily separates it from them.

Though collectors consider the pachycaulous species desirable, it is generally agreed that the most interesting members of the genus are several low-growing or mound-forming dwarfs. Perhaps the best known of these rare extreme endemics is **Othonna euphorbioides**. Typically

Othonna euphorbioides in its typical habitat, a cleft in a southern Richtersveld low granite *koppie*. Photo by Kurt Zadnik.

Othonna herrei, its sculptural qualities more apparent during its leafless summer dormancy.

Essentially growing on bare rock, *Othonna cacalioides* benefits from winter mist on a Namaqualand mountain. Photo by Rob Skillin.

Othonna clavifolia, growing on vertical carbonate rock where it receives only a little sea fog, yet still produces its anomalous daisy flowers.

Othonna cf. *protecta*, in Richtersveld quartz, with leaves like black onions over a 3-inch (3-cm) tall caudex.

Othonna opima, growing near the Orange River in Namibia, with leaves almost as big as bananas. Photo by Kurt Zadnik.

found in narrow clefts on low granite koppies in the southeastern Richtersveld, it is best known for its dense covering of thin, curving spines. Mature multibranched plants form low mounds up to a foot (30 cm) across and half as tall. Its foliage, glaucous and entire, resembles that of many of the pachycaulous species.

Othonna herrei has blue-green, wavy-margined leaves and is primarily valued for its stems, which are somewhat elongated, sparsely branching, and covered with prominent, irregularly shaped brown tubercles. *Othonna armiana*, sometimes considered a subspecies of *O. herrei*, is similarly tubercled, but remains low. Mature plants look like a typical *O. herrei* turned on its side. The quartz field–dwelling *O. lepidocaulis* resembles *O. herrei* as well, but its flattened, overlapping, scalelike tubercles are lighter in color. The similar *O. wrinkleana* is darker and even smaller. These four bizarre species actually look more interesting when dormant, as when actively growing their large leaves and flowers obscure their stems and in effect, normalize them.

Although its blue-green leaves and little yellow-daisy flowers resemble those of many other species, *Othonna cacalioides* retains its distinctive appearance whether growing or dormant and leafless. It forms a squat, almost spherical, aboveground caudex up to several inches (about 10 cm) in diameter and generally shorter than wide. Old plants may branch with multiple caudices. This species is found in localized pockets running from the southern edge of Namaqualand into coastal Namibia. It often grows in shallow sandy grit on top of rocky plates, sometimes, in the southern part of its range, next to the miniature *Anacampseros comptoniana*.

The thick, succulent leaves of a few other choice othonnas differentiate them from the rest. *Othonna clavifolia* grows in the tiniest cracks in sometimes vertical rocks near the Richtersveld seacoast. It forms miniature spreading plants with thick, almost spherical, succulent leaves. Unfortunately, in cultivation, it is almost impossible to keep the leaves from elongating (etiolating) unrecognizably.

Othonna protecta, another Richtersveld plant, forms a short, thick stem topped by a tuft of very elongated, terete, dark green leaves, and occasional thin, short-lived side shoots. *Othonna opima* is a larger species with smooth succulent stems. It grows on both sides of the Orange River. On the South African side the leaves are usually terete, narrow and curving, with pointed tips, while on the Namibian side of the river, they are proportionately enormous, over 6 inches (15 cm) long, and perfectly cylindrical with rounded apices.

Several species of these odd othonnas come well from seed or cuttings and occasionally show up in specialist nurseries. They all want the maximum amount of light possible, and during their winter growing season they should receive water about once a week when the weather is good. When they are dormant, water every three or four weeks will not hurt most of them, though species such as *O. lepidocaulis* and *O. clavifolia* may rot unless kept very dry. Othonnas do well in a leaner-than-average, extremely fast draining succulent soil mix. Though a challenge both to find and to grow, othonnas, with their annual transformation from picturesque, sculptural apparent stumps to flowering daisies and back, put on a show that justifies the effort.

Chapter 21

Dioscorea, Cucurbits, and Other Succulent Caudiciforms

ALTHOUGH SOME PLANTS with a caudiciform habit crop up in almost all the plant families discussed so far, in a number of families caudiciforms comprise the majority of their succulent species. Speaking technically, the caudex of a true caudiciform derives from the embryonic plant's hypocotyl, located between its incipient leaves and roots. In horticultural circles the definitions are less clear cut, and caudiciform may be applied to any succulent with a dramatically enlarged base. Regardless of terminology, several groups of entirely unrelated succulents develop a large basal caudex obviously distinct from its roots as well as its usually much less succulent upper parts. These caudices, often picturesque, knobby, fissured, or ridged, have ensured the popularity of these plants with collectors.

DIOSCOREA

The monocotyledonous family Dioscoreaceae consists of several hundred mostly tropical species of vining plants, often with tuberous roots, and best known for their edible representatives, yams and sweet potatoes. Within this family of tropical tubers, however, a relatively few species have gained special recognition because of their large woody caudices. These succulent dioscoreas occur sparingly in widely separated parts of the world: southern Mexico and southern and eastern Africa.

The caudiciform dioscoreas are furnished with an either partly or completely aboveground caudex equipped with a thick, woody outer layer that both maximizes water retention and protects against predation. These caudices vary from tall and tapering, to flat and ground hugging, to nearly cubical. Additionally, many of them are divided into regular polygonal plates that become protuberant with age, and are separated by deep fissures. The annual vines that grow from these bases bear gen-

erally cordate (heart-shaped) leaves not that dissimilar from a typical sweet potato vine.

Dioscorea mexicana (synonym *D. macrostachys*), from Mexico, grows in the understory of both dense tropical forests and more open woodlands. In its search for light it sends out an alarmingly vigorous vine in late spring that may stretch over 30 feet (9 m) long before dying back in winter. Unaffected by the high overall rainfall of its habitat, *D. mexicana* typically lives on steep rocky slopes characterized by extremely fast runoff. Moreover, much of its habitat fluctuates between wet conditions in late spring through early fall and relative drought for the remainder of the year. The low, dome-shaped caudices of *D. mexicana* may reach 3 feet (90 cm) in diameter and perhaps 8 to 10 inches (20 to 25 cm) in height. Along with its longer vines, it has larger leaves than the African species.

Dioscorea mexicana, its twin vines disappearing upward into the canopy above.

Among the several South African succulent dioscoreas, **Dioscorea sylvatica** has a cone-shaped caudex and remains mostly underground in habitat. As a result it has less need for the knobby protrusions that decorate and protect some of the other species. Its leaves may be typically cordate or fairly deeply lobed.

Dioscorea paniculata (synonym *D. sylvatica* var. *paniculata*) has an almost pancake-flat caudex, rather similar to *D. mexicana*, and large cordate leaves. The more irregularly shaped caudex of **D. hemicrypta** can grow 4 or 5 feet (1.2 to 1.5 m) high and about half as wide. It looks like the stump of a tree, half hidden by the mix of shrubs and succulents with which it grows in the Little Karoo and surrounding areas. What looks at first glance like an unassociated vine growing out of its top turns out to be its foliage, small-leafed, glaucous, and arranged in short secondary branches. Among several more-or-less caudiciform, rarely seen East African species, **D. buchananii**, from Mozambique to Tanzania, resembles *D. sylvatica*.

Certainly the most famous and probably the most interesting dioscorea is **Dioscorea elephantipes**, the elephant's foot plant, fairly widely distributed though never common in the South African winter-rainfall area. In this species the depth of the furrows, height of the knobs, and geometrical regularity of the plates attain their greatest development. The caudices of old plants can reach over 3 feet (90 cm) in diameter with a height to match.

Because South African dioscoreas grow in areas of mixed succulent scrub where they receive more light than the Mexican forest dwellers, their vines remain more compact. *Dioscorea elephantipes* and *D. hemicrypta* start their growth in autumn and go dormant in early summer, while species such as *D. paniculata* and *D. sylvatica*, from farther east, generally grow in the warm months of the year.

Although none of these odd plants is particularly difficult to raise, the various species do have certain quirks. The roots of *Dioscorea mexicana* grow from the sides of its caudex rather than from the bottom. Consequently, raising the caudex too high in a container for purposes of display will eliminate any possibilities for new root growth, leading to the eventual death of the plant. *Dioscorea elephantipes* has a more typical root system, and though it generally goes dormant in summer, sometimes both it and its Mexican cousin ignore their proper growing seasons, either keeping their vines long into their seasonal rest period or producing new vines earlier than expected. If this should occur, paying attention to the plants instead of the calendar is recommended. Perhaps surprisingly, *D. elephantipes* is fairly cold hardy. Specimens can survive light frosts outdoors if given excellent drainage, particularly in areas where the winter rain and overcast is rapidly replaced by bright sunshine.

Entirely different from both the Mexican and African species, **Dioscorea basiclavicaulis**, from dry forests in southern Brazil, is a good-sized shrub that sends out multiple thick stems heavily armed with spines that taper

Dioscorea hemicrypta looks like an abruptly cut off stump with a bush on top.

An old plant of *Dioscorea elephantipes* with very prominent tubercles.

The Brazilian *Dioscorea basiclavicaulis*: spiny bases emerging out of a cluster of separate tuberous roots. Photo by Rob Skillin.

into vines. Strikingly fierce looking, though very rarely cultivated, it is sure to make its way more generally into horticulture eventually.

Large specimens of *Dioscorea mexicana* show up for sale from time to time, and command high prices. It is important to realize that these are collected plants, either legally imported years ago or acquired by less reputable means. Though they do well in cultivation their caudices grow either imperceptibly or not at all.

Large legally imported specimens of *Dioscorea elephantipes* also show up from time to time but they are extremely expensive. Seed of *D. elephantipes* is available and germinates fairly easily, so that nursery grown plants, though rather slow growing, are frequently obtainable. Seedlings begin to develop their characteristic fissures after four or five years.

Because they are vining plants, often growing near trees, dioscoreas do not need as much light as many succulents. Any standard, fast-draining succulent soil mix will serve them well. When in growth they should receive water about once a week. When dormant they should get enough water to prevent them from desiccating, generally every three to four weeks.

KEDROSTRIS, MOMORDICA, GERRARDANTHUS, AND RELATED CUCURBITS

A second family of plants more widely known for their edible qualities is the Cucurbitaceae, or gourd family. It includes cucumbers and melons, but also a good number of caudiciform and other succulents, distributed over a wide swathe of the world's warmer zones.

Typically, succulent cucurbits consist of a large caudex with an annual climbing vine. In the wild these caudices may hide underground, protrude partly above the surface, or live entirely above ground. Those that remain below ground generally have a smooth surface, while the aboveground ones often develop a protective woody exterior, with fissures and protuberances of the type that appeal to succulent enthusiasts. The leaves vary considerably among the different genera, a few having an entire, rhomboidal, rather ivylike shape, while in most species the leaves are lobed and often finely dissected.

Most of the tuberous cucurbits in cultivation come from southern and eastern Africa. *Kedrostris*, *Momordica*, and *Gerrardanthus* are probably the best-known genera, but *Coccinia* and *Corallocarpus* are also cultivated.

Kedrostris, with a few dozen species that range as far afield as Yemen, forms caudices varying in shape from a

Kedrostris nana var. *zeyheri*, its pancakelike caudex usually buried in the ground.

rough-textured approximate sphere to a flattened disc. **Kedrostris nana** has a disc-shaped caudex that sends out a vine up to several yards (meters) long, with small multi-lobed leaves.

A number of other cucurbits share the characteristics of *Kedrostris*, namely, a more-or-less rounded caudex, often marked with bumps and irregularities, and three-, five-, or seven-lobed leaves growing from an elongated, thin-stemmed vine. These include the more typically grown species of *Coccinia* and *Corallocarpus* such as **Coccinia sessiliflora** from Namibia and more eastern species such as **Corallocarpus bainesii** and **C. welwitschii**. These plants, however, tend to be quite alike aside from details of their small odd-shaped flowers and number of lobes on their leaves.

Rarely seen, the Namibian **Corallocarpus dissectus** develops an elongated, somewhat pachycaulous stem, as does the Somali **C. glomeruliflorus**. The East African **Momordica rostrata** has an elongated, flask-shaped caudex that can reach several feet into the air and tapers into a clambering vine with three-part leaves. **Momordica africana**, more frequently encountered in cultivation, develops a more conventional, rounded caudex.

Gerrardanthus macrorhizus, also widely grown though never common, has a squat caudex up to 2 feet (60 cm) across and thin shining green leaves with angu-

The tapering caudex of *Momordica rostrata* can reach high into a supporting tree.

Gerrardanthus macrorhizus develops a vigorous vine with lush foliage. Photo by Terry Thompson.

The distinctive lobed leaves of *Cephalopentandra ecirrhosa* emerge from a fissured, multitoned caudex. Photo by Susan Carter.

Dormant *Ibervillea sonorae*, its elongated caudex characteristically set at an angle (and unrelated to the nearby flowers). Photo by Brian Kemble.

lar lobes. **Cephalopentandra ecirrhosa**, from Uganda to as far north as Ethiopia, may be the most interesting of these plants. Its caudex, fissured like a *Dioscorea*, good-sized squash blossom flowers, and large leaves lobed like an oak distinguish it from its relatives. *Ibervillea*, the New World equivalent to the African caudiciform cucurbits, comprises a number of species, the best known of which is the northwestern Mexican **I. sonorae**. This species has an aboveground, asymmetrical, boat-shaped caudex with its vine emerging out from prow, as it were. The

generally smooth-skinned tubers of **I. tenuisecta** and other ibervilleas, some of which grow as far north as Texas, tend to remain underground.

Madagascar has its own succulent cucurbits, the largest, **Odosicyos bosseri**, with a huge, somewhat disc-shaped underground caudex up to 3 feet (90 cm) across, and a correspondingly large annual vine.

The most distinctive Madagascan succulent cucurbits, however, comprise two small genera, *Seyrigia* and *Xerosicyos*. Although eventually (after many years in the case of *Xerosicyos*) plants develop somewhat tuberous bases, horticulturally they are more valued for their odd stems or leaves. Actually, *Seyrigia* leaves are tiny and ephemeral; the plants resemble other dead stick succulents, with somewhat thickened stems that conceal their chlorophyll behind a screen of other colors. With limited horticultural appeal, mature plants of most species look like a mass of barren twigs. The most popular seyrigia, however, **S. humbertii**, has stems so densely covered with soft white fuzz that they look as if they were made of felt.

Seyrigia humbertii, its new growths covered in white felt. Photo by Brian Kemble.

Xerosicyos danguyi, with leaves shaped like coins, clambers over nearby vegetation in habitat. Photo by Terry Thompson.

The few species of *Xerosicyos* have thin, woody stems, arrayed with remarkably thick, succulent yellow-green leaves the size and shape of coins. ***Xerosicyos danguyi***, fairly common in cultivation, has round leaves the size of silver dollars and twice as thick, while ***X. perrieri*** has slightly thinner leaves the size of quarters. In the wild xerosicyos clamber over trees in dry places, but in cultivation their stems grow fairly slowly, in contrast to the vines of most cucurbits. They root readily from stem cuttings.

A number of more-or-less succulent cucurbits grow in dry northwestern South Africa, among them ***Acanthosicyos***. It has a large underground caudex, stiff, spiny branches that sprawl for many feet in all directions, and very bitter fruit that look like watermelons growing in the desert.

Finally, in common with so many other unique Socotra endemics, ***Dendrosicyos socotrana*** grows into a thick-trunked, pachycaulous tree close to 20 feet (6 m) tall and 5 feet (1.5 m) thick, with multilobed, elongated leaves with bristly margins. Certainly the most spectacular succulent in the Cucurbitaceae, it remains rare in cultivation, though seedlings become available from time to time.

Tropical East Asia also provides a home to cucurbits, and one of them, ***Neoalsomitra podagrica***, is a climbing plant with a jointed, thick, succulent base that tapers gradually into climbing stems. With a fierce armament of spines, it resembles a smaller version of the odd Brazilian *Dioscorea basiclavicaulis* and needs warmth and more water than most succulents.

The caudiciform cucurbits do well in cultivation, though finding any to purchase may be a problem. Since most of them are climbing or clambering vines that grow at the bases of other plants, they do not need as bright light as many free-standing succulents. Any standard succulent mix should work fine as soil, though a little more organic matter than average will not hurt.

Most of the cucurbits come from places where it never freezes. They are rarely grown outdoors, but they will do well in a greenhouse or a bright window. Start watering them regularly when they begin to vine, which in some forms of *Ibervillea sonorae* from Baja California may be in fall or winter. When the vine dies back, reduce but do not eliminate water. About every three weeks will do during this dormant time. The stem and leaf succulents from Madagascar respond well to the same treatment. *Dendrosicyos socotrana* needs excellent drainage and much brighter light than the others, although its watering requirements are similar. Because many of the more readily obtainable plants look very similar to each other, few growers feel the need for a comprehensive collection of these plants, but everyone who likes the exotic in xerophytes should try a cucurbit or two.

Dendrosicyos socotrana, the world's largest cucumber, with *Dracaena cinnabari* and *Adenium socotranum* in the background. Photo by Rob Skillin.

IPOMOEA

Ipomoea is the sole genus of the Convolvulaceae, or the morning glory family, with succulent species. Distributed worldwide, its succulent members grow both in Africa—in northern Namibia and northeastern South Africa—and at the opposite side of the Earth, in Mexico. The free-flowering African species include *I. holubii* and *I. transvaalensis* and the Namibian *I. inamoena*. Caudiciforms with big, underground tubers and thin, leafy stems, they differ completely from the Mexican ones in morphology. The Mexican plants, in contrast, are somewhat succulent shrubs and trees with thickened stems and branches. Two examples are *I. arborescens*, from south-central Mexico, and *I. cuernavacana*, growing farther north and east. These pachycaulous plants lack the

Ipomoea holubii—in the wild it would look like an uninteresting small shrub. Photo by Terry Thompson.

A small, somewhat pachycaulous *Ipomoea* species in Oaxaca.

A colony of *Pyrenacantha malvifolia*, looking almost identical to the surrounding boulders. Photo by Susan Carter.

A smaller *Pyrenacantha malvifolia*, easier to visualize but still with a stone-like caudex. Photo by Terry Thompson.

spectacular weirdness of their caudiciform cousins, but they have attractive foliage and their morning glory-like flowers offer a surprising additional bonus.

PYRENACANTHA

The obscure family Icacinaceae includes a few species in the genus *Pyrenacantha*, from East Africa as far as northern Kenya and Somalia. Best known, and one of the most extraordinary of all caudiciforms, **P. malvifolia** forms an enormous aboveground caudex sometimes over 6 feet (1.8 m) tall and wide, looking very much like a rough gray boulder, with one or more thick-stemmed branching vines emerging out of its top. Other species, exceptionally rare in cultivation, look similar and would do well with the same treatment: bright light, a typical succulent soil mix, water once a week when growing and every three to four weeks when dormant. Larger plants can withstand an entire dry season without water and in areas of low light and high humidity this may be the best winter-growing strategy for them.

HYDNOPHYTUM AND MYRMECODIA

A final group of caudiciforms belong to the Rubiaceae, the family best known for the coffee plant. Two genera, *Hydnophytum* and *Myrmecodia*, differ both in geographic habitat and specific adaptations from the other plants mentioned so far. From Southeast Asia and the tropical parts of northern Australia, they grow in areas with heavy seasonal rains and live epiphytically, resembling a canteen-type pachypodium attached to the side of a tree trunk. Their fat, swollen, often very spiny bases are up to a foot (30 cm) or more in diameter. Rather than serving primarily as water-storing devices, these bases are filled with pockets and holes which function as living quarters for the tropical ant colonies that inhabit and defend them. Consequently their cultural needs differ from those of typical succulents.

Hydnophytum and *Myrmecodia* require considerable warmth, and during their growing season they enjoy humidity and more frequent water, about every five days. During the colder months they should receive much less water even though they do not necessarily drop their slightly leathery, deep green leaves. Their soil mix should be extremely quick draining, either with a considerable amount of acidic organic matter or with regular fertilizing over a mix more suitable for an orchid than a typical succulent. They can also be mounted on a slab, although in a home or dry greenhouse it could be difficult to supply them with adequate humidity.

The species of both genera resemble each other, and though none are common, the largely spineless **Hydnophytum formicarum** and the spiny **Myrmecodia echinata** occasionally show up in collections. Some Australian species such as **H. ferrugineum** and **M. tuberosa** are becoming better known.

Chapter 22

Adenia, Cissus, Ficus, and *Pterodiscus*: Succulent Passion Vines, Grapes, Figs, and Sesames

SEVERAL PLANT FAMILIES better known for ornamental or fruit-bearing plants also include a few succulent species. The genus *Adenia* resides within Passifloraceae, the passionflower family. The grape family, Vitaceae, includes *Cissus* and *Cyphostemma*; the fig family, Moraceae, *Dorstenia* and *Ficus*; and the sesame family, Pedaliaceae, *Pterodiscus*, *Sesamothamnus*, and *Uncarina*.

The succulents in these four families include further variations on the caudiciform theme, along with pachycauls and some that defy easy description. They also include many rarities, plants once found only in major botanic gardens, sought after by collectors and now very gradually becoming available from specialist growers.

ADENIA (PASSIFLORACEAE)

Although the passionflower family, Passifloraceae, is known for tropical vines, complex, beautiful flowers, and endless varieties of foliage, it also includes succulents from the genus *Adenia*. Mostly climbing tropical vines up to 150 feet (46 m) long and bearing comparatively drab flowers, the approximately one hundred species of *Adenia* range from Southeast Asia through India and tropical Africa, to South Africa and Namibia. A number of adenias grow from underground tubers. As various species have adapted to drier environments their tubers have grown proportionately larger with some finally turning into aboveground caudices with a concomitant decrease in the exuberance of their vining stems.

As would be expected, the more succulent adenias live in the drier parts of Africa, southwestern Arabia, and Madagascar. These species share a few basic forms. In those most frequently encountered the caudex is at least partly above ground and covered with a thin, often waxy, woody bark. Their stems, originating from their caudices, may either be woody, thick, and relatively short or liana-like, capable of climbing high into surrounding vegetation.

The South African ***Adenia fruticosa*** has a tall, curving or spindle-shaped, sometimes multistemmed caudex topped with a few thin, arching branches and usually trilobed foliage. In ***A. firingalavensis***, from Madagascar, the caudex is more compact, although its branches grow very tall and climb high into any nearby trees.

Other species develop a roughly globose to shallowly hemispherical caudex. In digitate-leafed (leaves lobed like the fingers of a hand) ***Adenia glauca***, the caudex grows up to 3 feet (90 cm) across, rapidly tapering into

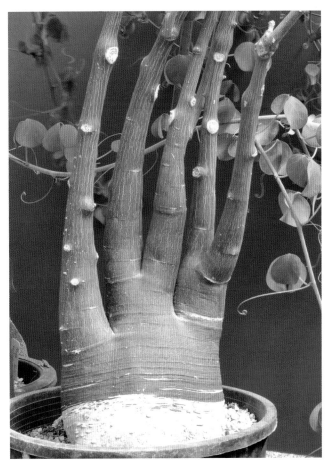

A large *Adenia fruticosa,* with multiple stems like the fingers of an elongated hand.

Adenia firingalavensis, out in the open in a Madagascar garden. Photo by Inge Hoffman.

Adenia spinosa—the subject of years of careful grooming. Photo by Terry Thompson.

Adenia glauca with its vine emerging from its suddenly truncated caudex.

Adenia venenata in Yemen, with a flask-shaped, tapering caudex. Photo by Rob Skillin.

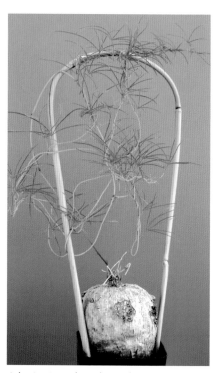

Adenia stenodactyla, with its narrow-lobed leaves twining around a support.

one or more narrow woody stems. In the multistemmed *A. spinosa*, the caudex can grow over 6 feet (1.8 m) in diameter though less than 2 feet (60 cm) tall. From the same general eastern South African region as *A. glauca*, *A. spinosa* produces tendrils at the base of its nonlobed, ovate leaves that harden into thin, curved spines.

With their smooth, green-gray, waxy surfaces, sharply demarcated into dull brownish at soil level, these adenias resemble small islands with a few vines or little leafy trees growing out of them. *Adenia repanda*, which has an elongated, narrower caudex and nonlobed leaves, also sends its few branches into surrounding vegetation, while *A. volkensii* and *A. ellenbeckii* grow vigorously but compactly, looking like small bushy shrubs.

Adenia keramanthus, from Kenya and Tanzania, with serrate margins on its bristly leaves, the Somali *A. ellenbeckii*, and the East African and Arabian *A. venenata* grow tall, green, photosynthesizing stems, thickest at their bases and tapering gradually with a few secondary branches. All the stems emerge from tuberous roots or a rudimentary caudex. *Adenia venenata* may display a great variety of leaf shape on a single plant; the first leaves of the season are angular with long, sharply pointed lobes, subsequent leaves steadily becoming less angular, and concluding with short-lobed, gently rounded palmate leaves.

Species with a somewhat similar habit include *Adenia karibaensis*, from Zimbabwe. It has palmate leaves and a rounded caudex similar to *A. glauca*, but a main stem that elongates into a thick, mottled gray and green trunk up to 8 feet (2.4 m) tall. The Madagascan *A. epigea*, has variable trilobed or entire foliage. The rare Somali *A. aculeata* also has a subsurface caudex and thick main stems ending in long vines. Its caudex and stems are covered with pale spines when young that become jet black with age and look as if made of cast plastic.

A number of adenias have markedly digitate or palmate leaves, striking enough in one case to have given a name to the most notorious adenia. *Adenia digitata*, which is distributed widely in Africa, has the possibly justifiable reputation as the most poisonous plant in the world. It combines two deadly toxins within its tubers: one a fast-acting cyanide, and another all its own, slower, but also lethal. Rather disappointingly, its up to 2-foot (60-cm) diameter caudex remains underground in the wild. Though it can be lifted for display in cultivation it lacks the texture and dramatic appearance of its less toxic cousins.

Another adenia with an underground, unornamented caudex, the rarely seen *Adenia stenodactyla*, comes from Tanzania and Zambia. Its leaves are so finely dissected as to look like masses of green hair or swarms of tiny vines. Rather than developing tendrils, the leaf tips themselves twine onto nearby plants for support.

A few geographically disparate species share another growth form, with an enormous aboveground, somewhat hemispherical caudex topped by stiff, nonvining branches. The Namibian *Adenia pechuelii* has been called the strangest plant in a region of amazingly strange plants. Its enormous caudex can approach 10 feet by 6 feet (3 m by 1.8 m) and over 3 feet (90 cm) high, covered with randomly distributed stubby branches that make it look something like a hedgehog. As the caudices age they change from relatively spherical to more amorphous and boulderlike, looking as if they had melted into the ground. The plants wedge themselves in little crevices in boulders or grow in slightly larger bare patches between rocks. They prefer rocky ridges elevated above the surrounding desert plains, unlike the climbing species that grow in the understory of thin, semiarid woodlands. In contrast to those adenias that resemble islands with a few small trees, mature plants of *A. pechuelii* look like oddly shaped boulders covered on top with a dense growth of *A. glauca*-like caudiciforms—in reality their own stems. Seedling plants resemble *A. glauca* as well, differing only in their stubbier branches and undivided leaves. How long it takes a seedling with a 2- or 3-inch (5- to 8-cm) caudex to grow into one of the giants is anyone's guess.

Far to the northeast, *Adenia globosa* and *A. ballyi*, though not closely related to *A. pechuelii*, share something of its habit and its preference for arid, stony places. *Adenia globosa* resembles a dark green, hemispherical boulder up to 8 feet (2.4 m) across and tall, dotted with rigid arching branches, several feet long and defended by thick spines. The overall effect is something like a spiky crewcut with all its hairs suddenly on end. Rarer and slightly smaller than *A. globosa*, the Somali *A. ballyi* has vertically

Adenia pechuelii, a 5-foot (1.5-cm) wide plant merging into the Namibian rocks. Photo by Kurt Zadnik.

Impressive as it may seem, compared to wild plants this *Adenia globosa* is little more than a seedling. Photo by Terry Thompson.

Adenia ballyi: beneath this tangle of branches lies a caudex. Photo by Susan Carter.

striped gray branches that may conform to the shape of its caudex. It resembles its cousin, with similarly spiked branches and equally sharp-angled, trilobed leaves. *Adenia pechuelii* grows in small scattered colonies but in some parts of northeastern Africa large populations of *A. ballyi* may dominate an otherwise bleak landscape.

Adenias are still fairly rare in cultivation, with *Adenia glauca* and *A. fruticosa* probably the most common. The different species have different cultural needs. The plants are dioecious, that is, plants are either male or female only, and production of seed, much less obtaining stock from which to get seed, has never been easy. Many of them, including *A. globosa* and *A. pechuelii*, however, will come from cuttings, and given time and enough root room, may develop quite respectable caudices of their own.

Once obtained, the southern African plants such as *Adenia fruticosa*, *A. glauca*, and *A. spinosa* are not difficult to grow. Any good, rapidly draining succulent soil mix suits them. As low growing climbers they do not need as much light as most succulents and will do fine in any spot that gets some direct sun. They can take quite a bit of cold, but are not reliably hardy outdoors in places that receive occasional frost. They like regular, typically weekly watering when their leaves begin to grow in spring, and a fairly strict dry period, with watering reduced to once every three or four weeks when their leaves drop in late fall.

In contrast, adenias from East Africa and Madagascar can be very sensitive to cold. Furthermore, some of them seem to like a great deal of water during their leafy growing season. *Adenia globosa* and *A. ballyi* produce their small leaves only briefly if at all, but they too need warmth and generous water, followed by a strict dry rest period in winter. *Adenia pechuelii* has habits similar to the *A. glauca* group, but it is susceptible to rotting if too wet and is even slower growing than its painfully slow-growing cousins; contrarily, it sometimes acts as a winter grower, even though in habitat it receives its rain in summer.

Adenias want to become large and will do much better if potted in containers that offer them generous root room. Several species besides *Adenia digitata* have reputations as toxic plants, with local uses noted such as "used to poison hyenas." Unless you have an irresistible Hitchcockian penchant for obscure means of murder, they are probably safe to have around the house.

CISSUS AND CYPHOSTEMMA (VITACEAE)

Along with more familiar plants, Vitaceae, the grape family, includes a number of spectacular succulents. The succulent grapes fall into three general categories: vining plants, clambering plants with thickened, segmented, often angular stems, and plants straddling the caudiciform-pachycaul divide with enormously swollen bases either elongated into trunks or squat as egg-shaped boulders. All the succulent grapes were once included in the genus *Cissus*, but after *Cyphostemma* was split off from it only a relatively few succulent species remained in a genus better known for ornamental tropical and temperate vines.

The succulent species left in *Cissus* encompass clambering, annual vining and slightly pachycaulous plants from semiarid regions in both Africa and Mexico. Most of the annually vining plants are Mexican, usually with underground caudices. With a good-sized, aboveground caudex, *C. tuberosus*, from the northwestern Mexican state of Sonora is the exception. *Cissus tuberosus* grows easily but needs a lean soil mix in a proportionately small container, a winter rest after its leaves fall, and careful watering when growth resumes to develop a large caudex.

Cissus tuberosus—if given too much soil and water, it will not develop this type of caudex. Photo by Terry Thompson.

Cissus cactiformis on the ground in search of something to climb. Photo by Susan Carter.

Along with most members of its genus, it propagates readily from cuttings, and stem segments that come in touch with the soil often spontaneously root.

Many clambering species, such as ***Cissus quadrangularis*** and ***C. cactiformis***, both from East Africa and Arabia, have perennial succulent, often jointed stems and quickly ephemeral leaves. They develop thickened tuberous bases in time, and in habitat they can cover small trees and shrubs. In contrast, ***C. subaphylla***, from Socotra, with smaller, elongated, flattened stems, remains compact. The climbing, vining stems of ***C. rotundifolia***, from East Africa and Arabia, bear large thick, three-lobed leaves. These species live in fairly arid regions, and, not surprisingly, do best with very bright light and fairly strict winter dry periods.

Although *Cyphostemma* was separated from *Cissus* because of technical details of its inflorescence, once seen, few of the cultivated succulent cyphostemmas could be mistaken for a cissus. These African species occupy the indefinite border between caudiciforms and pachycauls. Even as young plants they are prized because of their striking massive stems and peeling, papery bark.

From seasonally arid, semitropical parts of northern Namibia, ***Cyphostemma juttae*** may grow to over 6 feet (1.8 m) in height and more than 2 feet (60 cm) in diameter at the base. Often with only a few small branches and growing with a slight curve, plants have been fancifully compared to swollen elephant tusks protruding from the ground, topped with very large trilobed, fleshy green leaves.

Cyphostemma uter from dry hillsides and sandy flats in northern Namibia has long-lasting, toothy-margined

Cyphostemma juttae in Berkeley, a survivor of 17°F (-8°C), with its multiple stems the result of frost damage. Photo by Terry Thompson.

The swirling, architectural structure of *Cyphostemma uter*, from northern Namibia. Photo by Rob Skillin.

The extremely shaggy *Cyphostemma bainesii*, dormant in arid surroundings in southern Namibia. Photo by Rob Skillin.

In the mountains of central Namibia with *Cyphostemma currori*, over 15 feet (4.5 m) tall. Photo by Rob Skillin.

leaves. It makes intricate whorls of fat, curved, mostly horizontal branches, up to 5 feet (1.5 m) tall with an 8-foot (2.4-m) spread.

Cyphostemma currori, the largest species, is also Namibian, growing on steep dry hills in the north and center of the country. It has very large round-lobed leaves covered in white to golden-brown felt, complementing its often golden-yellow bark. It can reach close to 20 feet (6 m) in height, with a massive, sometimes multitrunked base up to 8 feet (2.4 m) in diameter surmounted by a crown of spreading 2-foot (60-cm) thick branches.

Cyphostemma bainesii, the southernmost Namibian cyphostemma, may be single-stemmed to a few feet tall, or remain low with multiple stems. It has exceptionally shaggy bark, and its three-lobed leaves have a covering of fine short, white hair. Closely related and generally considered to be just a form of *C. bainesii*, *C. seitzianum* is from a few spots at altitudes over 6000 feet (1800 m) in the mountains separating the central Namibian highlands from the fog-bound coastal plains. It forms an egg-shaped caudex up to a foot (30 cm) tall and almost twice as wide. Its one to two short branches put out two or three large trilobed leaves during its four- or five-month growing season. The leaves are extra densely covered in silvery-white felt.

Other species, such as the relatively slender *Cyphostemma hardyi* and *C. oleraceum*, and the tuberous-rooted *C. quinatum* with thick, hairless, pale green leaves, live in eastern South Africa. Cyphostemmas occur sporadically along the eastern side of the continent as well, including very rarely cultivated cucurbit-like species with underground caudices and thin, climbing vines, such as *C. adenocaule* from Kenya. Plants continue as far north as Somalia, where the scarce *C. betiforme* (see photo on page 28) resembles the squat, branching Namibian species.

A number of cyphostemmas grow in Madagascar, and like the East African plants, these send out fairly long vines from strange, flasklike caudices which can

Cyphostemma seitzianum, a form of *C. bainesii*, with heavily felted leaves.

The relatively thin-bodied *Cyphostemma hardyi*.

An extremely rare *Cyphostemma* aff. *betiforme* in Somalia. Photo by Susan Carter.

Looking like a looming vegetable skyscraper, the Madagascan *Cyphostemma laza*. Photo by Brian Kemble.

endure frosts in habitat, but in conditions of extreme aridity. *Cyphostemma uter* must be protected from cold and kept very dry when dormant, while *C. seitzianum*, which should be given less-than-average water when growing and a strict winter rest period, often does not leaf out until midsummer and can go dormant as early as midautumn.

Cyphostemmas will grow from cuttings or seed, but in some cases seed is very difficult both to produce and to germinate, ensuring the continuing scarcity of the rarer species. Even *C. juttae* is still somewhat uncommon in cultivation, and the more unusual cyphostemmas are among the most coveted of collector's items. Although cyphostemma fruits resemble grapes, they are filled with oxalic acid and are best left uneaten.

DORSTENIA AND FICUS (MORACEAE)

The first dorstenia I saw looked more like a sculpture of some alien plant form from a science fiction movie than anything that actually existed. With its nearly spherical base, short upright branches that seemed made of shiny, brown plastic, and its apparent flowers—small stars with irregular rays radiating out from a central disc filled with sparkling grains the size of beach sand—it seemed like nothing from Earth, but it was, from Somalia.

There are as many as two hundred species of *Dorstenia* in the Moraceae, the fig family. Found in both the New and Old World tropics, most are small herbaceous plants in the rain forest understory. The succulent species, however, cluster around the Great Rift Valley of eastern Africa and the shores of its watery extension, the Red Sea, where the plants have had to adapt to an increasingly arid environment. In response, some species have developed underground tubers with rosettes of annual leaves, some have evolved into true stem succulents, and one species has turned into a small "bottle tree," like a miniature baobab, with a greatly enlarged main trunk.

Dorstenias are defined by their unique flowering structure, the asymmetrical little stars that first caught my attention. Correctly called a hypanthodium, the inflorescence consists of a fleshy, flat or concave, typically disk-shaped structure filled with tiny simplified flowers and usually surrounded by anywhere from a few to over a dozen "rays." Think of a fig turned inside out and carved into a child's drawing of the sun with its rays and you will get the general picture. Although in some dorstenias the hypanthodium can be triangular or even almost linear, the star shape is the rule for most species.

attain surprisingly large dimensions. A large plant of **Cyphostemma laza** resembles an obelisk, cylindrical and barely tapering throughout its length until it suddenly divides into a number of trailing, woody stems at its top. Perhaps the best-known Madagascan species, **C. elephantopus**, consists of a very large disc-shaped underground caudex that elongates into a thick, succulent, aboveground stem ending in a narrow, leafy vine.

The tropical cyphostemmas need much the same care as the East African *Cissus* species: lots of light, protection from cold, reasonable amounts of water when growing, and a fairly rigorous dry period when their leaves drop in winter until their new growth starts in spring. *Cyphostemma juttae*, by far the most common cyphostemma in cultivation, requires the same general treatment, but is surprisingly cold hardy, capable of surviving cold-snaps below 20°F (–7°C). Both *C. currori* and *C. bainesii* also

The most common succulent dorstenia in cultivation is **Dorstenia foetida**, a plant from both sides of the Gulf of Aden at the mouth of the Red Sea, and south to coastal Kenya as well. The species comes in an overwhelming variety of forms, some quite tiny, some fairly large, more or less erect and barely branched or freely producing small stubby branches, and with thin leaves curly or uncurled. Some forms are prolifically self-fertile, some barely so, others self-sterile and difficult to propagate. Even the largest will do well in a 4-inch (10-cm) pot, while smaller forms are suitable for a 2- or 3-inch (5- to 8-cm) container. One very distinct appearing variation was recently described as **D. lavranii**; it is one of the few single-sexed (dioecious) species.

Also a good candidate for a small pot, **Dorstenia hildebrandtii** will develop a small rounded base and an erect 3- or 4-inch (8- to 10-cm) stem if kept container-bound, but becomes leggy if allowed too much root room. **Dorstenia crispa** and **D. lanceolata**, from farther south in coastal Kenya, resemble *D. foetida*, but with more elongate leaves and stems, while **D. radiata** and **D. zanzibarica** look like taller, skinnier versions of *D. hildebrandtii*.

The rarely grown tuberous dorstenias can be fussy in cultivation, but they are remarkably strange little plants, with small rosettes of leaves and hypanthodia raised up at the ends of tall peduncles. **Dorstenia barnimiana**, with thin, almost rectangular leaves and elongated, nearly linear hypanthodia, probably is the most frequently encountered of these in cultivation, but species such as **D. ellenbeckiana**, with annual stemless rosettes of soft leaves and a hovering, spiderlike inflorescence, are worth seeking out.

The most striking succulent dorstenias are relatively large-growing, such as the multibranched **Dorstenia**

Dorstenia foetida, a common form with little star-shaped hypanthodia.

A symmetrically grown specimen of *Dorstenia lanceolata*.

Dorstenia lavranii, endemic to a few Somali gorges.

Dorstenia barnimiana, with thin leaves wrapped over its caudex and odd elongated hypanthodia.

Dorstenia ellenbeckiana, soft leaves and arachnoid hypanthodia above its caudex.

Dorstenia gypsophila—a few plants clinging to the crumbling gypsum slopes of their Somali hill. Photo by Susan Carter.

Dorstenia gigas, growing in a crack in a cliff, nurtured by the Socotran sea mists. Photo by Rob Skillin.

gypsophila from a couple of overgrazed gypsum hills in Somalia. It has squared off leaves and a basal caudex shaped as if it had melted and then amorphously re-hardened. The largest dorstenia is the amazing **D. gigas**. Endemic to Socotra, *D. gigas* develops a pachycaulous trunk to 6 feet (1.8 m) tall and 2 feet (60 cm) wide at the base. It grows in tiny cracks in vertical cliff faces, and in habitat the plants look as if they simply were glued to the rock.

Dorstenias all need warmth; some cannot tolerate cool temperatures at all. Even though they grow in arid regions, they do not like drying out, and should be watered more frequently than most succulents. Every five to seven days in summer, and every ten to fourteen in winter is appropriate for them. Most are not fussy about soil as long as it drains quickly. If grown in sufficient light, either in habitat or in cultivation, their branches will remain short and their bases will widen. Otherwise they will elongate. *Dorstenia foetida* and its relatives are pretty easy to grow and do well on sunny windowsills. The other types, however, can be considerably more difficult to grow and to find.

Ficus, the most familiar member of the Moraceae, includes a great number of trees, many with massive bases, but only a small number that can justifiably be termed succulent. **Ficus petiolaris**, growing from northern Mexico to as far south as Oaxaca, becomes a large tree, with a broad trunk that spreads along the rocky ground where it usually makes its home. It is typically at home in seasonally dry forests that vary from junglelike during the summer rainy season to quite barren during the winter.

Closely related forms such as **Ficus brandegeei** and **F. palmeri**, which very possibly are just variants of *F. petiolaris*, occur in rockier, drier regions, and remain dwarfed,

Ficus palmeri, developing its multiple trunks in a large pot.

developing a caudexlike base early in their lives. African and mid-Eastern equivalents such as **F. abutilifolia** and the potentially gigantic **F. sycomorus** also sometimes near the line separating odd tropical trees from pachycaulous succulents.

Amenable to container culture, the smaller varieties of these figs need warmth and ample water when growing. When leafless, they do best in relative dryness, with

Pterodiscus ngamicus, with tubular, open-ended flowers typical of the genus.

The Somali Pterodiscus kellerianus, with its caudex completely hidden from view. Photo by Susan Carter.

Sesamothamnus lugardii grows into a large wide-based shrub.

water every two or three weeks. Without bright light they will grow leggy and lose much of their charm.

PTERODISCUS, SESAMOTHAMNUS, AND UNCARINA (PEDALIACEAE)

The succulent members of the Pedaliaceae, the sesame family, live in a strip of northern Namibia and northern South Africa, and again farther northeast in countries such as Kenya and Somalia and the island of Madagascar. *Pterodiscus*, with several relatively obscure species, exhibits variety of form both in stem and leaf. Members of the genus rarely grow more than a foot (30 cm) high, and some, with underground caudices, barely protrude from the ground at all. Others, such as the East African **P. ruspolii** and **P. ngamicus** send out many thin, leafy, usually annual shoots from their caudex, which may be flask- or bottle-shaped or nearly cubical, either single or branching underground.

Pterodiscus foliage varies from simple and ovate, to dentate, as in the pink- to purple-flowered **P. speciosus** from eastern South Africa, to deeply and narrowly pinnate, as in the golden-flowered Somali caudiciform **P. kellerianus**. The flowers are proportionately large, open ended, and tubular, almost like those in the genus *Columnea*. *Pterodiscus* flowers are often brightly colored, as with the golden-orange, relatively tall-stemmed **P. aurantiacus** from northern Namibia and Angola, or the purple- to dark red-flowered **P. elliottii**, from Zimbabwe and Zambia.

In contrast to *Pterodiscus*, the half dozen or so species of *Sesamothamnus* essentially look alike. They cover the same range as *Pterodiscus*, from northern Namibia across the top of South Africa and up the eastern edge of Africa

Sesamothamnus guerichii grows taller, though just as wide.

to Somalia, but they grow quite a bit larger, up to 15 feet (4.5 m) tall, with a complex, multiaxial base that may extend several feet. Their underground caudices, shaped like a giant football, merge imperceptibly into a basket-like mass of woody, succulent stems surrounding a central main trunk. Sesamothamnus bear long-tubed, generally white or pale pink flowers that flare open at their tips, and their small pale green or blue-green soft leaves grow all along their primary and secondary branches.

Sesamothamnus lugardii, from the southern part of their range, probably is the most common in cultivation. It is similar to the Namibian **S. guerichii** as well as the very rarely cultivated **S. benguellensis**. **Sesamothamnus**

Uncarina roeoesliana: possibly the smallest and most obviously succulent of the genus.

busseanus from Somalia and **S. rivae**, from Kenya occasionally show up in choice collections, but are less succulent and striking in their form.

Native to Madagascar, *Uncarina* takes on a wide variety of aboveground shapes, from short-stemmed caudiciforms, to tree-types with a somewhat caudiciform base, to small more-or-less pachycaulous trees. All species develop underground caudices. **Uncarina decaryi** is more treelike, while the pachycaulous **U. grandidieri** has a thicker stem and a fatter bottom. **Uncarina platycarpa**, with a deep black throat in its yellow flowers; **U. abbreviata**, with pink or purple blossoms; and **U. stellulifera**, a relatively small plant with a thick stem and rose-colored flowers mottled white, offer contrasts from the completely yellow flowers of most species. **Uncarina roeoesliana** may be the most amenable for container culture with its thick caudex and short branches.

Uncarinas leaf out in spring and drop their very variably lobed, often slightly fuzzy foliage in late autumn. Their compound fruits, surrounded by a halo of nastily barbed hooks, adhere to any animal unlucky enough to pass by them.

Pterodiscus species, although they may look like inhabitants of severe climates, like more water than most succulents, perhaps every five days or so during their peak summer growing period. During their dormant season they can rot if kept too wet or too cold, but should not go for extremely long periods without water either, perhaps every three or four weeks. *Uncarina* species need water every five to seven days when growing, and even when dormant should receive water every two to three weeks.

Sesamothamnus species also like very bright light and warmth, though perhaps a slightly leaner soil mix. They will leaf out when they want to, generally in spring, but may drop their leaves at any time and can start up again regardless of the calendar. In any case, when they leaf out, give them reasonable amounts of water, once a week or so, and some water every three or four weeks when they are leafless; as with the others in this group they need protection from temperatures below 50°F (10°C). All succulent Pedaliaceae are unusual plants, hard to find, and often quite slow growing, but they are all worthwhile additions to any succulent collection, sought after and highly valued by those in the know.

Chapter 23

Succulent Trees and Pachycauls

I N CHAPTER 1 we learned that the term *pachycaul* was devised to describe the growth form of those succulent plants whose extremely thickened trunks and main branches make them resemble squat, very thick trees, sometimes in miniature, sometimes enormous. As a group of otherwise unrelated plants, pachycauls can be distinguished from more typical stem succulents by their generally woody stems and branches and their typically thin, seasonally deciduous leaves. Pachycauls can further be differentiated from true caudiciforms by the morphology of their succulent parts, derived from embryonic stems rather than their hypocotyl.

All this notwithstanding, as with succulents in general, the term is less than perfectly precise. Though it is used to describe plants for which no other descriptive term seemed really applicable, environmental factors often determine the shape of an individual plant, and unambiguous sounding terminology can become quite blurry. To a degree, it is equally satisfactory to think of these plants simply as succulent trees.

Pachycauls occur in a number of plant families: Burseraceae, Anacardiaceae, Bombacaceae, Moringaceae, with a few species in Fabaceae, Araliaceae, and Caricaceae as well. With a very different look, the Fouquieriaceae and Didiereaceae also consist of plants that might be considered pachycauls.

BURSERA, COMMIPHORA, AND BOSWELLIA (BURSERACEAE)

With about a dozen and a half genera and about five hundred species, the bursera family, Burseraceae, consists of small to medium-sized trees from the semitropics and tropics, generally with aromatic sap and pinnate foliage. A significant number of them have evolved a pachycaulous habit, and plants from several genera have adapted to extremely arid environments.

Bursera itself, with about one hundred species, ranges from southernmost Arizona and California, through Mexico, home to around eighty of the species, east to the Caribbean region and south into South America. Burseras show three general growth forms; these are of little botanical significance but handy for sorting out the species. The thin, peeling bark that is a striking attribute of many burseras occurs in species from all of these growth forms.

The largest burseras live in the tropics, including some true rain-forest denizens. The gumbo-limbo tree, **Bursera simaruba**, is open branched and to 50 or 60 feet (15 to 18 m) tall, with soft, light wood and pale, peeling bark. It has a range that reaches the Florida Keys. Similar, larger growing species live in wetter areas, where their smooth, often reddish bark makes them look a little like madrones (*Arbutus*), although with an entirely different leaf structure. This habit typifies the larger members of the genus. A number of these have trunks, typically of a dark brownish green to almost blue-green hue, that photosynthesize beneath their paperlike outer bark layer. In addition, they have modified their soft woody tissues for water storage. As these succulents-in-the-making have colonized increasingly arid environments, these incipient characteristics have come to the fore, with the species decreasing in size even as the portion of their stems devoted to water-storage increased.

Burseras of this second type inhabit areas either with lower total rainfall, or with drastic differences between wet and dry seasons, a climate that characterizes much of mainland Mexico. Burseras may form a significant component of low scrub forest, and are one of the dominant tree groups of the taller, seasonally dry forests as well, coexisting with agaves, opuntias, and large columnar cacti (see photo on page 21). These mid-sized, arboreal burseras include **Bursera galeottiana** and **B. schlechtendalii**, both to about 25 feet (7.6 m) tall with a foot (30 cm) thick trunk and reddish brown bark, and **B. bolivarii**, with glaucous foliage and a blue-gray stem that shows under the bark. They develop somewhat swollen main stems, and when small look like good subjects for natural bonsai. As they grow taller, however, their diameters do not increase proportionally with their height. Rarely cultivated, some of them nonetheless would probably respond to careful pruning and a regime of reduced water.

Last but certainly not least in terms of horticultural desirability, in several widely separated parts of Mexico a small number of burseras have adapted a third growth habit and become true succulents. These species specialize in arid habitats, where they often take the form of multistemmed or densely branched woody shrubs up to 6 or even 8 feet (1.8 to 2.4 m) tall, and almost as wide. In the most extreme cases, the exigencies of their environments have compelled dwarfed, twisted, picturesque growth, giving plants the look of natural bonsais. **Bursera fagaroides**, widely distributed in scattered pockets from Jalisco state as far south as Oaxaca, has light golden, peeling bark, a vaguely cigar-shaped trunk, and leaves with from three to five or more pairs of leaflets. It may grow in ground composed largely of limestone chunks in the company of true desert cacti such as *Astrophytum myriostigma*, or in tiny pockets in solid rock in areas with higher seasonal rainfall. Under these harsh conditions plants develop greatly thickened trunks and grow almost horizontally.

Bursera hindsiana, from Baja California and parts of neighboring Sonora, has reddish, nonpeeling bark, smaller leaves with fewer segments, and typically develops into a loosely branched shrub. **Bursera microphylla**, also from Baja and Sonora and extending north in small numbers into deserts of southwestern Arizona and Southern California, has undergone the most radical modifications of all in the face of extreme aridity. Its tiny distinctly dark green, pinnate leaves drop off readily under drought conditions while the plant continues to photosynthesize from beneath a thin layer of peeling outer bark. In form an ordinary *B. microphylla* resembles a typical *B. hindsiana*, a good-sized multibranched shrub with a thickened main stem. Under the right circumstances, though, both these species take on a greatly modified aspect, and *B. microphylla*, in particular, may develop into a classic "canteen" plant, with a proportionately huge rounded base and a few succulent main branches. These thick-footed plants are one of two Baja California pachycauls known as elephant trees.

On a few hills in central coastal Baja, in areas of wind-swept fog desert almost devoid of regular rainfall, ancient specimens of *Bursera microphylla* grow completely horizontally, sprawled along the ground with swollen trunks and equally ground-hugging branches close to a foot (30 cm) wide and less than 6 inches (15 cm) tall. In contrast, their leaf-bearing branches are nothing more than a few pencil-thick twigs a couple of inches (about 5 cm) long. *Bursera hindsiana*, though less common in these situations, shows up as well, its skeletal stems also bleached and sprawling, with only a few leaves here and there demonstrating it is still alive.

Several other rarely seen *Bursera* species from mainland Mexico equal the better-known species as natural bonsais when grown under appropriate conditions. Examples are **B. diversifolia** from as far south as Chiapas, **B. morelensis** and **B. multifolia**, with tiny leaf segments similar to *B. microphylla*, and the nonpinnate **B. simplici-**

Bursera fagaroides, an old cultivated plant.

An ancient *Bursera hindsiana,* stunted by wind and drought.

Bursera microphylla, growing very low to the ground in central Baja California.
Photo by Terry Thompson.

Commiphora dinteri, in a particularly desolate part of central Namibia.

Commiphora cf. *wildii,* on the edge of an old Namibian lava bed.

folia. In addition to their other features, these burseras are so filled with dense, highly aromatic sap that they readily release clouds of pine-scented fragrance into the air. Walking through a "grove" of these 6- or 12-inch (15- to 30-cm) tall trees, with incense wafting up into the air at the slightest touch, is truly memorable. Called *copal* in Mexico, the sap has been used for ceremonies since ancient times.

When collecting wild plants was still legal, some of these Baja burseras would occasionally show up for sale. Fortunately, the largest ones were too big to collect and we can hope they are still there today, living in areas of almost total isolation.

Crossing the ocean to Africa brings us to the central habitat of the genus *Commiphora*, closely related to and very similar to *Bursera*. There may be as many as two hundred species of *Commiphora*, and they live in Madagascar, Arabia, western India, and possibly southern Brazil (these may actually be burseras) as well as the African mainland. Typically smallish trees, commiphoras dominate much of the semiarid East African landscape in company with acacias. Their spongy, moisture-retaining wood serves as elephant fodder during droughts.

In even drier regions, *Commiphora*, like *Bursera*, has evolved dwarf species with low-growing caudiciform-like bases. The arid, rocky landscapes of west-central Namibia, for example, provide a home to several *Commiphora* species, their bark variously gray, tan, or almost white, in some species peeling, in others not. Namibian species such as *C. saxicola* and particularly the white-barked *C. dinteri* and the gray-brown *C. wildii* equal the natural "bonsai" form of the best burseras.

Pressed against a rocky cliff, *Boswellia nana* shows its white bark and almost black foliage. Photo by Rob Skillin.

In the semiarid northwestern Namibian grasslands, *Commiphora* cf. *mollis* shows its typical contorted growth habit. Photo by Kurt Zadnik.

Other species resemble the small tree or large shrub-sized burseras. These include the widely distributed **Commiphora africana** and the Somalia **C. holtziana**, with a photosynthesizing blue-green epidermis underneath its peeling, golden outer bark. Madagascar, rich with pachycaulous plants, includes larger growing but highly contorted species such as **C. monstruosa** and **C. madagascariensis**, matched by the localized Namibian knobby-trunked **C. mollis** and the more widespread **C. glaucescens**.

A third genus, *Boswellia*, from the Horn of Africa, Socotra, Yemen, and points east, consists largely of marginally pachycaulous, tortuously branched small trees (see photo of *B. elongata* on page 19). An exception, the dwarf, rock dwelling, Socotran **B. nana**, has entered cultivation as a slow-growing miniature plant suitable for treatment as a succulent bonsai. The sap of boswellias has been valued for millennia as a source of frankincense. Various commiphoras also provide frankincense as well as myrrh.

These succulent burseras, and almost all pachycauls and succulent trees, though slow growing, are not difficult to cultivate. They need fast-draining soil, although not as lean as the driest growing succulents, and very bright light. Watering depends on when the plants grow. They signal the start of dormancy by dropping their leaves and the start of the growing season by putting out new ones. For most of them, that will be in spring, but *Bursera microphylla* and *B. hindsiana*, from Baja California's winter rain and fog area, start their growth in early or midautumn and begin to go dormant by mid or late spring. When dormant the plants should not be kept bone dry; water every three or four weeks will be plenty, and once a week should be adequate during their growing seasons.

Some burseras regularly withstand light frost in their environments, and if one has surplus plants it might be worth trying to grow them outdoors, with the warning that an exceptionally cold or wet winter will probably finish them off. Most other succulent Burseraceae, and most pachycauls in general, are more tropical growing, and best kept protected from cold.

Although some of these plants are almost nonexistent in cultivation, a surprising number are available thanks to the efforts of a few specialist growers. The seeds of burseras generally germinate easily, but it takes a great deal of patience and some careful pruning to convert them from twiggy baby trees to fantastic succulent pachycauls. Burseras will root from cuttings, and these rooted branches will develop a bit of thickness over the years, but given sufficient time, seed-grown plants will look more natural.

Even as seedlings the most arid growing species have a tendency to assume odd shapes that with time and perseverance will result in a nice looking specimen. Just remember that in cultivation the goal is to produce a situation equivalent to a habitat defined by constant wind, intense sun, and very little rain to end up with a compact, horizontally oriented piece of living sculpture.

PACHYCORMUS AND OPERCULICARYA (ANACARDIACEAE)

Dispersed throughout much of the world, the family Anacardiaceae includes useful and decidedly unpleasant species—mango and cashew nut trees as well as poison oak. Its few succulent, pachycaulous members, however, occur only in localized situations half a world apart from each other.

Pachycormus discolor, the sole member of its genus, thrives in the dry heart of Baja California. Plants may reach 8 to 10 feet (2.4 to 3 m) in height and a couple of feet (60 cm) in diameter in deep soil. Under more trying conditions in rocky or windswept areas, plants become dwarfed with fantastically thickened trunks. Pachycormus often grows alongside the more widely distributed *Bursera microphylla*, and though both are called elephant trees, pachycormus always has greatly thickened trunks and seems more deserving of the name.

The two species resemble each other in their general appearance. In addition, they have superficially similar pinnate leaves composed of very small leaflets. The easiest way to tell the two apart is by the scent, or lack thereof, that emanates from their foliage. Whether crushed or just gently rubbed, bursera leaves will immediately perfume the surrounding air, while the leaflets of pachycormus are essentially odor-free.

When flowering, pachycormus produce dense sprays of tiny blossoms, again, quite distinct from the few, inconspicuous flowers of burseras. In a few windswept coastal parts of Baja, and on occasional stony outcroppings and old lava flows, exceptionally dwarfed ancient specimens of this species never exceed 2 feet (60 cm) in height, with great swollen bases almost as wide. Some of these plants, collected many years ago, still show up in cultivation and in appearance equal *Fouquieria columnaris* as probably the most interesting, unique members of the Baja California flora.

Ten feet (3 m) tall and composed of spongy, water-holding wood, *Pachycormus discolor* makes a stand on a Baja California hillside. Photo by Terry Thompson.

The Madagascan genus *Operculicarya* shares both the succulent lifestyle and the tiny pinnate leaflets of *Pachycormus discolor*, although it never develops as extreme a form. The few *Operculicarya* species remain somewhat uncommon in cultivation. **Operculicarya decaryi**, the most widely grown, forms a pachycaulous trunk, heavily wrinkled in more-or-less vertical strips and shaped like an elongated cone, suddenly tapering at its tip. Its short, thin branches often grow quite horizontally, accentuating the odd appearance of its trunk's furrows and ridges. In cultivation *O. decaryi* maintains its leaves for most of the year. Though its main trunk develops relatively slowly, seedlings reach an adult form more quickly than either pachycormus or bursera.

The other *Operculicarya* species are somewhat larger, sometimes multistemmed plants, less obviously pachycaulous. An exception is the rare **O. pachypus**, with an irregular, lumpy trunk up to about 5 feet (1.5 m) tall and close to 2 feet (60 cm) broad at its base.

The succulent Anacardiaceae do well in cultivation given standard pachycaul treatment, though *Operculicarya* requires more protection from cold and will respond to a slightly richer soil mix than *Pachycormus* and perhaps more frequent water when dormant, particularly in very arid climates. Succulent specialty nurseries sometimes offer *Operculicarya*, and *Pachycormus* (considerably slower growing) also shows up from time to time.

FOUQUIERIA (FOUQUIERIACEAE)

Difficult to spell and awkward to pronounce, the family Fouquieriaceae includes some of the most spectacular succulents in the New World among its relatively few species. One of the world's strangest plants, *Fouquieria columnaris* shares its otherworldly appearance with two other, much more obscure Mexican species. In contrast, the more common members of the family help define the unique appearance of the North American deserts

Fouquieria splendens, the ocotillo, is by far the most widely distributed member of the family and has become a mainstay of U.S. Southwest desert landscaping, in private homes as well as along freeway shoulders and airport entryways. Sometimes considered an indicator plant of the Chihuahuan Desert, *F. splendens* ranges beyond that desert's borders, far enough west to have the town of Ocotillo Wells in San Diego County, California, named after it. Ocotillos show up in all the fairly low altitude deserts in the United States, the Chihuahuan in Texas and New Mexico, the Sonoran mostly in Arizona, and the Mojave in California and southern Nevada. They also extend far south into Mexico.

Ocotillos take the form of a spray of spiny stems, growing from a central point in curves that may form an upright urn shape, or flare outward like sprays of water from a fountain. The plants put out their leaves all along the stems from between their spines. When conditions are right in spring or early summer, a spray of orange-red, tubular flowers extends from their branch tips. The stems can reach a substantial height, well over 8 feet (2.4 m), and the plants become quite large.

Not suited as landscaping subjects for anywhere with chilly, damp winters, ocotillos also grow too large to make good container plants, but in desert cities such as Palm Springs, they are ubiquitous both as cultivated plants and wild ones. A thousand miles (1600 km) to the east, ocotillos cover the arid flats of Big Bend National Park in Texas. And, south another 600 or 700 miles (965 to 1125 km) into Mexico, hillsides of ocotillos dot the countryside.

Species resembling *Fouquieria splendens* grow over much of Mexico, but most of the other members of the family have more restricted ranges. Many of these possess a definite main stem and some can turn into trees.

Operculicarya decaryi, the Madagascar equivalent of *Pachycormus*.

Opeculicarya pachypus, even thicker and more horizontally inclined than its relative.

Among them, *F. diguetii*, from the eastern part of central Baja California down to its southern tip, may grow like an ocotillo with distinctly thicker stems and may develop into a small barely succulent tree. The very tree-like *F. formosa* is a resident of seasonally dry tropical forests, where its appearance varies with the time of year, transforming from a leafy, mid-sized tree with sprays of brilliant red flowers to a leafless, golden-barked semi-pachycaul. *Fouquieria macdougalii*, from northwestern Mexico, also resembles an ocotillo, but one with a distinct trunk and peeling, golden-yellow bark on its major limbs.

In contrast to these freely branching types, the three most interesting fouquierias have maximized their central stems and water-retaining capacities. Though *Fouquieria columnaris* is relatively widespread in comparison to the other two species, it nonetheless is restricted to the north-central coastal fog desert of Baja California (see photo on page 25), except for a tiny outlying population found in coastal Sonora. The species has achieved a certain renown, as its colloquial names suggest. In Spanish it is called *cirio* ("candle") and in English, either idria, after the now-invalid name of its former monotypic genus, or the boojum tree, after the ultimate unknown object in the Lewis Carroll poem, "The Hunting of the Snark."

In their environment, idrias are impossible to miss, unmistakable upright objects that resemble slightly tapering telephone poles gone astray. Often rather than simply growing vertically, they may bend over (sometimes almost completely), fork at the top to make a Y shape, and on hilltops form silhouettes against the sky that look like crowds of whimsically misshapen people. The plants can become large, close to 80 feet (24 m) tall in rare cases, and a few feet thick, though most are smaller and too twisted and turned for any height measurement to be applicable. Thin, spiny branches poke out of their thick, corky trunks, and, in the manner of ocotillos, put out small green leaves between the spines during their late fall and winter growing season. Their orange to yellow flowers grow from the tops of their mature trunks.

Idrias perform well as container plants, although they are very slow. In the wild, plants growing in fissures in rock develop with excruciating slowness, while those that take root in sandy, deep-soiled flats may grow quite rapidly. Their general weirdness has led to various stories about them, including unsupportable statements about their great age. It is reasonable to assume, however, that any idria over 60 feet (18 m) tall, or even a few feet tall but growing in a crack in a rock, is a very old plant. Idrias will survive outdoors in areas free from hard frosts and

Part of a small idria (*Fouquieria columnaris*) colony with a toehold in coastal Sonora, across the gulf from Baja California. Photo by Inge Hoffman.

where winter rain alternates frequently with sunny days. Too much rain or severe cold snaps even in such climates will often disfigure the plants if not kill them outright.

The two other spectacular fouquierias are rare endemics, occurring only in few spots in their respective states. *Fouquieria fasciculata*, from Hidalgo, lives by the great Barranca de Metztitlán Biosphere Reserve where it sometimes grows on the very edges of highly unstable limestone cliffs. *Fouquieria purpusii* comes from farther south, near the border between Puebla and Oaxaca, and grows on steep, rocky ridges, though not quite as suicidally precipitous as the cliffs favored by its relative. Dormant in winter, the two begin growing in spring and retain their abundant foliage until late in autumn.

Fouquieria fasciculata—partway up its base, composed of a series of enormous, woody, water-storing spheres, in Mexico's Hidalgo state. Photo by Rob Skillin.

Smaller plants of *Fouquieria purpusii*, growing on cliffs near the border of Puebla and Oaxaca states. Photo by Brian Kemble.

Small cultivated plants of both species resemble idrias. Although their thickened trunks taper more rapidly, they have similar thin, spiny branches with slightly larger, more elongated leaves, almost linear in *Fouquieria purpusii*. In the wild, however, mature specimens of *F. fasciculata* may become enormous. From huge, swollen aboveground caudices grow several 2-foot (60-cm) thick and 6- or 7-foot (1.8- to 2.1-m) high trunks topped with multibranched fascicles of tiny white flowers. With their dark gray-green stems perched precariously on the very edge of crumbling white limestone cliffs, the plants look truly unearthly.

Plants of *Fouquieria purpusii* may look very much like idrias, with trunks upright as a telephone pole, as much as 30 feet (9 m) tall and 2 feet (60 cm) wide at the base, or they may spread, occasionally resulting in plants with multiple trunks. They also have a penchant for picturesque habitats, deeply eroded limestone knobs shared with burseras, agaves, and unpleasant wasps. The trunks and thicker branches of both species are partially covered with bands and patches of white or gray bark, but their green water-storing tissue creeps beyond the protective

boundaries of the bark like an abundant abdomen peeking from the gaps between the buttons on an overstretched shirt.

In regard to cultivation, the species modified from the basic ocotillo model such as *Fouquieria macdougalii* and *F. diguetii* will grow reasonably well in containers when given standard pachycaul culture, taking their various seasonal requirements into account. Rather surprisingly, small plants of *F. macdougalii* can produce their red hummingbird flowers in a 5-inch (13-cm) pot. Usually a winter grower, *F. columnaris* will also do well with the same light and soil, but should be rested after its leaves drop anytime from early spring to early summer until it leafs out again, typically in midautumn. Even during its rest period, however, some water every three or four weeks will not hurt.

Fouquieria fasciculata and *F. purpusii* require the same treatment as *F. columnaris*, adjusted to accommodate their reversed growing and dormant periods. Unlike the boojum tree, it is doubtful if they can withstand frost. Finding these plants used to be impossible, but a few specialized growers now produce seedlings of both species (and idrias) from time to time. Though seedlings grow quite rapidly, it is hard to imagine them reaching a truly mature form in cultivation.

DIDIEREA, ALLUAUDIA, DECARYIA, AND ALLUAUDIOPSIS (DIDIEREACEAE)

The members of the Didiereaceae, found almost nowhere but in Madagascar, may be the most distinctive of that island's many distinctive succulents. These tree-sized, heavily spined deciduous plants have leaves growing from between their spines. Several genera make up a major component of the remarkable southwestern Madagascan thorn forests. Oddly enough, these forests are the habitat of several lemurs, the native primates of Madagascar. These arboreal animals leap from one fiercely spiny stem to another without any hesitation or apparent harm. Aside from serving as lemur habitat, the succulent trees and shrubs of the Didiereaceae are sufficiently interesting in their own right to have fascinated several generations of plant collectors.

The eponymous genus *Didierea* consists of two species, **D. madagascariensis** and **D. trollii**. At maturity both species grow into tree-sized shrubs, with spiny central stems surrounded by whorls of equally spiny branches. *Didierea madagascariensis* is the larger of the two, and mature plants can resemble thickets, with the branches curling out and upwards and nearly obscuring their trunks. Frequently less neatly symmetrical, full-grown plants of *D. trollii* may develop a less cluttered trunk, with swirling branches radiating out nearer to the top.

The leaves of *Didierea madagascariensis* are linear, almost terete, and grow from inch (2.5 cm) long, narrow cylindrical projections (abortive branches), at the center of a terminal spine cluster. In contrast, *D. trollii* has ovate, flat leaves and almost nonexistent stem projections. Nonetheless, as mature plants the two species look very much alike. In contrast, the juvenile forms could hardly be more different.

Seedlings of *Didierea madagascariensis* resemble miniature unbranched mature plants and grow upright, straight as a ruler. If given enough root-room they begin producing their mature branches when they reach 4 or 5 feet (1.2 to 1.5 m) in height. Plants of *D. trollii* branch when still young, but rather than upright their limbs grow parallel to the ground, and juvenile plants turn into a sprawl of horizontal, spiny branches, without a visible main trunk. At a certain size and age, however, a branch will begin to grow vertically; this, in fact, is the main

A large *Didierea madagascariensis* standing apart from its thorny surroundings. Photo by Brian Kemble.

trunk, and as it reaches 5 or 6 feet (1.5 to 1.8 m) in height, it too starts to send out branches from near its apex. In the meantime, the juvenile, ground-hugging branches slowly die off, resulting in adult plants that look completely different from the immature ones.

The six species of *Alluaudia* probably include the most interesting members of the family. All grow into medium-sized trees and shrubs, though of very strange appearance. In contrast to didiereas, which bear flowers in short, dense fascicles along the lengths of their branches, alluaudias flower from their branch tips.

The most widespread of these six species in the wild and probably in cultivation is **Alluaudia procera**, which can reach over 45 feet (13.7 m) in height. In maturity the plants develop a main trunk with a large number of sharply ascending branches that rise up almost parallel to it. Both trunk and branches bear small thin, rounded leaves between their spines for the whole of their lengths. In the larger branches and trunk the spines and leaves spiral up from bottom to top, in widely separated, parallel rows. When small, the leaf-covered branches resemble ocotillos; when mature they look a little like tall multi-stemmed idrias (completely unrelated, of course).

A stand of *Alluaudia procera*: one flowering, others displaying the various forms they can assume. Photo by Brian Kemble.

Alluaudia ascendens looming in the Madagascar morning mist. Photo by Inge Hoffman.

The shrublike **Alluaudia humbertii**, the least interesting species horticulturally, makes a spiny, 8-foot (2.4-m) tall thicket when full grown. In contrast, *A. ascendens* resembles an elongated caricature of *A. procera*, with vertical branches stretched out beyond all reason. **Alluaudia montagnacii**, similar looking but with fewer, even more elongated if not quite so vertical branches, and leaves only a third as long as its spines, may be the most attractive species. The linear leaves of *A. dumosa* are quickly ephemeral. Plants grow into small trees with thin, leathery brown, photosynthesizing, slightly thorny branches, while *A. comosa* becomes a densely branched short tree with a distinctive upswelling, almost mushroom-shaped silhouette (see photo on page 253).

The two remaining genera of Didiereaceae have either dispensed with or never evolved extreme modifications for enduring droughts. With only minimally succulent stems they behave like many generalized semixerophytic plants in cultivation, with less need for significant rest periods. The only species of its genus, **Decaryia madagascariensis** forms a small scraggly tree. Its branching habit has given rise to the name zig-zag plant; its secondary branches turn at an angle after each leaf-

bearing node, creating an overall impression of a tangle of endlessly zigzagging, slightly succulent twigs supplied with small thorns and leaves at their nodes.

Alluaudiopsis consists of two species, also with just slightly succulent stems and branches, bearing spines and linear, semisucculent leaves along the length of their stems. They grow into medium-sized, densely branched shrubs. **Alluaudiopsis marnieriana** is noteworthy because of its attractive, open red flowers, which are structurally so close to those of cactus that botanists have placed the Didiereaceae next to the Cactaceae in their phylogenetic models.

All these plants are reasonably easy to grow. Most do well with standard pachycaul culture though *Decaryia madagascariensis*, *Alluaudia humbertii*, *A. dumosa*, and, in particular, both species of *Alluaudiopsis*, need more water than most succulents. Plants of alluaudiopsis should never be allowed to go bone dry, while the others will do fine with water once a week or a little more often in very hot weather and every two to three weeks during winter. The remaining species tend to drop their leaves more-or-less all at once, signaling the start of their winter rest period, which ends when their new leaves begin peeking out in spring.

Almost artificially neat, *Alluaudia comosa* typically attains this very groomed look. Photo by Brian Kemble.

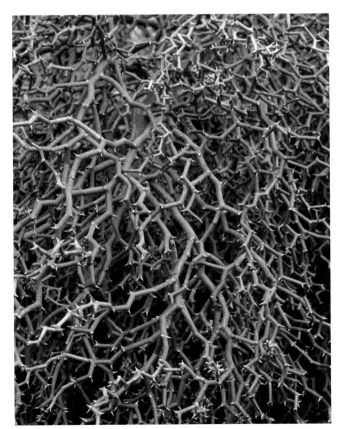

The zig-zag plant close up: *Decaryia madagascariensis*. Photo by Inge Hoffman.

Aside from *Alluaudia humbertii* and *A. procera*, all the other species are fairly uncommon in cultivation. Though sensitive to cold, many will survive outdoors in the most sheltered parts of Southern California. While they will never attain their mature form in a container, they can reach imposing proportions and provide an exotic touch to a grouping of succulent plants.

ADANSONIA, CAVANILLESIA, CEIBA, ERIOTHECA, AND PSEUDOBOMBAX (BOMBACACEAE)

Bombacaceae, the bombax family, includes the largest succulent plants of all and is widely dispersed over much of the warmer parts of both the Old and New Worlds. Many of its genera consist of trees with compound, usually trilobed leaves and sometimes enormously swollen trunks.

Its most famous genus is *Adansonia*, the baobab, which although impractical for cultivation, nonetheless continually attracts the attention of succulent growers. Baobabs grow over most of the drier parts of Africa and Madagascar, and one species, *A. gibbosa*, occurs in Australia. Most people have at least some idea of what a

A huge, multitrunked baobab, *Adansonia digitata* in the Kaokoveld of northern Namibia. Photo by Rob Skillin.

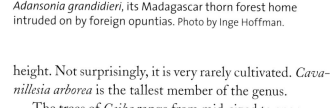

Adansonia grandidieri, its Madagascar thorn forest home intruded on by foreign opuntias. Photo by Inge Hoffman.

baobab looks like, an enormously thick trunk, growing upright and abruptly dividing into several thickened main limbs, which then subdivide into more ordinary branches and twigs.

Adansonia digitata, the single continental African species, has a trunk over 60 feet (18 m) tall and up to 30 feet (9 m) thick, filled with soft, spongy wood. It is the best-known species in the genus, but some of the seven species from Madagascar are even more fantastic.

Madagascar is home to a famous stand of huge **Adansonia grandidieri** that rivals any avenue of giant redwoods. **Adansonia rubrostipa**, to only 40 feet (12 m) tall, looks like a miniaturized giant (see photo on page 253), while the lesser-known **A. za** includes both the largest and the most wildly contorted members of the genus (see photo on page 17). People like to raise adansonias, but unless you can allow them to grow up to 20 or 30 feet (6 to 9 m) tall, and can protect them from cold, they will remain permanent spindly seedlings.

Cavanillesia, with a number of Brazilian species, resembles *Adansonia* and can reach over 100 feet (30 m) in height. Not surprisingly, it is very rarely cultivated. *Cavanillesia arborea* is the tallest member of the genus.

The trees of *Ceiba* range from mid-sized to enormous and grow in tropical locations from Mexico through Central and South America. They vary from giants that look as if they were made of smooth, gray cement, with thick, buttressed trunks and enormously swollen bases, to smaller, spiny-trunked, more modestly proportioned species. As with other members of the family, the seeds that fill their pendent elliptical fruits are attached to fluffy appendages, the original source of kapok. With one exception their need for tropical climates and their often enormous mature size of well over 150 feet (46 m) tall in the largest species removes them from horticultural consideration. The exception, **Ceiba insignis** (synonym *Chorisia speciosa*), is from Brazil and is widely used in Southern California as a landscape tree. It ultimately grows into a large sparsely branched tree with compound leaves, a bottle-shaped trunk covered with pyramidal spines, and a spectacular display of large pink flowers.

Another South American genus, *Eriotheca*, has slight-

Cavanillesia arborea, a baobab-like tree from the dry forests of Brazil. Photo by Rob Skillin.

A tree in a pot—a developing seedling of *Eriotheca peruviana*.

Kept confined to a container, *Pseudobombax ellipticum* will retain its pachycaulous nature.

The well-defended pachycaulous lower trunk of *Ceiba rubriflora*, another Brazilian species. Photo by Rob Skillin.

ly smaller bottle trees. **Eriotheca peruviana** is endemic to Peru and very rare, though not difficult, in cultivation.

The genus of the Bombacaceae most suitable for container culture is the rather lamentably renamed *Pseudobombax*. This small group of Mexican trees was previously included in *Bombax*. The plants can become quite large, but in drier climates and rocky settings remain stunted, with a short, irregular caudiciform base divided into geometric patterns and branches that reach at most 6 feet (1.8 m) into the air.

In favorable circumstances, **Pseudobombax ellipticum**, the most common in cultivation, may reach well over 50 feet (15 m) in height. Wild specimens growing wedged around boulders attain fantastic shapes that cannot easily be duplicated by seed grown plants. Seedlings grow fairly swiftly and by the time they are large enough for a 6- or 8-inch (15- to 20-cm) container they will have developed a thick, semispherical base and thickened main branches approaching those of collected plants.

Pseudobombax palmeri, from northwestern Mexico, is rare in cultivation and never becomes as large as its more widespread cousin. It develops a similar form as an even smaller plant.

Though most of the succulent Bombacaceae grow too large to make satisfactory cultivated specimens, people are always trying various species of *Adansonia*, which ultimately turn into what can legitimately be called the world's largest succulents. Curiously, baobabs do well with a surprisingly large amount of water. In the warmer months they should not dry out, with water twice a week or even more a good idea. In winter they do not appreciate long droughts either.

In contrast, *Pseudobombax* flourishes with typical pachycaul care. Too much water and root room, however, will produce more treelike, less succulent growth. Seedlings of *P. ellipticum* appear from time to time; *P. palmeri* is less common but occasionally obtainable.

MORINGA (MORINGACEAE)

Moringa, the only genus of the Moringaceae, consists of less than a dozen species native to Africa and western and central Asia. The two Indian species are arborescent and nonsucculent, while the several species that live around the Horn of Africa grow as multistemmed shrubs emerging out of an underground tuberous base. The latter are essentially nonexistent in cultivation. The remaining moringas, however, from Madagascar and southern and eastern Africa are medium-sized, definitely pachycaulous trees. The two Madagascan species, **M. drouhardii** and **M. hildebrandtii**, along with **M. ovalifolia**, from Namibia and southern Angola, occasionally make their way into succulent collections.

The pachycaulous moringas grow over 50 feet (15 m) tall, with thick, almost sausage-shaped trunks topped with a few swollen branches. They produce a sparse complement of compound leaves and white to yellow flowers. *Moringa drouhardii*, sometimes with a disturbingly anthropomorphic curvaceous trunk, shares its stark white bark with *M. ovalifolia*, the most widely grown species.

Though *Moringa ovalifolia* reaches less than half the height of the Madagascan species, plants, often growing in rocky outcrops, occasionally develop a proportionately much thicker base. In northern Namibia, on the edge of Etosha National Park, a dense stand of moringas displays multiple, twisted stems growing out of enormous bases, the result of elephant damage. These have become a minor tourist attraction, showing up on locally produced postcards, and known as the *sprokieswoud* ("haunted forest").

No moringas grow in completely arid deserts; instead

Moringa drouhardii, leafless in Madagascar. Photo by Brian Kemble.

they usually come from warm to hot semiarid habitats with a reasonable amount of rain followed by a more-or-less strict dry period that lasts for many months. Although a mature *Moringa ovalifolia* looks like it could withstand years of no rain, the plants actually like a good amount of water when growing, a fairly nutritious though fast-draining soil, warm temperatures, and water every two to three weeks even when dormant. Moringas like more root room than many succulents, and rather than trying to expose the thickened stem base that even small seedlings will develop, it is better to pot them deeper and wait for the stems to thicken higher up naturally.

ERYTHRINA (FABACEAE), CUSSONIA (ARALIACEAE), AND JACARATIA (CARICACEAE)

A surprising number of other plant families have a few infrequently grown semisucculent members as well. Among these, the legumes, Fabaceae, include a few species of **Erythrina** from southern Africa that grow from underground caudices and remain relatively small. Also

Moringa ovalifolia, leafed out in central Namibia. Photo by Kurt Zadnik.

The leguminous *Delonix floribunda*, with *Alluaudia comosa* and *Adansonia rubrostipa* in the background. Photo by Brian Kemble.

included are the odd East African and Madagascan species of ***Elephantorrhiza***, with underground caudices and thin stems bearing mimosa-like pinnate foliage. ***Delonix*** and ***Senna*** are genera of leguminous flowering trees with rarely grown Madagascan pachycaulous representatives.

The Araliaceae, along with tropical shrubs and ginseng, includes the genus *Cussonia*, plants locally known as cabbage trees. Several generally similar African cussonias grow into small trees with distinctly enlarged bases, marginally succulent stems, and characteristic large digitate leaves similar to the decorative foliage of other members of the family. Surprisingly hardy, ***C. paniculata*** will survive freezes into the twenties Fahrenheit (around −4°C) if given good drainage, but the plants are more commonly grown in containers where they do well with standard pachycaul treatment.

Perhaps the least likely family of all, the Caricaceae, best known for the papaya, also includes several species of New World tropical and semitropical pachycaulous shrubs in the genus ***Jacaratia***. These are also amenable to dwarfing and container culture with standard pachycaul treatment.

Cussonia paniculata developing its swollen base.

Chapter 24

Aloe

STARTING FROM A basic theme of a rosette of long, narrow succulent leaves and an erect inflorescence of orange-red flowers, aloes display an astonishing diversity. With at least five hundred species, *Aloe* consists of more than enough plants to justify the many published books devoted solely to it; in this chapter I will provide an overview.

Aloe has been variously considered the main genus in the family Aloaceae, a major component of the more inclusive family Asphodelaceae, or a member of a much expanded family, the Xanthorrhoeaceae. Aloes range in size from large multibranched trees to tiny rosettes no more than 2 or 3 inches (5 to 8 cm) across. Species may grow tall, form shrubby bushes, remain small and solitary or produce so many offsets that they dominate a landscape; a few odd ones hang pendently downward from cliffs. Some aloes will bloom and remain permanently happy in a 4-inch (10-cm) pot; others need great amounts of root room to thrive, much less flower.

Fortunately, the many species more or less sort themselves out into logical groups. The tree aloes, for example, are easily separated from the dwarf aloes. Other groups are united by their geography, such as the aloes of eastern South Africa versus those of western South Africa. Still other groups share a particular growth habit or have distinctly spotted leaves and distinctively shaped flowers.

TREE ALOES

The most immediately impressive members of the genus are the largest, those plants typically referred to as tree aloes. Most are native to eastern and southern South Africa, Namibia, Mozambique, and surrounding regions, as well as Madagascar. The aloes in this group usually form single trunks from 6 to over 25 feet (1.8 to 7.6 m) in height. Occasionally they branch high on the stem.

Some tree aloes occur in large colonies in open, brushy areas and steep hillsides where they are exposed to hot sun and occasional frosts. One example is the very widespread ***Aloe marlothii***, to 20 feet (6 m) tall, with spiny blue leaves, usually yellow or orange flowers, and very cold resistant. Another is the equally common *A. ferox*, slightly shorter, generally orange flowered, and spiny only on its leaf margins. A third, *A. speciosa*, has tilted rosettes of small-spined leaves and flowers that change from red to greenish white as they open.

Other tree aloes, from better-watered, generally lower

Aloe marlothii: very hardy, usually but not always with yellow flowers. Photo by Brian Kemble.

Aloe ferox: variable and extremely wide spread in South Africa. Photo by Brian Kemble.

altitudes in eastern South Africa, grow among arborescent euphorbias and semitropical trees, and can withstand only a little frost or none at all. These include the uncommon **Aloe angelica**; **A. rupestris** and **A. pluridens**, both a little more cold hardy; and the tall **A. excelsa**. Also included here are several species with deeply channeled, recurved, long, narrow leaves, such as **A. thraskii**, found near the warm Indian Ocean coast and well suited for outdoor growing in Southern California, less so in colder climates, and **A. alooides**, a little hardier and with a narrow, unbranched, yellow-flowered inflorescence quite different from most of the other tree types.

Aloe lineata, not as tall, occurs in mountains, sometimes growing incongruously among imported pine trees, and **A. comosa**, also a smaller tree type but with a lofty unbranched inflorescence, both withstand fairly low temperatures in nature. Atypically for this group, *A. comosa* comes from the winter-rainfall region of western South Africa and does not like excessive rain and humidity. Despite its name which means "of the seashore," **A. littoralis** extends in a more northerly band from Angola and Namibia all the way to Mozambique, usually very far from

A colony of *Aloe littoralis* in central Namibia-it often chooses very hot habitats. Photo by Kurt Zadnik.

Aloe divaricata, half tree, half shrub, with invasive agaves behind it. Photo by Brian Kemble.

Aloe barberae, the largest species, flowering in subtropical eastern South Africa. Photo by Inge Hoffman.

the ocean. To 12 or 15 feet (3.6 to 4.5 m) tall and with distinctly gray leaves, sometimes spotted white, it often grows in large colonies; some forms may be quite cold hardy, others from hot, arid interior regions, less so.

Not surprisingly, the tree aloes of Madagascar also do not do well outdoors anywhere it occasionally freezes. *Aloe vaombe*, with a size, shape, and multibranched inflorescence reminiscent of *A. ferox*, but often red-tinged in the sun, may be the best known of these Madagascan plants. Others, such as *A. vaotsanda* and *A. helenae*, more localized and each to about 15 feet (4.5 m) tall, develop long, deeply channeled, recurving leaves similar to *A. thraskii*. *Aloe suzannae* grows slightly taller, with 3-foot (90-cm) long, sword-shaped, almost terete leaves that cluster at its apex and a narrow, unbranched inflorescence that stretches an additional 10 feet (3 m) into the air. Highly endemic, it is restricted to a small section of the driest parts of far southern Madagascar. *Aloe divaricata*, more widely distributed on the island, is decidedly less robust than the others even though its slender main stem, surrounded by a few smaller subsidiary ones, may reach as much as 10 feet (3 m) in height. A few tall tree aloes, very rare in cultivation, live in East Africa and southwestern Arabia, such as the Yemeni *A. sabaea*, single-stemmed, tall and slender.

Almost all these plants will do well outdoors in

coastal parts of Southern California, but not many will survive for long in areas with lower minimum temperatures. Species unable to withstand cold nights in the ground will grow adequately in containers, but unless given lots of height and root room, they will never develop their adult forms. Nonetheless, there are enough large aloes with at least some frost hardiness to ensure a good variety suitable for most succulent gardens.

The largest aloe of all, *Aloe barberae* (synonym *A. bainesii*), grows into a tall, gracefully branching tree up to 60 feet (18 m) high. From a distance it looks like an ordinary tree, but its branches end in aloe rosettes, and it produces typical upright inflorescences of close-packed orange flowers. Native to the semitropical east coast of South Africa, it can withstand slight frost, but a hard freeze will kill it. If given shelter, warmth, adequate root room, and a decent amount of water, however, it grows remarkably quickly. The very similar *A. eminens*, from Somalia, is much rarer and even less tolerant of cold weather.

The other aloes related to *Aloe barberae*, however, grow under much more arid circumstances in northwestern South Africa and Namibia. *Aloe dichotoma* reaches over 20 feet (6 m) in height. It has a thick, almost caudiciform trunk divided into leathery, ridged plates and crowned with a burst of dichotomous branches. The species ranges widely through northwestern South Africa

Called the *kokerboom* or quiver tree, *Aloe dichotoma*, 20 feet (6 m) tall and very compact in southern Namibia. Photo by Rob Skillin.

Aloe plicatillis, much taller growing in the wild than in cultivation. Photo by Brian Kemble.

Aloe ramossisima in dry country just north of the Orange River.

and southern Namibia. The most compact plants grow in the driest parts of its range; laxer forms appear in the slightly moister climate of the uplands separating Bushmanland from the Namaqualand plains.

Even taller growing, to over 30 feet (9 m), with a massive base, a tall, tapering trunk, and a few thick

branches is the very rare **Aloe pillansii**. Found only in a few Richtersveld and southern Namibian hilltop localities, it may be the most surreal looking aloe of them all (see photo on page 18). Unlike the upright inflorescences of *A. dichotoma*, those of *A. pillansii* hang downward; flowers of both species are yellow. **Aloe ramossisima**, a much smaller plant, looks like the top of a densely branched *A. dichotoma*. The significant botanical differences between the two species are not all that clear. *Aloe ramossisima* ("most branched"), however, rarely exceeds 6 feet (1.8 m) in height, lacks a distinct central trunk, and branches more abundantly than any other aloe. It lives in the same arid winter-rainfall region of the Richtersveld and southern Namibia, but is less sensitive to excess humidity than the other two species. It comes well from cuttings and grows fairly rapidly.

Not closely related to these species but also tall-growing and branching, the commonly cultivated **Aloe plicatillis** has fans of soft, fleshy distichous leaves at the ends of its branches. It grows in fynbos in the mountains north of Cape Town where it receives more than 30 inches (760 mm) of winter rain and a fair amount of frost as well. In cultivation it usually forms a relatively short, thick trunk, but it the wild it grows much taller, with its broad soft leaves giving it a misleadingly tropical look. In its northwest South African and southern Namibian home *A. dichotoma* also regularly withstands hard frosts, but its habitat is so dry that in cultivation winter humidity can turn it to mush; in central, coastal California it is only marginally hardy outdoors, while *A. pillansii* is at least as sensitive to excess humidity and less cold hardy as well.

SHRUBBY ALOES

Another selection of aloes consists of good-sized, often freely branching plants, including the extremely common **Aloe arborescens**, which forms a sort of multistemmed hedge or thicket, perhaps 8 feet (2.4 m) tall and considerably broader. It occurs over much of South Africa except the arid northwest, and extends into neighboring countries as well. Stemless, blue-leafed and much slower growing, **A. mutabilis** is rarer but closely related. Beyond

the limits of its range *A. arborescens* is replaced by other less commonly cultivated shrubby species that continue north as far as Somalia. Among these is the smaller **A. cameronii**, from Zimbabwe, Malawi, and Mozambique, with leaves that turn brick red in good sun.

Aloe pearsonii, lending color to its Richtersveld canyon home. Photo by Brian Kemble.

Aloe mutabilis near Pretoria, less robust than the related *A. arborescens*. Photo by Brian Kemble.

Aloe castanea, a small tree with a dense "bottlebrush" inflorescence. Photo by Brian Kemble.

From exceedingly arid surroundings, *Aloe pearsonii*, a north Richtersveld endemic, sends out masses of upright stems up to 4 feet (1.2 m) tall, densely clad with flat-topped, very thick leaves that color up deep purple-red as they face the sun. It occurs in large numbers in its very limited range, reddening whole hillsides. Other often multistemmed, rather large aloes include the South African *A. spicata*, *A. vryheidensis*, and *A. castanea*, and the Zimbabwean *A. taurii*, all with unbranched inflorescences that resemble giant cattails thickly covered with small sessile (stemless) brown to orange flowers. In bright light, the foliage of *A. taurii* turns bright red.

Enjoying more shade than most species, a number of smaller, semivining aloes include the commonly grown *Aloe ciliaris*, with deep orange flowers; *A. striatula*, with yellow flowers; and *A. tenuior*, with either orange or yellow flowers. This last trio of plants can withstand cold and a lot of water.

SPOTTED ALOES

One of the major divisions of the genus, the maculate aloes include over three dozen species of plants with distinctly spotted leaves, botanically differentiated because of the swollen bases of their flowers, which otherwise vary widely in color and shape of inflorescence. Stemless or very short stemmed, and ranging from about a foot (30 cm) to perhaps 3 feet (90 cm) in diameter, most of these aloes come from central and eastern South Africa, though about a half dozen others cover most of the rest of the continent.

By far the best-known species, *Aloe maculata* (synonym *A. saponaria*), is typical of the group, with gray-green leaves bordered by a toothed margin that turns orange in good light, and with its upper leaf surface heavily spotted with whitish marking. *Aloe maculata* grows very easily with no particular special needs, and can offset so readily as to become a nuisance after a while. Several closely allied, generally similar looking species, much less common in cultivation, include *A. grandidentata*, *A. greatheadii* and its variety *davyana* (synonym *A. davyana*), *A. affinis*, and the somewhat less hardy *A. greenii*.

The most common northern maculate aloe, *Aloe zebrina*, grows in Namibian and Angolan grasslands and continues all the way east to Mozambique. More distinctive, *A. branddraaiensis* has its spots arranged linearly. Its leaves turn orange-red in good light, while *A. mudenensis*, also with reddish leaves, forms a short stem. The broadly triangular leaves of the somewhat smaller *A.*

Aloe affinis, typifying dozens of similar, spotted aloes. Photo by Brian Kemble.

prinslooi typically die back at their tips, while the narrow leaves of *A. suffulta*, small and frost-sensitive, with a twining inflorescence, color up almost purple-brown in good light. *Aloe verdoorniae*, typically solitary and fairly small, has leaves that turn blue-gray to almost black in strong light, contrasting vividly with their bright white spots.

These species, along with the others in this section, range from extremely easy to somewhat sensitive in cultivation. They may remain solitary or form small to very large clumps. In contrast to the all-too-common *A. maculata*, they can prove quite difficult to find.

MEDIUM AND SMALL ALOES OF WESTERN SOUTH AFRICA AND NAMIBIA

Many distinctive aloes occur over much of western South Africa and Namibia, both in arid regions and better-watered places. The best known of these may be *Aloe microstigma*, a variable but always attractive medium-sized plant, sometimes clumping a bit, sometimes forming a short stem. Its typically gray-green leaves are covered top and bottom with white dots and it readily puts

A spectacular red form of the normally gray *Aloe microstigma*. Photo by Brian Kemble.

Aloe comptonii flowering in the Robertson Karoo, accompanied by *Crassula* cf. *rupestris*.

Aloe hereroenis growing on a limestone outcrop in northern Namibia along with *Pachypodium lealii* var. *lealii*. Photo by Kurt Zadnik.

On the way to the western ocean, *Aloe arenicola*, whose name means "sand-growing," appropriately sprawls in sand, its rosettes tightening toward their flowering tips.

up its unbranched flower stalk in outdoor gardens, not minding even fairly hard freezes. Some forms color up brilliantly under bright desert sun.

Looking like a dwarf, more delicate *Aloe microstigma*, with gray-pink, narrow, heavily dotted leaves, *A. picti-*

folia still is uncommon in cultivation, though it should become increasingly popular as it becomes better known. Highly endemic, it is restricted to a few steep cliffs in the Eastern Cape Province. Although it offsets fairly readily, with its compact habit it will not outgrow a decent-sized container.

Aloe hereroenis, found in the interior of South Africa and most of the summer-rainfall parts of Namibia, is a small plant, often growing in groups, though its rosettes remain solitary. Its leaves, gray and spotted with white, blend in with the limestone outcrops where it typically grows, and its orange flowers turn to yellow in its northern Namibian forms.

With a totally different growth form, *Aloe comptonii*, *A. mitriformis*, and *A. arenicola* sprawl rather than cluster. These related species elongate as they move westward.

Aloe comptonii forms blue, upturned rosettes about 1.5 to 2 feet (45 to 60 cm) across at the end of its stems, *A. mitriformis* is smaller but longer stemmed, and *A. arenicola*, from sandy areas along the Atlantic coast, develops long, procumbent stems with alternating white-spotted leaves that at maturity reach up and develop into small rosettes.

The very odd, very rare *Aloe haemanthifolia* grows high in the mountains of the Western Cape, in peaty soil on steep slopes where it receives much winter rain and frost. The plant, low, distichous leafed, with soft, spineless leaves, looks rather like a tiny stemless *A. plicatillis*, but is much more difficult to grow.

The arid areas of Namaqualand, the Richtersveld, and southern Namibia provide a home for several of the most interesting small to mid-sized aloes. One of the nicest of these, *Aloe krapohliana*, rarely even a foot (30 cm) across, remains solitary although a miniature form, **var. dumoulinii**, endemic to the northwest Richtersveld, forms small dense clusters. Both varieties have blue leaves with darker bands and very small marginal teeth. *Aloe krapohliana* is one of the few aloes from the winter-rainfall areas that will not successfully switch to a summer watering regime, and instead should be kept fairly dry in summer, with water given more frequently in fall, winter, and early spring.

Two other choice aloes, closely related to each other,

Aloe krapohliana flowering near the edge of a Namaqualand quartz field.

A loose clump of *Aloe melanacantha* in northern Namaqualand. Photo by Rob Skillin.

Aloe gariepensis, widely distributed along both sides of the Orange River, formerly known as the Gariep River. Photo by Kurt Zadnik.

Aloe claviflora, a small clump with horizontal inflorescences facing outward in Bushmanland. Photo by Kurt Zadnik.

An old "fairy ring" of *Aloe asperifolia* in a particularly arid part of northern Namibia. Photo by Rob Skillin.

Aloe melanacantha and *A. erinacea*, form small clusters of very spiny green rosettes. *Aloe melanacantha*, to about 2 feet (60 cm) across, grows on hilly ground from Namaqualand into Namibia. Its many stiff, narrow, upward-curving green leaves are rimmed with black spines. The rare *A. erinacea*, endemic to a small area in southern Namibia, resembles its relative but is even spinier. Its spines remain translucent and pale rather than black and its leaves appear covered with a faint coating of whitish glaze. Although very slow growing, it ultimately forms a short procumbent stem and makes larger clusters than *A. melanacantha*. Both species live in very arid regions, but both are reasonably cold hardy and *A. melanacantha* will survive several degrees of frost outdoors as long as it has excellent drainage.

Aloe framesii is another rare plant, from the western South Africa. Basically gray leafed with white spots, it grows along the arid but foggy coastal strip and forms dense clusters of rosettes. In the northern part of its range it may meet up with *A. gariepensis*, a usually solitary plant with narrow leaves marked with parallel longitudinal lines that vary from gray to brown to orange to red. *Aloe gariepensis* makes its home along the hot margins of the Orange (or Gariep) River but will survive a surprising amount of cold.

Also with linear markings on its nearly white leaves, **Aloe glauca** has margins of orange-brown teeth. It forms small clumps of rosettes to as much as 2 feet (60 cm) across. Although from dry habitats, it will grow successfully in well-drained gardens throughout much of California.

Another group of arid-growing aloes produces numer-

Aloe dewinteri on a steep cliff face. Photo by Rob Skillin.

MEDIUM AND SMALL ALOES OF EASTERN SOUTH AFRICA

The eastern half of South Africa is also rich in small and medium-sized aloes, many of them good subjects for gardens. **Aloe peglerae**, from higher elevations in the northeast, forms tight, inward-curving rosettes about a foot (30 cm) across, with blue to pinkish leaves and a tight, dense inflorescence. Somewhat similar, *A. petricola* is more open growing, spinier, and slightly larger, while the blue-leafed *A. pratensis* is smaller with large marginal spines.

Aloe suprafoliata grows distichously as a young plant, but matures into a 2- or 3-foot (60- to 90-cm) wide rosette. Contrasting with its deep scarlet flowers, its flower stalk often is covered with a silvery bloom. Another usually solitary plant, *A. aculeata* has leaves covered with bands of spines ranging from pure white to pure black on all parts of its leaf surfaces.

Aloe broomii, with broader leaves and a more open, bowl-shaped rosette, sometimes develops a short stem, rarely clumps, but is best known for its tall, unbranched inflorescence which broadens at the top, fancifully compared to the hooded head of a cobra. The rare, always

ous rosettes that face outward from a central point. The best known of these is **Aloe claviflora**, a widespread species of the harsh deserts of the South African interior, with gray leaves and flower stalks that lie along the ground as they point out from the circle of rosettes. **Aloe falcata**, from the Namaqualand coast, *A. pachygaster*, very rare, from southern Namibia, and the blue-pink leafed *A. asperifolia*, from the Namibian north, all share this same general growth form. These plants cannot withstand much rain or humidity outdoors. Fully grown clumps are too large for a container, but smaller, single-rosette plants of this group are still highly valued by collectors.

A peculiar niche exploited by a few widely separated *Aloe* species consists of steep cliff faces. Several species, mostly but not exclusively from northwestern South Africa and scattered spots along the entire length of Namibia, specialize in these precarious habitats, each one typically confined to a single mountain complex. Some, such as *A. dewinteri*, from the far north of Namibia, bend upward to the light and produce upright inflorescences, while others, such as the Richtersveld species *A. meyeri*, hang absolutely upside down, with their flower spikes also growing pendently until finally turning up at their tips.

Aloe peglerae, somewhat threatened from development and over collection. Photo by Brian Kemble.

The pointed tubercles of *Aloe aculeata* range from pure black to pure white. Photo by Brian Kemble.

coveted *A. polyphylla* also has broadly triangular leaves arranged in a unique spiral, either right- or left-handed. Its habitat consists of steep slopes high in the mountains of Lesotho where it regularly endures hard freezes. It has survived 9°F (–13°C) in a California garden). It is difficult to keep healthy without a quick-draining soil mix rich in organic matter.

The spineless ***Aloe striata*** also forms a 2- or 3-foot (60- to 90-cm) rosette composed of broad, tan to orange

A left-handed version of *Aloe polyphylla*.

A field of flowering *Aloe striata* subsp. *striata*. Photo by Brian Kemble.

Aloe broomii, with its thick, flaring inflorescence at an early stage. Photo by Brian Kemble.

An exceptional specimen of *Aloe striata* subsp. *karasbergensis*, now apparently collected. Photo by Brian Kemble.

Aloe deltoideodonta ranges from purple to pink to orange; some substitute lines for spots. Photo by Brian Kemble.

Aloe viguieri, with turquoise leaves, usually found on slopes. Photo by Brian Kemble.

leaves outlined in deeper orange, but it is extremely easy to grow. **Subspecies *karasbergensis***, from farther north and west into Namibia, is similar in size and shape but has almost pure white leaves covered with linear blue lines, giving it a seersucker appearance. One of the few aloes to grow both in winter- and summer-rainfall areas, subsp. *karasbergensis* receives very little rain wherever it grows. Accordingly, it is only borderline hardy outdoors except in the most benign climates.

Considerably smaller but otherwise quite similar in appearance and much easier under garden conditions, ***Aloe reynoldsii***, from the southeast corner of South Africa, forms rosettes of thin, pale green leaves covered with dotted dark green and white lines, and H-shaped white markings. It rather resembles *A. deltoideodonta* from Madagascar.

MEDIUM AND SMALL ALOES OF MADAGASCAR AND EAST AFRICA

Aloe deltoideodonta, with numerous forms and varieties, includes some of the prettiest of the many mid-sized and smaller Madagascan aloes. Plants, which make small clusters, reach about 10 inches (25 cm) in diameter, their broad, fairly thin leaves densely covered with a variety of white markings, and with a color range from lavender to orange when given bright light.

Rather similar, but unspotted and with thinner rosy-purple and blue leaves, ***Aloe imalotensis*** is about the same size, though slower to offset. Other attractive Madagascan plants include *A. laeta*, with blue-gray leaves bordered with pink, fringelike tiny teeth and *A. viguieri*, a small plant with light blue, almost turquoise leaves that

Once called *Aloe hemmingii*, this form of *A. somaliensis* has an exceptionally shiny texture.

One of few cultivated succulents from Sudan, yellow-flowered *Aloe sinkatana* retains its pink edge in good light.

typically grows pendently on steep slopes. *Aloe compressa* grows on ridges composed of easily shattered rock where its distichous form helps it wedge itself securely in tiny cracks. Forms range from mid-sized to quite small.

A number of Madagascan aloes have stiff blue leaves margined with purple teeth, including two yellow-flowered species, *Aloe conifera* and *A. capitata*. The latter has a distinctive globular inflorescence. Varieties of *A. capitata* range from small to almost arborescent, and some occur only on specific types of rock, often growing in small soil-less pockets floored with a layer of decayed sedges, a unique habitat that also supports various pachypodiums and other succulents.

Many other mid-sized aloes with patterns of spots or stripes decorating their leaves grow in eastern Africa. One of the most attractive of these species is *Aloe somaliensis*, including the form once known as *A. hemmingii*.

Superficially similar to the maculate group from the south, its dark green leaves, mottled heavily with zigzagging white marking almost like lightning bolts, have a distinctly glossy appearance.

The Ethiopian species *Aloe harlana*, as seen in cultivation, is rather similar though somewhat larger growing, but its original description states that only juvenile plants have spotted leaves, suggesting that cultivated plants under this name may be suspect, either hybridized or misidentified.

In its habitat, barren eastern Sudan, *Aloe sinkatana* grows either with or without spots. Cultivated plants were selected for their spots, white dots decorating their flat-topped, narrow, gray-green leaves with bright red margins. Oddly, considering the species's hot, arid home, it is fairly cold hardy and will tolerate subfreezing temperatures if kept dry.

Several small shrubby aloes with erect stems, like miniature versions of *Aloe arborescens*, include the misleadingly named *A. zanzibarica* (synonym *A. concinna*), from Kenya, and *A. tororoana*, from Uganda. Both have green leaves marked with white spots, and both are quite happy in relatively small containers.

The dozens of unspotted aloes native to the vast sweep of land from the Horn of Africa to Mozambique include *Aloe scobinifolia*, from Somalia, with a rough-textured, leathery skin; the freely clumping, plain green (red in the sun), toothy-margined *A. dorotheae* from Tanzania; and the blue-gray leafed, widespread *A. chabaudii*, which ranges from Mozambique and Zimbabwe north to Tanzania and southeastern Congo, yet which is surprisingly cold-hardy if kept dry.

The somewhat similar, almost as widely distributed *Aloe cryptopoda* and *A. globuligemma* reach into northern South Africa; neither is extremely cold resistant. *Aloe ortholopha*, up to 3 feet (90 cm) across, gray leafed, with a secund inflorescence (flowers all arranged in an upward direction on the flower stalk), is a striking species from Zimbabwe. *Aloe tomentosa*, a medium-sized plant from Somalia, has gray leaves and white, densely fuzzy flowers, unique in the genus.

Across the Red Sea, the Arabian peninsula has its own mid-sized aloes, including *Aloe audhalica*, with gray to pinkish leaves; *A. dhufarensis*, with thick, channeled, occasionally white-spotted gray leaves; the larger, also pinkish gray *A. rubroviolacea*; and the plain gray, black-toothed *A. vacillans*. *Aloe fleurentinorum*, from Yemen, has brown, arching leaves that curve over beyond and below the edge of a container in near perfect symmetry.

One of a number of distinctly gray Arabian species, *Aloe vacillans* has leaves edged with jet black teeth. Photo by Rob Skillin.

Once common in the wild, *Aloe aristata* at least remains secure in cultivation. Photo by Brian Kemble.

The most northern-growing aloe, **Aloe porphyro-stachys**, was relatively recently discovered. It grows in Arabia and as far north as Jordan. Several other recently described Arabian aloes are gradually making their way into cultivation, with a number still waiting in the wings. Most of the ones mentioned here, however, are at least sporadically available. All are worthwhile, colorful, not too hard to grow, and content to remain in a 6- or 8-inch (15- to 20-cm) pot for many years.

DWARF ALOES

Along with large and medium-sized aloes suited for gardens, the genus also includes a number of dwarf species ideal for growing in small to medium-sized pots. Though a number of these grow in South Africa, at least as many are Madagascan and East African.

Probably the most widely cultivated dwarf aloe, very satisfactory either in a container or in the ground, is the South African **Aloe aristata**. It used to be common in the wild as well, but a local belief that plants placed on a house can provide protection from lightning has caused a serious decline in its population. *Aloe aristata* grows to about 6 inches (15 cm) in diameter and height, and sends out a branched flower stalk about two or three times as high. Some forms offset freely, others less so, and the tight, little rosettes, composed of large numbers of dark gray-green leaves, will ultimately form small mounding clumps if given partial shade and not too much water.

Aloe ecklonis, the broad-leafed grass aloe, looks more like an iris than a grass. Photo by Brian Kemble.

Other South African miniatures include **Aloe humilis**, with an urn-shaped 4-inch (10-cm) rosette composed of pale blue-gray, spiny, bumpy leaves. It is easy to grow, but the similar looking *A. longistyla*, about the same size but even spinier and with a very short but proportionately huge inflorescence, can be quite difficult to cultivate.

Aloe chortolirioides, though widely distributed, remains uncommon in cultivation.

The Madagascan dwarf *Aloe albiflora* will not outgrow a 5-inch (13-cm) pot.

Aloe variegata has a huge range in Namibia and South Africa, with remarkably little variability. Photo by Kurt Zadnik.

The slow-growing *Aloe parvula* has teeth reduced almost to hairs and rosettes at most a few inches across. Photo by Terry Thompson.

Aloe bowiea, which was formerly given its own genus as *Chamaealoe africana*, is a small clumping plant with rosettes of soft leaves and barely discernable spines. It does well in containers and can survive surprisingly low temperatures. *Aloe bowiea* resembles a group of generally inconspicuous plants known as grass aloes, which make their living concealed among the grasses of the South African veldt. Some of these plants are quite tiny. Others such as *A. ecklonis* resemble an iris more than a grass, but none are commonly cultivated. Closely associated with the grass aloes, *A. chortolirioides* forms elongated stems for its clumps of soft, elongated rosettes.

Finally, among the small southern African species, we find the partridge breast aloes, which make little rosettes of a few very thick, vividly marked triangular leaves. *Aloe variegata*, with a wide natural range over much of South Africa and Namibia, has a long history as a popular cultivated plant. It has two much scarcer relatives: *A. dinteri* from northern Namibia and Angola, and the very localized central Namibian *A. sladeniana*. *Aloe dinteri* is smaller, with narrow, upright leaves, chocolate-brown when given enough light. *Aloe sladeniana* is almost impossible to find in the grass-covered rock in which it grows. It resembles a miniaturized *A. variegata* with a slightly more open rosette. Some forms of *A. variegata* can reach a foot (30 cm) across, *A. dinteri* only about half that size, although as much as 18 inches (45 cm) tall, while a cluster of *A. sladeniana* will have room to spare in a 5- or 6-inch pot (13- to 15-cm). Though harder to find than to grow, these two small species should be given a great deal of light and a very rapidly draining soil. They need protection from winter cold, humidity, and rain as well.

The dwarf aloes of Madagascar include both extremely distinct plants and some which look like miniaturized versions of the ubiquitous spotted aloes that range over almost the entire continent of Africa in suitably dry areas. With leaves having the slightly roughened texture of a lizard tail, *Aloe albiflora* and *A. bellatula* form small clumps of stemless rosettes 3 or 4 inches (8 to 10 cm) across and about 8 to 10 inches (20 to 25 cm) tall. The two species look almost identical out of flower, but the blossoms of *A. albiflora* open into little pure white bells while those of *A. bellatula* keep the pinkish orange color and shape of ordinary aloe flowers. Neither plant causes difficulty in cultivation, although *A. bellatula* seems a bit more delicate than its cousin. Both need reasonable warmth, less light than most aloes, and a bit more water than average during their winter rest.

With similar needs in cultivation but a different appearance, *Aloe haworthiodes* is a tiny plant, with rosettes rarely more than 3 inches (8 cm) in diameter. Its narrow, dark brown leaves are edged with soft, fuzzy spines, and its tiny yellow-orange flowers smell of honey. Some forms offset fairly rapidly and consequently it has become quite common in cultivation.

Aloe parvula is a very small still-uncommon plant, with individual rosettes rarely more than 3 inches (8 cm) across. Though the plants slowly clump, a 4- or 5-inch (10- to 13-cm) pot will easily hold a multiheaded specimen. *Aloe parvula* likes very bright light, and when properly grown its almost fuzzy leaves, equipped with tiny harmless spines, will turn gray-purple.

From a habitat of limestone hills, another odd, rare, tiny Madagascan aloe, *Aloe calcairophila*, grows distichously rather than in a rosette. Its two-ranked leaves look like an opened fan no more than 3 or 4 inches (8 to 10 cm) from tip to tip.

Aloe descoingsii, with thick, bright, shiny leaves marked with white spots, forms rosettes that are even smaller, rarely 3 inches (8 cm) across. Its bright orange flowers, shaped like tiny closed bells, are among the smallest in the genus. It needs bright light, but otherwise is easy to grow and surprisingly cold hardy for an almost equatorial plant.

Aloe rauhii, with rosettes to about 4 inches (10 cm) across, thinner, narrower leaves, and more typical looking flowers, tolerates lower light, but under brighter conditions its leaves will turn from green to lavender or even somewhat orange, always with an attractive pattern of white H-shaped spots and dots. This species is a parent of many of the increasingly popular small highly patterned aloe hybrids.

Aloe bakeri differs from these other Madagascan miniatures in that it forms dense growths of elongated more-or-less upright stems up to 8 inches (20 cm) tall with rosettes of narrow, semiterete, shiny greenish brown, often spotted leaves. It grows readily and can survive outdoors in sheltered, mostly frost-free areas if given some sun and good drainage.

East Africa also has its share of small and near-miniature aloes. *Aloe jucunda*, from Somalia, looks like a larger version of *A. descoingsii*, with shiny green leaves decorated with patterns of white spots and lines. *Aloe dumetorum*, from the dry north of Kenya, grows slightly larger, up to about 5 inches (13 cm) across. Its pale, soft, narrow but thickly succulent leaves are further embellished with dark lines and patterns of almost square white markings. Although the species offsets freely, a multiheaded plant will grow contentedly in a 5- or 6-inch (13- to 15-cm) pot. The Ethiopian *A. jacksonii* has flat-topped, gray-green, white-spotted leaves, and a growth habit much like *A. bakeri*, producing clusters of small upright stems. Although this is just a sample, as a group the dwarf aloes offer a lot for collectors with limited space.

Most aloes grow quite easily. They enjoy sun, good drainage, soil with some organic matter, and, typically, water about once a week in the warmer months and about once a month in winter. Many of them will adapt to winter rainfall without difficulty if planted outdoors.

The truly dry-growing species should be kept in containers and protected from rain, and given a longer stay between watering when they are dormant, but only a few really demand accommodation to their native rainfall patterns. In fact, despite their extremely arid habitats a number of the winter-growing species, among them *Aloe pillansii* and *A. pearsonii*, need water about once a week in summer, and never should be left completely dry.

A surprising number of aloes from tropical regions will tolerate a fair amount of cold and even some frost, but it is always wise to be cautious when dealing with plants from East or West Africa, Arabia, or Madagascar.

In addition enthusiastic growers are increasingly producing surprising *Aloe* hybrids that generally require no out of the ordinary care. Aloes are one of the mainstays of any outdoor succulent garden, and the small and medium-sized plants make fine container plants whether on a windowsill or in a greenhouse.

Chapter 25

Haworthia

CLOSELY RELATED TO aloes and therefore subjected to the same taxonomic dissonance regarding family, *Haworthia* trumps its larger cousin by extending the confusion down to the level of species. Deciding which haworthias do or do not represent valid species has caused unending contentious debate. This confusion, due in part to the plants' natural variability and compounded by a vast number of garden hybrids and indeterminable cultivated plants lacking adequate locality or habitat data, led to an oversupply of species names in the last century and a half. Sorting out the taxonomic mess has occupied the efforts of numerous specialists, at least two journals, several books, and innumerable articles. Further complicating the issue, new forms, varieties, and species continue to be discovered.

Years of study in the wild by several experts, who do not necessarily agree among themselves, first reduced the number of accepted species from more than one hundred and fifty to around sixty. More recently the leading student of *Haworthia* has further reduced the number to fewer than thirty. For horticulturalists more likely to encounter plants in nurseries or collections than in the wild, however, having sixty or so reasonably plausible species names with a large accompanying complement of subspecies, varieties, and forms at least somewhat consistently referable to specific plants may be more helpful than botanically more accurate compilations of endlessly variable continuums of individual specimens. It is important to remember, nonetheless, that species in *Haworthia* should be understood as a very broad, flexible concept, and that given names apply to a wider variety of forms than can be indicated by a single photograph.

Haworthias achieved their popularity in the early nineteenth century and have maintained it ever since. Their small rosettes of fleshy leaves vary from stemless to more-or-less columnar. Confined almost entirely to South Africa, many have mastered the art of concealing themselves from prying eyes and wandering, plant-munching mouths. Their relatively long flower stalks bear small tubular, generally asymmetrical flowers, basically white, but sometimes with green, pink, or brownish tints. Flower structure and shape are the basis for the current division of *Haworthia* into three subgenera, which, with some exceptions, also tend to look different from each other. Some members of subgenus *Haworthia*, with distinctly windowed or stainglass-like colored leaves, have the most eye appeal in the genus. The choicer species in subgenera *Hexangulares* and *Robustipedunculares*, however, often appeal to more sophisticated collectors who appreciate their subtle interplay of geometry, pattern, and texture, and can see them as unique living miniature sculptures.

Most people will recognize some of these light green, often rather translucent little rosettes or short columns of darker green leaves marked with white tubercles as common inhabitants of dish gardens and windowsills. Some thrive with little care in gardens given partial shade and not too much water. People familiar with these easily grown, rapidly multiplying haworthias may be astounded at the high prices collectors will pay for rare specimens, and dumbfounded at the slow rate of growth of some of these rare forms. Common or rare, haworthias illustrate the endless variations within a restricted basic growth form that appeal to most succulent plant enthusiasts. Though many of the most widely grown haworthias are really hybrids, prolific and almost indestructible, the much more interesting world of true species is worth a closer look.

SUBGENUS *HAWORTHIA*: SOFT, TRANSLUCENT, AND SPIDERWEB-LEAFED PLANTS

The largest subgenus of *Haworthia*, also called *Haworthia*, consists mostly of low-growing, stemless plants and comprises about two thirds of the species. There are several basic growth types within the subgenus, and treating these more-or-less similar-looking species as informal groups makes it easier to navigate through the genus, even though the plants may not necessarily be closely related. Most of the more widely distributed haworthias vary tremendously in appearance across their range and the presence of bristles, windows, and spots on leaves has very little significance in determining relationships between species, although it has a lot to do with determining which plants people consider desirable to grow and collect.

The first group consists of plants with generally pale-green, somewhat translucent, usually rather soft leaves. The best known of these is *Haworthia cymbiformis* ("boat-form") from the Eastern Cape, with leaves shaped something like a rowboat, curving on the outer surface, concave on the inner, and coming to a little point. The typical variety produces offsets rapidly, but some forms, with larger, more triangular leaves may remain solitary for many years. **Variety *incurvula*** is smaller, with more curving leaves and **var. *ramosa*** forms long, pendent stems. Both **var. *transiens*** and **var. *obtusa*** have rounded leaf tips, veined and almost transparent, quite similar in appearance to forms of *H. cooperi*.

Haworthia cooperi may grow in more exposed situations than *H. cymbiformis*, and in such settings it often at least partially withdraws underground. The transparent tips of its **varieties *pilifera*** and ***truncata*** die back leaving flattened, windowed surfaces exposed to the sun while the bulk of the plant takes shelter below the surface.

Some varieties of *Haworthia mucronata*, particularly the form alternatively called *H. helmiae*, also closely resemble *H. cymbiformis*. Others such as **var. *inconfluens*** and **var. *morrisiae*** have leaves more yellow-green, and often narrower and less rounded or boat-shaped (see photo on page 22).

Another very variable species, *Haworthia reticulata*, has pale, generally lightly patterned leaves, often flat or even convex on their upper surfaces in contrast to the concave or trough-shaped upper surfaces of *H. cymbiformis* and its look-alikes. The attractively patterned leaves of the inch (2.5 cm) wide *H. reticulata* **var. *hurlingii***, the smallest variety, often remain concealed beneath surrounding bushes. When in active growth, *H. lockwoodii*, from extreme climatic zones bordering Bushmanland and the Great Karoo, and somewhat difficult in cultivation, resembles forms of *H. mucronata*, but when dormant, its outer leaves shrivel to paper thinness, forming a

Haworthia cymbiformis var. *transiens* reproduces less rapidly than some forms of the species and develops more definite rosettes.

Very variable *Haworthia reticulata* occurs in relatively well watered places. Photo by Rob Skillin.

Haworthia lockwoodii, in summer dormancy, can withstand climatic extremes.

protective sheath. Plants during these times look rather like little onions.

A somewhat catch-all group of haworthias includes several small-growing, mostly abundantly offsetting species. **Haworthia chloracantha** resembles some forms of *H. reticulata*, but its narrow leaves are opaque rather than semitranslucent. The tiny rosettes of **H. chloracantha var. denticulifera**, at most an inch (2.5 cm) in diameter, have nearly linear leaves fringed with minute teeth and reproduce so rapidly that a single plant will fill a 4-inch (10-cm) pot in four or five years. The other varieties of *H. chloracantha*, larger and with broader leaves also grow very easily, although not quite as rapidly.

The fountain-shaped rosettes of the relatively uncommon **Haworthia floribunda** tend to be darker green and slower growing, with twisted leaves. Other somewhat similar species with small many-leafed rosettes and proportionately long, narrow leaves include **H. outeniquensis** (with translucent spots), restricted to a small mountain range that separates the Little Karoo from the coastal plains and hills, and **H. maraisii var. meiringii** (other varieties of this species have considerably broader, recurved leaves resembling *H. retusa*). **Haworthia angustifolia**, and the odd, long-leafed **H. wittebergensis** share this general configuration, while the very variable **H. gracilis** includes forms that would fit here, some forms similar to *H. mucronata*, as well as some that look more like the *H. arachnoidea* group discussed later in this chapter. Most of these plants grow in the shade of bushes or on hillsides facing away from the sun, but certain forms (usually pale or yellow-green) can withstand considerably more light.

The defining characteristic of another group in subgenus *Haworthia* is their retuse leaf tips, flattened and often provided with windows as well. These plants present a taxonomic muddle of related and intersecting forms, the largest number concentrated in an area not far from the coast and about 150 to 200 miles (240 to 320 km) east of Cape Town. Well worth getting to know, they include some of the most sought after haworthias, attaining an amazing range of colors if given adequate light: purple, turquoise, pink, gold, and streaked and dotted with white, gold, and silver as well. When grown properly, the nicest forms of these species resemble little sculptures of stained glass. In habitat many of them grow flush with the soil, and their baroque coloring actually serves to camouflage them amid the pebbles and sparse bushes. Their transparent leaf tips and tops act as windows, letting light into their interiors so they can photo-

The rare *Haworthia outeniquensis* manages to thrive in a forest of imported pine trees. Photo by Kurt Zadnik.

Haworthia retusa, large growing and rarely offsetting in its Western Cape home. Photo by Kurt Zadnik.

synthesize from inside, without having to expose more of their mass to the potential threats of the great outdoors.

Best known of them, **Haworthia retusa** is most often represented in cultivation by a rapidly offsetting, medium-sized, rather chunky plant with firm, glassy green leaves. Unfortunately, this form probably is a hybrid, possibly involving *H. turgida*. Although generally similar to its impersonator, the real *H. retusa* becomes considerably larger to over 4 inches (10 cm) in diameter, and is much shyer about producing offsets. It often grows in relatively well-watered localities amid grass and small shrubs, sheltered in their shade or fully exposed in the gaps between them. *Haworthia retusa* may have attractive silvery-gray lines marking the upper surfaces of its leaves. Quite sim-

A minutely papillose "crystalline" form of *Haworthia pygmaea*.

Genes and culture combine in this spectacularly colored *Haworthia magnifica* var. *splendens*.

Haworthia magnifica var. *atrofusca*: other forms of the species are the color of eggplant; all are tiny with a pebbled texture.

A golden form of *Haworthia emelyae* var. *emelyae*, hunkered down and blending in with the landscape of the Little Karoo.

ilar but smaller, darker and frequently somewhat glaucous, *H. mutica* grows in rocky ridges farther west and rarely if ever offsets.

The inappropriately named *Haworthia pygmaea* is an average-sized retuse species, growing on hillsides near the coast. It offsets very slowly and has a somewhat frosted texture which in some cases results in plants with surfaces that look as if they were covered with sugar crystals. A related form, *argenteo-maculosa* ("silver-spotted"), at times considered a variety, a separate species, or a variety of *H. magnifica*, does not offset and is covered with silver-white dots that may lie flush on its surface or be raised up. Other less taxonomically blurry subsets of *H. magnifica* include **var. magnifica** itself, smaller, often darker, and more heavily veined than *H. retusa* and frequently slightly rough textured. **Variety atrofusca** remains small and grows very slowly. It can be smooth

textured or rough, covered with minute papillae, and it varies from dark green to distinctly purple-black, to forms which are colored like red molten glass. **Variety dekenahii**, sometimes considered a separate species, has a somewhat bumpy texture and distinct silver veins. The remarkable *H. magnifica* **var. splendens** consists of a few extremely localized forms with pink and silver flecks covering their bumpy leaf surfaces, in between bright silver veins. In good light plants may color up completely in shades of pink and gold.

The variable and beautiful *Haworthia emelyae*, another nonoffsetting species, lives farther inland in the Little Karoo. *Haworthia emelyae* **var. major** resembles forms of *H. magnifica*, sometimes blue-purple and intensely papillate. *Haworthia emelyae* **var. emelyae** is either slightly rough or smooth textured. Some of its forms, such as the one called *picta*, for example, can turn completely golden, or a blend of gold, turquoise, and pink, dotted, white veined and rivaling *H. magnifica* var. *splendens*. Larger, to 4 inches (10 cm) across, **H. emelyae var. comptoniana** lacks the range of coloration of var. *emelyae*, but as compensation its broad, smooth, almost plastic-textured, shining green leaves usually display a pattern of checkerboard tessellations. **Haworthia emelyae var. multifolia** sometimes offsets but lacks the spectacular colors and patterns of the other varieties.

Occasionally with tessellations on its upper surfaces similar to those of *Haworthia emelyae* var. *comptoniana*, **H. bayeri**, a Little Karoo species, may also have linear markings or none at all, but plants are always dark green to nearly black with a granular texture on their translucent surfaces. **Haworthia mirabilis** resembles *H. emelyae* var. *multifolia*, with flat-surfaced, bluish, clear leaves marked by a few longitudinal veins that turn red in bright light. Its **variety badia** has fewer but larger leaves with very translucent tips and a color range from golden to chestnut brown to glassy blue-purple. The even larger **var. beukmannii**, to 5 inches (13 cm) across, also has only a few leaves per rosette and tends to remain green; it, along with the previous two, does produce offsets but only very slowly, particularly in cultivation where plants may remain solitary for decades. Other varieties, such as **calcarea**, the somewhat bristly **paradoxa**, and **triebneriana**, with long, narrow leaves, offset more readily, though they never form large clumps.

In contrast, **Haworthia turgida** may form clumps several feet across. It is more widespread than most of the other retuse types, and often grows on steep slopes and in mountainous areas. Accordingly, it is one of the more

cold hardy haworthias, although almost all of them will withstand at least a few degrees of frost. Unlike most of the others in this group, *H. turgida* rarely withdraws into the soil, and in some forms the leaf-tips are barely retuse at all. Some *H. turgida* forms, such as **f. rodinii** are covered with dots and lines, almost as strongly patterned as the real show-stoppers of the group and would undoubtedly be coveted and expensive if they were not fairly proliferous. Nonoffsetting and growing far to the east of the other retuse species, the rare **H. springbokvlakensis** keeps mostly underground. It reaches 4 inches (10 cm) or more in diameter and its leaves turn bluish with contrasting red veins in good light, but it is outstanding because of its almost bubblelike leaf-tip windows (see photo on page 23).

Perhaps the most accomplished of the haworthias at concealment in the wild, and always the most attention grabbing in cultivation, **Haworthia truncata**, and its **variety maughanii** (synonym *H. maughanii*), grow flush with the soil, with their leaf apices so flattened that they look as if they'd been cut off with a knife. Rather than form a rosette, the leaves of *H. truncata* are distichous (growing in two ranks), resulting in a shape like an old-

A small piece of the Little Karoo supports a dense population of *Haworthia truncata*. Photo by Rob Skillin.

A select form of another Little Karoo species, *Haworthia bayeri*.

fashioned fan. Both varieties also are notable because of their massive roots, equal to the rest of the plant in size. Usually offsetting but sometimes permanently solitary, *H. truncata*, scattered over several parts of the Little Karoo, shows considerable variation, with some forms much broader leafed than others, some glassy textured, some with papillate, almost hairy surfaces, and some with highly decorative leaf patterning. Nestled in a tiny habitat in the middle of *H. truncata* territory, var. *maughanii* forms a rosette in standard haworthia fashion, but with its angularly faceted, cut-off, occasionally highly patterned leaf tips, it looks more like a tiny glass model of a modern sculpture than it does a plant (see photo on page 37).

Often associated with the retuse species, **Haworthia parksiana** is perhaps the only plant ever inadvertently named in honor of a city park. It is also one of the small-est and rarest haworthias, slow to offset and found in only a few locations very near the seacoast, one of them a hill right in the middle of a South African town. It forms tiny rosettes barely an inch (2.5 cm) across, composed of many recurved, long, narrow leaves dark green to almost black. In the wild it is well hidden in grass on steep slopes, visible only when flowering when its stalks rise up beyond the concealing grass.

Haworthia pulchella, another small dark, rare species has leaves armed with small white teeth, and usually remain solitary. There is a proliferous variety. A third diminutive endemic, *H. pubescens* substitutes a dense covering of bristly hairs for teeth. Along with *H. pulchella* it has a western, though extremely limited, distribution.

Taking a step beyond the bristly hairs of *Haworthia pubescens*, several haworthias have leaves with greatly elongated, hairlike marginal teeth that in the most extreme cases make them look like small spherical silvery spider webs. These haworthias are perhaps best represented by the various varieties and forms of the appropriately named *H. arachnoidea*. Various varieties of this form, which all have at one time been considered separate species, range as far northwest as the Richtersveld, through Namaqualand, the hills bordering Bushmanland, the Little Karoo, and much of both the Western and Eastern Cape Provinces. They more-or-less form a continuum ranging from the less hairy, more spiny looking **varieties *xiphiophylla*, *nigricans*, *scabrispina*,** and ***namaquensis*** (northwestern, with by far the widest distribution, though never abundant), to the **varieties *aranea*, *arachnoidea*** itself, and the most extreme, **var. *setata*,** which resembles a little ball composed of fine, silvery threads or hairs.

Haworthia parksiana, with 1-inch (2.5-cm) rosettes: effectively invisible in the wild.

A relatively new discovery, *Haworthia pulchella* looks like a miniature aloe.

Haworthia arachnoidea var. *setata,* growing in deep shade. Photo by Rob Skillin.

Haworthia decipiens, wedged between rocks on the border of the Little and Great Karoo. Photo by Kurt Zadnik.

Haworthia semiviva, growing near the equally hairy Crassula barbata. Photo by Rob Skillin.

The very similar **Haworthia bolusii**, from farther east, forms smallish rosettes of leaves, each narrow leaf densely edged with translucent bristles that completely screen the plant. A number of other haworthias share this general look, but with their elongated spines less numerous and not as fully transformed into soft threads. These include the Namaqualand species **H. nortieri**, sometimes with distinctly yellow flowers; **H. decipiens**, which ventures into the desolate environment of the southern Great Karoo; most varieties of **H. herbacea**; and the delicate **H. marumiana** var. **archeri**. **Haworthia semiviva** specializes in harsh areas such as the fringes of Bushmanland and the Great Karoo, where temperatures soar in summer and plummet during winter nights. It shares its habitat with dwarf mesembs such as *Titanopsis* and *Aloinopsis*, but unlike them it grows under small bushes where it does receive a little shelter. Related to the nonserrate-

leafed **H. lockwoodii**, when dormant its thin, white leaves similarly close into a tight, quite dead-looking ball.

Many of the faster growing, readily offsetting species in subgenus *Haworthia* grow very easily. Most of the more interesting members grow in the western half of South Africa, whether along the coastal strip of Western Cape Province, the semidesert of the Little Karoo, the more intense desert of the Great Karoo, or the arid mountains and plains of the northwest part of the country. All these areas share a general precipitation pattern of dry summers and rain from fall through spring. The easiest growing haworthias do not need a specialized watering regime to do well, and watering them about once a week in spring, summer, and fall and about every two weeks in winter will keep them alive. A better choice that's almost mandatory for the more delicate species is water about every two weeks in summer and winter, and once a week in spring and fall. Keeping these haworthias too wet in summer frequently leads to a loss of their roots, and although the plants often regenerate, over time they will disappear.

A couple of species, such as **Haworthia nortieri**, from the far west, need a somewhat stricter summer drought, more careful watering in spring and fall, and water every week to ten days in winter, depending on the weather. Many spiderweb plants also do better with water every ten days during their growing period, rather than once a week. *Haworthia truncata* and its variety *maughanii* thrive with water every two weeks during the growing season, and every three weeks or less during summer and winter. These plants and other species with massive tuberous roots can rot if kept too wet.

No haworthias are terribly fussy about soil, as long as it drains rapidly and contains a bit of organic matter. Again, the easy growing species will do well in almost any mix while the more refractory ones will benefit from extra drainage.

Light is the variable most often misapplied to haworthias. They all can tolerate quite low light for succulent plants, and species such as *Haworthia cymbiformis*, which grows in shaded spots in the wild, do well under such conditions. Most people do not give haworthias enough light. In inadequate light the retuse species, and those forms of *H. cooperi* and *H. cymbiformis* that develop windowed leaf tips, will simply never display the brilliant colors and patterns that mark them in the wild. For better results give the plants as much light as they can take without burning. Note that the irregular, discolored splotches of leaf-burn look nothing like the symmetrically patterned bands and lines of color that define well-grown plants. Most haworthias will thrive in an east-facing window that gets good morning light with some sun; in a south- or west-facing window they should receive light shade to protect them from the hotter sunlight. In real desert climates, however, haworthias will need considerable shade and may prove fairly difficult to keep healthy.

SUBGENUS *HEXANGULARES*: STEM-FORMING, TUBERCLED, AND STIFF-LEAFED HAWORTHIAS

The second and third subgenera of *Haworthia*, distinguished from the first and from each other by details of flower structure, include many species with shared features, including stiff, opaque green leaves marked by white tubercles, and often an upright, somewhat columnar growth form. Not surprisingly, a number of species in each subgenus are exceptions to these broadly described types, included among them some of the most interesting haworthias.

The subgenus *Hexangulares*, with flowers with a somewhat hexagonal shape at the base, includes both very common and very rare species. The most common ones, hard to kill and quick to offset, have made their way into many everyday gardens where they thrive with a mix of sun and shade. The most frequently seen develop into masses of small highly proliferous rosettes heavily dotted with white tubercles. Many of these plants are unidentifiable garden hybrids with **Haworthia attenuata** somewhere in their ancestry, although the authentic species *H. attenuata* does not look all that different. The smaller, slower offsetting **var. radula** (synonym *H. radula*), although still hardy, is less rugged than typical *H. attenuata*. At first glance resembling *H. attenuata*, **H. fasciata** actually is both slower growing and more attractive, with tubercles only on its outer leaf surfaces that form definite bands almost like a zebra's stripes. **Haworthia fasciata f. browniana** is a drier growing form, with an elongated stem and heavier leaves that attain a glossy, almost frosted sheen in good light.

A second group of plants in this subgenus consists of smaller leafed, usually heavily tubercled species that slowly grow into clusters of little columns. The two main species with this habit, *H. coarctata* and *H. reinwardtii*, encompass a wide diversity of growth types, complicating identification. **Haworthia coarctata** and **H. reinwardtii** come from distinctly different parts of the East-

Haworthia fasciata, growing in a surprisingly bright spot. Photo by Brian Kemble.

Red, but not sunburned, this *Haworthia coarctata* f. *greenii* has barely visible tubercles.

ern Cape Province of South Africa, but that is little help in distinguishing plants growing in adjacent pots. Typically, but not always, *H. coarctata* has proportionately thicker leaves, arranged less densely on its stems. An attractive, almost tubercle-free form of *H. coarctata*, a type of distinction now thought taxonomically meaningless, was once called *H. greenii*. The most striking members of this group have smaller leaves and form more distinctive columns. These include **H. coarctata var. tenuis**; **H. reinwardtii f. kaffirdriftensis**, with small overlapping leaves and extremely distinct tubercles in longitudinal rows, **H. reinwardtii f. chalumnensis**, a relatively quick column maker; **H. reinwardtii f. zebrina**, with tubercles arranged in distinct lateral bands; and **H. reinwardtii var. brevicula**, a miniature rather delicate variant. Some of these plants are almost as common in cultivation as the various versions of *H. attenuata*, while others are ex-

Haworthia reinwardtii var. brevicula, a small version of this more freely offsetting species.

A heavily sculpted form of the slow-growing Haworthia nigra.

A very old Haworthia viscosa, growing in full sun. Photo by Rob Skillin.

tremely slow growing and rather easy to rot, guaranteeing their desirability to collectors.

A third group of plants in this subgenus consists of mostly summer-growing plants that make columns of three-ranked, triangular, solid-colored leaves. Both **Haworthia viscosa** and **H. nigra** form masses of upright, trifold columns that range from red to olive-orange to almost black. Both species grow slowly, though *H. viscosa* and its various forms (as many as fifteen varieties, now largely disregarded) are relatively quicker and larger as well, with columns ultimately up to a foot (30 cm) tall and 2 inches (5 cm) across. *Haworthia nigra* remains small, with leaves that often display heavily sculpted surfaces, marked with patterns of dark lines and ridges. Some of its forms, such as the plant once known as *H. nigra* var. *schmidtiana*, can be almost unbelievably slow growing, producing no more than one or two leaves a year, and remaining content in a 2-inch (5-cm) pot for decades.

A fourth group of plants diverges from almost all of the previously mentioned characteristics of the subgenus other than flower form. Best known of these, the extremely widely distributed **H. venosa** **subsp.** **tessellata** forms compact, low-growing rosettes with flat-topped, translucent leaves. Plants range from the winter-rainfall regions of southern Namibia to the summer-rainfall areas of the Free State and Eastern Cape Provinces of South Africa a thousand miles (1600 km) to the east. Most forms have an attractive checkerboard pattern on the tops of their leaves. Leaf color varies from bright green to bronze to almost black, but almost all of the forms grow easily and produce offsets from the ends of short underground stolons. Other subspecies of *H. venosa* show up much less frequently and include **subsp. venosa** itself, looking like a somewhat dried out, checkerboard-free version of *tessellata*; **subsp. granulata**, almost opaque leafed and very slowly forming rough, black columns somewhat resembling *H. nigra*; and the extreme endemic, possibly now extinct **subsp. woolleyi**, a small delicate barely offsetting plant that looks somewhat like a

Haworthia venosa subsp. *tessellata* hiding under a Bushmanland bush. Photo by Rob Skillin.

Haworthia limifolia, easy to grow but possibly doomed to extinction in the wild.

Haworthia venosa subsp. *granulata*, from dry areas and very slow growing.

Haworthia koelmaniorum var. *mcmurtryi*, an extreme endemic from northeastern South Africa.

miniaturized subsp. *tessellata* with thinner, more elongated, upright leaves. It was native to a tiny strip of land which ended up as a severely overgrazed, eroded gully on the wrong side of a fence. Fortunately, the species has been propagated by seed, and so still exists in cultivation if not in its habitat.

Also under imminent threat of extinction, ***Haworthia limifolia***, typically forming flat, star-shaped rosettes of green-black leaves with lateral ridges on the surfaces like a tiny washboard, was once quite widespread and common. It and a couple of associated haworthias live far to the east and north of the others, extending almost to the South Africa-Mozambique border. Unfortunately, local people have decided that the plants offer protection from lightning strikes if pulled out of the ground and placed on their homes, and consequently *H. limifolia*, along with some other only vaguely similar succulents,

are in the process of being eradicated in habitat. Its pink-tan, smooth-leafed **variety *umbomboensis***, though originally rarer in nature, is safe at least from this human-engendered threat.

Related rare endemics also from the South African northeast, ***Haworthia koelmaniorum*** and its distinctive **variety *mcmurtryi*** look like a cross between *H. limifolia* and one of the windowed retuse species. Unlike the proliferous, easy-to-grow *H. limifolia*, these two haworthias only rarely offset and develop very slowly, but with leaves that can be deep wine-red with blue tessellations, or almost purple-black, they have become popular in the relatively short time since they were discovered. Not closely related but equally rare in habitat, *H. bruynsii* forms tiny rosettes of brown, translucent leaves and looks like a miniature retuse species except for its flowers. Difficult to grow, it remains solitary, and in the wild retracts into

Haworthia scabra var. *starkiana*, growing in full sunlight on the top of a cliff. Photo by Kurt Zadnik.

Haworthia longiana growing in the Eastern Cape. Photo by Brian Kemble.

With leaves like the claws of a dinosaur, *Haworthia scabra* var. *scabra* is another very slow grower.

Haworthia sordida ("dirty") attracts dust in habitat, hence its name.

the ground, its light-transmitting leaves usually coated with a fine covering of dust.

A number of the other species in the subgenus form chunky, stiff-leafed rosettes. One of these, **Haworthia scabra var. starkiana**, grows in crumbling rock at the edge of a Little Karoo canyon in bright sunlight that turns its leaves brilliant yellow-orange. Its stiff rosettes were once described as resembling a cluster of small upright bananas. As with many of these uncommon haworthias, the habitat of *H. starkiana* is better measured in acres than square miles. Its relatives, **var. lateganiae** and **var. scabra** itself, grow in the same system of small canyons. Interesting, slow-growing plants, their rosettes, sadly, bear less of a resemblance to a bunch of bananas. **Haworthia longiana** ultimately forms massive clusters of slow-growing rosettes with narrow elongated leaves up to

1.5 feet (45 cm) long, while the even slower **H. sordida** puts forth smaller rosettes of rough-textured sometimes recurved, green to blackish leaves. These plants offset only gradually, but other somewhat similar-looking species, such as **H. glauca**, often long-stemmed or with tubercles, grow and clump more quickly.

Most members of this subgenus grow fairly easily, with the eastern forms better treated as summer growers, receiving weekly water in spring, summer, and fall, and a partial winter rest, while the others do better with water once a week in spring and fall, and every other week in summer or winter. As with all haworthias, maximum light short of burning will bring out the best in the plants, but most will survive considerably less than optimum conditions without too much complaint.

Haworthia pumila, a big plant on a steep, wet slope.

SUBGENUS *ROBUSTIPEDUNCULARES:* FLOWERS ON BRANCHED STALKS

The third subgenus, *Robustipedunculares*, consists of a small number of species which produce slightly larger flowers on long, often-branched stalks. Most of these plants can become quite large and many remain solitary. They include **Haworthia pumila**, the biggest species, with rosettes up to nearly a foot (30 cm) across, and with often ornately tubercled leaves, glistening white and pearly, and in some forms, shaped like little pearly glazed doughnuts (see photo on page 36). **Haworthia minima**, slightly smaller and in some instances comparatively freely offsetting, also has pearly tubercles, sometimes arranged in orderly, shining rows, while in the larger, usually solitary **H. kingiana** the tubercles lie almost flat. Most forms of the last species of this subgenus, **H. marginata**, lack tubercles, and form large rosettes which, with their often sharp-tipped leaves, look superficially similar to some smaller agaves.

Most of these plants remain scarce in cultivation, although hybrids of *Haworthia pumila* are common enough, looking like larger, more striking versions of *H. attenuata*. The plants in this group grow in western winter-rainfall areas and can be fairly touchy in cultivation. The most frequently seen, *H. pumila*, may grow on soaking wet steep hillsides, half-hidden by dense shrubs, or may live quite exposed to the sun on level ground. As with so many of these plants the trick is to give them as much light as they can take without burning, plant them in fast-draining soil that nonetheless has some organic mat-

A hybrid of *Haworthia pumila* and *H. springbokvlakensis*, looking like neither of its parents.

ter in it, and be careful of too much water in summer. Water every two or three weeks in summer is probably a safe bet, with water once a week in fall and spring, and slightly less often in winter, providing there is at least occasional sunlight.

HAWORTHIA HYBRIDS

Finally, over the last several years a number of skilled growers have created haworthia hybrids. These plants, a far cry from the random garden crosses of the past, have expanded the possibilities of the genus, adding colors, shapes and textures never found in nature. Most of the choicer hybrids remain scarce for the time being, but will undoubtedly become a major force in continuing haworthia cultivation.

Chapter 26

Gasteria, Astroloba, and Poellnitzia

L IKE *ALOE* AND *Haworthia*, the smaller, less-familiar genera *Gasteria*, *Astroloba*, and *Poellnitzia* are members of the inclusive family Asphodelaceae or the even-larger family Xanthorrhoeaceae, depending on which authority is followed. *Gasteria* is closely related to *Aloe*, while *Astroloba* and *Poellnitzia* are closest to *Haworthia* and at one time were included in that genus. Gasterias make great indoor plants and are fairly common in cultivation. Astrolobas and the single poellnitzia are somewhat slow but not difficult to grow.

GASTERIA

Gasterias are small to medium-sized South African aloe relatives. They might strike many people as a rather unassuming genus of succulent plants, good for dish gardens and window-sills, but not really all that exciting. And, at least to a degree, there would be some truth in such a judgment. Since the late seventeenth century, when gasterias were first discovered by Europeans, they have served as reliable horticultural subjects, without the strict requirements of light or water shared by many more spectacular or bizarre South African succulents. Gasterias are, nonetheless, interesting plants, with new discoveries in the genus being made even today, and with several extremely intriguing attractive species and forms quite unlike the norm of the genus.

The genus was named for the assumed resemblance of the flower shape to a stomach. Instead of the cylindrical flowers of *Aloe*, the flowers of *Gasteria* generally curve or bend in the middle, resulting in a shape something like a kidney bean, or a human stomach. Most gasteria flowers are orange-red with a green tip, arranged along relatively long, simple or branching stalks.

Gasterias hybridize freely, and it took the work of skilled botanists and field researchers to determine which plants were naturally occurring species. Currently about two dozen species and varieties are accepted, ranging from the tiny *Gasteria bicolor* var. *liliputana*, with leaves barely an inch (2.5 cm) long, to surprisingly large plants such as *G. excelsa*, which may grow into a rosette 2 feet (60 cm) tall and almost 3 feet (90 cm) across. With a few exceptions, however, the species generally form stemless plants, with long, comparatively narrow leaves arranged either in rosettes or in the shape of a spread out fan (distichous). Though the leaves often have pointed tips, they lack true spines and may have a somewhat cartilaginous margin, often white, along their edges. For the most part green, often with white spots, the leaves may be variously smooth, rough-textured, or covered with tubercles.

Growing in a wide geographical band that parallels the South African coastline, gasterias avoid the intense aridity and climatic extremes characteristic of the higher altitudes of the South African interior. Most grow amid scrub brush and succulent bushes, which provide them with the relative shade almost all gasterias prefer, though some larger species will outgrow the surrounding vegetation and end up almost fully exposed to the sun. Gasterias typically are found on steep slopes and rocky ledges, in the company of other succulents such as crassulas and adromischus. Several species occur in the *fynbos* community of drought resistant, but not generally succulent plants. Because they grow in less uninhabitable areas than many succulents, the habitats of various gasterias are subject to human development. Many of the plants, which generally once were common, are finding their future in the wild increasingly precarious.

Less frequently grown because of their size at maturity, the three largest species, *Gasteria excelsa*, *G. acinacifolia* and *G. croucheri*, though superficially similar in appearance, differ in significant details of inflorescence and flowers, leaf size and shape, and geographic distribution. All of them, presumably less dependent on concealment as they grow, are equipped with protective serrated leaf margins.

Gasteria excelsa, from southeastern South Africa, forms a large rosette composed of broadly triangular, thick, sharp-tipped leaves that are channeled above, keeled below, and edged with sawlike marginal teeth. The dense white dots that cover juvenile plants turn at maturity into scattered white markings that contrast with the overall glossy, dark green leaf surface. The large branched inflorescence dwarfs that of any other gasteria. In common with the other two large species, *G. excelsa* usually avoids full exposure to the sun in habitat, but in cultivation it can tolerate full sunlight quite easily in areas with moderate climates.

Less common than *Gasteria excelsa*, **G. croucheri** grows well to the north, along the eastern coast of South Africa, a region of hot summers, frost-free winters, and considerable precipitation. Smaller than *G. excelsa*, it nonetheless can form a rosette 2 feet (60 cm) across and 18 inches (45 cm) tall and, unlike its solitary southern cousin, it clusters fairly readily. Mature plants tend to be more heavily spotted than *G. excelsa*, the variably shaped dark green leaves less sharply tipped, the marginal teeth smaller. *Gasteria croucheri* frequently grows on steep slopes, where the extra drainage mitigates the high rainfall. A closely related plant, smaller and with drooping leaves, **G. pendulifolia**, is confined exclusively to the faces of steep cliffs.

Gasteria acinacifolia, with a restricted habitat along the southern and eastern South African coast, ultimately becomes bigger than the other two large species, with a rosette a few feet across and at least as tall. It often grows on the sides of stabilized sand dunes in the shade of vegetation. Its youthful, distichous leaves are covered with tubercles, while in mature plants the tubercles generally disappear, replaced by bands of white dots. *Gasteria acinacifolia*, along with the other large species, does very well as a container plant; even if slightly dwarfed by confinement, its bold, upturned rosettes formed of a relatively few massive leaves contrast dramatically with the other gasterias.

The remaining gasterias are considerably smaller. Even those with long leaves are much less bulky. Most of these remain distichous for a long time, sometimes permanently, and when the rosette forming species change into their mature configuration they often surprise their growers. The rosettes of these species generally are wider than tall, and most of the plants rarely exceed a foot (30 cm) in diameter or height.

One of the permanently two-ranked species, **Gasteria disticha**, grows inland from the coastal regions, edging past the mountains into the harsh Great Karoo, where it experiences comparatively extreme degrees of both heat and cold. It also grows to the south, in somewhat more benign circumstances (see photo).

Gasteria carinata **var.** *retusa* closely resembles *G. disticha* and shares the southern part of its range before continuing farther west and south. The two differ in that *G. carinata* var. *retusa* has pearly-white tubercles on its leaves and a smooth surface on the nontubercled parts of its leaves, in contrast to the unraised white dots and roughened epidermis of *G. disticha*.

Gasteria carinata **var.** *verrucosa*, formerly considered a separate species, tends to have long leaves, very densely covered with tubercles either white or noncontrasting

Gasteria acinacifolia, a large rosette protruding from the surrounding Eastern Cape undergrowth. Photo by Brian Kemble.

Gasteria disticha in typical gasteria habitat at the base of a sheltering bush.

Gasteria carinata, the plant shaded, inflorescence in more light. Photo by Rob Skillin.

Gasteria batesiana 'Barberton', a selected form with black to red coloration.

Gasteria batesiana, the typical form, a smaller plant growing in almost vertical surroundings. Photo by Brian Kemble.

green. **Gasteria carinata var. carinata** ultimately forms dense clusters of rosettes each up to a foot (30 cm) in diameter or a bit more.

A third medium-sized species, **Gasteria brachyphylla** from the Little Karoo, remains distichous throughout its life. It also resembles G. *disticha*, differing in its smooth skin and pointed leaf tips, and sometimes developing an appealing orange-brown mottling when given sufficient light.

The distichous forms of these three medium-sized species look quite similar, but a fourth species, **Gasteria pulchra**, from farther east, generally has proportionately much longer and narrower leaves than the others. Although it shares the common gasteria marking of bands of white dots, the remaining green parts of its leaves can become very dark, almost black in some forms. Between the four of them, these plants more-or-less define the classic form of a gasteria.

A mid-sized plant with a frequent penchant for growing on steep slopes and near-vertical cliffs, **Gasteria batesiana** also lives far to the northeast of the other species, in the provinces of KwaZulu-Natal and Mpumalanga. Smaller than G. *pulchra*, it is immediately recognizable because of its densely spotted, somewhat tuberculate leaves which are thick, rough-textured and leathery, and deeply channeled on their upper surface. Though distichous when juvenile, it develops a rosette rather quickly and offsets slowly but steadily. Typically dark green, some forms, such as 'Barberton', have almost black leaves that will turn strikingly red-black in good light, their almost velvety appearance belied by their pebbly, tough surface.

Looking somewhat like a miniature version of *Gasteria batesiana*, **Gasteria ellaphieae** rarely exceeds 6 inches (15 cm) in diameter. Relatively recently discovered, it grows in a limited area not far from the middle of the southern South African coast. Its approximate similarity to G. *batesiana* extends to its preference for steep, almost inaccessible habitats, where it conceals itself, sunk down among rocks and scattered vegetation, its color and markings further helping to camouflage it. One of the most recently described gasterias, **G. glauca**, was discovered in the same small river drainage system as G. *ellaphieae*. Similar in size, it offsets much more freely and has a rougher, more tuberculate leaf surface texture as well as a slightly blue, glaucous color.

Two other dwarf species, **Gasteria baylissiana** and **G. glomerata**, remain distichous, while a third, **G. vlokii** ultimately forms a small relatively few-leafed rosette. All

Left: *Gasteria ellaphieae*, wedged into a crack between rocks filled with organic debris. Photo by Brian Kemble.
Right: *Gasteria bicolor* var. *bicolor*, a colorful clone, showing its elongated stem.

Gasteria bicolor var. *liliputana*, completely different: miniature, clumping, with very sharp leaf tips.

Gasteria pillansii, brownish in the bright light of the South African west coast.

three are highly localized, comparatively recently described, and still not very widely distributed in cultivation. *Gasteria glomerata* forms dense clusters of 2- or 3-inch (5- to 8-cm) plants, the clusters themselves rarely exceeding 8 inches (20 cm) in diameter. Its unmarked, glaucous green leaves, short, wide, and thick, give it the look of a miniature version of *G. armstrongii* (described below). Similarly shaped, with thick leaves densely spotted with white tubercles, *G. baylissiana* will offset in a 2.5-inch (6-cm) pot, though it is far slower than *G. glomerata* to make large clumps. Typical of the miniature gasterias, it is a plant of mountain tops and steep slopes.

Gasteria bicolor, widely distributed in Eastern Cape Province, includes among its varieties the smallest gasteria, **G. bicolor var. liliputana**, along with completely dissimilar, much larger plants exceptional in the genus because of their upright stems. These larger forms may remain distichous or their leaves may spiral in a swirling pattern rather than a true rosette, while the plants can reach almost 2 feet (60 cm) in height, half of it leafless stem. Some forms may have bands of white dots or the dots may merge into patches and bands that stretch across the leaf width, contrasting with the otherwise very dark, almost black-green coloration in a sort of zebra effect. *Gasteria bicolor* exhibits a continuum of shapes, and at its most diminutive, *G. bicolor* var. *liliputana*, looks completely different from the larger forms, with narrow leaves 1 or 2 inches (2.5 to 5 cm) long. It may remain distichous or spiral, and does not form an elongated stem. Variety *liliputana*, armed with a sharp leaf tip, offsets prolifically,

grows very easily, and has been a popular dish garden subject for decades.

The greatest variety of succulent plants live in northwestern South Africa, but only one gasteria has found a home in this land of fog and winter rain. **Gasteria pillansii** first appears not far north of Cape Town and continues along the coastal plain and facing hills through Namaqualand and the Richtersveld, then just crosses the Orange River into a strip of Namibia. Its range encompasses some of the driest parts of South Africa, but it selects relatively sheltered places to live, avoiding the quartz fields in favor of gentle coastal hills that funnel the fog from the cold ocean current. The plants remain distichous, their upper leaf surfaces flat, and the leaves themselves rather strap-shaped (lorate), leathery, spotted with white, and in good light, chocolate brown. Plants from drier parts of the range tend to be smaller (one of these

Gasteria pillansii var. *ernst-ruschii*, a highly endemic Richtersveld miniature, filling a crack in the rocks with offsets.

Gasteria nitida var. *armstrongii* sunk into the soil, its semi-translucent leaves allowing some light to filter inside. Photo by Brian Kemble.

was once called **G. neliana**), and the smallest version, **var. *ernesti-ruschii*** is very small, with leaves occasionally up to 3 inches (8 cm) long. Confined to the Richtersveld, in nature *G. pillansii* var. *ernesti-ruschii* is a fairly uncommon plant, but as is sometimes the case with rare succulents, where it does grow it is abundant, capable of filling a rocky crevice with hundreds of offsets.

In contrast to these outlying or oddly proportioned gasterias, ***Gasteria nitida* var. *nitida*** seems quite typical, growing over a large portion of the coastal Eastern Cape, where it forms rosettes of triangular, pointed, white-dotted leaves. The plant, up to 8 inches (20 cm) tall and 10 inches (25 cm) in diameter, rather resembles a small version of *G. excelsa*, and would hardly be worth mentioning if it were not for a close relative. Variably considered a variety of *G. nitida* or a separate species, **G. armstrongii** is the most distinctive looking gasteria of all. Good clones of it retain their distinct appearance, with always distichous, two-ranked, extremely thick leaves that look like tongues cast in dark green glass, sometimes tubercled or humped, then recurved toward their tips. In habitat the plants often remain partially underground, quite hidden. Their glassy, slightly translucent design may allow a bit of light to filter through, a step in the direction of a true window.

Very different from all the rest, ***Gasteria rawlinsonii***, from the central southern coastal regions of South Africa, has stems as much as 3 feet (90 cm) long clad in strap-shaped, lightly toothed leaves for their entire length. Plants first arc out, then hang straight down from the almost inaccessible cliff faces where they grow. In cultivation plants remain erect for 3 or 4 inches (8 to 10 cm), then bend over; presumably a sufficiently large specimen would complete the arc and face downward. The plants branch slowly from the base and produce typical unbranched gasteria inflorescences.

Almost all gasterias are easy to grow. Most will thrive in any reasonably fast draining soil mix, and can take either partial shade or bright sunlight. Water once a week, with a winter rest period of water perhaps every three weeks works best. Most will take a little frost with no problem if kept dry, but wet and cold conditions in winter can foster permanent disfiguring black spots on the leaves. Other than that, the plants generally remain disease- and pest-free. Many gasterias thrive outdoors given a slightly shaded spot in a succulent garden. *Gasteria nitida* var. *armstrongii* may want somewhat longer intervals between water in winter, and *G. pillansii*, though tolerating standard treatment, will do best if treated as a winter grower, with a moderate rest period in summer.

There also are a number of variegated gasterias and clones selected for intense leaf color or unusual shape. These may be slower growing and hard to find, but not particularly difficult in cultivation. In addition, an increasing number of hybrid gasterias, purposefully bred rather than the product of random garden crossings, have become popular, selected and propagated for their unusual leaf colors and textures.

Gasteria rawlinsonii in habitat grows pendently, with stems approaching 3 feet (90 cm) long.

ASTROLOBA AND POELLNITZIA

Astroloba and *Poellnitzia*, though closely related to *Haworthia*, significantly differ from that larger genus and from *Gasteria* and *Aloe* as well. At first glance they resemble columnar haworthias such as *H. viscosa*, but where those produce leaves in whorls of three, astrolobas generally have four- or five-ranked leaves, each new whorl looking like a little crown on top of a column composed of very hard leaves with sharply pointed tips. Additionally, *Astroloba* has symmetrically organized flowers. They swell, narrow at the tips, and flare open again in the little lobed star shape that gave a name to the genus.

With only six currently named species and lingering confusion about some natural hybrids and uncertainly identified plants, astrolobas are not grown or seen that often. They occupy a swathe of land that runs from the central part of the Western Cape, through the Little and southern Great Karoo into the Eastern Cape, always well back from the coast, where they endure hot summers and very cold winters.

Astroloba bullulata, the westernmost species, grows and branches very slowly, remaining small at only 3 or 4 inches (3 to 10 cm) tall. It has stiff dark, brownish green to almost blue-black leaves marked with distinctive rows of darker tubercles. *Astroloba congesta* and *A. spiralis* have unmarked, very pointed leaves that turn sharply upwards, while the upper surfaces of the leaves of *A. foliolosa* and *A. herrei* remain largely horizontal. *Astroloba corrugata*, a widely distributed species, shows the horizontal leaf configuration of *A. foliolosa* and *A. herrei*, but its dark green leaves, with sometimes paler, almost translucent margins, are ridged, dotted and corrugated.

Gasteria 'Silver King', one of many highly colored or variegated gasteria hybrids.

Astroloba cf. *bullulata*, slow growing and either solitary or very sparsely branched.

Astroloba spiralis, in the shelter of bushes but in very bleak surroundings. Photo by Kurt Zadnik.

Astroloba cf. foliolosa from the Eastern Cape, enjoying good light.

Astroloba cf. corrugata, a large somewhat sun-scorched plant at the east end of the Little Karoo.

Poellnitzia rubriflora, slow growing, with very hard, stiff blue leaves and orange aloe-like flowers.

Most astrolobas make large clusters of stems, often growing among other succulent shrubs that support them as they elongate. They may be fully exposed to the sun in conditions surprisingly bright for plants that look so much like shade-loving haworthias. In cultivation they grow slowly and sometimes the older stems lose their leaves, but they often look similarly weather beaten and tattered in the wild as well. Despite this, and an occasional tendency for the slower growing species to lose their roots when overwatered, they are attractive plants, deserving more recognition among growers than they typically receive.

Poellnitzia rubriflora, the only member of its genus, has four- or five-ranked leaves just as hard as those of *Astroloba*, smooth, blue-green, and with a slightly waxy coating that can be rubbed off if touched too vigorously. It would certainly be included in *Astroloba* except for its orange-red flowers that look very much like those of an *Aloe*. It is found in the Robertson Karoo, a relatively well watered area west of the Little Karoo that has largely been given over to agriculture. Often found under bushes, *Poellnitzia* also sometimes grows nearly fully exposed on almost bare rock outcrops. It too grows slowly, gradually branching from the base. Although not difficult, if given too much water, particularly during summer, it can lose its roots.

Chapter 27

Succulent Bulbs

ALONG WITH ITS huge population of succulent plants, South Africa also supports an extraordinary array of bulbs, many of them winter growers. A good number of these have established themselves in general horticulture, where genera such as *Ixia*, *Babiana*, *Gladiolus*, *Freesia*, and *Sparaxis* have become winter- and spring-blooming mainstays. Others with similar growing habits that have not achieved widespread recognition include *Romulea*, *Ferraria*, *Lapeirousia*, *Tritonia*, *Cyanella*, *Geissorhiza*, and *Ornithoglossum*, each with species rivaling the better known genera when in flower.

Along with the other monocots, these bulbous plants have recently undergone complete taxonomic reorganization. Placed years ago for the most part in the lily family (Liliaceae), then split over time into several new families (Hyacinthaceae, Colchicaceae, Asphodelaceae, Amaryllidaceae), they are currently being relocated into greatly expanded versions of the Xanthorrhoeaceae and the Asparagaceae. Many of the most frequently grown plants belong to the iris family, but despite their enlarged nutrient- and water-storing underground parts, they would never be considered succulents.

Bulbs and other plants that have developed a lifestyle of underground dormancy for much of the year are termed *geophytes*. In the course of this book we have encountered many totally unrelated succulent geophytes. These plants typically have an underground caudex or tuber and include members of the Euphorbiaceae, Passifloraceae, Moraceae, Apocynaceae, and more. Though geophytes, there is little possibility of confusing them with a bulb.

There are, however, a number of plants that venture close to the boundary between a geophytic succulent and a bulb, some sitting on both sides at once. Most bulb growers have ignored them, and almost by default they have fallen into the domain of things sought out by succulent growers, often because of their striking, if tem-porary, foliage, or the strange forms of their thickened, underground parts. Moreover, a number of these plants develop bulbs that partially rise above the soil surface, defying the protective logic behind the evolution of a bulb but making them seem more desirable to succulent collectors.

In this chapter we will look first at plants that produce generally upright leaves: *Bulbine* in Asphodelaceae, and *Bowiea*, *Lachenalia*, *Ledebouria*, *Veltheimia*, *Nerine*, and *Drimia* in Hyacinthaceae. Then we will consider the plants that develop flat, sometimes fleshy leaves that remain prostrate on the ground. These come from several unrelated groups and are among the most striking succulent bulbs: *Massonia* in Hyacinthaceae; *Haemanthus*, *Brunsvigia*, *Ammocharis*, *Boophane*, *Rauhia*, and *Gethyllis* in Amaryllidaceae; and *Eriospermum* in Eriospermaceae.

Before dealing with these purely bulbous genera, however, it is worth mentioning **Aloe buettneri**, an aberrant member of that undeniably succulent genus. This species is almost unknown in cultivation though with a huge distribution from Angola through the Congo and north as far as Mali. It looks exactly like an ordinary aloe when in growth, but in dormancy completely drops its leaves and retreats into an underground bulb until the next rainy season.

BULBINE (ASPHODELACEAE)

More closely related to *Aloe* than most of the other bulbs, *Bulbine*, from the asphodel group, is one of the genera that skirts the border between bulb and succulent. Generally small plants, bulbines typically form rosettes of fleshy, often patterned leaves that in many cases die back completely in summer. One exception is **B. latifolia**, from the Eastern Cape; it may keep the soft, thick leaves of its large aloelike rosettes year-round (see photo on page 18). On the opposite extreme, the tiny **B. mesembryanthe-**

Bulbine mesembryanthemoides subsp. *namaquensis* rivals *Lithops* in its reduction to essentials: two windowed leaves and an inflorescence. Photo by Rob Skillin.

Bulbine cf. *fallax*, with translucent leaves forming a rosette in Namaqualand. Photo by Kurt Zadnik.

From the Richtersveld coast, the rare *Bulbine rhopalophylla* does not resemble any typical bulb. Photo by Rob Skillin.

moides, widely distributed in the winter-rainfall parts of South Africa, sends out one, or infrequently two, glassy-green, half-inch (13-mm) leaves that look like transparent, watery bubbles. In conditions of intense sunlight, the leaves die back to ground level, transformed into little, flat, transparent "windows" that allow photosynthesis to take place below the soil line.

Bulbine fallax, common on the fringes of Namaqualand quartz fields, lies somewhere in between the two, with a stemless, flat rosette several inches (centimeters) across made of windowed green leaves. A much rarer species from the Richtersveld coastal strips, **B. rhopalophylla** puts out a taller rosette of thick, waxy, ovoid leaves that resemble those of Mexican crassulaceous succulents such as *Pachyphytum*.

Various other bulbines, often highly endemic and poorly known, may form very small many-leafed fountainlike rosettes or grow into thumb-sized, nearly transparent green domes. All of them bear very similar flowers, usually yellow, with inflorescences that vary from long, thickly flowered racemes to single-blossomed. No matter how firm-textured and solid their leaves may appear, the winter-growing ones dry up and vanish into their underground bulbs with every summer dry season; many of these species must be kept completely dry when dormant or they will rot.

BOWIEA, LACHENALIA, ORNITHOGALUM, AND RELATIVES (HYACINTHACEAE)

Another genus that straddles the bulb-succulent boundary, *Bowiea*, comes from the hyacinth contingent. It has large shiny bulbs to 6 or 8 inches (15 to 20 cm) in diameter that remain above ground and annually produce a flower stalk with long, twining tendrils and only a few tiny flowers. The modified flower stalk acts as the main photosynthesizing organ, substituting for the barely noticeable, rudimentary leaves. *Bowiea* bulbs are poisonous, so handle with caution! **Bowiea volubilis** comes from eastern South Africa, but may grow at any time of year; some of its forms live as far north as Tanzania. The rare **B. gariepensis**, with a thicker, less twining flower stalk, grows strictly in winter.

Other somewhat related genera that seem more firmly on the bulb side of the division include *Lachenalia* and *Ledebouria*. *Lachenalia*, with tubular to campanulate, brightly colored flowers, is widespread in the summer dry parts of South Africa. A few lachenalias occasionally show up in nurseries, but **L. viridiflora**, with brilliant, turquoise-colored blossoms, and **L. anguinea**, with a single thick, succulent, erect or arching leaf with trans-

Bowiea volubilis, the glass onion, with its photosynthesizing inflorescence. Photo by Terry Thompson.

Ledebouria socialis, a decorative dwarf form of this popular succulent bulb.

The striped and very thick-leafed *Lachenalia anguinea*, in deep sand south of Namaqualand.

verse banding, remain, respectively, rare and almost unknown in cultivation.

Ledebouria, with spotted, sometimes perennial leaves and small but pretty flowers, comes from eastern and central South Africa. It consists of one very well known evergreen species, **L. socialis**, and a number of obscure and uncertainly determined ones. Their ovoid bulbs typically proliferate fairly rapidly and often partially protrude above the soil line. In cultivation most people raise them entirely above ground.

Often solitary, **Veltheimia** and **Nerine** become much larger than lachenalias. Some share similar autumn through spring growing seasons and general cultural requirements. More are summer growers, however, and some of these species and hybrids have crossed over into more general horticultural communities. *Nerine* has brightly colored tubular flowers.

Drimia consists of a number of species. **Drimia haworthioides** is one of the few bulbs more interesting during its resting period than when it is actively growing. It flowers with unprepossessing green-white blossoms before putting out narrow, strap-shaped leaves. When the leaves dry off they leave a rosette of scales that look something like an upturned pinecone or the rosette of a weather beaten haworthia.

Looking very different, but also in the hyacinth group, *Albuca* and *Ornithogalum* both have rather plain, somewhat campanulate flowers, striped white and green or yellow-green. They vary from small plants with rosettes of narrow, almost terete foliage, to genuine miniatures with a single cigar-shaped succulent leaf, to much larger plants with heavy, fleshy, sometimes channeled leaves that may be several feet long and grow in a loose, swirling rosette. **Albuca spiralis**, fairly small and with a bulb that remains underground, produces a dramatically spiraled rosette of narrow leaves around the time its nodding flowers start to fade.

ANDROCYMBIUM (COLCHICACEAE)

Unlike the previously described genera which generally produce upright leaves, the uncommonly cultivated genus *Androcymbium*, related to the giant crocus, *Colchicum*, includes several species from the South African west equipped with a single pair of flattened, elongated, ovoid leaves, along with several less interesting species from northern Africa. Androcymbiums bloom from their centers, their small flowers dominated by enclosing cuplike or even tentlike bracts. The more common **Androcymbium ciliolatum**, from central and northern Namaqua-

Growing in one of the harshest climates in South Africa, *Androcymbium latifolium* stays low. Photo by Kurt Zadnik.

Massonia pustulata, a miniature species with white rather than yellow flowers.

Massonia depressa, large flat leaves may cool the underground bulb or collect dew.

Massonia bifida, growing in a vertical crack in a Richtersveld hill. Photo by Kurt Zadnik.

land, has pure white bracts that look like tissue paper, while in ***A. latifolium*** (synonym *A. pulchrum*), from the arid, stony plateaus bordering Bushmanland, the bracts may be glowing red.

MASSONIA (HYACINTHACEAE)

Massonia, from the hyacinth family, is another desirable succulent bulb with a prostrate growth form. Occurring as far north as the Richtersveld and well beyond Cape Town to the southeast, it also flowers from between its two outstretched, often thick, flat leaves. Up to 6 inches (15 cm) wide, the paired leaves of ***M. depressa*** may stretch over a foot (30 cm) from tip to tip. Its dense tuft of yellow, simplified flowers with protruding stamens and untidy masses of pollen contrasts with the pristine white, tubular flowers of other species such as ***M. pustulata***, named

because of its rugose (bumpy) leaves, or with those of several truly miniature Richtersveld species. These plants tend to grow in flat areas, whereas ***M. bifida*** (formerly sole member of the genus *Whiteheadia*) has a predilection for cracks in vertical cliff faces. Its short, erect flower column is densely clad with bracts. All of these plants flower when fully leafed out, in contrast to several of the amaryllid genera, which develop their flattened pairs and rosettes of leaves only after completing flowering.

HAEMANTHUS, BRUNSVIGIA, AMMOCHARIS, BOOPHANE, AND RELATIVES (AMARYLLIDACEAE)

Perhaps the best known of the succulent amaryllids, *Haemanthus* inhabits a fairly wide area in Africa and so has varying flowering and growth periods. The flowers of the best-known species, which are very narrow and lack petals, look like a dense mass of pollen-dusted bristles growing out of a cup and raised up on a short stalk. The most commonly cultivated species, the white-flowered **H. albiflos**, comes from summer-rainfall regions and of-

ten retains its foliage year-round. The most-sought-after haemanthus, however, are winter growers, with flowers that range from orange to pink to deep red. **Haemanthus coccineus**, with a tulip-shaped flower cup, puts out a pair of flat-growing, very fleshy leaves up to 2 feet (60 cm) long from its large subterranean bulb. In contrast, the rare, pink-flowered **H. nelsonii** will bloom and grow in a 4-inch (10-cm) pot. Numerous other species of haemanthus are cultivated, all interesting but none common.

Most species of *Brunsvigia* also keep their leaves, whether paired, multiple and radiating, or otherwise oddly arranged, flat on the ground. When in leaf, **B. bosmaniae** and **B. marginata** look something like green starfish that somehow had wandered into the desert. They bloom from an often spectacular tall-stalked, wheel- or ball-like inflorescence composed of a swarm of large dazzlingly pink and red flowers. The radius of the flowering

Haemanthus coccineus exhibiting hysteranthy (flowering before leafing out).

Brunsvigia cf. *bosmaniae,* with leaves like an aberrant starfish.

The same plant a month later.

Brunsvigia marginata, in leafless flower at the University of California Botanical Garden at Berkeley.

Boophane disticha, flowering from its leafless, aboveground bulb. Photo by Brian Kemble.

Equally distichous, *Boophane haemanthoides*, from the South African west, grows in winter.

A spiraling, hairy *Gethyllis* species, growing from a crack in a rock near the Namaqualand town of Springbok. Photo by Kurt Zadnik.

ball almost reaches its total height including stalk. After pollination, the dry flower capsules elongate until the inflorescence radius precisely matches its height. Subsequently the inflorescences tumble along for miles, blown by the wind and scattering seed as they go. ***Brunsvigia josephinae***, with huge, partially aboveground bulbs, keeps its long, narrow leaves in a semierect rosette. The miniature **B. radulosa** produces much smaller, flat-to-the-ground leaves with a roughened, bristly texture. It is one of the few brunsvigias that will flower in a small container.

Ammocharis coranica, growing from the western Karoos far into East Africa, forms a multileafed rosette with an inflorescence similar to a brunsvigia. ***Ammocharis longifolia*** (synonym *Cybistetes longifolia*), from Namaqualand and the Richtersveld, produces an inflorescence even closer to a brunsvigia, and holds its leaves very low

to the ground, but unlike brunsvigias, it flowers when in full growth.

The few species of *Boophane*, with very large, often aboveground bulbs, send out distichous rows of long, strap-shaped leaves. They may grow either in the winter-rainfall west or the summer-rainfall east of South Africa and neighboring countries. ***Boophane disticha***, from Zimbabwe and eastern South Africa, can develop bulbs the size of bowling balls and leaves 3 feet (90 cm) long, the latter sometimes straight, sometimes with curly margins. Its inflorescences, along with those of the much less commonly seen, winter-growing **B. haemanthoides** resemble those of *Brunsvigia*, and similarly tumble along and scatter their seeds.

Most of the prostrate-leafed bulbs grow in western South Africa and Namibia. As the two or three species of the Peruvian amaryllid *Rauhia* leaf out, their exceptionally thick, paired leathery leaves first grow erect, the second of the pair unfurling from within the grasp of the first like a piece of origami. As the leaves mature, however, they bend down and ultimately lie prostrate on the ground. Slow growing and slow to bloom, their greenish white pendent flowers are borne from a tall stalk and lack the striking form and color of their South African cousins. Generally, ***Rauhia decora*** and ***R. multiflora*** are grown for their foliage alone. The leaves of *R. decora* look like striped, flattened green sausages and are marked with silver streaks when young. The larger *R. multiflora* has broad, thick, sometimes perennial leaves.

Many species of *Gethyllis*, a genus of smaller amaryllids, largely confined to arid parts of western South Africa, produce tightly coiled spirals of leaves, sometimes densely tomentose or hairy. Mostly small flowered, a few have large striking ivory to light pink or yellow blooms. They usually flower after their leaves have dried up, but only develop their fruit several months later, before leafing out for the next season. **Gethyllis grandiflora** forms dense, aboveground clusters of bulbs that resemble a caudex, topped with long, almost hair-thin leaves.

ERIOSPERMUM (ERIOSPERMACEAE)

Concluding this brief overview of succulent bulbs, the infrequently grown members of the South African *Eriospermum*, often considered the only genus of the Eriospermaceae, may produce one or two simple, flat leaves that look almost like stylized ears lying on the ground. Other species develop amazingly extended and ramified tubercles from their very reduced leaves and resemble a 2-inch (5-cm) tall, densely branched juniper tree. Small-flowered, their foliage distinguishes them from any of the other bulbs.

Most of the plants described in this chapter, if known at all, have remained in the domain of succulent fanciers, rather than general gardeners. Not only are their forms more in keeping with the bizarre than the conventional, their cultural needs also are similar to those of succulent plants. Some evergreen types, but not *Rauhia*, respond

All this "foliage" derived from tubercles: an *Eriospermum* species from the Richtersveld.

well to a slightly richer soil and only a minimal winter rest period. Most succulent bulbs, however, need a quick-draining soil mix, with water about once a week when they are growing. Typically, water every three or four weeks when dormant will not hurt them. Since some of the more arid-growing kinds will rot in summer if they receive any water at all, knowledge about climate conditions in their habitats is vital. The larger-growing species need lots of root room to grow well and flower, either in large containers or in very well drained soil in a succulent or rock garden. Most of them will easily withstand several degrees of frost outdoors, and then there are those few that will thrive and flower in a small pot.

Chapter 28

Agave

IN MANY WAYS agaves are the New World equivalent of the somewhat similar looking aloes. The few hundred *Agave* species offer almost as much variety from a correspondingly, very limited range of forms—essentially a larger or smaller rosette of thick, fibrous, somewhat succulent leaves with marginal teeth and a terminal spine. Agaves populate vast stretches of the deserts, semiarid and seasonally arid lands of Mexico, the American Southwest, Central America and the West Indies, whether in enormous colonies or as individual plants, and provide a foundation for dry gardens the world over. In addition, agaves are inextricably tied to the past and present populations of Mexico and neighboring lands, supplying local people with food, beverages, and fiber for rope and weaving. Several species have been cultivated for so long and disseminated so widely that their original habitats are now lost forever.

After bouncing back and forth between the eponymous family Agavaceae and the more inclusive Amaryllidaceae, the genus is currently being fitted into the greatly expanded Asparagaceae. Monocarpic, after eight to thirty years or even longer—but far less than a century—agaves produce spectacular flower stalks as much as 40 feet (12 m) tall, and then die. Of course that is not really the end for the majority of agaves, which give rise to numerous offsets before flowering. The most prolific species eventually develop into large colonies of plants. A number of species never offset at all, however, and can only be propagated from seed, while a few others have developed a third way to reproduce, forming bulbils (tiny plantlets) directly on the flower stalk. As the dying parent plant begins to collapse, the bulbils fall to the ground and almost immediately root.

Differences in inflorescence and flower structure, which are undetectable during the many years before flowering, determine botanical relationships within the genus. Most noticeably, the majority of species are grouped in subgenus *Agave* and bloom with inflorescences that produce panicles (small flowering side branches), while the species in subgenus *Littaea* send up unbranched flower spikes, densely clad with clustered blossoms. The very distinctive species of subgenus *Manfreda*, at times considered a genus of its own, consist of smaller, soft-leafed plants with unbranched, sparse-flowered inflorescences.

As a result of human intervention *Agave americana* in particular has spread over much of the world, adapting successfully and fitting in so well as part of the landscape that it sometimes appears in nineteenth-century paintings portraying Biblical times. Besides those few made extremely abundant through human agency, a number of agaves have enormous natural ranges; others occur only on a single mountain or island. Certain areas, among them parts of Sonora and Sinaloa, Oaxaca and the isolated islands of the Sea of Cortez, are centers of agave endemism, while the vast central plains and deserts of much of Mexico harbor a smaller number of species that may range over hundreds of miles.

LARGE, WIDESPREAD, OR PROLIFIC AGAVES

Although **Agave americana**, the almost indestructible, prolifically offsetting century plant is certainly the most common agave in existence, it has never been located in the wild, and it is probably best to regard it as a cultivated clone rather than a normally constituted species. The rosettes are up to 7 feet (2.1 m) tall and as much as 10 feet (3 m) across, and the sword-shaped leaves are 6 feet (1.8 m) long. The very similar **A. americana subsp. protamericana**, variable but usually with noticeably shorter leaves than the typical century plant, grows in the Sierra Madre Oriental of northeastern Mexico. The variegated **A. americana 'Mediopicta Alba'**, with a broad white stripe running down the middle of its leaves, has achieved popularity among collectors. It is rather slow to offset, and somewhat smaller and less robust than ordinary century plants or more common, yellow-margined cultivars.

Almost as large as *Agave americana* and nearly as widespread in Mexico, where it is often used to make *pulque*, *A. salmiana* has shorter, proportionately broader leaves with larger spines than those of the century plant. Toward the southern part of its range it blends in with *A. salmiana* var. *ferox* (synonym *A. ferox*).

Only about half the size of *Agave americana*, *A. asperrima* (synonym *A. scabra*) forms large colonies of plants that spread over a significant portion of the Chihuahuan Desert of northern Mexico, and cross over into parts of southern Texas. It shares the same proliferous habits and blue-gray coloration of its larger cousin, but its more prominent, larger teeth, and its often-incurving, channeled leaves serve to distinguish typical forms from the century plant.

Agave asperrima shares a colonizing habit and affinity for extremely arid areas with *A. deserti*, but is not closely related. *Agave deserti* occurs farther west throughout much of the Sonoran Desert, from Southern California through Baja California, and into Arizona and the Mexican state of Sonora. Very variable, its different subspecies range in size from close to *A. asperrima* to only about half as large, and its leaves, often heavily glaucous and blue-white, are less curved as well as not quite as heavily armed. With its attractive individual rosettes, if it were not so proliferous it probably would be a very popular plant.

Agave lecheguilla ("little lettuce") is also attractive as an individual plant, but offsets so heavily as to take over any area where it is allowed to become established. Offsets of cultivated plants have been known to break through asphalt paving in their search for more room. To call *A. lecheguilla* abundant is a serious understatement; its wild population must be in the billions and it is considered an indicator plant of the Chihuahuan Desert ecosystem where stands of many thousands of plants per acre commonly occur. It continues far to the south of that desert as well and is equally abundant in southwestern Texas. Within its range it grows almost anywhere, but shows a predilection for rocky areas, particularly limestone. Individual plants are bright green to yellow-green and have relatively small teeth along their leaf margins, made up for by a sharp, good-sized terminal spine. The closely packed rosettes may reach almost 2 feet (60 cm) across and tall, but often are smaller. The unbranched, 6-foot (1.8-m) tall inflorescences reveal this species as a member of subgenus *Littaea*.

Agave americana subsp. *protamericana*, with comparatively stubby, broad leaves. Photo by Brian Kemble.

Also in subgenus *Littaea*, the closely related *Agave lophantha* resembles a larger, usually darker green, sometimes gray or blue-green, *A. lecheguilla* with a more open rosette. *Agave lophantha* grows along the eastern edge of *A. lecheguilla* territory. Although far from rare, it is less proliferous than its smaller relative.

Agave filifera, another small species rarely to 2 feet (60 cm) across, comes from a somewhat restricted range in central Mexico. It also produces so many offsets as to hinder its ultimate usefulness as an ornamental plant. Its leaves, toothless though with a sharp terminal spine, are recognizable because of the white, shredding fibers along their margins. In common with many agaves, it will survive several degrees of frost, and if managed carefully can be kept under control along the edges of a rock garden or wall. If left alone, though, it will start to take over.

Along with these proliferating, usually widespread plants, there are a number of larger plants, often bluegray, much slower to offset and from relatively restricted areas. These, though harder to find, achieve a dominant

Agave havardiana, with the typical paniculate inflorescence of subgenus *Agave.* Photo by Brian Kemble.

Agave atrovirens, stretching close to 10 feet (3 m) from leaf tip to leaf tip.

Agave obscura in a high-altitude Mexican pine forest. Photo by Brian Kemble.

presence in a succulent garden or a suitably large container. One of them, ***Agave havardiana,*** grows both in the Big Bend area of West Texas and across the border in Coahuila and Chihuahua, usually at fairly high altitudes, and most often in level areas and meadows. Its rosettes reach to 4 or 5 feet (1.2 to 1.5 m) in diameter, considerably less in height, with broad, sharply tapered, spiny, often glaucous leaves.

Agave montana (see photo on page 36) and ***A. gentryi,*** both good-sized green to glaucous species from high elevations in northeastern Mexico, show up occasionally in cultivation. Though not as enormous as some species, they have thick, heavy leaves, often patterned with the toothy bud imprint of emerging leaves that add to the impact of their heavy spines. With massive inflorescences, quite cold hardy, and often solitary, they are uncommon plants gradually becoming better known.

Also growing at high elevations of up to 11,000 feet (3300 m), but farther south in Oaxaca state and adjacent areas, ***Agave atrovirens*** is one of the largest agaves, with

normally nonoffsetting rosettes to 10 feet (3 m) tall and more than 12 feet (3.6 m) across. Its enormous, elongated cone-shaped flower stalk can reach 40 feet (12 m) in height, but its most interesting feature is its color, dark blue-green but sometimes with a surface so reflective it shines with a silvery sheen in the sun. Rather than a desert dweller, it often grows on cloud forest slopes in areas that rarely if ever dry out completely. Its related to somewhat similar but smaller species that range southward through Chiapas and northern Central America.

From farther north, at medium altitudes along the Sierra Madre Oriental in Mexico, *Agave obscura* also often lives in relatively wet, somewhat shaded, forested areas. To several feet across and with small marginal teeth on its glaucous gray leaves, *A. obscura* has proven to be quite frost hardy and does well in surprisingly chilly, damp climates. It is often grown under the invalid name *A. polyacantha*.

BROAD-LEAFED, BIG-TOOTHED OR GLAUCOUS, SMALL TO MEDIUM-SIZED AGAVES

A second aggregation of agaves consists of species with the common denominators of small to medium overall size and spreading, broad-leafed rosettes. Of these several species, some closely related to each other, some not, the most commonly cultivated is *Agave parryi*, a medium-sized plant related to the previously described *A. havardiana*. It produces bowl-shaped rosettes occasionally as much as 4 feet (1.2 m) in diameter.

Its varieties, inconsistently larger or smaller, occur in Arizona, New Mexico, and farther along the western Sierra Madre Occidental several hundred miles into Mexico. **Variety *huachucensis***, though restricted to a few fairly high altitude locations in southeastern Arizona, has become widely cultivated largely because of some extremely proliferous individual clones. As with all versions of this species, it has gray-blue leaves with black spines in a tight rosette and resembles an artichoke or a giant sempervivum. Somewhat smaller and less commonly seen, **var. *parryi***, often with slightly taller growing, less globular rosettes, has a much larger range, from central Arizona through Chihuahua and Durango states in Mexico. The rarely grown **var. *couesii*** lives farthest north on limestone areas in central Arizona, while **var. *truncata***, very compact and from the Durango-Zacatecas border, though popular in cultivation is the smallest and the rarest in nature. **Variety *neomexicana*** has narrower leaves with smaller marginal teeth than the others. Not commonly grown, some of its forms offset in great quantity.

Endemic to high altitudes in a few Chihuahuan Desert limestone mountains in the state of Coahuila, *Agave parrasana* looks a little like a dwarfed *A. parryi*, at most reaching 2 feet (60 cm) in diameter. Its prominent pale, sometimes white, marginal teeth curl and twist

Growing high and dry in the Chihuahuan Desert, *Agave parrasana* forms very tight rosettes. Photo by Brian Kemble.

in any direction. It is another of the agaves with striking tooth imprints stamped onto its developing leaves. Typically, with only a few offsets, it remains somewhat uncommon in cultivation.

From farther south in Mexico, *Agave guadalajarana* also has flat leaves, very glaucous white and armed with prominent copper-colored teeth. It's another plant of rocky, semiarid grasslands sprinkled with oaks.

The isolated peaks of Sonora and Sinaloa states have fostered the development of a number of endemic *Agave* species. One of them, *A. bovicornuta*, grows in several northwestern localities in the Sierra Madre Occidental of Mexico. The undulating margins of its yellow-green leaves, sometimes with an almost shimmering texture, typify several related, crenate-leafed agaves, most of which are solitary or just slightly offsetting.

From farther south, in Oaxaca and Puebla, *Agave potatorum* is another more widespread, very variable, frequently cultivated decorative species. To about 3 feet (90 cm) across, its broad, occasionally green but usually blue glaucous leaves are also highly crenate, with marginal projections bearing large teeth. Plants grow both in grassy meadows and on steep slopes at moderate alti-

Agave potatorum, with exceptionally large marginal teeth. Photo by Brian Kemble.

Agave isthmensis, growing with *Jatropha* sp. in Oaxacan limestone; none of the rosettes exceed 8 inches (20 cm) in diameter.

Chalk white *Agave guiengola* with the unbranched flower spike of subgenus *Littaea*, growing with *Pilosocereus* cacti. Photo by Brian Kemble.

tudes. Mescal distilled from *A. potatorum* is prized to the extent that the plants, though currently abundant, might eventually come under threat.

Numerous dwarf agave cultivars, many bred by Japanese growers, appear to be forms or hybrids of *Agave potatorum*. A smaller horticulturally confused plant, very glaucous with an almost frosted texture, called ***A. verschaffeltii***, is very close, if not identical to ***A. isthmensis***. This appealing diminutive agave, looking much like some of the dwarf cultivars, grows in a few dry spots in Oaxaca where it rarely reaches a foot (30 cm) across. Some plants are so glaucous that they seem dusted with powdered sugar. As with *A. potatorum*, *A. isthmensis* offsets but not heavily and is susceptible to frost, unlike most members of the genus.

BANDED AND COLORFUL AGAVES

A number of agaves deserve mention because of the bright colors, extremely heavy glaucous coatings, or dis-

tinctive banding of their leaves. Plants fitting this description occur across the whole of the genus, but discussing them as a unit may serve to link them together in the minds of growers as particularly attractive plants.

Agave guiengola, from subgenus *Littaea*, occurs in substantial numbers in its very localized lowland Oaxacan habitat. Armed only with weak, not very numerous teeth, it is good sized and may offset or remain solitary. In its best forms it is almost pure, sometimes silvery, white. Although it grows at low altitudes in a tropical region, it can withstand a few degrees of frost without complaint.

Another medium-sized, blue-white species, ***Agave gypsophila***, has loose rosettes of undulating narrow leaves and specializes in limestone and gypsum areas. It lives near the Pacific coast of Oaxaca as well as farther north in Guerrero state at low altitudes, and shows very limited tolerance to cold temperatures.

Agave macroacantha, fairly abundant in its mostly Oaxacan habitat, forms rosettes to about 2 feet (60 cm) in diameter and not quite as tall. Its many leaves, narrow,

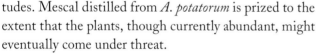

The perfectly symmetrical rosettes of *Agave macroacantha*. Photo by Brian Kemble.

Agave colorata, one of the nicest of the many species endemic to isolated Sonoran hills. Photo by Brian Kemble.

One of the most decorative agaves, *Agave cupreata*. Photo by Brian Kemble.

stiff, and blue-gray, resemble those of various other agaves, but juxtaposed with its pure black teeth and large black terminal spines the plants seem distinctly two-toned. *Agave macroacantha* offsets, but not too freely; plants do well in containers but they are only somewhat frost hardy.

From one of the groups of Baja California agaves, **Agave sebastiana**, native to a few islands off the Pacific coast and the neighboring shores, has developed distinct coloration. Plants are light green overlaid with a pale

glaucous powder, in some cases approaching pure white. The species belongs to the paniculate-flowering sub-genus *Agave*. It becomes good sized and offsets, but grows slowly and can remain in an appropriate container for years. It also is reasonably frost-hardy if planted outdoors.

From the mountains of southern Mexico, **Agave cupreata**, a fairly large species, has deeply undulate leaf margins, with each marginal prominence tipped with a large often copper-colored tooth, sharp tipped from a broader base. The wide, flat leaves resemble those of *A. potatorum* in shape, but their bright green color is immediately indicative. The imprinted bud patterns incised onto its new leaves add to its appeal.

Several of these decorative agaves come with distinct lateral bands. In **Agave marmorata**, the very light gray and darker blue-gray broad bands may be separated by an almost white strip. Otherwise, these large plants resemble agaves in the *A. americana–A. asperrima* complex, but unlike those rugged species, *A. marmorata*, from the warm dry lands of Oaxaca, is not particularly frost hardy.

Agave zebra, endemic to a few arid Sonoran mountains, is considerably smaller, with thinner, deeply chan-neled leaves that come to a very sharp point. Narrow, dark gray bands set against its otherwise pale gray, glau-cous leaves suggested its name. Hardier as well as smaller than the related *A. marmorata*, it will survive outdoors in suitable climates, but does not like overwatering. An-other one of the Sonoran endemics, **A. subsimplex**, is a small, big-toothed, narrow-leafed species, sometimes so glaucous as to almost shine, with striking bud imprints marking its leaves.

Perhaps the most colorful agave of all is the appropri-ately named **Agave colorata**, also from coastal slopes in Sonora. The glaucous and often almost white leaves oc-casionally develop distinct narrow, dark bands. In the brightest light the leaves turn red and purple, sometimes complete with pink cross banding. The rosettes, up to 3 feet (90 cm) in diameter and composed of relatively few broad, almost rhomboidal leaves, remain fairly manageable, offsetting sparingly and able to survive moderate frost outdoors.

Similarly though far less vividly banded, the medium-sized **Agave sobria** was named because it was mistakenly supposed not to be used in making alcoholic beverages. Occasionally grown, it is one of the more easily recognizable of the endlessly introgressing agaves of Baja California.

WHITE-MARGINED AGAVES

Another group of agaves consists of several related species from subgenus *Littaea* distinguished by the white margins, sometimes with a hornlike texture, that surround the perimeters of their leaves. By far the best known of these colorful species, **Agave victoriae-reginae** grows in scattered Chihuahuan Desert localities in northeastern Mexico. Its best forms look as if they had been carefully painted with precise, brilliant white stripes in geometric patterns along the surfaces as well as along the margins of their stiff, dark green, toothless leaves, tipped with black spines. Up to 2 feet (60 cm) across but usually smaller, plants make almost perfect rosettes. Typically a solitary plant that reproduces only from seed, several aberrant vigorously offsetting dwarf forms have also become common in cultivation.

The long, narrow leaves of some taxonomically confused plants gathered together as **Agave peacockii** generally are white margined with black or white curving teeth and form tight rosettes, taller than wide. Restricted to a small part of Puebla and neighboring Oaxaca states, they grow in seasonally arid conditions and share part of their habitat with the spectacular pachycaul, *Fouquieria purpusii*. Plants do not offset, unlike the somewhat similar **A. triangularis**, with weaker teeth spaced farther apart on its thinner, light-colored leaf margins. Its rosettes, about 3 feet (90 cm) across, with broad-based, strongly triangular leaves, do not match *A. peacockii* in size. Even though its range, which is also near the Puebla-Oaxaca border, barely exceeds that of the bigger plant, it is much more abundant in the wild.

From farther north, in the Mexican states of Hidalgo, San Luis Potosí, and beyond comes white-margined **Agave xylonacantha**. With flat, fairly narrow leaves wavy-edged as a Malayan *kris* and armed with extremely large, jagged, white teeth, it grows in drier areas, often in limestone, where it is sometimes accompanied by 30-foot (9-m) tall plants of *Cephalocereus senilis*, the old man cactus, famous for its long, coarse white hairs. *Agave xylonacantha* may reach 4 feet (1.2 m) in diameter, but its comparatively few-leafed, tortuous, loose rosettes lack the symmetrical grace of the broad-leafed species. *Agave xylonacantha* compensates for its deficiencies with its eccentric, extra heavy duty armament of spines and teeth.

The relatively recently discovered **Agave titanota**, endemic to northern Oaxaca and rare, may reach 3 feet (90 cm) in diameter but often remains smaller. Its rosettes, composed of several very broad, flat leaves, range from green to almost pure glaucous white. Its wide white leaf margins and enormous teeth equal those of *A. xylonacantha*. It offsets slowly and sparingly. Like most of its rela-

Agave victoriae-reginae, fit to be named after a queen. Photo by Julia Etter and Martin Kristen.

Agave titanota has perhaps the most extravagant teeth in the genus. Photo by Brian Kemble.

With white shark-teeth and bright green leaves, *Agave horrida* stands out against the dark lava in its habitat. Photo by Brian Kemble.

A Sonora mountain endemic, *Agave pelona* exemplifies dangerously sharp-tipped symmetry. Photo by Brian Kemble.

Agave utahensis f. *eborispina,* in central Nevada limestone.

tives, *A. titanota* can withstand at least a little frost, but does better if kept out of the rain, particularly in the colder months.

More rugged in cultivation, with broad white leaf margins and teeth like those of a great white shark, **Agave horrida** forms medium-sized, nonoffsetting rosettes to 3 feet (90 cm) across. Native to a few ancient lava flows in central Mexico, it does well in succulent gardens and withstands moderate frosts. Unlike many agaves, *A. horrida* can attain a miniaturized version of its mature form even if confined to a 6-inch (15-cm) pot. The very similar, more northern *A. obscura* (previously described), sometimes considered a variant of *A. horrida*, forms more crowded-looking, less symmetrical rosettes of narrower margined leaves.

SMALL TO MEDIUM-SIZED, NARROW-LEAFED AGAVES

With its narrow white leaf margins, **Agave pelona**, not clearly related to other agave groups, is most noteworthy because of its symmetrical rosettes, composed of many toothless, narrow, dark green to almost purple leaves tipped with an extremely long spine. Rare in nature, it is another Sonoran coastal mountain endemic, sometimes growing alongside *A. zebra* in its very dry home. *Agave pelona* remains solitary, with a massive, dark-red flowered, nonpaniculate inflorescence that resembles a giant cattail.

Confined to the southwestern United States, the few species and subspecies in the **Agave utahensis** complex typically form dense clusters of smallish rosettes. **Subspecies *utahensis***, with individual plants to a foot (30 cm) tall and a little more in diameter, has narrow, slightly channeled leaves, sharp-tipped, and with relatively few marginal teeth. About twice as large, **subsp. *kaibabensis*** occurs only in northwestern Arizona. **Subspecies *nevadensis***, actually more common in California than Nevada, is smaller, with glaucous blue-gray leaves and very long terminal spines and larger teeth. It forms extremely dense, compact clusters. Largely confined to Nevada, on limestone outcrops in the mountains northeast of Las Vegas, **forma *eborispina*** also makes clusters of usually small rosettes, greener than subsp. *nevadensis*, white margined and with strong white teeth. It really stands out, however, because of its extremely long, often undulating terminal spines. These may almost equal the length of the whole leaf and curve back over the rosette, enclosing it like spiny basketwork. All forms of *A. utahensis* come from very dry surroundings, with blazing hot summers and winters that drop far below freezing.

Agave arizonica, found in only a few places in north-central Arizona, resembles a more open growing, smaller *A. utahensis*. It clumps, but not with the density of the other species. With an extremely limited range, it will always be potentially threatened in the wild.

DWARF AGAVES

Another Arizonan species, from the far south of the state and crossing the Mexican border into Sonora, *Agave parviflora*, has the smallest flowers in the genus and is probably the smallest plant as well. Its decorative, often solitary rosettes may reach 8 inches (20 cm) in diameter and only about 6 inches (15 cm) in height. In habitat, growing among grasses in semiarid surroundings, it is difficult to see until it sends out its narrow, 6-foot (1.8-m) tall, unbranched inflorescence. Rather than marginal

Just 6 inches (15 cm) across, *Agave parviflora* keeps hidden in southern Arizona grasslands.

Completely manageable in a pot, *Agave nizandensis* requires more attention than most species.

teeth, its leaves fray along their edges into fibrous strands. Closely related, with slightly larger rosettes and flowers a little larger and pink as well, *A. polianthiflora*, from farther south in Sonora and a few points eastward, offsets more readily, but never forms large groups. The two species look very similar and, though both do well outdoors in relatively mild climates, unlike most agaves they also will reach flowering maturity in a pot.

From central Arizona, *Agave toumeyana* looks like a slightly larger *A. parviflora*, with more sharply tapering, curving leaves. It offsets readily and forms dense stands; if it were less prolific it would be more desirable. The same could be said about *A. schottii*, larger still at 18 inches (45 cm) wide and tall, with narrower, less fraying, yellow-green leaves.

Barely larger than *Agave parviflora*, *A. nizandensis* is from far away in southern Oaxaca. Its very distinctive flat, two-toned leaves, light green to brown with a pale green to yellow mid-stripe, combine tiny harmless marginal serrations with a terminal point substituting for a sharp spine. It is another of the few agaves that will flourish in a container though in the wild it forms dense, small clusters. It wedges itself in the gaps along rocky slopes in the low-altitude, hot, humid places where it grows and where it never endures frost.

UNARMED AGAVES

Compared to most agaves, *Agave nizandensis* might reasonably be called unarmed, despite its tiny innocuous teeth. It shares a close relationship with several other species equally harmless to passers by though considerably larger. Most similar in regard to leaf shape and texture, *A. bracteosa*, from the far northeast of Mexico, also grows on cliffs and steep slopes, but in much drier environments. Its pale yellow-green, flat-topped, somewhat rough-textured leaves grow to about twice the length of those of *A. nizandensis* and curl at their tips. *Agave bracteosa* offsets from its leaf axils rather than from its rootstock, resulting in a humped up mound of rosettes.

Agave attenuata, so commonly grown as an outdoor ornamental in Southern California as to have become a horticultural cliché, develops a fairly tall, offset-producing stem. Its thin, wide leaves, usually pale gray green, are soft, flexible, nearly toothless, and end in a bendable terminal point. It grows in isolated colonies at fairly high altitudes in central Mexico, often on the edges of forests where it receives a good amount of rain. It can tolerate a few degrees of frost but no more, and does better in slightly shaded areas than almost any other agave.

Two other essentially unarmed agaves live in isolated pockets in the mountains of western Mexico. ***Agave pedunculifera***, closely related to *A. attenuata*, differs from it in neither developing an elongated stem nor offsetting. More often than not, it colonizes sheer cliff faces, a habit it has in common with *A. vilmoriniana*. This second species, with a generally similar distribution, has proportionately longer and narrower leaves and in its perpendicular habitats covers cliff faces in great numbers like dangling colonies of giant octopi. Its leaf colors, ranging from yellow-green to almost turquoise blue, contrast with the glaucous, pale gray of *A. pedunculifera*. After flowering, *A. vilmoriniana* produces bulbils, which eventually fall and occasionally lodge onto a minute ledge and root. As a consequence of its easily grown bulbils *A. vil-*

Agave bracteosa, oddly tropical looking in its arid habitat. Photo by Brian Kemble.

moriniana has become fairly widespread in cultivation, though it is rarely planted in the near-vertical settings where it can develop to its best advantage.

Quite distinct from the others in this group, ***Agave mitis*** (synonym *A. celsii*), forms mid-sized rosettes to 3 or 4 feet (90 to 120 cm) in diameter and develops into multi-headed dense clusters in cultivation. In the wild, where it typically grows on limestone cliffs in seasonally dry areas, it offsets less profusely. *Agave mitis* has soft, broad, upturned leaves, margined with small teeth and tipped by a fairly long but also soft spine. Its most popular cultivated form, **var. *albicans***, is heavily glaucous and almost white. Plants from the massive Barranca de Metztitlán, in Hidalgo state, approach var. *albicans* in color, growing on precipitous, crumbling limestone cliffs accompanied by species of *Echeveria*, *Pachyphytum*, globular and columnar cacti of various types, enormous specimens of the pachycaulous *Fouquieria fasciculata*, and the ever-present *mala mujer*, *Cnidosculus*, waiting for an unwary climber to grab at for a hand hold.

A few species from subgenus *Agave* have developed shapes approximating these nearly unarmed members of subgenus *Littaea*. Among them *A. desmettiana*, found growing in Sinaloa on the Mexican Pacific coast, looks a little like a stemless *A. attenuata*. Just slightly toothed, it forms a fountain-shaped rosette, with leaves more brittle than soft and flexible, armed with a fairly stiff apical spine. It grows fairly rapidly to as much as 4 feet (1.2 m) across and flowers quickly—within eight or ten years—but cannot withstand much in the way of frost. A good deal larger at 7 or 8 feet (2.1 to 2.4 m) in diameter, with long, narrow, soft and flexible leaves, ***A. weberi*** grows over a large area, from San Luis Potosí as far north as southern Texas, where it may have escaped after being planted as an ornamental. With its nearly unarmed leaves, it resembles a slightly smaller, somewhat less proliferous, more people-friendly version of *A. americana*.

THIN-LEAFED AGAVES

A small number of agaves from subgenus *Littaea* produce rosettes composed of up to hundreds of extremely thin, cylindrical or flattened, elongated, often rigid leaves. Plants within this group look very much alike. The most widely dispersed, ***Agave striata***, from much of northeastern Mexico, covers almost the entire Chihuahuan Desert, the moister regions just east of it, and a few outlying areas to the west. Its rosettes to almost 4 feet (1.2 m) across often form large dense clusters. Extremely similar and

A colony of *Agave stricta* in Oaxaca.

most easily differentiated by its more southern habitat in Oaxaca and adjacent parts of Puebla, *A. stricta* also generally is smaller, with slightly smaller, shorter flowers. Both of these sharp-spined species form beautifully wavy colonies with a deceptively soft, almost pillowlike appearance.

A couple of rare endemics, cliff dwelling and much less proliferous, include *Agave petrophila*, which hangs off vertical canyon walls in dry tropical parts of Oaxaca. Far to the north, tucked away in a massive canyon complex not far from the city of Monterrey, *A. albopilosa* was described in 2007. It is unique in the genus because of the tufted fibers that surround its terminal leaf tips like wedge-shaped paint brushes. Otherwise this plant resembles a straighter-leafed *A. stricta*, though solitary or barely offsetting.

The two better known members of this group do very well outdoors, sharing a reasonable degree of frost hardiness. The other two, currently almost unknown in cultivation, might reasonably be expected to need stringent drainage, with *Agave petrophila* at least very possibly unable to withstand much if any frost.

MISCELLANEOUS AGAVES

A number of other agaves worth mentioning do not readily fit into any of these very informal groups. *Agave*

shawii, which makes massive colonies along the Pacific seashore of northern Baja California, grows procumbently, its elongated stems stretched out along the pebbly ground. Dark green, with variably black or white marginal teeth and a black terminal spine, it is another of the species that would be quite desirable except for its propensity to spread without restraint.

Variously light gray or dark green, medium-sized, broad-leafed and only weakly toothed, *Agave chiapensis* grows amid orchids and bromeliads in the rocky hills of Chiapas, in the far south of Mexico. Its tolerance for cold temperatures, despite its southern habitat, reflects the 8000-foot (2400-m) altitude at which it grows, in an area that experiences at least a little frost almost every winter. Several other agaves, all rarely cultivated, medium-sized to large green or glaucous, continue southward into Central America. A number of them, such as *A. boldinghiana* and *A. vicina*, speciated by isolation, have made homes for themselves on the drier island environments of the West Indies.

Among the interminable introgressing agaves from Baja California, *Agave margaritae* deserves mention because of its combination of small size, deeply crenate margins, and proportionately large eccentrically curved teeth. Restricted to a few islands off the southwestern coast of the peninsula, uncommon white-margined forms

Agave shawii dominates parts of its northern Baja California habitat. Photo by Terry Thompson.

of *A. margaritae* resemble offsetting, smaller versions of the unrelated *A. horrida*.

Agave karwinskii is another of the many species from the Puebla-Oaxaca area. Atypically for the genus, at times it forms an elongated trunk up to 6 or 8 feet (1.8 to 2.4 m) tall, an agave on a stick. It tends to grow in dry areas, often on slopes. From the same general region, *A. kerchovei* may have white leaf margins or a paler, yellow-green mid-stripe on its narrow leaves.

Still often called *Agave angustifolia* in acknowledg-

ment of its even narrower leaves, *A. vivipara* occurs from Sonora all the way to Costa Rica, probably embellished by human efforts. It shows up in deserts, open spots in tropical forests, and everything in between. Often grown as a source of fiber, some of its many varieties have been cultivated and selectively bred for centuries. Plants vary from 2 to 6 feet (60 to 180 cm) across, with leaf color from green to glaucous blue to almost white. **Variety marginata**, yellow- or white-margined and stem forming, is often cultivated.

Very similar but somewhat larger, with heavier leaves, **Agave tequilana** is important economically as the source of tequila, but rarely grown except for commercial purposes. Wild plants matching its description, nonetheless, do occur in Jalisco, the traditional home of tequila production.

SOFT-LEAFED, SPARSE-FLOWERED: MANFREDAS

Most members of the subgenus *Manfreda* stand apart from other agaves not only in their inflorescence but also in their general appearance, choice of environments and, to a degree, their horticultural needs. Growing in the United States as far as the mid-Atlantic states as well as in Mexico, manfredas often develop from a somewhat bulbous base and form small low rosettes of soft, semi-succulent leaves, frequently spineless and in the more popular species, covered with irregular displays of purple to brown dots.

Typical of these, **Agave maculosa** ranges from Texas far into central Mexico, with similar plants growing even farther south. The plants grow in a wide variety of habi-

Agave kerchovei—not all forms have the lighter mid-stripe.

Agave cf. *maculosa*, growing in a high-altitude Oaxacan cloud forest.

Agave cf. *brunnea,* a miniature highly patterned plant from dry parts of eastern Durango state.

tats, from semiarid areas to rainy cloud forests. The more xerophytic-living **A. brunnea**, with marginal teeth and firmer leaves, looks more like a typical agave but remains small, with dwarf forms only 6 or 7 inches (15 to 18 cm) across. Plants may have leaves heavily patterned with random black lines and spots. Many manfredas respond to normal garden cultivation, but hybrids between them and other agaves, which often retain their spots, do well with typical agave treatment.

Almost without exception, agaves are easy to grow. Their only drawback often is their mature size. Since most agaves when small give no indication either of their ultimate dimensions or their offsetting proclivities, it is important to obtain them from reliable, knowledgeable sources, especially if planting them in the ground (and be careful about placing them too close to where people walk!). Any quick-draining succulent soil will work for them. For container plants, water once a week during the warmer months and about every three weeks during winter will suffice.

Several other species besides *Agave americana* can endure hard frosts and will survive outdoors in a surprising variety of places. The tropical growers, from low altitudes in regions such as Oaxaca, along with some of the true desert dwelling species from Sonora, parts of Baja California, and the interior higher altitude deserts of the U.S. Southwest may not tolerate rainy winters outdoors regardless of minimum temperatures. These plants do best in containers except in appropriate climates. That still leaves a very large number of agaves available as essential subjects for any succulent garden featuring plants from the Western Hemisphere.

Chapter 29

Agave Relatives and Terrestrial Bromeliads

AGAVE RELATIVES INCLUDE the closely related *Furcraea* and *Yucca*, the more distantly related members of the *Nolina* group, and from Africa and surrounding lands, *Dracaena* (with just a few succulent species) and *Sansevieria*. Some of these plants are generalized xerophytes, but many of them cross the boundary into true succulence. Only distantly related, a large number of bromeliads have adapted to life in arid surroundings and, particularly in South America, have filled the ecological niches taken up by agaves and their relatives to the north, and aloes in Africa.

FURCRAEA AND *YUCCA* (AGAVACEAE)

The plants of *Furcraea* are closely related to *Agave* and form monocarpic spiny rosettes, though they also often develop trunks as well. Their leaves typically are thinner and softer-textured than agaves, however, and they flower with paniculate inflorescences (usually followed by multitudes of bulbils) on long, drooping branches. In bloom they look like a fountain of stems and blossoms.

Probably the most striking species, ***Furcraea macdougalii***, grows in a small section of seasonally dry country

Twenty-five-foot (7.6-m) tall plants of *Furcraea macdougalii* in Oaxacan scrub.

Yucca aff. *harrimaniae*, possibly intro-gressed with another species, in flower.

Yucca faxoniana, on the way to San José de las Flores, in Tamaulipas state, Mexico.

in Oaxaca. Its wild origins remain mysterious; plants, though not actively cultivated, tend to appear near areas of human habitation. The long, narrow leaves arrange themselves in neat rosettes on thick stems to 20 feet (6 m) that are marked with the geometric patterns of old leaf bases. In flower these enormous plants look as if someone had placed a straggly Christmas tree directly on their tops. Hardy to several degrees of frost, *F. macdougalii* is one of the best plants available for an outdoor succulent garden in suitable climates. Its cultural needs are identical to those of agaves from similar semitropical environments.

Fundamentally distinguished from agaves because of their nonmonocarpic habit, most yuccas are more xerophytic than truly succulent, with fibrous, stringy foliage and stems. Nonetheless, almost anywhere succulent plants occur in North America yuccas grow as well. In cultivation their needs are very similar to agaves.

Yuccas show a great variety in growth habit with the greatest number consisting of good-sized plants with mostly single or slowly clustering, sparsely branched trunks that range from 2 or 3 to about 10 feet (60 to 90 cm to 3 m) tall with rosettes of long, sword-shaped, often fibrous-margined and sharp-tipped leaves. Plants that fit this general description cover a geographic continuum from *Yucca schidigera* in California deserts to the Arizonan *Y. schottii*, the New Mexican *Y. elata*, the Texan *Y.*

torreyi, occasionally found in a dwarf form, and a number of Mexican species.

Other yuccas remain largely stemless or grow short stems very slowly. Some of these cluster freely, others very sparingly or remain solitary. They include *Yucca baccata*, the banana yucca, with edible fruits; *Y. baileyi*; and the Californian *Y. whipplei* (synonym *Hesperoyucca whipplei*). Similar but smaller, usually stemless, and with many, often narrow-leafed rosettes that can become almost hemispherical are *Y. angustissima*; the smaller *Y. harrimaniae* which usually grows to 1 to 2 feet (30 to 60 cm) in diameter; and the even smaller *Y. nana*. These last three all grow in the high deserts of Utah, western Colorado and northern Arizona, and New Mexico.

Several yuccas from much wetter regions also form slowly clumping, stemless or short-stemmed rosettes. The best known, *Yucca aloifolia*, comes from the southeastern United States and resembles other species that grow as far north as New England and south to the Yucatán peninsula and Chiapas in southern Mexico.

Yuccas cross with each other readily in nature, making species identification difficult. The largest plants are among the most distinctive. *Yucca brevifolia*, the Joshua tree, is representative of these very large yuccas, with a single massive trunk that subdivides into numerous spiny limbs radiating out in all directions. Joshua trees grow in

With terete, sharp-tipped leaves, *Yucca queretaroensis* resembles few other species. Photo by Brian Kemble.

A colony of very blue *Yucca rigida* in the Durango hills. Photo by Rob Skillin.

the Mojave Desert of the American Southwest, always at moderately high elevations. They have a relictual distribution, stands of plants suddenly emerging seemingly out of nowhere upon reaching a certain altitude. With sharp, pointed leaves shrunk down to minimize water loss, *Y. brevifolia* can grow to over 30 feet (9 m) in height, and its trunks can reach up to 3 feet (90 cm) in diameter. Quite similar in appearance but considerably larger, **Y. filifera** and **Y. decipiens** dominate parts of the Chihuahuan Desert, while **Y. valida**, from central Baja California shares the same growth habit but is somewhat smaller.

Another very large plant, **Yucca faxoniana** (including plants formerly called *Y. carnerosana*), generally remains single stemmed and unbranched. The more southeastern plants originate from Tamaulipas and Nuevo León, have surprisingly slender trunks reaching well over 30 feet (9 m) in height, and dwarf the Texan forms from the Big Bend area. Smaller, with more slender, sometimes forking trunks, **Y. mixtecana** and **Y. periculosa**, both from Oaxaca state, along with the more northern **Y. jaliscana** and **Y. potosina**, are all endemics, relatively uncommon in the wild and rarely cultivated.

Yuccas that combine medium-sized trunks with rosettes formed of many very narrow leaves, sometimes hemispherical or arranged in latitudinal bands, include

Mexican endemics such as **Yucca queretaroensis**, with long, extremely narrow, almost terete leaves, and the stiff-leafed, very glaucous **Y. rigida** from southeastern Durango. **Yucca rostrata**, which crosses the border into Texas, has flattened rosettes of flat, narrow leaves as well.

Finally, **Yucca endlichiana**, restricted to a few Chihuahuan Desert localities in Coahuila state, produces a series of close growing, few-leafed, stemless rosettes from an enlarged underground caudex. Among the smallest

Yucca endlichiana, plants emerging from an underground caudex. Photo by Brian Kemble.

species it is not common in cultivation despite being one of the few yuccas with truly succulent leaves and one of the best choices for growing in a container.

Seedling yuccas tend to look alike, giving few hints of their mature appearance. They can be very slow growing and those that branch from the base, or from underground rootstocks, may survive for many centuries, sending up long-lived stems and replacing them with new ones as the years go by. Their fruits can be either dry or quite fleshy and sometimes very large. Their attractive white flowers are sometimes striped with green, brown, or pale pink and often share a symbiotic relationship with specific species of night-flying moths. Most of them will tolerate severe cold and many regularly experience temperatures below 0°F (–18°C) in habitat. As is the case with many Mojave Desert species, Joshua trees will not tolerate excess humidity, and generally do not do well if grown or transplanted out of their native environment.

NOLINA, BEAUCARNEA, DASYLIRION, AND CALIBANUS (NOLINACEAE)

Separated out of Agavaceae and placed in Nolinaceae because of significant details of flowering structure, *Nolina* and its relatives have now been reunited with *Agave* within the enlarged Asparagaceae. Nonetheless, it is worth recognizing the nolina tribe's distinctiveness from yuccas, agaves, and the like.

Beaucarneas, sometimes submerged into *Nolina*, are certainly the best known of these plants in cultivation. They develop greatly swollen bases that taper into distinct trunks surmounted with dense rosettes of leaves. The commonly grown ***Beaucarnea recurvata***, or ponytail palm, has ribbony leaves up to 3 feet (90 cm) long that curl downward. Native to warm, seasonally moist southern Mexican hillsides, it sometimes grows under a thin canopy of taller trees, and as a result does not need as much light as the other species. While it can take bright light and even full sun outdoors, it also survives reasonably well indoors. It begins to develop its enlarged base when still small. In the wild or when planted in the ground in suitable areas plants ultimately become huge.

The several other species of *Beaucarnea* have more compact, stiffer foliage and a more xerophytic habit. Both ***B. gracilis*** and the shorter-leafed ***B. stricta*** attain a considerable size with massive bases. Plants may grow in arid situations surrounded by agaves and cacti or on well-drained slopes in cloud forests where they may become hosts to epiphytes: orchids, bromeliads, peperomias, and,

Beaucarnea recurvata growing in limestone under mixed, quite tropical forest cover.

somewhat disconcertingly, mammillarias and even epiphytic agaves. Easy to grow but only moderately frost hardy, beaucarneas thrive outdoors in warm areas such as Southern California, but do not do that well in cold, rainy, or frosty winters.

Nolinas are most easily distinguished from yuccas by the multitudes of much smaller flowers on their gracefully branched inflorescences. Although some are barely succulent and resemble coarse, clumping grasses, many larger Mexican species such as ***Nolina nelsonii*** and ***N. parviflora*** look very much like arborescent yuccas. The gigantic ***N. bigelovii***, with 10- to 12-foot (3- to 3.6-m) wide rosettes of narrow leaves and huge inflorescences that look like fountains of white flowers, can be seen for miles when in bloom on Mojave desert hillsides.

Dasylirions resemble nolinas, with narrow, rigidly straight leaves and very slow growing trunks that may eventually exceed 10 feet (3 m) in height. As with nolinas and beaucarneas they do not die after blooming and send up tall flower spikes at intervals once they mature. The Mexican ***Dasylirion quadrangulatum*** and the very similar ***D. longissimum*** have stiff, pointed terete leaves 5 or 6 feet (1.5 to 1.8 m) long and a quarter inch (6 mm) in

Beaucarnea gracilis, highly xerophytic, 4 feet (1.2 m) thick in dry surroundings. Photo by Brian Kemble.

A very old plant of *Dasylirion quadrangulatum* in the Chihuahuan Desert. Photo by Kurt Zadnik.

Nolina nelsonii, like an arborescent *Yucca*, but with tiny individual flowers. Photo by Brian Kemble.

Looking like stiff grass growing out of a rock, *Calibanus hookeri* keeps a low profile even when fully exposed. Photo by Brian Kemble.

diameter. Other species that also grow in the American Southwest, such as **D. wheeleri** and **D. leiophyllum**, often referred to as *sotols*, have wider, spiny, flattened leaves with swollen bases.

Probably the best suited of all these plants for container culture, **Calibanus hookeri** (named after the monstrous creature in Shakespeare's *Tempest*) consists of a boulderlike caudex with small grassy, nolina-like rosettes growing from it. In their central Mexican home calibanus are reputed to reach over 6 feet (1.8 m) in diameter, and if planted in the ground they grow surprisingly quickly. Unfortunately, large plants, always scarce, have been collected almost out of existence. An extremely rare second species, *C. glassianus*, resembles a short-stemmed beaucarnea, with longer, broader leaves than *C. hookeri*.

In any case, calibanus, along with dasylirions, nolinas, and most furcraeas are perfectly hardy in areas with moderate climates. Beaucarneas are somewhat less so. These plants do best with lots of sun, good drainage such as on a slope or in rocky soil, and not too much water, but many kinds can adapt to a wide range of conditions. In summer they should be watered from time to time, more often for the miniature or less succulent ones and less for the giant species after they are established. In pots they will thrive in a standard succulent soil mix combined with water once a week in the warm months and about every three weeks or so in winter. Along with agaves, furcraeas, and yuccas, these plants, with their striking sculptural shapes, can function as the foundations of a dry garden, although it is important to realize how large they may become in maturity and arrange them accordingly.

DRACAENA AND SANSEVIERIA (DRACAENACEAE)

The family Dracaenaceae was established for a large group of Old World plants separated out from Agavaceae and has since undergone reclassification into Ruscaceae and then to Asparagaceae. Members of the namesake genus *Dracaena* generally live in the understory of tropical rain forests but a small number have adapted to thoroughly arid circumstances and approach a degree of succulence.

These xerophytic dracaenas occupy ecological niches similar to yuccas, although with a much smaller distribution. Best known of them, though the least succulent, *Dracaena draco*, the Canary Island dragon tree, was valued by alchemists because of its dried red sap, thought to be dragon's blood. Plants live a long time and become very large, with thick, deeply furrowed trunks and limbs which branch and rebranch dichotomously. Their flat, lanceolate leaves, fibrous rather than succulent, form dense rosettes. Although they will thrive and grow fairly rapidly in Southern California, and can withstand dry conditions, they are only marginally hardy to frost, particularly in combination with rainy, humid winters. In drier climates they will withstand temperatures to the high twenties (about –2°C), but still will not survive a hard freeze.

With similar dichotomously branched stems and narrower, slightly succulent leaves, *Dracaena serrulata* does not become as large as *D. draco*, but good-sized specimens occur in the mountains of southern Arabia, including Yemen and farther east in Oman. This species and the very similar if not identical *D. ombet* (synonym *D. schizantha*), from mountainous parts of northeast Africa, grow more slowly than *D. draco*, and can take more cold, but are less tolerant of excess moisture.

The most interesting xerophytic dracaena, the Socotran endemic *Dracaena cinnabari*, grows up to 30 feet (9 m) tall (see photo on page 225). A solid mass of stiff, short-leafed rosettes covers the top of the plant, looking like a dome-shaped green shell fitted over the close-packed intricately divided and redivided dichotomous limbs. Plants occur in fairly dense stands or follow each other in lines up ridges. Rarely cultivated, *D. cinnabari* grows extremely slowly and does best in very mild climates.

An all-too-familiar-seeming genus of plants, *Sansevieria* nonetheless includes a large number of unfamiliar, very interesting species. A few sansevierias resemble agaves or yuccas, but others have distinct habits of their own. The old common name for the genus, mother-in-law tongue, suggests that the plants are sharp tongued and impossible to get rid of.

Only two forms of sansevieria, both semisucculent, constitute the vast majority of cultivated plants. One of these, *Sansevieria trifasciata*, has long, narrow, sword-shaped, patterned and mottled leathery leaves. In cultivation for a very long time, various selected forms and cultivars, such as **variety** *laurentii*, with distinct cross-banding and yellow leaf margins, still show up in dish gardens and mixed indoor plantings. Other forms of *S. trifasciata*, however, remain somewhat rare and choice; among these, **'Bantel's Sensation'** often evokes interest, with leaves almost completely white except for occasional linear green streaks. As with many highly variegated plants, it grows slowly enough to stay uncommon.

Odd forms of *Sansevieria trifasciata* and of *S. hahnii* attract collectors. The latter, a rosulate plant of uncertain horticultural origins, resembles a small flat-leafed, spineless agave. **'Golden Hahnii'** is a common form with golden-yellow leaf margins. The much scarcer **'Loop's Pride'** develops small rosettes that are almost black when well grown. Other variants are still rarer, very slow growing, and command high prices.

The dichotomously branched *Dracaena cinnabari*, a natural topiary on the island of Socotra. Photo by Rob Skillin.

Sansevieria forskaalii, reproducing from underground stolons, in Yemen. Photo by Rob Skillin.

Sansevieria deserti in the blazing Namibian sun. Photo by Kurt Zadnik.

The many other species of sansevieria, rarely encountered in the general nursery trade, exhibit a considerable diversity of shape combined with a greater degree of succulent modification. Many species form rosettes, usually offsetting on rhizomes. Of these, some remain quite small, no more than 5 or 6 inches (13 to 15 cm) across. Examples are **Sansevieria subspicata** or the relatively uncommon, confusingly named **S. aethiopica**, from southern Africa. The narrow leaves of these species have soft tips. In contrast, **S. ballyi** and **S. phillipsiae** have small tight rosettes composed of spike shaped, sharp-tipped leaves. In still other species the rosettes reach well over a

foot (30 cm) in diameter. In nature these plants often cluster around the bases of acacia trees in the seasonally arid East African plains.

Another group, typified by **Sansevieria grandis** or **S. forskaalii**, the latter from Arabia and the Horn of Africa, form vase-shaped rosettes, with wide, flattened, elongated leaves. A third growth habit, displayed by species such as **S. stuckyi**, **S. cylindrica**, and **S. deserti**, produces thick, terete leaves that point upright into the air. Other species make dense clumps of broad-leafed rosettes, or rosettes of spoon-shaped leaves on thin stalks, or columns of distichous (two-ranked) leaves, almost like a

Sansevieria suffruticosa, from Kenya. Photo by Susan Carter.

Sansevieria kirkii var. pulchra, a form mixing pink, bronze, and green.

Sansevieria pinguicula, supporting itself on stilt roots whether in cultivation or in the wild. Photo by Terry Thompson.

pillar made of curving cow horns. Distichous-leafed species such as **S. powellii** can grow quite tall, or, as in **S. ehrenbergii**, **S. robusta**, or the densely clustering **S. suffruticosa**, develop individual leaves that become tall and massive, with adult plants looking like crowds of many-fingered outspread hands or open fans.

Somewhat analogous to yuccas, immature sansevierias often bear absolutely no resemblance to their mature forms. For example, juveniles of **Sansevieria fischerii** (synonym *S. singularis*) make rosettes of mottled green leaves, thick, curving, and channeled. The rosettes can become quite large, and the plants appear full grown. Upon reaching actual maturity, however, their subsequent growths consist of just a single leaf, very thick, and to several feet tall, protruding straight out of the ground with no sign of the rosettes from which they began.

Vaguely similar in appearance, though not rosette-

making, **Sansevieria hallii**, introduced as *S.* 'Baseball Bat', is composed of several individual or paired leaves, connected by an underground rhizome and shaped more like a dowel sawed down the middle than a cylinder. Another unusual species, **S. pinguicula**, from Kenya, slowly makes clumps of extremely thick-leafed small rosettes that taper sharply into vicious points. Plants resemble miniature versions of *Agave victoriae-reginae*, but their rosettes often become airborne, held aloft on thickened stilt roots. **Sansevieria kirkii var. pulchra**, with elongated, flattened leaves, has striking patterns of cross-hatching, and, in the best clones, mixes pink and gray with hardly a trace of green visible. Rare and coveted, **S. eilensis**, from Somalia, produces juvenile upright single leaves about the size and shape of a finger scattered along its underground rhizome, very gradually replaced by decumbent pairs of distichous leaves up to about 8 inches (20 cm) long. Another Somali species, known as **S. horwoodii** (possibly a form of *S. forskaalii*), has thick, flattened leaves that in time grow into approximate rosettes.

Suffering from chaotic taxonomy, many sansevierias in cultivation have never been formally described. Some of these are known by numbers assigned them by the United States Agriculture Department, dating from World War II when many plants were collected in hopes of producing usable fiber for ropes and netting. Other have names given them by collectors and growers, sometimes giving way to official botanical names after many years have passed. The popularity of the plants waxes and wanes; when the unusual ones first came into cultivation they caused quite a stir, but many of the best ones grow painfully slowly and will always remain uncommon, while others gradually become larger and larger until they are simply difficult to accommodate. Sansevierias usually reside on the fringes of succulent-growing popularity, although there are a number of people who concentrate on them to the exclusion of almost anything else.

Often close to indestructible, most sansevierias tolerate much lower light than other succulents; they will survive almost any soil mix and endure neglect and abuse without complaint. Under ideal conditions they should receive a little morning sunlight, or bright indirect light, water about once a week and perhaps every three weeks or so in winter. They do fine in a standard succulent mix.

A few are touchier. *Sansevieria pinguicula* will rot if water remains in its rosettes; it also will do better with a slightly leaner soil and somewhat brighter light. *Sansevieria eilensis* can be difficult to keep alive. Skilled growers sometimes raise it in soil heated by underground cables to prevent it from rotting.

BROMELIA, PUYA, DYCKIA, HECHTIA, AND OTHER XEROPHYTIC BROMELIADS (BROMELIACEAE)

Most bromeliads, with their unique method of storing water in living vases made of their own leaves, certainly do not meet the definition of a succulent plant. Particularly in South America, however, certain terrestrial bromeliads, though only very distantly related to agaves, occupy many of the same niches taken by agaves, yuccas, and similar plants in North America. Many of these plants approach the ill-defined boundaries of what is and what is not a succulent.

The bromeliad family (Bromeliaceae) consists of three subfamilies or tribes. The Bromelioideae consists of mostly epiphytic plants with berrylike fruit and spiny leaves such as *Aechmea* and *Neoregelia*. The Tillandsioideae, also mostly epiphytic, with spineless leaves and tiny wind-distributed seeds, includes the silvery tillandsias and the vaselike vrieseas. Finally, the Pitcairnioideae, comprises generally terrestrial plants with tubular flowers and dry fruits.

Even though most members of the first two tribes are epiphytes in humid tropical forests, several of their genera have made themselves at home on the ground. Among the Bromelioideae, *Bromelia* and *Ananas* (pineapple) are terrestrial, medium or large rosettes with sharp spines along the edges of their leaves. Bromelias often serve as living fences, fierce enough to keep out hungry wandering cattle. More succulent, the few species of *Ochagavia* form clusters of medium-sized, spiny leafed rosettes,

Ochagavia cf. *carnea* in bloom.

with short, globular inflorescences and dense heads of brightly colored flowers.

The great majority of plants from the Tillandsioideae live in rain and cloud forests, but a few interesting *Tillandsia* species have adapted to life in one of the driest places on Earth, the coastal deserts of Peru, where some places literally never receive rain. Tillandsias absorb moisture through their leaf surfaces, which are covered with tiny cells that look almost like open jugs. Species such as *T. purpurea* manage to thrive on coastal sand dunes, absorbing water from the fog in places where not even cactus can survive. These plants are true xerophytes, but they have evolved a way of survival in dry climates entirely different from those used by plants we think of as succulents.

Many species from the Pitcairnioideae have adapted more thoroughly to the succulent lifestyle. *Pitcairnia* generally grows under moist conditions, but several of the other genera range throughout the American deserts from South Texas all the way down to Chile, often cohabiting with agaves and sharing their predilection for precipitous slopes.

Hechtia occurs in both extremely dry and semiarid habitats. Atypically for bromeliads, plants are either exclusively male or female. Most form viciously spiny rosettes of narrow, sometimes curving, hard leaves, definitely succulent and often covered with minute whitish or silvery scales. Their flowers, usually white and unimpressive, also come in brighter colors, red or purple, in some species.

Sometimes called the false agave, ***Hechtia scariosa*** (synonym ***H. texensis***) crosses the Rio Grande into the Big Bend Region of Texas where it grows on limestone. Its narrow, heavily spined leaves turn red in the bright

Relatively unarmed, this *Hechtia* species was growing alongside orchids, tillandsias, and semiepiphytic echeverias in a moist Oaxacan forest.

Hechtia rosea, a messier species, with unusually bright flowers for the genus.

More heavily armed and adapted for dry life, *Hechtia marnier-lapostollei* is clad in silvery scurf.

Dyckia aff. *leptostachya*, large colonies hanging off an Argentinean cliff. Photo by Inge Hoffman.

sun of its habitat. **Hechtia glomerata**, widely distributed throughout Mexico, forms a 2- or 3-foot (60- to 90-cm) wide rosette composed of many long, narrow spiny leaves, either vaguely silver-gray or tinged red. **Hechtia argentea**, and particularly the localized **H. marnier-lapostollei**, combine very fierce spines with fairly small size and bright silver coloring.

At least a few other, unidentified Mexican hechtias also shine in the sunlight with silver, yellow, or red leaves. With red flowers, **Hechtia rosea** may have foliage tinged red and yellow as well, in common with other, smaller, less fiercely spined Oaxacan species. In contrast, **H. caerulea**, from extremely arid hillsides in northern Mexico, has flat, thick, channeled, pale green leaves with barely visible spines, and puts out a spray of dozens of tiny pale purple flowers that nod in the faintest breeze. The white-

flowered **H. tillandsioides** looks quite similar; both plants resemble *Agave bracteosa*, another plant unlike the others in its genus.

Dyckia, centered in Brazil but extending into neighboring countries and as far west as Chile, more-or-less resembles *Hechtia*, but its flowers generally are brightly colored, yellow, orange, or red. Some dyckias grow along stone outcroppings in areas of seasonally dry tropical forest, while others live in genuinely arid places. The usually many-leafed rosettes range from less than 6 inches (15 cm) to a couple of feet (60 cm) across, and most species ultimately form dense clumps. **Dyckia rariflora**, small and with relatively few spines, grows low to the ground. **Dyckia leptostachya**, larger and with fewer leaves, looks more like a hechtia. **Dyckia fosteriana**, with small silvery almost metallic-looking rosettes made of many narrow,

Dyckia fosteriana, atypical in the genus because of the number and narrowness of its leaves and the intensity of its silver coloring.

A *Deuterocohnia* species (*Abromeitiella* type) threatening to swallow up *Parodia tilcarensis* in Argentina. Photo by Inge Hoffman.

The gigantic *Puya raimondii*, rosettes 10 feet (3 m) across, high in the Peruvian Andes. Photo by Inge Hoffman.

spiny, spiraling leaves, and **D. marnier-lapostollei** (not to be confused with the hechtia of that name) with thick, bright silver leaves of a soft, almost velvety texture, fringed with relatively innocuous spines, probably are the most desirable species. **Dyckia odorata**, almost unknown in cultivation and possibly now extinct in the wild, makes dense-leafed rosettes only 5 or 6 inches (13 to 15 cm) across, decorated with small but effective spines.

Encholirium and *Deuterocohnia* consist mostly of good-sized, fiercely spined, rarely grown plants, except for the miniature species of *Deuterocohnia* previously included in the now-sunken genus *Abromeitiella*. From Argentina and Bolivia, these tiny plants grow into deceptively cushionlike mounds composed of thousands of few-leafed rosettes that range from a couple of inches (centimeters) in diameter to less than a half inch (13 mm). Armed with

dagger-sharp, stiff little leaves, some forms are so small they resemble mounds of moss; their flowers are green and tubular. The dense, almost sculptural mounds formed by these plants fill the crevices in which they grow or, fully exposed, mimic smallish, green boulders.

The most famous terrestrial bromeliads are a few members of the large mostly Andean genus *Puya*. These plants, though lacking succulent leaves, grow in some of the harshest conditions on the planet, sometimes in high-altitude deserts with an average day to night temperature range of 100°F (38°C), sometimes in high-altitude swamps that freeze every night of the year, sometimes in the coastal, almost rainless deserts of Chile.

Puyas range from fairly small, such as the Peruvian **Puya laxa**, found near the ruins of Machu Picchu, to enormous species such as **P. raimondii**, with a 10-foot (3-m) wide rosette and a 35-foot (11-m) tall flower spike. Other species form trunks that branch and resemble Joshua trees.

Many puyas have extraordinary inflorescences; among these **Puya alpestris** produces 30-inch (76-cm), nastily

Puya alpestris, aggressive, with nasty spines, but the flowers may be worth it.

spined rosettes and a 3-foot (90-cm) tall, densely blossomed flower spike. Its tubular flowers are silky textured and unearthly turquoise blue, with an upright stalk of bright orange anthers topped with chartreuse-green stigmas. The flowers are filled with deep purple nectar that both smells and tastes just like the artificial butter used on cineplex popcorn. Very similar, but with larger rosettes and metallic green rather than turquoise blossoms, **P. berteroniana** is much rarer than *P. alpestris* in cultivation and is regarded as even more spectacular when in flower.

Terrestrial bromeliads grow readily, thriving in full sun and any fast-draining soil mix. Though drought tolerant, they can withstand both winter rain and a considerable amount of frost and will almost all survive outdoors. In pots they should be watered about every week in the warm months and in winter from once every two weeks to about half that often depending on where they originate. The smaller ones make very striking container plants in a sunny window or outdoors. Some puyas, however, can be very aggressive and if growing them in the ground one should make sure they have plenty of room to spread. Transplanting or dividing clumps of these plants cannot be considered fun. Still, they make distinctive, attractive and hardy candidates for outdoor growing.

Chapter 30

Succulent Odds and Ends

IN ADDITION TO the major succulent plant families and those less well known ones that include some of the most desired plants for enthusiasts, a number of comparatively unfamiliar succulents belong to a surprising variety of other families. For the most part not frequently grown, these often-overlooked succulent leftovers come from genera not usually thought of as succulent at all.

PEPEROMIA (PIPERACEAE)

The pepper family, Piperaceae, consists largely of tropical vining plants, some commercially important, others horticulturally interesting because of their colorful foliage. The family also includes nonvining genera, among them commonly grown houseplants.

Peperomia is a large well-known genus of small tropical plants, either forming multistemmed upright small shrubs or growing as spreading creepers with minute but brightly patterned leaves. Species from tropical rain forests generally require high humidity. Many peperomias, however, produce thickened, slightly succulent leaves and stems that help them live on the bare trunks of trees in tropical forests. Despite the high overall rainfall, these epiphytic plants must be able to withstand temporary dryness to survive.

A number of peperomias have crossed the blurry divide between "typical" and succulent plants, with more extensive physical modifications than slightly thickened leaves alone. These modifications towards succulence have enabled them to thrive in fairly harsh environments, or perhaps more accurately, stressful microclimates in the middle of what still tend to be quite well-watered, tropical habitats. The greatest diversity among succulent peperomias occurs in Andean countries such as Peru. There many of the most succulent species have abandoned trees for sheer cliffs and the life of a lithophyte (a plant that characteristically grows on rocks). In response, their

leaves have thickened and often have become proportionately reduced in size as well, limiting surface area while maximizing internal (and water-holding) volume. Several of these have developed the special trick of turning their leaves in part into translucent windows. One of these is *Peperomia dolabriformis*, probably the best-known peperomia in cultivation.

Peperomia dolabriformis is a small to medium-sized shrub, with somewhat thickened green stems and succulent yellow-green leaves, shaped something like a scimitar blade turned upside down. Its "window" runs along the upper part of the curve and allows light to filter inside the leaf, providing more room for photosynthesis to be carried out. In contrast to typical window-leafed succulents, which keep mostly below ground in their harsh, sun-beaten, arid environments, the leaves and entire plant of these tropical forest-dwelling peperomias remain exposed.

Peperomia asperula resembles *P. dolabriformis*, with slightly less succulent leaves, but similar placement of windows. *Peperomia nivalis*, somewhat smaller, has more rounded, more succulent foliage, with wider windows running down the middle of its leaf-tops. *Peperomia graveolens* has earned a degree of popularity because of its

Peperomia graveolens, with a growth habit reminiscent of a *Crassula*.

bright red stems and bicolored, falcate (sickle-shaped) leaves, also vividly red except for a longitudinal channel on top, covered with a green-gray translucent window.

These peperomias grow as miniature bushes, with their leaves distributed either regularly or more sporadically along the erect or arching stems. The leaf form and arrangement of the most interesting succulent peperomias deviates from this model; these species face the world with stems either largely or entirely concealed by thick, imbricate foliage.

Peperomia congesta, which was also described as *P. rauhii* before it was realized that the plant actually had been discovered and named long before, is large for a peperomia. Its few, unbranched inch (2.5 cm) thick stems can reach 2 feet (60 m) in height. The leaves resemble a dark green lemon bisected along its length, oval when viewed from above, very succulent and somewhat translucent, functioning as a window. Like many succulent peperomias, *P. congesta* congregates at moderately high elevations, around 6000 feet (1800 m) and up, where it shares its precipitous home with multitudes of soft-leafed bromeliads and other lithophytes.

The most striking succulent species, **Peperomia columella**, grows at considerably lower altitudes. It is a tiny plant, with thin stems to about 6 inches (15 cm) tall, covered with thick leaves which overlap and completely obscure the stem. The bright green leaves cling to the stems like shingles on a roof or the scales of a fish and rarely exceed a quarter inch (6 mm) in length, width, or thickness. They inflate the sliced lemon shape of *P. congesta* into something more like a bisected sphere. Their translucent outer surfaces face upward at the tips of the branches then reorient themselves outward farther down the stem.

Additional succulent peperomia species, some fairly recently described, occasionally appear in cultivation. Since they are very much plants with only niche appeal, they may remain uncommon for a long time.

Most succulent peperomias are fairly easy to grow. They need fast drainage, a soil fairly rich in organic matter, and more water than most succulents. Watering them like a typical houseplant, however, will prove fatal, with the more succulent ones most susceptible to overwatering. *Peperomia columella* can be quite touchy. It needs a little more warmth than the other species, a minimum of at least 55°F (13°C). Although it does not like to dry out completely, it rots fairly easily if too wet. When grown in less than ideal conditions, its lower leaves drop off, diminishing the densely shingled, imbricate leaf arrangement that is its best feature. The unique appearance of *P. columella* when grown well, however, has ensured its presence in many collections.

Peperomia congesta, a tall shingle-leafed bush, preparing to flower from its two main stems.

Peperomia columella, sheathed in fat, windowed little leaves.

BEGONIA (BEGONIACEAE)

Begonias may seem even less likely candidates for inclusion among succulent plants than peperomias, but a few

South American and African species approach the physical modifications that enable a plant to be called a succulent. One, **Begonia peltata** (synonym *B. incana*) from Peru, could reasonably be described as a leaf succulent. When grown with bright light, very fast draining soil, and relatively limited water, its leaves become quite thick, asymmetrically elliptical and covered with a dense, almost furry grayish white covering.

Brazil is also home to several species of somewhat succulent begonias. One of these, **Begonia venosa**, resembles *B. peltata*, with similarly whitish, scurfy, but somewhat less succulent leaves, and slightly more succulent stems.

Other rarely grown Brazilian species include plants with more significantly thickened stems and multilobed nonsucculent leaves. **Begonia dregei**, from eastern South Africa, forms an underground caudex from which it sends out elongated stems, also with multilobed, sharp-angled leaves. With its caudex raised above the soil line, it makes a surprisingly effective looking small caudiciform.

OXALIS (OXALIDACEAE)

Members of the oxalis family, Oxalidaceae, occur over much of the world in habitats ranging from moist woodlands to stony deserts where rain may not fall for several years. More than two hundred species come from southern Africa. Oxalis grow from underground corms.

The South African species rarely attract the interest of succulent growers. One that might, **Oxalis bullulata** (synonym *O. beneprotecta*), grows on the edge of Namaqualand quartz fields along with lithops, or in Richtersveld quartzite hills and ridges with a host of other succulents. This tiny ground-hugging succulent has leaves in a half-inch (13-mm) rosette and a usually solitary flower larger than the rest of the plant. In cultivation *O. bullulata* presumably would respond to careful water when in leaf, followed by near total dryness when dormant.

Across the ocean, **Oxalis rubra**, widely cultivated as an ornamental, produces a proportionately large amorphously shaped underground tuber. If raised above soil

Oxalis aff. *bullulata,* in bud and in flower, at the edge of a Namaqualand quartz field.

An unidentified succulent-stemmed Brazilian *Begonia.*

Oxalis aff. *rubra,* very effectively treated as a caudiciform. Photo by Terry Thompson.

level, *O. rubra* undergoes a transformation into a very unusual small caudiciform. It grows in southern Brazil through Argentina.

Across the Andes, particularly in Chile, several more typically succulent oxalis have found homes. **Oxalis carnosa** quickly forms a forked underground tuber with a perennial succulent stem topped with a rosette of succulent trilobed leaves. If it did not scatter its seed all too readily it would be appreciated more; unfortunately it deserves its reputation as a quick-spreading succulent weed. **Oxalis herrerae**, with a taller, pencil-thick stem and succulent leaves on long petioles, behaves better.

Oxalis gigantea, also Chilean, develops into a multistemmed arching plant several feet tall, shaped like a small ocotillo. Its brittle brown stems, completely leafless when dormant, produce leaves all along their length when growing, along with yellow flowers. In cultivation *O. gigantea* may lapse into dormancy at irregular intervals, during which it should receive water only very occasionally. In general it and the other succulent oxalis grow easily, sometimes too easily.

CALLISIA AND TRADESCANTIA (COMMELINACEAE)

Most members of the Commelinaceae, known as the dayflower or spiderwort family, grow as small creeping or vining plants, some adapted to temperate conditions but most to life in the tropics. Among the tropical species, some have adapted an epiphytic habit and look almost identical to bromeliads, with leaves that form a water-holding vase. Others have somewhat thickened leaves and approach a succulent appearance. One of these is **Callisia macdougallii**, a diminutive vining plant with thick, wedge-shaped, white-striped leaves, which produces small but extremely fragrant white flowers. It occurs in southern Mexico.

Another commelinid, the wider ranging **Tradescantia navicularis**, manages to thrive in the northeastern Mexican Chihuahuan Desert, where it seeks out slightly shaded places often within reach of truly arid growing cacti, such as *Thelocactus* and *Turbinicarpus*. *Tradescantia navicularis* can become a somewhat rampant, not notice-

Oxalis gigantea in Chile, displaying typical oxalis flowers and leaves scattered along tall succulent stems. Photo by Inge Hoffman.

Tradescantia navicularis growing in the shade on a gypsum cliff in northeastern Mexico.

ably succulent grower if given too lush conditions, but in habitat its short, alternate leaves, shaped something like a deep channeled rowboat, are quite succulent and the plants themselves are dwarfed and compressed.

Other Mexican commelinids resemble the East African *Cyanotis somaliensis*, a species with elongated, slightly succulent, hairy leaves distributed along succulent stems. All these do well with moderately bright light, standard soil and slightly more frequent than average watering.

PLECTRANTHUS (LAMIACEAE)

Though it might seem unlikely for the mint family, Lamiaceae (formerly Labiatae), to have any succulent representatives, a number of *Plectranthus* species ranging from South Africa to southwestern Arabia and Madagascar have distinctly succulent leaves and show up from time to time in comprehensive collections. Small somewhat creeping plants, many of these not very well known species resemble kalanchoes. A few, such as the South African **P. ernstii** and **P. dolomiticus** form decumbent or erect-growing bushes, superficially similar to a small *Crassula ovata*. Their fuzzy, moderately succulent leaves and in some cases thickened stems grant them admission into the world of succulents. They respond satisfactorily if cultivated in the manner of kalanchoes.

SINNINGIA (GESNERIACEAE)

In the gesneriad family, Gesneriaceae, the South American genus *Sinningia* includes a few epiphytic species that produce good-sized tubers with annual rosettes. **Sinningia cardinalis**, with fuzzy green foliage, is one of these, as is **S. leucotricha**, with leaves covered in silky white hairs. Both species bloom with spectacular heads of large bright red, tubular hummingbird flowers. They need warmth, quick-draining soil, and somewhat more than average water both when in flower and when dormant.

ZAMIOCULCAS AND PHILODENDRON (ARACEAE)

Rather surprisingly, a few stray aroids, members of the family Araceae, could reasonably be called succulents, although in most cases with certain qualifications. A number of aroids are geophytes from seasonally dry regions. **Dracontium**, with deeply pinnate leaves, and the rarely grown Bolivian **Synandrospadix vermitoxicus**, with thick, undivided foliage, disappear into their under-

A succulent *Plectranthus* species from southern Madagascar. Photo by Inge Hoffman.

A hybrid of *Sinningia leucotricha,* very similar to its parent.

ground tubers when dormant and emerge above ground with the spring rains. Cultivating them in the manner of succulent bulbs will prove successful.

A unique aroid, the East African **Zamioculcas zamiifolia**, consists of a series of thickly swollen succulent stems bearing opposing leaves that grow out of a central root stalk. In the wild, it receives a good deal of rainfall during the wet season, but has to withstand dry winters, during which time it often drops many of its leaves. In cultivation, if grown in fast-draining soil and watered generously year-round, it will grow taller, lusher and more quickly, though it will lose its natural character. It can survive a lot of neglect, and in the last few years has become widely grown as the result of mass production by tissue culture. Since it does not look much like a typical aroid, or anything else for that matter, it has apparently been sold as a palm, a cycad, even an orchid. To those unfamiliar with it, it may look more like a plastic plant

Zamioculcas zamiifolia, treated as a typical succulent.

greenhouse, *Philodendron martianum* responds well to high humidity and weekly watering year-round. It would be an appropriate companion for a collection of the other odd succulent epiphytes that exist in somewhat similar ecological niches here and there in the world.

OECEOCLADES AND EULOPHIA (ORCHIDACEAE)

Another family likely to be overlooked by succulent growers, Orchidaceae, the orchids, includes a few plants legitimately classifiable as succulents. Among the thousands of tropical epiphytic and lithophytic orchid species, quite a few have developed thick water-storing leaves and pseudobulbs (modified stems). Some of these, such as the Brazilian terete-leafed miniature plants of *Leptotes*, can endure considerable drought, and along with some Brazilian dwarf lithophytic laelias, have undergone mod-

Oeceoclades roseovariegata, with the pink and charcoal colors of various unrelated Madagascan succulent plants.

than anything else, but it actually is a pretty interesting species, the only member of its genus.

A couple of purely epiphytic *Philodendron* species have had to develop a degree of succulence to survive in their bright, often windy treetop environments. The most interesting of these is **Philodendron martianum** (synonym *P. cannifolium*), from northeastern South America, where it lives exposed to the sun, high in the tallest trees and probably receives a minimum of 100 inches (2500 mm) of rain a year. It has developed strikingly succulent petioles (the stalked bases of its leaves). These become large and very thick, larger than the leaves themselves; the plants look something like a cattleya orchid with its large pseudobulbs and single leaf.

If cultivated under typical lush, moist tropical conditions, the leaves of this philodendron will grow larger and lose their red tinge, though the swollen petioles remain. If given very bright light and a rapid-draining soil, such as an orchid mix, the plants will gradually return to their natural appearance. Hardly a plant for a desert

An *Oeceoclades* species, leaves exposed to the light in a Madagascan grassland. Photo by Brian Kemble.

ifications that bring them quite close to a kind of succulent morphology.

Several Old World terrestrial orchids, however, have taken this process even further, and the primarily Madagascan genus *Oeceoclades*, with rounded or pear-shaped pseudobulbs and leathery, usually pink and gray mottled leaves, has entered the world of succulent trade. Interesting oddities, one of them, **O. spathulifera**, blooms with reasonably large attractive flowers as a bonus. **Oeceoclades roseovariegata**, with fiber-covered bulbs and flat, cardboard-textured leaves is probably the most unusual looking of the genus. A related species, **Eulophia petersii**, from northeastern Africa, grows terrestrially in arid areas, often among the aloes which it vaguely resembles. It develops fairly good-sized, upright pseudobulbs and heavy, succulent, sword-shaped leaves. These orchids will do well in a slightly richer-than-average succulent mix, such as one suitable for echeverias, and will respond to similar treatment: very bright light, water about once a week in summer and every two or three weeks in winter.

Orchids and philodendrons may seem very far removed from plants such as lithops and crassulas, but I hope I have shown that the definition of succulence in plants is both expansive and flexible. The development of succulence in all its forms has allowed widely divergent plants to prosper in some of the least hospitable places on Earth. Perhaps we might learn something from the succulent survival strategy of carefully conserving limited resources. In any case gaining an appreciation of the strange beauty developed in response to the stringent demands of environmental necessity is something we all can carry with us and apply to a variety of experiences.

Further Reading

Bally, Peter R. O. 1961. *The Genus Monadenium*. Berne, Switzerland: Benteli Publishers.

Bayer, Bruce. 1999. *Haworthia Revisited*. Hatfield, South Africa: Umdaus Press.

Bruyns, Peter V. 2005. *Stapeliads of Southern Africa and Madagascar*, 2 vols. Hatfield, South Africa: Umdaus Press.

Carter, Susan, John J. Lavranos, Leonard E. Newton, and Colin C. Walker. 2011. *Aloes: The Definitive Guide*. Kew, United Kingdom: Royal Botanic Gardens.

Court, Doreen. 2000. *Succulent Flora of Southern Africa*. Rev. ed. Rotterdam, Netherlands: A. A. Balkema.

Craib, Charles. 1995. *The Sarcocaulons of Southern Africa*. Hystrix Natural History and Cultivation Series. Gauteng, South Africa: South African Pelargonium and Geranium Society.

de Wilde, W. J. J. O. 1971. *A Monograph of the Genus Adenia Forsk. (Passifloraceae)*. Wageningen, Netherlands: H. Veenman.

Eggli, Urs, ed. 2001–2003. *Illustrated Handbook of Succulent Plants*, 6 vols. Berlin: Springer.

Gentry, Howard Scott. 1982, 1988. *Agaves of Continental North America*. Tucson, Arizona: University of Arizona Press.

Hammer, Steven. 2010. *Lithops: Treasures of the Veld*. 2d ed. British Cactus and Succulent Society.

Hammer, Steven. 1993. *The Genus Conophytum*. Pretoria, South Africa: Succulent Plant Publications.

Hammer, Steven. 2002. *Dumpling and His Wife: New Views of the Genus Conophytum*. Norwich, United Kingdom: E.A.E. Creative Colour.

Irish, Mary, and Gary Irish. 2000. *Agaves, Yuccas, and Related Plants*. Portland, Oregon: Timber Press.

Pilbeam, John. 2010. *Stapeliads*. Hornchurch, United Kingdom: British Cactus and Succulent Society.

Pilbeam, John. 2008. *The Genus Echeveria*. Hornchurch, United Kingdom: British Cactus and Succulent Society.

Pilbeam, John, Chris Rodgerson, and Derek Tribble. 1998. *Adromischus*. The Cactus File Handbook 3. Southampton, United Kingdom: Cirio Publishing.

Rauh, Werner. 1995, 1998. *Succulent and Xerophytic Plants of Madagascar*, 2 vols. Mill Valley, California: Strawberry Press.

Reynolds, Gilbert W. 1966. *The Aloes of Tropical Africa and Madagascar*. Mbabane, Swaziland: Trustees of the Aloe Book Fund.

Rowley, Gordon. 2003. *Crassula: A Grower's Guide*. Venegono, Italy: Cactus & Company International Society.

Rowley, Gordon. 1999. *Pachypodium and Adenium*. The Cactus File Handbook 5. Southhampton, United Kingdom: Cirio Publishing.

Rowley, Gordon. 1995. *Anacampseros, Avonia, Grahamia: A Grower's Guide*. British Cactus and Succulent Society.

Rowley, Gordon. 1994. *Succulent Compositae: A Grower's Guide to the Succulent Species of Senecio and Othonna*. Mill Valley, California: Strawberry Press.

Rowley, Gordon. 1993. *Caudiciform and Pachycaul Succulents*. Mill Valley, California: Strawberry Press.

Rowley, Gordon. 1992. *Didiereaceae: Cacti of the Old World*. British Cactus and Succulent Society.

Schulz, Rudolf. 2007. *Aeonium in Habitat and Cultivation*. San Bruno, California: Schulz Publishing.

Schwartz, Herman, Ron LaFon, and Daryl Koutnik, eds. 1983–1996. *The Euphorbia Journal*, vols. 1–10. Mill Valley, California: Strawberry Press.

Smith, Gideon, et al. 1998. *Mesembs of the World*. Pretoria, South Africa: Briza Publications.

Smith, Lyman. 1974. *Pitcairniodeae*. Flora Neotropica Monograph 14, part 1. New York: New York Botanical Garden.

Steyn, Marthinus. 2003. *Southern Africa Commiphora*. Polokwane, South Africa: M. Steyn.

Van der Walt, J. J. A., and P. J. Vorster. 1981, 1988. *Pelargoniums of South Africa*, 3 vols. Purnell & Sons (vol. 1), Juta (vol. 2), National Botanic Gardens, Kirstenbosch (vol. 3), Cape Town, South Africa.

van Jaarsveld, Ernst, and Daryl Koutnik. 2004. *Cotyledon and Tylecodon*. Hatfield, South Africa: Umdaus Press.

van Jaarsveld, Ernst J. 1994. *Gasterias of South Africa*. Capetown, South Africa: Fernwood Press.

van Jaarsveld, Ernst J., and U. de Villiers Pienaar. 2000. *Vygies: Gems of the Veld*. Venegono, Italy: Cactus & Company International Society.

Van Wyck, Ben-Erik, and Gideon Smith. 2004. *Guide to the Aloes of South Africa*. Pretoria, South Africa: Briza Publications.

White, Alain, R. Allen Dyer, and Boyd L. Sloane. 1941. *The Succulent Euphorbieae (Southern Africa)*, 2 vols. Pasadena, California: Abbey Garden Press.

Williamson, Graham. 2000. *Richtersveld: The Enchanted Wilderness*. Hatfield, South Africa: Umdaus Press.

Index of Plant Names

Agave gentryi, 298
Agave guadalajarana, 299
Agave guiengola, 300
Agave gypsophila, 300
Agave havardiana, 298, 299
Agave horrida, 303, 307
Agave isthmensis, 300
Agave karwinskii, 307
Agave kerchovei, 307
Agave lecheguilla, 297
Agave lophantha, 297
Agave macroacantha, 300, 301
Agave maculosa, 307
Agave margaritae, 306, 307
Agave marmorata, 301
Agave mitis, 305
    var. albicans, 305
Agave montana, 36, 298
Agave nizandensis, 304
Agave obscura, 298, 299, 303
Agave parrasana, 299
Agave parryi, 299
    var. couesii, 299
    var. huachucensis, 299
    var. neomexicana, 299
    var. parryi, 299
    var. truncata, 299
Agave parviflora, 35, 304
Agave peacockii, 302
Agave pedunculifera, 305
Agave pelona, 303
Agave petrophila, 306
Agave polianthiflora, 304
Agave polyacantha. See A. obscura
Agave potatorum, 299, 300, 301
Agave salmiana, 297
    var. ferox, 87, 297
Agave scabra. See A. asperrima
Agave schottii, 304
Agave sebastiana, 301
Agave shawii, 306, 307
Agave sobria, 302
Agave striata, 305
Agave stricta, 306
Agave subsimplex, 301
Agave tequilana, 307
Agave titanota, 302, 303
Agave toumeyana, 304
Agave triangularis, 302
Agave utahensis, 303, 304
    forma eborispina, 303
    subsp. kaibabensis, 303
    subsp. nevadensis, 303
    subsp. utahensis, 303
Agave verschaffeltii. See A. isthmensis
Agave vicina, 306
Agave victoriae-reginae, 302, 316

Agave vilmoriniana, 305
Agave vivipara, 307
    var. marginata, 307
Agave weberi, 305
Agave xylonacantha, 302
Agave zebra, 301, 303
Aichryson, 77
Aichryson tortuosum, 77
Aizoaceae (family), 15, 23, 136
Albuca, 291
Albuca spiralis, 291
Alluaudia, 247
Alluaudia ascendens, 248
Alluaudia comosa, 248, 249, 253
Alluaudia dumosa, 248
Alluaudia humbertii, 248, 249
Alluaudia montagnacii, 248
Alluaudia procera, 247, 248, 249
Alluaudiopsis, 248
Alluaudiopsis marnieriana, 248
Aloaceae (family), 254
Aloe, 23, 39, 161, 218, 254, 269, 270,
    282, 287, 289, 296, 309, 327
Aloe aculeata, 263, 264
Aloe acutissima, 71
Aloe affinis, 259
Aloe albiflora, 268, 269
Aloe alooides, 255
Aloe angelica, 255
Aloe arborescens, 258, 266
Aloe arenicola, 260, 261
Aloe aristata, 267
Aloe asperifolia, 262, 263
Aloe audhalica, 266
Aloe bainesii. See A. barberae
Aloe bakeri, 269
Aloe barberae, 256
Aloe bellatula, 269
Aloe bowiea, 268
Aloe branddraaiensis, 259
Aloe broomii, 263, 264
Aloe buettneri, 289
Aloe calcairophila, 269
Aloe cameronii, 258
Aloe capitata, 266
Aloe castanea, 258, 259
Aloe chabaudii, 266
Aloe chortolirioides, 268
Aloe ciliaris, 259
Aloe claviflora, 262, 263
Aloe comosa, 255
Aloe compressa, 266
Aloe comptonii, 260, 261
Aloe concinna. See A. zanzibarica
Aloe conifera, 266
Aloe cryptopoda, 266

Aloe davyana. See A. greatheadii var.
    davyana
Aloe deltoideodonta, 264, 265
Aloe descoingsii, 269
Aloe dewinteri, 14, 263
Aloe dhufarensis, 266
Aloe dichotoma, 256, 257, 258
Aloe dinteri, 268
Aloe divaricata, 256
Aloe dorotheae, 266
Aloe dumetorum, 269
Aloe ecklonis, 267, 268
Aloe eminens, 256
Aloe erinacea, 262
Aloe excelsa, 255
Aloe falcata, 263
aloe family. See Aloaceae
Aloe ferox, 254, 255, 256
Aloe fleurentinorum, 266
Aloe framesii, 262
Aloe gariepensis, 262
Aloe glauca, 262
Aloe globuligemma, 266
Aloe grandidentata, 259
Aloe greatheadii, 259
    var. davyana, 259
Aloe greenii, 259
Aloe haemanthifolia, 261
Aloe harlana, 266
Aloe haworthiodes, 269
Aloe helenae, 256
Aloe hemmingii. See A. somaliensis
Aloe hereroensis, 260
Aloe humilis, 267
Aloe imalotensis, 265
Aloe jacksonii, 269
Aloe jucunda, 269
Aloe krapohliana, 47, 261
    var. dumoulinii, 261
Aloe laeta, 265
Aloe lineata, 255
Aloe littoralis, 255
Aloe longistyla, 267
Aloe maculata, 259
Aloe marlothii, 254
Aloe melanacantha, 261, 262
Aloe meyeri, 263
Aloe microstigma, 259, 260
Aloe mitriformis, 260, 261
Aloe mudenensis, 259
Aloe mutabilis, 258
Aloe ortholopha, 266
Aloe pachygaster, 263
Aloe parvula, 268, 269
Aloe pearsonii, 259, 260, 269
Aloe peglerae, 263
Aloe petricola, 263

Bowiea, 289, 290
Bowiea gariepensis, 290
Bowiea volubilis, 290, 291
Brachystelma, 196, 201, 202
Brachystelma barberae, 201
Brachystelma foetidum, 201
Bromelia, 317
Bromeliaceae (family), 317
bromeliad family. See Bromeliaceae
Bromelioideae (tribe), 317
Brownanthus, 165
Brownanthus pubescens, 165, 166
Brunsvigia, 289, 294
Brunsvigia bosmaniae, 293
Brunsvigia josephinae, 294
Brunsvigia marginata, 293
Brunsvigia radulosa, 294
bryophyllum-type kalanchoes, 66, 67, 68
Bulbine, 289
Bulbine fallax, 290
Bulbine latifolia, 18, 289
Bulbine mesembryanthemoides, 289, 290
  subsp. *namaquensis*, 290
Bulbine rhopalophylla, 290
Bursera, 11, 19, 21, 239, 240, 241, 242, 243, 246
Bursera bolivarii, 240
Bursera diversifolia, 240
Bursera fagaroides, 240
bursera family. See Burseraceae
Bursera galeottiana, 239
Bursera hindsiana, 240, 242
Bursera microphylla, 240, 241, 242, 243
Bursera morelensis, 240
Bursera multifolia, 240
Bursera schlechtendalii, 239
Bursera simaruba, 239
Bursera simplicifolia, 240
Burseraceae (family), 239, 242

cabbage trees. See *Cussonia*
Cactaceae (family), 15, 248
cactus family. See Cactaceae
Calandrinia. See *Cistanthe*
Calibanus, 314
Calibanus glassianus, 314
Calibanus hookeri, 313, 314
Callisia, 329
Callisia macdougallii, 329
Calochortus kennedyi, 99
Canary Island dragon tree. See *Dracaena draco*
Caralluma, 184, 186, 188, 192, 200
Caralluma europaea, 186
Caralluma frerei, 186
Caralluma gracilipes, 186

Caralluma penicillata, 186
Caralluma priogonium, 186
Caralluma socotrana, 186
Caralluma somalica, 186, 187
Caralluma speciosa, 186, 187
Caricaceae (family), 253
Carpobrotus, 166
cashew, 243
cattleya, 326
caudiciforms, 11, 16, 128, 130, 172, 174, 175, 201, 203, 206, 211, 217, 220, 225, 226, 231, 239
Cavanillesia, 250
Cavanillesia arborea, 250, 251
Ceiba, 250
Ceiba insignis, 250
Ceiba rubriflora, 251
Cephalocereus senilis, 302
Cephalopentandra ecirrhosa, 223
Cephalophyllum, 166
Cephalophyllum alstonii, 166
Cephalophyllum compactum, 166, 167
Ceraria, 168, 173, 174
Ceraria fruticulosa, 174
Ceraria namaquensis, 174, 175
Ceropegia, 196, 197, 199, 200
Ceropegia adrienneae, 199
Ceropegia ampliata, 197, 198
Ceropegia armandii, 199
Ceropegia bosseri, 199
Ceropegia cimiciodora, 198
Ceropegia dichotoma, 199
Ceropegia dimorpha, 198, 199
Ceropegia elegans, 198
Ceropegia fusca, 199
Ceropegia haygarthii, 198
Ceropegia lindenii, 198
Ceropegia linearis, 198
Ceropegia radicans, 198
Ceropegia robynsiana, 198
Ceropegia sandersonii, 198
Ceropegia somaliensis, 198
Ceropegia stapeliiformis, 198
Ceropegia woodii, 197, 198
Chamaealoe africana. See *Aloe bowiea*
Cheiridopsis, 153, 154
Cheiridopsis brownii, 153
Cheiridopsis cigarettifera, 153
Cheiridopsis denticulata, 153, 154
Cheiridopsis peculiaris, 55, 153
Cheiridopsis pillansii, 153
Cheiridopsis umdausensis, 153, 154
Cheiridopsis verrucosa, 153
Chorisia speciosa. See *Ceiba insignis*
cirio. See *Fouquieria columnaris*
Cissus, 227, 231, 234
Cissus cactiformis, 231

Cissus quadrangularis, 231
Cissus rotundifolia, 231
Cissus subaphylla, 231
Cissus tuberosus, 231
Cistanthe, 168, 175
Cistanthe guadalupensis, 175
club moss. See *Lycopodium*
Cnidosculus, 134, 305
Cnidosculus basiacanthus, 134
Coccinia, 222
Coccinia sessiliflora, 222
Colchicaceae (family), 289, 291
Colchicum, 291
Columnea, 237
Commelinaceae, 325
commelinid. See Commelinaceae
Commiphora, 241, 242
Commiphora africana, 242
Commiphora dinteri, 241
Commiphora glaucescens, 242
Commiphora holtziana, 242
Commiphora madagascariensis, 242
Commiphora mollis, 242
Commiphora monstruosa, 242
Commiphora saxicola, 241
Commiphora wildii, 241
common rosary vine. See *Ceropegia woodii*
Compositae (family). See Asteraceae
composite family. See Asteraceae
Conicosia, 166
Conophytum, 23, 44, 136, 140, 141, 145, 146
Conophytum achabense, 145
Conophytum angelicae subsp. *tetragonum*, 143
Conophytum bilobum, 140
  subsp. *altum*, 141
Conophytum bolusiae, 141
Conophytum burgeri, 144, 145
Conophytum calculus, 16, 142
Conophytum cubicum, 143
Conophytum elishae, 140
Conophytum ernstii, 143
Conophytum ficiforme, 143
  f. *placitum*, 143
Conophytum flavum, 141
Conophytum friedrichiae, 144
Conophytum frutescens, 141
Conophytum fulleri, 142, 143
Conophytum gratum, 142
  subsp. *marlothii*, 62, 142
Conophytum herreanthus, 141
Conophytum hians, 141
Conophytum khamiesbergense, 143
Conophytum limpidum, 144
Conophytum lithopsoides, 143

Fouquieria formosa, 245
Fouquieria macdougalii, 245, 246
Fouquieria purpusii, 245, 246, 302
Fouquieria splendens, 244
Fouquieriaceae (family), 239, 244
Freesia, 289
Frerea indica. See Caralluma frerei
Frithia, 23
Frithia pulchra, 154
    var. minor, 154
Furcraea, 309, 314
Furcraea macdougalii, 309, 310

Gasteria, 34, 282, 283, 286–287
Gasteria acinacifolia, 282, 283
Gasteria armstrongii, 285, 286
Gasteria batesiana, 284
    'Barberton', 284
Gasteria baylissiana, 284, 285
Gasteria bicolor, 285
    var. bicolor, 284, 285
    var. liliputana, 285
Gasteria brachyphylla, 284
Gasteria carinata, 284
    var. carinata, 284
    var. retusa, 283
    var. verrucosa, 283
Gasteria croucheri, 282, 283
Gasteria disticha, 283, 284
Gasteria ellaphieae, 284, 285
Gasteria excelsa, 282, 283, 286
Gasteria glauca, 284
Gasteria glomerata, 285
Gasteria neliana. See G. pillansii
Gasteria nitida, 286
    var. armstrongii. See G. armstrongii
    var. nitida, 286
Gasteria pendulifolia, 283
Gasteria pillansii, 285
    var. ernesti-ruschii, 286
Gasteria pulchra, 284
Gasteria rawlinsonii, 286, 287
Gasteria 'Silver King', 287
Gasteria vlokii, 284
Geissorhiza, 289
Geraniaceae (family), 177
Gerrardanthus, 222
Gerrardanthus macrorhizus, 222
Gesneriaceae (family), 325
Gethyllis, 289, 294
Gethyllis grandiflora, 295
giant crocus. See Colchicum
Gibbaeum, 23, 49, 151
Gibbaeum album, 152
Gibbaeum dispar, 152
Gibbaeum heathii, 152
Gibbaeum johnstonii, 152

Gibbaeum nebrownii, 152
Gibbaeum pachypodium, 152
Gibbaeum petrense, 152
Gibbaeum pubescens, 45, 152
Gibbaeum shandii, 152
ginseng, 253
Gladiolus, 289
Glottiphyllum, 49, 160, 161, 162
Glottiphyllum cruciatum, 161
Glottiphyllum grandiflorum, 160, 161
Glottiphyllum linguiforme, 160
Glottiphyllum longum, 160
Glottiphyllum neilii, 160, 161
Glottiphyllum nelii, 160
Glottiphyllum oligocarpum, 160
Glottiphyllum petersii, 161
Glottiphyllum pygmaeum, 160, 161
Glottiphyllum regium,
gourd family. See Cucurbitaceae
grape family. See Vitaceae
grapes, succulent, 230, 231
Graptopetalum, 19, 92, 96, 97, 98
Graptopetalum amethystinum, 92, 93
Graptopetalum bartramii, 93
Graptopetalum bellum, 93
Graptopetalum filiferum, 93
Graptopetalum grande, 92
Graptopetalum macdougallii, 93
Graptopetalum pachyphyllum, 93
Graptopetalum paraguayense, 31, 34, 92
Graptopetalum pentandrum, 92
Graptopetalum rusbyi, 93
Graptoveria, 90, 92
    'Silver Star', 93
Greenovia. See Aeonium
gumbo-limbo tree. See Bursera sima-
    ruba
Gymnocalycium, 124

Haemanthus, 289, 293
Haemanthus albiflos, 293
Haemanthus coccineus, 293
Haemanthus nelsonii, 293
half man. See Pachypodium nama-
    quanum
Haworthia (genus), 11, 23, 30, 31, 32,
    39, 218, 270, 271, 276, 280, 281,
    282, 287
Haworthia (subgenus), 270, 272, 276–
    277
Haworthia angustifolia, 272
Haworthia arachnoidea, 275
    var. aranea, 275
    var. archnoidea, 275
    var. namaquensis, 275
    var. nigricans, 275
    var. scabrispina, 275

    var. setata, 275
    var. xiphiophylla, 275
Haworthia argenteomaculosa. See H.
    pygmaea f. argenteomaculosa
Haworthia attenuata, 277, 281
    var. radula, 277
Haworthia bayeri, 274
Haworthia bolusii, 276
Haworthia bruynsii, 279
Haworthia chloracantha, 272
    var. denticulifera, 272
Haworthia coarctata. 277
    var. tenuis, 277
Haworthia cooperi, 271, 276
    var. pilifera, 271
    var. truncata, 271
Haworthia cymbiformis, 271
    var. incurvula, 271
    var. obtusa, 271
    var. ramosa, 271
    var. transiens, 271
Haworthia decipiens, 276
Haworthia emelyae, 273
    var. comptoniana, 274
    var. emelyae, 273
    var. major, 273
    var. multifolia, 274
Haworthia fasciata, 277
    f. browniana, 277
Haworthia floribunda, 272
Haworthia glauca, 280
Haworthia gracilis, 272
Haworthia helmiae. See H. mucronata
    f. helmiae
Haworthia herbacea, 276
Haworthia kingiana, 281
Haworthia koelmaniorum, 279
    var. mcmurtryi, 279
Haworthia limifolia, 279
    var. umbomboensis, 279
Haworthia lockwoodii, 271, 276
Haworthia longiana, 280
Haworthia magnifica, 273
    var. argenteomaculosa. See H. pyg-
    maea f. argenteo-maculosa
    var. atrofusca, 273
    var. dekenahii, 273
    var. splendens, 273, 274
Haworthia maraisii var. meiringii, 272
Haworthia marginata, 281
Haworthia marumiana var. archeri, 276
Haworthia maughanii. See H. truncata
    var. maughanii
Haworthia minima, 281
Haworthia mirabilis, 274
    var. badia, 274
    var. beukmannii, 274

var. *calcarea*, 274
var. *paradoxa*, 274
var. *triebneriana*, 274
Haworthia mucronata, 271
f. *helmiae*, 271
var. *inconfluens*, 271
var. *morrisiae*, 22, 271
Haworthia mutica, 273
Haworthia nigra, 278
var. *schmidtiana*, 278
Haworthia nortieri, 276
Haworthia outeniquensis, 272
Haworthia parksiana, 275
Haworthia planifolia. See *H. cymbiformis* var. *cymbiformis*
Haworthia pubescens, 275
Haworthia pulchella, 275
Haworthia pumila, 36, 281
Haworthia pygmaea, 273
f. *argenteo-maculosa*, 273
Haworthia radula. See *H. attenuata* f. *radula*
Haworthia reinwardtii, 277
var. *brevicula*, 277, 278
f. *chalumnensis*, 277
f. *kaffirdriftensis*, 277
f. *zebrina*, 277
Haworthia reticulata, 271, 272
var. *hurlingii*, 271
Haworthia retusa, 272, 273
Haworthia scabra, 280
var. *lateganiae*, 280
var. *scabra*, 280
var. *starkiana*, 280
Haworthia semiviva, 45, 276
Haworthia sordida, 280
Haworthia springbokvlakensis, 23, 274
Haworthia truncata, 274, 275, 276
var. *maughanii*, 37, 275, 276
Haworthia turgida, 272, 274
f. *rodinii*, 274
Haworthia venosa, 278
subsp. *granulata*, 278, 279
subsp. *tessellata*, 278, 279
subsp. *venosa*, 278
subsp. *woolleyi*, 278
Haworthia viscosa, 278, 287
Haworthia wittebergensis, 272
heath family. See Ericaceae
Hechtia, 19, 87, 317, 318
Hechtia argentea, 318
Hechtia caerulea, 318
Hechtia glomerata, 318
Hechtia marnier-lapostollei, 318
Hechtia rosea, 318
Hechtia scariosa, 317
Hechtia tillandsioides, 318

hen and chickens. See *Sempervivum tectorum*
Hereroa, 163
Hereroa calycina, 163
Herreanthus meyeri. See *Conophytum herreanthus*
Hesperoyucca whipplei. See *Yucca whipplei*
Hexangulares (subgenus), 270, 277
Hoodia, 181, 192, 193, 195
Hoodia currorii, 192
Hoodia gordonii, 192
Hoodia parviflora, 192, 193
Hoodia pedicellata, 192
Hoya, 196, 197
Hoya australis, 196
Hoya bella, 196
Hoya carnosa, 196, 197
Hoya kerri, 196, 197
Hoya macgillivrayi, 196
Hoya minima, 197
Hoya pubicalyx, 196
Hoya purpureo-fusca, 196
Hoya serpens, 196, 197
Hoya shepherdii, 196
Huernia, 184
Huernia caespitosa, 185
Huernia confusa, 185
Huernia hystrix, 185
Huernia insigniflora, 185
Huernia kennedyana, 185
Huernia levyi, 185
Huernia loeseneriana, 185
Huernia oculata, 185
Huernia pendula, 185
Huernia pillansii, 185, 186, 191
Huernia primulina, 185
Huernia procumbens, 185
Huernia reticulata, 185
Huernia verekeri, 184
Huernia zebrina, 185
Huerniopsis atrosanguineus. See *Piaranthus atrosanguineus*
hyacinth family. See Hyacinthaceae
Hyacinthaceae (family), 289, 291, 292
Hydnophytum, 226
Hydnophytum ferrugineum, 226
Hydnophytum formicarum, 226
Hylotelephium, 73, 74
Hylotelephium sieboldii, 74
Hylotelephium spectabile, 74

Ibervillea, 223
Ibervillea sonorae, 223, 224
Ibervillea tenuisecta, 223
Icacinaceae (family), 226
ice plant, 162, 166, 167

idria. See *Fouquieria columnaris*
inchworm plant. See *Senecio pendulum*
Ipomoea, 225
Ipomoea arborescens, 225
Ipomoea cuernavacana, 225
Ipomoea holubii, 225
Ipomoea inamoena, 225
Ipomoea transvaalensis, 225
Ixia, 289

Jacaratia, 253
jade plant. See *Crassula ovata*
Jatropha, 133, 134, 135, 300
Jatropha aceroides, 133
Jatropha berlandieri. See *J. cathartica*
Jatropha capensis, 133
Jatropha cathartica, 133
Jatropha cinerea, 133
Jatropha conzattii, 134
Jatropha cuneata, 133
Jatropha dioica, 133
Jatropha ferox, 133
Jatropha fissispina, 134
Jatropha giffordiana, 134
Jatropha hyssopifolia, 133
Jatropha lagarinthoides, 133
Jatropha macrocarpa, 134
Jatropha malacophylla, 133
Jatropha marginata, 134
Jatropha moranii, 134
Jatropha multifida, 133
Jatropha pelargonifolia, 133
Jatropha podagrica, 133
Jatropha spathulata. See *J. dioica*
Joshua tree. See *Yucca brevifolia*
Juttadinteria, 151
Juttadinteria albata, 151
Juttadinteria ausensis, 151
Juttadinteria elizae, 151
Juttadinteria simpsonii, 151
Juttadinteria suavissima, 151

Kalanchoe, 66, 72, 167, 215, 365
Kalanchoe arborescens, 70
Kalanchoe beauverdii, 66
Kalanchoe beharensis, 70, 71, 72
'Fang', 70
Kalanchoe bentii, 70
Kalanchoe blossfeldiana, 70
Kalanchoe campanulata, 66
Kalanchoe citrina, 68, 69
Kalanchoe daigremontiana, 66, 67
Kalanchoe delagoensis, 66, 67
Kalanchoe dinklagei, 70
Kalanchoe eriophylla, 72
Kalanchoe fadeniorum, 69
Kalanchoe farinacea, 68, 69

Kalanchoe fedtschenkoi, 67
Kalanchoe figueiredoi. See K. humilis
Kalanchoe gastonis-bonnieri, 67
Kalanchoe grandidieri, 72
Kalanchoe humilis, 69
Kalanchoe laetivirens, 67
Kalanchoe lanceolata, 68, 69
Kalanchoe laxiflora, 66
Kalanchoe luciae, 68
Kalanchoe manginii, 67
Kalanchoe marmorata, 68, 69
Kalanchoe marnieriana, 67
Kalanchoe nyikae, 69
Kalanchoe orgyalis, 71
Kalanchoe pinnata, 67
Kalanchoe prolifera, 67
Kalanchoe pumila, 68
Kalanchoe rhombopilosa, 70
Kalanchoe rotundifolia, 67
Kalanchoe suarezensis, 67
Kalanchoe synsepala, 70, 71
Kalanchoe teretifolia. See K. bentii
Kalanchoe thyrsiflora, 69
Kalanchoe tomentosa, 71, 72
    'Chocolate Soldier', 72
Kalanchoe tubiflora. See K. delagoensis
Kalanchoe uniflora, 67
Kedrostris, 222
Kedrostris nana, 222
    var. zeyheri, 222
Kleinia. See Senecio
Kleinia gregorii. See Senecio stapelii-
    formis
Kleinia neriifolia. See Senecio kleinia
Kleinia obesa. See Senecio deflersii
Kleinia petraea. See Senecio jacobsenii
Kleinia pusilla. See Senecio iosensis
Kleinia saginata. See Senecio mwero-
    ensis subsp. saginatus
kokerboom. See Aloe dichotoma

Labiatae (family). See Lamiaceae
Lachenalia, 289
Lachenalia anguinea, 290, 291
Lachenalia viridiflora, 290
laelia, 326
Lamiaceae, 325
Lampranthus, 167
Lampranthus glaucoides, 167
Lampranthus haworthii, 167
Lampranthus roseus, 167
Lapeirousia, 289
Lapidaria, 136, 149, 151
Lapidaria margaretae, 148
Larryleachia, 193, 195
Larryleachia cactiformis, 193
Larryleachia marlothii, 193, 194

Larryleachia perlata, 193
Lavrania, 193
Ledebouria, 289, 290, 291
Ledebouria socialis, 291
legume family. See Fabaceae
Lenophyllum guttatum, 98, 198
Leptotes, 326
Lewisia, 168, 175
Lewisia maguirei, 175
Lewisia rediviva, 175
    subsp. maguirei. See L. maguirei
Liliaceae (family), 289
lily family. See Liliaceae
Lithops, 23, 136–138, 140, 147, 149,
    150, 151, 161, 290, 323, 327
Lithops aucampiae, 139
    'Bellaketty', 139
Lithops bromfieldii, 139
Lithops comptonii, 137
Lithops dinteri, 138
Lithops divergens, 137
    var. amethystinum, 138
    var. divergens, 137
Lithops dorotheae, 139
Lithops gesinae, 139
Lithops helmutii, 137
Lithops herrei, 139
Lithops hookeri, 139
Lithops julii, 139
    subsp. fulleri, 139
Lithops karasmontana, 35, 139
    var. bella, 139
Lithops lesliei, 139
Lithops meyeri, 138
Lithops olivacea, 137, 139
Lithops optica, 138
    'Rubra', 30, 138
Lithops otzeniana, 138, 139
Lithops pseudotruncatella, 139
Lithops ruschiorum, 138
Lithops salicola, 139
Lithops schwantesii, 138
Lithops terricolor, 137
Lithops verruculosa, 139
Lithops viridis, 137
Littaea (subgenus), 296, 297, 300,
    302, 305
living stones, 136, 149, 150
Lycopodium, 42

madrone. See Arbutus
Mammillaria albilanata, 87
Mammillaria elongata, 85
Manfreda (genus). See Manfreda (sub-
    genus)
Manfreda (subgenus), 296, 307, 308
mango, 243

Massonia, 289, 292
Massonia bifida, 292
Massonia depressa, 292
Massonia pustulata, 292
Matelea, 196, 202
Matelea cyclophylla, 202
melons, 222, 224
Mesembryanthema (subfamily), 136
Mesembryanthemaceae (family), 136
Mesembryanthemum, 167
Mesembryanthemum barklyi, 167
Mesembryanthemum crystallinum, 167
mesembryanthemums, 15, 23, 30, 35,
    136, 159, 163, 168
Mestoklema, 164
Mestoklema arboriforme, 164
Mestoklema tuberosum, 164
Mexican jelly bean. See Sedum
    rubrotinctum
Meyerophytum, 156, 158
Meyerophytum meyeri, 158
    var. holgatense, 158
milkweed family. See Asclepiadaceae
milkweed subfamily. See Asclepiadoi-
    deae
miniature Joshua tree. See Sedum
    multiceps
mint family. See Lamiaceae
Mitrophyllum, 157, 158
Mitrophyllum clivorum, 157
Mitrophyllum grande, 157, 158
Mitrophyllum mitratum, 157
Momordica, 222
Momordica africana, 222
Momordica rostrata, 222, 223
Monadenium, 130, 132
Monadenium arborescens, 130
Monadenium coccineum, 130
Monadenium echinulatum, 130
Monadenium ellenbeckii, 131
    f. caulopodium, 131
Monadenium erubescens, 132
Monadenium guentheri, 131
Monadenium heteropodum, 131
Monadenium invenustum, 130
Monadenium lindenii, 130
Monadenium lugardae, 131
Monadenium magnificum, 131
Monadenium majus, 132
Monadenium montanum, 132
Monadenium reflexum, 131
Monadenium rhizophorum, 130
Monadenium ritchei, 131
    subsp. nyambense, 130
Monadenium rubellum, 132
Monadenium schubei, 131
Monadenium simplex, 132

Monadenium spectabile, 131
Monadenium spinescens, 132
Monadenium stapelioides, 130
Monadenium stellatum, 131
Monadenium torreyi, 132
Monadenium yattanum, 130
Monanthes, 76, 78
Monanthes brachycaulos, 78
Monanthes polyphylla, 78
Monilaria, 156, 157, 158
Monilaria chrysoleuca, 156, 157
Monilaria moniliformis, 156
Monilaria pisiformis, 156, 157
Monsonia, 161, 177, 180, 182, 183
Monsonia ciliata, 181
Monsonia crassicaule, 182, 183
Monsonia flavescens, 181
Monsonia herrei, 183
Monsonia inerme, 182
Monsonia lavranii, 181
Monsonia mossamedensis, 182
Monsonia multifida, 182
Monsonia patersonii, 181
Monsonia peniculinum, 182
Monsonia spinosa, 181
Monsonia vanderietiae, 182
Montiaceae (family), 168
Moraceae (family), 227, 235, 236, 289
Moringa, 252
Moringa drouhardii, 252
Moringa ovalifolia, 252, 253
Moringaceae (family), 239, 252
morning glory family. See Convolvulaceae
mother-in-law tongue. See *Sansevieria*
mother of millions. See *Kalanchoe daigremontiana*, *K. delagoensis*
Muiria, 152, 153
Muiria hortenseae, 152, 153
Myrmecodia, 226
Myrmecodia echinata, 226
Myrmecodia tuberosa, 226

Nananthus, 163
Nananthus wilmaniae, 163
Nelia, 151
Nelia schlechteri, 151
Neoalsomitra podagrica, 224
Neoregelia, 317
Nerine, 289, 291
Nolina, 309, 312, 314
Nolina bigelovii, 312
Nolina nelsonii, 312, 313
Nolina parviflora, 312
Nolinaceae (family), 312
Notechidnopsis, 190
Notechidnopsis framesii, 190

Ochagavia, 317
Ochagavia carnea, 317
ocotillo. See *Fouquieria splendens*
Odontophorus, 160
Odontophorus angustifolius, 160
    subsp. *protoparcoides*, 160
Odontophorus marlothii, 160
Odosicyos bosseri, 223
Oeceoclades, 328
Oeceoclades roseovariegata, 328
Oeceoclades spathulifera, 328
old man cactus. See *Cephalocereus senilis*
oleander family. See Apocynaceae
Oophytum, 156, 158
Oophytum nanum, 158
Oophytum oviforme, 158
Operculicarya, 243, 244
Operculicarya decaryi, 243, 244
Opeculicarya pachypus, 244
Ophionella, 190
Ophionella arcuata, 190
Ophthalmophyllum (genus), 23. Also see *Conophytum*
Ophthalmophyllum praesectum. See *Conophytum praesectum*
Opuntia, 120, 239, 250
Orbea, 184, 191
Orbea namaquensis, 188
Orbea variegata, 188
Orbeanthus, 188
Orbeanthus hardyi, 188
Orbeopsis, 188
Orbeopsis lutea, 188
orchid, 79, 83, 89, 94, 184, 306, 312, 318, 326, 327
orchid family. See Orchidaceae
Orchidaceae (family), 326
Ornithogalum, 291
Ornithoglossum, 289
Orostachys, 74
Orostachys malacophylla, 75
    var. *aggregata*, 75
    var. *iwarenge*, 75
Orostachys spinosa, 74
    var. *erubescens*, 75
Oscularia deltoides, 167
Othonna, 212, 217, 218, 219
Othonna arborescens, 218
Othonna arbuscula, 218
Othonna armiana, 219
Othonna auriculifolia, 218
Othonna cacalioides, 218, 219
Othonna cakilifolia, 218
Othonna capensis, 217
Othonna clavifolia, 218, 219
Othonna euphorbioides, 218

Othonna furcata, 218
Othonna herrei, 218, 219
Othonna intermedia, 217
Othonna lepidocaulis, 219
Othonna opima, 219
Othonna pachypoda, 218
Othonna protecta, 219
Othonna retrofracta, 218
Othonna rosea, 217
Othonna sedoides, 217
Othonna triplinervia, 217
Othonna wrinkleana, 219
Oxalidaceae (family), 323
Oxalis, 323, 324
Oxalis beneprotecta. See *O. bullulata*
Oxalis bullulata, 323
Oxalis carnosa, 324
oxalis family. See Oxalidaceae
Oxalis gigantea, 324
Oxalis herrerae, 324
Oxalis rubra, 323, 324

Pachycormus, 243, 244
Pachycormus discolor, 243
Pachycymbium, 184, 188
Pachyphytum, 85, 92, 98
Pachyphytum coeruleum, 93
Pachyphytum compactum, 94
Pachyphytum glutinicaule, 94
Pachyphytum hookeri, 31, 94
Pachyphytum longifolium, 94
Pachyphytum oviferum, 93
Pachyphytum rzedowskii, 93, 94
Pachyphytum saltense, 94
Pachyphytum viride, 93
Pachyphytum werdermannii, 94
Pachypodium, 37, 203, 206, 209, 211, 226, 266
Pachypodium ambongense, 209
Pachypodium baronii, 209
    var. *windsorii*, 210
Pachypodium bicolor, 210
Pachypodium bispinosum, 206, 207
Pachypodium brevicaule, 210, 211
Pachypodium decaryi, 211
Pachypodium densiflorum, 209, 210
Pachypodium eburneum, 210, 211
Pachypodium geayi, 208, 209
Pachypodium horombense, 209, 210
Pachypodium inopinatum, 210
Pachypodium lamerei, 36, 116, 208, 209, 210
    subsp. *ramosum*, 208
Pachypodium lealii, 207
    var. *saundersii*. See *P. saundersii*
Pachypodium makayense, 210
Pachypodium namaquanum, 208, 211

Sansevieria ballyi, 315
Sansevieria cylindrica, 315
Sansevieria deserti, 315
Sansevieria ehrenbergii, 316
Sansevieria eilensis, 316, 317
Sansevieria fischerii, 316
Sansevieria forskaalii, 315, 316
Sansevieria grandis, 315
Sansevieria hahnii, 314
    'Golden Hahnii', 314
    'Loop's Pride', 314
Sansevieria hallii, 316
Sansevieria horwoodii, 316
Sansevieria kirkii var. pulchra, 316
Sansevieria phillipsiae, 315
Sansevieria pinguicula, 316, 317
Sansevieria powellii, 316
Sansevieria robusta, 316
Sansevieria singularis. See S. fischerii
Sansevieria stuckyi, 315
Sansevieria subspicata, 315
Sansevieria suffruticosa, 316
Sansevieria trifasciata, 314
    'Bantel's Sensation', 314
    var. laurentii, 314
Sarcocaulon. See Monsonia
Sarcostemma, 196, 199, 200
Schwantesia, 151
Schwantesia borcherdsii, 151
Schwantesia herrei, 151
    f. major, 151
Schwantesia pillansii, 151
Schwantesia ruedebuschii, 151
Sclerocactus spinosior, 175
Sedeveria, 90
Sedum, 19, 33, 34, 73, 92, 95, 98
Sedum acre, 73
Sedum adolphii, 96
Sedum allantoides, 96
Sedum burrito, 15, 95
Sedum craigii, 96
Sedum dasyphyllum, 73
Sedum dendroideum, 95, 96
Sedum frutescens, 97
Sedum furfuraceum, 31, 96
Sedum guatemalense, 95
Sedum hernandezii, 95
Sedum hintonii, 96
Sedum hystrix. See S. hintonii
Sedum lucidum, 95
Sedum macdougallii, 96
Sedum moranense, 96
Sedum morganianum, 15, 95
Sedum multiceps, 73
Sedum nussbaumerianum. See S. adolphii
Sedum oxypetalum, 97

Sedum pachyphyllum, 87, 96
Sedum palmeri, 96
Sedum rubrotinctum, 95
Sedum sediforme, 74
Sedum sieboldii. See Hylotelephium sieboldii
Sedum spathulifolium, 74
Sedum stahlii, 95
Sedum suaveolens, 96
Sedum torulosum, 97
Sedum versadense, 95
    var. villadioides, 95
Sempervivum, 12, 33, 75, 76, 82
Sempervivum arachnoideum, 75
Sempervivum calcareum, 75
Sempervivum ciliosum, 75
Sempervivum tectorum, 75
    'Greenii', 75
Senecio, 23, 212, 213, 214, 215, 217
Senecio acaulis, 215
Senecio articulatus, 213
Senecio ballyi, 214
Senecio cephalophorus, 216
Senecio citriformis, 216
Senecio corymbiferus, 216, 217
Senecio crassissimus, 215
Senecio decaryi, 215
Senecio deflersii, 214, 217
Senecio descoingsii, 213
Senecio ficoides, 215
Senecio hallianus, 215
Senecio haworthiodes, 215
Senecio hebdingii, 213
Senecio implexus, 215
Senecio iosensis. See S. sulcicalyx
Senecio jacobsenii, 215
Senecio kleinia, 213, 216, 217
Senecio kleiniiformis, 213
Senecio longiflorus, 213, 214
Senecio medley-woodii, 214
Senecio mweroensis, 214
    subsp. saginatus, 214
Senecio pendulum, 213
Senecio picticaulis, 213, 217
Senecio praecox. See Pittocaulon praecox
Senecio radicans, 22, 216
Senecio rowleyanus, 216
Senecio scaposus, 215
    var. addoensis, 215
    var. caulescens, 215
    var. scaposus, 215
Senecio sempervivus, 214
    subsp. grantii, 214
    subsp. sempervivus, 214
Senecio stapeliiformis, 213
Senecio sulcicalyx, 216, 217
Senecio talinoides, 215, 217

subsp. mandraliscae, 215, 217
Senna, 253
sesame family. See Pedaliaceae
sesames, succulent, 227, 237
Sesamothamnus, 227, 237, 238
Sesamothamnus benguellensis, 237
Sesamothamnus busseanus, 238
Sesamothamnus guerichii, 237
Sesamothamnus lugardii, 237
Sesamothamnus rivae, 238
Seyrigia, 223
Seyrigia humbertii, 223, 224
Sinningia, 325
Sinningia cardinalis, 325
Sinningia leucotricha, 325
Sinocrassula, 74
Sinocrassula indica, 74
Sparaxis, 289
spekboom. See Portulacaria afra
spider web sempervivum. See Sempervivum arachnoideum
spiderwort family. See Commelinaceae
split rocks. See Pleiospilos
Stapelia, 182, 184, 188, 196, 202
Stapelia clavicorona, 187
Stapelia engleriana, 187
Stapelia flavopurpurea, 187, 188
Stapelia gettliffei, 187
Stapelia gigantea, 187
Stapelia glanduliflora, 187
Stapelia grandiflora, 187
Stapelia hirsuta, 187
    var. comata, 187
Stapelia paniculata var. scitula, 187, 188
Stapelia pearsonii, 187
Stapelia unicornis, 187
stapeliads, 184, 186, 187, 190, 191, 196, 200, 202. Also see Stapelieae
Stapelianthus, 191
Stapelianthus madagascariensis, 191
Stapelianthus pilosus, 191
Stapelieae (subfamily), 184
Stapeliopsis, 190, 191
Stapeliopsis saxatilis, 190
Stomatium, 159, 160, 162
Stomatium agninum, 160
Stomatium alboroseum, 160
Stomatium geoffreyi, 160
Stomatium suaveolens, 160
Strombocactus disciformis, 83
Stultitia hardyi. See Orbeanthus hardyi
succulent asters. See Othonna, Senecio
sunflower family. See Asteraceae
sweet potatoes, 220
Synadenium, 132

Synadenium cupulare var. *rubra*, 132
Synadenium grantii. See *S. cupulare* var. *rubra*
Synandrospadix vermitoxicus, 325

Tacitus bellus. See *Graptopetalum bellum*
Talinaceae (family), 168
Talinum, 168, 173, 175. Also see *Cistanthe*
Talinum caffrum, 173
Tanquana, 149, 150
Tanquana archeri, 150
Tanquana hilmari, 150
Tanquana prismatica, 150
Tavaresia, 192, 195
Tavaresia angolensis, 192
Tavaresia barklyi, 192
Thelocactus, 324
Thompsonella, 97
Thompsonella minutiflora, 97
Thompsonella mixtecana, 97
Thompsonella platyphylla, 97
tiger's jaws. See *Faucaria*
Tillandsia, 83, 89, 94, 317, 318
Tillandsia purpurea, 317
Tillandsioideae (tribe), 317
Titanopsis, 49, 155, 156, 162, 276
Titanopsis calcarea, 156
Titanopsis fulleri, 156
Titanopsis hugo-schlechteri, 156
Titanopsis schwantesii, 156
Tradescantia, 324
Tradescantia navicularis, 324
Trichocaulon, 192, 193
Trichodiadema, 164
Trichodiadema bulbosum, 164
Trichodiadema densum, 164
Tridentea, 184, 188
Tridentea pedunculata, 189
Tritonia, 289
Tromotriche, 184, 188, 189
Tromotriche longii, 189
Tromotriche longipes, 189
Turbinicarpus, 324
twin-spined euphorbias, 116, 119, 122, 123, 125
Tylecodon, 52, 56, 60, 61, 63, 64, 65, 161, 216, 217, 218

Tylecodon bodleyae, 63
Tylecodon buchholzianus, 63 var. *fascicularis*, 63
Tylecodon cacalioides, 61
Tylecodon decipiens, 63
Tylecodon ellaphieae, 53
Tylecodon grandiflorus, 62, 65
Tylecodon hallii, 62
Tylecodon hirtifolius, 61
Tylecodon leucothrix, 63
Tylecodon longipes, 63
Tylecodon nolteei, 63
Tylecodon occultans, 64
Tylecodon paniculatus, 60, 61, 65
Tylecodon pearsonii, 61
Tylecodon peculiaris, 64
Tylecodon pusillus, 64
Tylecodon pygmaeus, 64
Tylecodon ramosus, 62
Tylecodon reticulatus, 47, 62, 65
Tylecodon rubrovenosus, 62
Tylecodon scandens, 64
Tylecodon schaeferianus, 63
Tylecodon similis, 64
Tylecodon singularis, 64
Tylecodon sinus-alexanderii, 63
Tylecodon striatus, 64
Tylecodon suffultus, 64
Tylecodon sulphureus, 63
Tylecodon torulosus, 63, 65
Tylecodon ventricosus, 62, 65
Tylecodon viridiflorus, 63
Tylecodon wallichii, 61, 62, 65

Uncarina, 227, 238
Uncarina abbreviata, 238
Uncarina decaryi, 238
Uncarina grandidieri, 238
Uncarina platycarpa, 238
Uncarina roeoesliana, 238
Uncarina stellulifera, 238

Veltheimia, 289, 291
Villadia, 74, 98
Villadia aristata, 98
Villadia guatemalensis, 98
vining plants, 66, 173, 196, 199, 202, 220, 222, 227, 230, 231, 321, 324

Vitaceae (family), 227, 230
Vriesea, 317

Whiteheadia bifida. See *Massonia bifida*
Whitesloanea, 194
Whitesloanea crassa, 194

Xanthorrhoeaceae (family), 254, 282, 289
xerophytic bromeliads, 317
Xerosicyos, 223, 224
Xerosicyos danguyi, 224
Xerosicyos perrieri, 224

yams, 220
Yucca, 19, 309, 310, 312, 314, 316, 317
Yucca aloifolia, 310
Yucca angustissima, 310
Yucca baccata, 310
Yucca baileyi, 310
Yucca brevifolia, 74, 310, 311
Yucca carnerosana. See *Y. faxoniana*
Yucca decipiens, 311
Yucca elata, 310
Yucca endlichiana, 311
Yucca faxoniana, 310, 311
Yucca filifera, 311
Yucca harrimaniae, 310
Yucca jaliscana, 311
Yucca mixtecana, 311
Yucca periculosa, 311
Yucca potosina, 311
Yucca queretaroensis, 311
Yucca rigida, 311
Yucca rostrata, 311
Yucca schidigera, 310
Yucca schottii, 310
Yucca torreyi, 310
Yucca valida, 311
Yucca whipplei, 310

Zamioculcas, 325
Zamioculcas zamiifolia, 325
zig-zag plant. See *Decaryia madagascariensis*